The Russian Revolution, 1905–1921

Recent Titles in
Bibliographies and Indexes in World History

The Russian Revolution, 1905–1921

A Bibliographic Guide to Works in English

Compiled by
MURRAY FRAME

Bibliographies and Indexes in World History,
Number 40

Greenwood Press
Westport, Connecticut • London

Library of Congress Cataloging-in-Publication Data

Frame, Murray.
    The Russian Revolution, 1905–1921 : a bibliographic guide to works
in English / compiled by Murray Frame.
      p.   cm. — (Bibliographies and indexes in world history, ISSN
0742–6852 ; no. 40)
    Includes index.
    ISBN 0–313–29559–X (alk. paper)
    1. Soviet Union—History—Revolution, 1917–1921—Bibliography.
I. Title. II. Series.
Z2510.F73   1995
[DK265]
016.947084'1—dc20   95–2463

British Library Cataloguing in Publication Data is available.

Library of Congress Catalog Card Number: 95–2463
ISBN: 0–313–29559–X
ISSN: 0742–6852

First published in 1995

Greenwood Press, 88 Post Road West, Westport, CT 06881
An imprint of Greenwood Publishing Group, Inc.

Printed in the United States of America

The paper used in this book complies with the
Permanent Paper Standard issued by the National
Information Standards Organization (Z39.48–1984).

10 9 8 7 6 5 4 3 2

CONTENTS

PREFACE

The Russian Revolution of 1905 to 1921 has continued to provoke the passions and minds of observers for several decades now. Since the series of events which destroyed the Tsarist regime and led to the formation of Soviet power, participants, eyewitnesses, scholars and others have endeavoured to understand and explain the nature and significance of this central period in modern history. Their endeavours have been disseminated in English-language publications. But until now no catalogue of this literature has been available. Why produce one now?

The sheer quantity of accessible works necessitates a guide for students and specialists. Studies continue to appear with bewildering speed. In particular, there now exist countless relevant and scholarly articles. These are often dispersed throughout various "obscure" journals, some of which few people would consider consulting when studying the Russian Revolution. Students especially have precious little time to search through even the more obvious journals. And doctoral theses are steadily produced (if not in sufficient quantity). This bibliography goes some way in bringing the relevant English-language monographs, articles and doctoral theses together.

In addition to this practical consideration, there is a rather more philosophical reason for producing a bibliography of English-language materials on the Russian Revolution. The past informs us about the present (and vice-versa). Russia is presently experiencing another revolution. Economic collapse, political chaos, dissolution of empire, rejuvenation of nationalities, and the attendant quest for new ideologies and paths of development in Russia today have their nearest precedent in the revolution of 1905 to 1921. The fact that these two revolutions can be used to understand each other is reflected in various comparative articles which have appeared.[1] Far from being a redundant subject (as some have suggested), study of Russia's previous upheaval is more important than ever. Fortunately, fresh thinking on the Russian Revolution is being aided by increasing (but often expensive) access to archives in the former Soviet Union. As researchers process materials which until recently were available only to the most senior scholars in the Communist Party *privilegentsia*, a ready-to-hand catalogue of completed research is desirable. This bibliography will assist students and specialists in what continues to be a vital subject.

Bibliographic categorisation is by no means an objective process. It is determined by the interaction of the compiler's subjective opinions of the topic and the nature of the extant literature thereof. The final structure provides a definition of the topic. Moreover, the utility of a bibliography is determined by its structure. Therefore, the type of organisation utilised requires some explanation and justification.

The main criterion for the inclusion of a work was that it should concern the period of the Russian Revolution from 1905 to 1921 (though it could be a work which covers, in addition, events outside that period, as many of the entries do). However, the mere mention of the revolution was not an acceptable reason for the inclusion of a work because the logical conclusion of that criterion would be a bibliography listing practically every work on Russia and the Soviet Union published in the twentieth century. Boundaries had to be established and only the user can judge whether or not those boundaries are reasonable. Why 1905 to 1921?

It is impossible to say when a revolution begins and ends. The origins of the Russian Revolution pre-date 1905. They are to be found at least in the 1890s, probably in the 1860s, and perhaps in the eighteenth or even earlier centuries. Yet a "dividing line" had to be chosen. Otherwise, the bibliography would be endless. Inclusion even of the 1890s would have introduced a vast array of additional works which would have rendered the bibliography less specific and therefore less useful to students specialising in the Russian Revolution.

The first Russian Revolution (that of 1905) is an appropriate starting point. It marked an important stage in the development of the struggle between Tsarism and its enemies. The events of Bloody Sunday (9 January, Old Style) were the first open clash between government and people since the eighteenth century. The Tsar's alleged complicity in the unprovoked massacre of peaceful demonstrators transformed his image in the eyes of the populace. The Little Father became Bloody Nicholas. The remainder of the year witnessed an upsurge of the three main forces which would make the revolutions of 1917. The first force, the peasantry, had always displayed a propensity for rebellion, symbolised most spectacularly in the uprisings of the seventeenth and eighteenth centuries. A relatively dormant force for much of the nineteenth century, they vented their anger at land shortages once more in the *jacquerie* of 1905. The second force was the nascent Russian proletariat. The 1890s had witnessed the emergence of a substantial and discontented urban working class. Increasingly receptive to the preachings of Russian Marxists, they struck in 1905. The third force was the intelligentsia, both liberal and revolutionary. The nineteenth century, in a sense, had been the age of the Russian intelligentsia. Russian thinkers began to question many aspects of life in their country, including the utility and morality of the autocracy. But in the absence of mass uprisings they were denied a powerful force to bolster and sanction their opposition to the regime. In 1905, provoked by the strains imposed by the Russo-Japanese War, these three forces came together. There was no conspiracy as such, but an evident coincidence of interests. For the first time, mass discontent and articulate political opposition erupted simultaneously. Tsarism was compelled to make its first political concessions.

The year 1905 witnessed the first serious manifestation of the nature of the struggle which was to continue, with varying degrees of intensity, until 1921 - the struggle, broadly defined, between old Russia and new Russia. That is not to suggest that 1917 was in any sense "inevitable". Lenin called 1905 a "dress rehearsal" for 1917, implying a preordained line of development. Yet Western scholars tend to regard the 1905 Revolution "not as an event that made any one path of development inevitable, but rather as a critical juncture that opened up several paths".[2]

By 1907 the regime had regained its composure and authority. The following ten years (the decade of the "Duma Monarchy") were relatively tranquil. Yet the deep fissures in the Tsarist polity and Russian society which had been illuminated during the 1905 Revolution did not heal and, under immense pressure inflicted by the First World War, the forces of discontent reappeared in 1917, this time toppling the monarchy and facilitating the Bolshevik coup.

This bibliography does not treat 1917 as a great "turning-point". The Bolsheviks did not seize power in October 1917 - they asserted their control of the second All-Russian Congress of Soviets in Petrograd. In fact, although the central Russian provinces turned to the Bolsheviks within a few weeks, it took the new regime three years to establish any authority that would have been acceptable to the later Tsars. But 1917 was certainly a pivotal moment in the on-going conflict, and that is reflected in the chronological sub-divisions of the bibliography.

The year of 1921 as a dividing line is quite common. The spring of that year is traditionally regarded as the end of the Civil War: the remnants of internal political opposition were routed (most famously at Kronstadt), a peace treaty with Poland was signed, the New Economic Policy was announced, and a trade agreement was made with Britain. The defeat of the Whites had marked the end of the most intense phase of the struggle between old Russia and new

Russia. With the defeat of the internal opponents of the Bolshevik dictatorship, the hegemony of the Communist Party was established. It might be said, therefore, that the central period of transition from Tsarist Russia to Soviet Russia (that is, the Russian Revolution) occurred between 1905 and 1921.

Certain bibliographic categories and sub-categories used by the compiler might require explanation. The *Documents* sub-category in section A contains only general collections of primary sources relating to the Revolution. More specific documentary collections are to be found under appropriate subject categories and sub-categories. Similarly, the *The 1905 Revolution, The February Revolution* and *The October Revolution* sub-categories in section A contain only general works on those subjects. Studies of more specialised aspects of those events are to be found in specific categories (for example, detailed works on the peasantry during the October Revolution are to be found under **Society:** *Peasants,* 1917).

Political Structures describes the political framework of Tsarism and Bolshevik attempts to create political institutions. *Provisional Government* is located in this section because it was essentially a political phenomenon. Indeed, it originated as the "Provisional Executive Committee of the Duma". The **Political Structures** section is followed by the **Society** which those structures governed and were part of. That is followed by categories relating to movements which supported the old regime, those who wanted to reform it, and those who wanted to overthrow it.

Perhaps the most unconventional sub-category of **Civil War** is the Kornilov Affair. Can the *Kornilov Affair* be considered part of the Civil War? Historians of the Russian Revolution have not agreed upon a precise date for the beginning of the Civil War but they all describe it as the struggle which took place against the Bolsheviks *in power*. Indeed, one recent study states that "the Civil War began with the October Revolution".[3] Yet this obscures the fact that the struggle between the revolutionaries and the old regime pre-dated the Bolshevik coup of October 1917. Was the Kornilov Affair part of that struggle? It has been written that "although contemporaries as well as historians have treated the Kornilov-Kerensky conflict exclusively as a struggle for power, for Kornilov it was first and foremost a critical, probably final effort to save Russia from defeat in the war".[4] That may be true. Yet even if Kornilov did not plan a coup, his statements and actions contributed to the oft-noted polarisation between left and right which occurred in the autumn of 1917. He detested the revolutionaries in the Soviet and believed that their influence over Kerensky was one of the main reasons for the lack of strong leadership in Russia. The reactionaries and Russian nationalists cheered Kornilov, while the revolutionaries backed Kerensky against the possibility of a right-wing takeover. Therein lay a conflict, and insofar as the Civil War was the most intensive and most brutal phase of that conflict between old Russia and new Russia, the Kornilov Affair might be considered, at the least, a prelude to the Civil War.

The qualification for membership in the **Main Non-Russian Nationalities and Regional Identities** category is two-fold: the nationality must have either gained independence from the Tsarist empire after 1917-18 (for example, Finland) and/or become a Republic of the USSR at some point (for example, the Baltics). The exceptions are the other large groups or areas with particularly strong identities, such as the Jews, the Cossacks, and Siberia. To the extent that the smaller nationalities within Russia proper are included, they tend to be in **Revolution in the Provinces**.

The only section which was truncated deliberately is "Literature". The reason for this is simple. There are so many works available on the writers and poets of the period that it would require another bibliography to compile them. Instead, a selection of some of the most relevant and accessible works is provided. The **Miscellaneous** category contains works which do not easily correspond to any of the categories used in the bibliography, but this is in no way to deny their importance (sometimes their centrality) to the study of the Russian Revolution. The section entitled **International Impact of the Revolution and World Opinion** is intended to indicate significant ramifications of the revolution such as the Red Scare in the United States between 1918 and 1920, yet without growing into a history of the United States in that period. The final category lists works dealing with the **Place and Significance of the Revolution in Russian and**

World History but it does not extend to general histories of Russia which nevertheless would deal with the same question.

All the categories should be used in conjunction with one another. For example, those interested in the Nestor Makhno movement should consult both the *Makhno and Makhnovshchina* and *Anarchists* sections, or those interested in the Okhrana should consult both *Police and Okhrana* and *Russian Espionage and Intelligence Abroad*. The Subject Index attempts to aid cross-consultation. Although this bibliography is not annotated, I have endeavoured to make the categories precise enough for the user to be able to gauge the main contents or themes of a work without any difficulty. It is my belief that the worth and utility of a book should be determined not by the compiler of the bibliography, but by the individual reader.

I wish to acknowledge my indebtedness to Professor Paul Dukes and to Cath Brennan, both of the Centre for Russian, East and Central European Studies at the University of Aberdeen, the first for providing me with the opportunity and encouragement to commence work on this project, the second for invaluable assistance in gathering article titles and for useful comments on the structure of the bibliography. Generous financial assistance from the Centre greatly facilitated my work on the bibliography. I am also grateful for the constructive comments of Dr R.B. McKean (University of Stirling) and Professor S.A. Smith (University of Essex). The staffs of the Queen Mother Library, Aberdeen, and the University Library, Cambridge, helped in various ways, often beyond the call of duty. Creidhe O'Sullivan (University of Cambridge) kindly granted me the benefit of her formidable computing skills. The shortcomings of the bibliography are, of course, my responsibility.

Murray Frame
St John's College
Cambridge University

Notes

[1] See, for example, H.G. Kyriakodis, "The 1991 Soviet and 1917 Bolshevik Coups Compared: Causes, Consequences and Legality," *Russian History* 18 (1991), no.3, pp.317-362 and J.Hiden, "Baltic Gold and Latvian Privatisation," *Journal of Baltic Studies* 23 (1992), no.1, pp.63-72. Hiden claims that his article (covering the immediate post-1917 period) "is not irrelevant to our understanding of Latvia's present odyssey towards economic change" (p.63).

[2] A. Ascher, *The Revolution of 1905: Russia in Disarray* (Stanford, 1988), p.2.

[3] E. Mawdsley, *The Russian Civil War* (London, 1987), pp.3-4.

[4] R. Pipes, *The Russian Revolution, 1899-1919* (London, 1990), p.448.

LIST OF JOURNALS USED

Where a journal is still current, the date (year and/or number) of the last volume/issue consulted is given. To avoid confusion title changes are indicated. Other periodical titles which appear in the text of the bibliography (but not in the following list) have not been systematically scanned. Occasionally, periodical references were taken from secondary sources, such as monographs.

1 *American Historical Review* 1-99 (June, 1994)
2 *American Slavic and East European Review* 1-20 [now *Slavic Review*]. The first three volumes
   are identical to the first three volumes of *Slavonic and East European Review*
3 *Australian Slavonic and East European Studies* 1-8 (no.1, 1994) [formerly *Melbourne Slavonic
   Studies*]
4 *Cahier du Monde Russe et Sovietique* 1-34 (1993)
5 *California Slavic Studies* 1-16 (1993)
6 *Canadian Slavic Studies* 1-5 [now *Canadian-American Slavic Studies*]
7 *Canadian-American Slavic Studies* 6-28 (no.1, 1994) [formerly *Canadian Slavic Studies*]
8 *Canadian Slavonic Papers* 1-34 (1992)
9 *Comparative Studies in Society and History* 1-36 (no.1, 1994)
10 *Cultures* 1-8 [formerly *Journal of World History*]
11 *East Central Europe* 1-19 (no.1, 1992)
12 *European History Quarterly* 14-24 (July, 1994) [formerly *European Studies Review*]
13 *European Studies Review* 1-13 [now *European History Quarterly*]
14 *Harvard Slavic Studies*
15 *Irish Slavonic Studies* 1-14 (1993)
16 *Jahrbucher fur Geschichte Osteuropas* 1-42 (no.1, 1994)
17 *Journal of Baltic Studies* 1-25 (1994, no.2)
18 *Journal of Contemporary History* 1-29 (July, 1994)
19 *Journal of Interdisciplinary History* 1-25 (summer, 1994)
20 *Journal of Modern History* 1-66 (June, 1994)
21 *Journal of World History* 1-19 [now *Cultures*]
22 *Melbourne Slavonic Studies* 1-19 [now *Australian Slavonic and East European Studies*]
23 *Oxford Slavonic Papers*
24 *Oxford Slavonic Papers (New Series)* 1-26 (1993)
25 *Past and Present* 1-143 (May, 1994)
26 *Revolutionary Russia* 1-7 (no.1, 1994)
27 *Russian History* 1-21 (Spring, 1994)
28 *Russian Review* 1-53 (July, 1994)
29 *Russian Studies in History* 31-32 (spring 1994) [formerly *Soviet Studies in History*]
30 *Sbornik (Study Group on the Russian Revolution)* 1-12
31 *Scando-Slavica* 1-39 (1993)
32 *Scottish Slavonic Review* 1-21 (1993)
33 *Slavic Review* 20-53 (Spring, 1994) [formerly *American Slavic and East European Review*]
34 *Slavonic and East European Review* 7-72 (April, 1994) [formerly *Slavonic Review*]. The first
   three volumes are identical to the first three volumes of *American Slavic and East
   European Review*. Volume 19 (1939-40) is entitled *The Slavonic Year-Book*

35 *Slavonic Review* 1-7 [now *Slavonic and East European Review*]
36 *Social History* 1-19 (May, 1994)
37 *Soviet Studies* 1-44 (1992)
38 *Soviet Studies in History* 1-30 (now *Russian Studies in History*)
39 *Soviet Union* 1-18 [now *The Soviet and Post-Soviet Review*]
40 *Stanford Slavic Studies* 1-7 (1993)

Doctoral dissertation titles were taken from J.J.Dossick, *Doctoral Research on Russia and the Soviet Union* (New York, 1960), J.J.Dossick, *Doctoral Research on Russia and the Soviet Union, 1960-1975* (New York & London, 1976), and the lists compiled by J.J.Dossick and published annually in the journal *Slavic Review.*

ABBREVIATIONS USED

Journals

AHR - American Historical Review
ASEER - American Slavic and East European Review
CASS - Canadian-American Slavic Studies
CSP - Canadian Slavonic Papers
EHQ - European History Quarterly
HSS - Harvard Slavic Studies
HT - History Today
IRSH - International Review of Social History
JCH - Journal of Contemporary History
JFGO - Jahrbucher fur Geschichte Osteuropas
JMH - Journal of Modern History
JSH - Journal of Social History
OSP - Oxford Slavonic Papers
OSP (NS) - Oxford Slavonic Papers (New Series)
RH - Russian History
RR - Russian Review
Sbornik (SGRR) - Sbornik (Study Group on the
          Russian Revolution)
SEER - Slavonic and East European Review
SR - Slavic Review
SS - Soviet Studies
SSH - Soviet Studies in History

Other

U.P. - University Press
ed. - editor
eds. - editors
trans.by - translated by
diss. - dissertation

A

REFERENCE, DOCUMENTS AND GENERAL

Reference:

A1. Baedecker, K. *Russia, with Teheran, Port Arthur, and Peking: Handbook for Travellers* (London: George Allen & Unwin, 1971 [facsimile of 1914 edition]).

A2. De Mowbray, S. *Key Facts in Soviet History, vol.I: 1917 - 22 June 1941* (London: Pinter, 1990).

A3. Jackson, G. (ed.) *Dictionary of the Russian Revolution* (New York, Westport, CT, London: Greenwood Press, 1989).

A4. Kennard, H.P. (ed.) *The Russian Year Book, 1908-1913* (London: 1908-1913).

A5. Shukman, H. (ed.) *The Blackwell Encyclopedia of the Russian Revolution* (Oxford: Basil Blackwell, 1988).

Bibliographies:

A6. Egan, D.R. & Egan, M.A. *Russian Autocrats from Ivan the Great to the Fall of the Romanov Dynasty: An Annotated Bibliography of English Language Sources to 1985* (Metuchen, N.J. & London: Scarecrow, 1987).

A7. Egan, D.R. & Egan, M.A. *V.I.Lenin: An Annotated Bibliography of English Language Sources to 1980* (Metuchen, N.J. & London: Scarecrow, 1982).

A8. Gibian, G. *Soviet Russian Literature in English: A Checklist Bibliography* (Ithaca: Center for International Studies, Cornell University, 1967).

A9. Lubitz, W. (ed.) *Trotsky: A Bibliography* (Munich: K.G. Saur, 1982).

A10. Nerhood, H.W. *To Russia and Return: An Annotated Bibliography of Travellers' English-Language Accounts of Russia from the Ninth Century to the Present* (Columbus, Ohio: Ohio State U.P., 1969).

A11.   Sinclair, L. *Trotsky: A Bibliography* (Brookfield, Ut., Scolar, Aldershot, Hants.: Gower, 1989).

A12.   Spath, M. *Bibliography of Articles on East-European and Russian History: Selected from English-Language Periodicals, 1850-1938*, edited by W.Philipp (Wiesbaden: Otto Harrassowitz, 1981).

Documents:

A13.   Bunyan, J. & Fisher, H.H. (eds.) *The Bolshevik Revolution 1917-8, Documents and Materials* (Stanford: Stanford U.P., 1934 [reprinted 1961, 1965]).

A14.   Dmytryshyn, B. (ed.) *Imperial Russia: A Source Book, 1700-1917* 2nd edition (Hinsdale: Dryden, 1974).

A15.   Golder, F. (ed.) *Documents of Russian History, 1914-1917*, trans. by E.Aronsberg (Gloucester, Mass.: Peter Smith, 1964).

A16.   Jones, M. *Storming the Heavens. Voices of October* (London: Zwan Publications, 1987).

A17.   McCauley, M. *Octobrists to Bolsheviks: Imperial Russia, 1905- 1917* (London: Arnold, 1984).

A18.   McCauley, M. *The Russian Revolution and the Soviet State 1917-1921. Documents* (London & Basingstoke: Macmillan, 1980).

A19.   Pethybridge, R. (ed.) *Witnesses to the Russian Revolution* (London: Allen & Unwin, 1964).

A20.   Vernadsky, G., Fisher, R.T. Jr., Ferguson, A.D., Lossky, A. & Pushkarev, S. (eds.) *A Source Book for Russian History from Early Times to 1917. Vol.3: Alexander II to the February Revolution* (New Haven & London: Yale U.P., 1972).

A21.   Von Mohrenschildt, D. (ed.) *The Russian Revolution of 1917: Contemporary Accounts* (London: Oxford U.P., 1971).

A22.   Vulliamy, C.E. (ed.) *The Red Archives. Russian State Papers and Other Documents Relating to the Years 1915-1918*, trans.by A.L.Hynes (London: Geoffrey Bles, 1929).

General surveys:

A23.   Abramovitch, R.R. *The Soviet Revolution, 1917-1939* (London: George Allen & Unwin, 1962).

A24.   Adams, A.E. (ed.) *Imperial Russia after 1861. Peaceful Modernization or Revolution?* (Boston: Heath, 1965).

A25.   Adams, A.E. (ed.) *The Russian Revolution and Bolshevik Victory. Why and How?* (Boston: Heath, 1960).

A26.   Alexinsky, G. *Modern Russia*, trans.by B.Miall (London: T.Fisher Unwin, 1913).

A27.   Bradley, J. *The Russian Revolution* (London: Brompton/Bison, 1988).

A28.   Brower, D.R. (ed.) *The Russian Revolution: Disorder or New Order* (St.Louis, Missouri: Forum, 1979).

A29.   Carmichael, J. *A Short History of the Russian Revolution* (London: Nelson, 1966 [reprinted by Sphere, 1971]).

A30.   Carr, E.H. *The Bolshevik Revolution 1917-1923*, 3 vols. (London: Macmillan, 1950-1953).

A31.   Carr, E.H. *The Russian Revolution from Lenin to Stalin (1917-1929)* (London: Macmillan, 1979).

A32.   Chamberlin, W.H. *The Russian Revolution, 1917-1921*, 2 vols. (London & New York: Macmillan, 1935 [republished by Princeton U.P., 1987]).

A33.   Chapnik, R.H. "Toward a General Theory of Political Revolution: An Historical Analysis of the Preconditions of the Russian Revolution of 1917," PhD diss., Colorado, 1979.

A34.   Charques, R.D. *The Twilight of Imperial Russia: the reign of Tsar Nicholas II (1894-1917)* (London: Phoenix House, 1958).

A35.   Chernov, V.M. *The Great Russian Revolution*, trans. & abridged by P.E.Mosely (New Haven: Yale U.P., 1936).

A36.   Crankshaw, E. *The Shadow of the Winter Palace: the Drift to Revolution 1825-1917* (London: Macmillan, 1976).

A37.   Curtiss, J.S. *The Russian Revolutions of 1917* (Princeton: D.Van Nostrand, 1957).

A38.   Daborn, J. *Russia: Revolution and Counter-Revolution, 1917-1924* (Cambridge: Cambridge U.P., 1991).

A39.   Dillon, E.J. *The Eclipse of Russia* (London & Toronto: J.M.Dent, 1918).

A40.   Dziewanowski, M.K. (ed.) *The Russian Revolution: An Anthology* (New York: Thomas Y.Crowell, 1970).

A41.   Farbman, M.S. *Bolshevism in Retreat* (London: Collins, 1923).

A42.   Fitzpatrick, S. *The Russian Revolution* (Oxford & New York: Oxford U.P., 1982; second edition 1994).

A43.   Florinsky, M.T. *The End of the Russian Empire* (New York: Collier, 1961 [first published 1931]).

A44.   Florinsky, M.T. "The End of the Russian Empire: A Study in the Economic and Social History of the War," PhD diss., Columbia, 1931.

A45.   Footman, D. *The Russian Revolutions* (London: Faber,1962).

A46.   Frankel, E.R., Frankel, J. & Knei-Paz, B. (eds.) *Revolution in Russia: Reassessments of 1917* (Cambridge: Cambridge U.P., 1992).

A47.   Frankel, J. "1917: the Problem of Alternatives," in: Frankel, E.R. et al (eds.) *Revolution in Russia: Reassessments of 1917* (Cambridge: Cambridge U.P., 1992), pp.3-13.

A48.   Geyer, D. *The Russian Revolution*, trans.by B.Little (Leamington Spa: Berg, 1987).

A49.   Golder, F. *The Russian Revolution* (Cambridge, Mass.: Harvard U.P., 1918).

A50.   Goldston, R.C. *The Russian Revolution* (London: Phoenix House, 1967).

A51.   Gronsky, P.P. *The War and the Russian Government* (New Haven: Yale U.P., 1929).

A52.   Harcave, S. *Years of the Golden Cockerel: The Last Romanov Tsars, 1814-1917* (London: Collier-Macmillan, 1968).

A53.   Hill, C. *Lenin and the Russian Revolution* (London: English Universities Press, 1947).

A54.   Hingley, R. *Russian Revolution* (London, Sydney, Toronto: Bodley Head, 1970).

A55.   Judge, E.H. & Simms Jr., J.Y. (eds.) *Modernization and Revolution: Dilemmas of Progress in Late Imperial Russia: Essays in Honor of Arthur P. Mendel* (New York: East European Monographs, distributed by Columbia U.P., 1992).

A56.   Katkov, G., Oberlander, E., Poppe, N. & Von Rauch, G. (eds.) *Russia Enters the Twentieth Century, 1894-1917*, (London: Temple Smith, 1971).

A57.   Keep, J. *The Russian Revolution - A Study in Mass Mobilization* (London: Weidenfeld & Nicolson, 1976).

A58.   Kerensky, A.F. *The Crucifixion of Liberty*, trans.by G.Kerensky (London: Arthur Barker, 1934).

A59.   Klimov, Y. *The Overthrow of Tsarism (1910-February 1917)* (Moscow: Novosti, 1975).

A60.   Kochan, L. *Russia in Revolution, 1890-1918* (London: Weidenfeld & Nicolson, 1966).

A61.   Kochan, M. *The Last Days of Imperial Russia, 1910-1917* (New York: Macmillan, 1976).

A62.   Korff, S.A. *Autocracy and Revolution in Russia* (London: Macmillan, 1923).

A63.   Kritsman, L. "The Heroic Period of the Russian Revolution (Introduction and Chapter One) (translated by Ronald I. Kowalski)," *Revolutionary Russia* 2 (1989), no.2, pp.*v-xvii* and 1-13.

A64.   Liebman, M. *The Russian Revolution: The Origins, Phases and Meaning of the Bolshevik Victory*, trans.by A.J.Pomerans (London: Jonathan Cape, 1970).

A65.   Lincoln, W.B. *In War's Dark Shadow: The Russians Before the Great War* (New York: Dial Press, 1983).

A66.   Lossky, N.O. "Reflections on the Origins and Meaning of the Russian Revolution," *RR* 10 (1951), no.4, pp.293-300.

A67.   Lynch, M. *Reaction and Revolutions: Russia, 1881-1924* (London: Hodder & Stoughton, 1992).

A68.   McKean, R.B. "Russia on the Eve of the Great War: Revolution or Evolution," PhD diss., East Anglia, 1971.

A69.   McKean, R.B. *The Russian Constitutional Monarchy, 1907-17*, Historical Association: General Series 91   (London: Chameleon, 1977, 1983, amended bibliography 1986).

A70.   McNeal, R.H. (ed.) *The Russian Revolution: Why did the Bolsheviks win?* (New York: Holt, Rinehart & Winston, 1959/60).

A71.   Maklakov, B. "On the Fall of Tsardom," *SEER* 18 (1939), no.52, pp.73-92.

A72.   Mavor, J. *The Russian Revolution* (London: Allen & Unwin,1928).

A73.   Maynard, J. *Russia in Flux: Before October* (London: Victor Gollancz, 1939).

A74.   Miliukov, P. *Russia To-day and To-morrow* (London: Macmillan, 1922).

A75.   Miliukov, P.N. *The Russian Revolution*, trans.by T. & R.Stites (vol.1) and G.M.Hamburg (vols.2 & 3) (Gulf Breeze, Florida: Academic International, 1978-1987).

A76.   Moorehead, A. *The Russian Revolution* (London & Glasgow: Collins with Hamish Hamilton, 1958).

A77.   Moynahan, B. *Comrades: 1917 - Russia in Revolution* (London: Hutchinson, 1992).

A78.   Nansen, F. *Russia and Peace* (London: George Allen & Unwin, 1923).

A79.   Page, S.W. *Russia in Revolution: Selected Readings in Russian Domestic History Since 1855* (Princeton, N.J.: D.Van Nostrand, 1965).

A80.   Pares, B. *The Fall of the Russian Monarchy: A Study of the Evidence* (London: Jonathan Cape, 1939).

A81.   Pearson, R. *Revolution in Russia* (Dublin: Gill and Macmillan, 1973).

A82.   Pethybridge, R.W. *The Spread of the Russian Revolution: Essays on 1917* (London: Macmillan, 1972).

A83.   Petrunkevich, A., Harper, S.N. & Golder, F.A. *The Russian Revolution* (London: Humphrey Milford / Oxford U.P., 1918).

A84.   Pipes, R. (ed.) *Revolutionary Russia* (London: Oxford U.P. 1968).

A85.   Pipes, R. *Russia under the Bolshevik Regime, 1919-1924* (London: Harvill/Harper Collins, 1994).

A86.   Pipes, R. *The Russian Revolution, 1899-1919* (London: Collins Harvill, 1990).

A87.   Pitcher, H. *Witnesses of the Russian Revolution* (London: John Murray, 1994).

A88.   Pushkarev, S. *The Emergence of Modern Russia, 1801-1917*, trans.by R.H.McNeal & T.Yedlin (New York: Holt, Rinehart and Winston, 1963).

A89.   Rogger, H. "Russia in 1914," *JCH* 1 (1966), no.4, pp.95-119.

A90.   Rogger, H. *Russia in the Age of Modernisation and Revolution, 1881-1917* (London & New York: Longman, 1983).

A91.   Ross, E.A. *The Russian Bolshevik Revolution* (New York: Century, 1921).

A92.   Ross, E.A. *The Russian Soviet Republic* (London: George Allen & Unwin, 1923).

A93.   Salisbury, H. *Black Night, White Snow: Russia's Revolutions 1905-1917* (Garden City, N.Y.: Doubleday, 1978).

A94.   Schapiro, L. *1917: The Russian Revolutions and the Origins of Present-Day Communism* (Hounslow: Maurice Temple Smith, 1984).

A95.   Serge, V. *Year One of the Russian Revolution*, trans.by P.Sedgwick (London: Allen Lane, Penguin, 1972).

A96.   Service, R. *The Russian Revolution 1900-1929*, 2nd ed. (Basingstoke & London: Macmillan, 1991).

A97.   Seton-Watson, H. *The Decline of Imperial Russia, 1855-1914* (London: Methuen, 1954).

A98.   Shukman, H. *Lenin and the Russian Revolution* (London: Batsford, 1966).

A99.   Stavrou, T.G. (ed.) *Russia Under the Last Tsar* (Minneapolis: University of Minnesota Press, 1969).

A100.   Steinberg, I.N. *In the Workshop of the Revolution* (London: Victor Gollancz, 1955).

A101.   Sukhanov, N.N. *The Russian Revolution 1917. A Personal Record*, trans.by J.Carmichael (London: Oxford U.P., 1955).

A102.   Suny, R. & Adams, A. (eds.) *The Russian Revolution and Bolshevik Victory: Visions and Revisions*, 3rd edition (Lexington, Mass., Toronto: D.C.Heath & Co., 1990).

A103.   Taylor, A.J.P. "Russia, 1917: the Last European Revolution," in: A.J.P.Taylor *Revolutions and Revolutionaries* (London: Hamish Hamilton, 1980), pp.141-160.

A104.   *The Russian Revolution* (New York: A CBS Legacy Book, 1967).

A105.   Thompson, J.M. *Revolutionary Russia, 1917* (New York: Charles Scribner's Sons, 1981).

A106.   Trotsky, L. *The History of the Russian Revolution*, 3 vols., trans.by M.Eastman (London: Victor Gollancz, 1965 [first published in England in 3 vols., 1932-33; first published in a single volume edition 1934; reissued 1965; published by Sphere in 3 vols., 1967]).

A107.   Tyrkova-Williams, A. *From Liberty to Brest-Litovsk. The First Year of the Russian Revolution* (London: Macmillan, 1919 [reprinted: Westport, Conn.: Hyperion, 1977]).

A108.   Voline *Nineteen-Seventeen. The Russian Revolution Betrayed*, trans.by H.Cantine (London: Freedom, 1954).

A109.   Von Laue, T.H. *Why Lenin? Why Stalin? A Reappraisal of the Russian Revolution, 1900-1930* (Philadelphia & New York: J.B. Lippincott, 1964).

A110.   Von Mohrenschildt, D. (ed.) *The Russian Revolution of 1917: Contemporary Accounts* (London: Oxford U.P., 1971).

A111.   Walkin, J. *The Rise of Democracy in Pre-Revolutionary Russia: Political and Social Institutions Under the Last Three Czars* (London: Thames & Hudson, 1963).

A112.   Walsh, E.A. *The Fall of the Russian Empire. The story of the last of the Romanovs and the coming of the Bolsheviki* (Boston: Little, Brown & Co., 1928).

A113.   White, J.D. *The Russian Revolution, 1917-1921: A Short History* (London: Edward Arnold, 1994).

A114.   Williams, B. *The Russian Revolution 1917-1921* (Oxford: Basil Blackwell, 1987).

A115.   Wilton, R. *Russia's Agony* (London: Edward Arnold, 1918).

A116.   Wolfe, B.D. *An Ideology in Power: Reflections on the Russian Revolution* (New York: Stein & Day, 1969).

A117.   Wolfe, B.D. "Titans Locked in Combat," Part I *RR* 23 (1964), no.4, pp.327-340; Part II *RR* 24 (1965), no.1, pp.13-24.

A118.   Wood, A. *The Origins of the Russian Revolution, 1861-1917* (London: Methuen, 1987; second edition, London & New York: Routledge, 1993).

A119.   Wood, A. *The Russian Revolution*, 2nd ed. (London: Longman, 1986).

The 1905 Revolution:

A120.   Ascher, A. *The Revolution of 1905. Russia in Disarray* (Stanford: Stanford U.P., 1988).

A121.   Ascher, A. *The Revolution of 1905. Authority Restored* (Stanford: Stanford U.P., 1992).

A122.   Askew, W.C. "An American View of Bloody Sunday," *RR* 11 (1952), no.1, pp.35-43.

A123.   Durland, K. *The Red Reign: The True Story of an Adventurous Year in Russia* (London: Hodder & Stoughton, 1907).

A124.   Edmondson, L. "Was there a Movement for Civil Rights in Russia in 1905?" in: O.Crisp & L.Edmondson (eds.) *Civil Rights in Imperial Russia* (Oxford: Clarendon, 1989), pp.263-285.

A125.   Emmons, T. "Russia's Banquet Campaign," *California Slavic Studies* 10 (1977), pp.45-86.

A126.   Floyd, D. *Russia in Revolt, 1905: the first crack in Tsarist power* (London: Macdonald, 1969).

A127.   Florinsky, M. "Twilight of Absolutism: 1905," *RR* 8 (1949), no.4, pp.322-333.

A128.   Harcave, S. *First Blood: The Russian Revolution of 1905* (New York: Macmillan, 1964).

A129.   Harrison, W. "MacKenzie Wallace's View of the Russian Revolution of 1905-7," *OSP(NS)* 4 (1971), pp.73-82.

A130.   Joubert, C. *Russia as it Really Is*, 7th ed. (London: Eveleigh Nash, 1905).

A131.   Joubert, C. *The Fall of Tsardom*, 2nd ed. (London: Eveleigh Nash, 1905).

A132.   Joubert, C. *The Truth about the Tsar and the Present State of Russia*, 4th ed. (London: Eveleigh Nash, 1905).

A133.   Miliukov, P.N. *Russia and Its Crisis* (New York: Collier,1962).

A134.   Pares, B. *Russia Between Reform and Revolution* (New York: Schocken, 1962 [originally published in 1907 as *Russia and Reform*]).

A135.   Perris, G.H. *Russia in Revolution*, 2nd ed. (London: Chapman & Hall, 1905).

A136.   Sablinsky, W. *The Road to Bloody Sunday: Father Gapon and the St.Petersburg Massacre of 1905* (Princeton: Princeton U.P., 1976).

A137.   Sablinsky, W. "The Road to Bloody Sunday: Father Gapon, His Labor Organization, and the Massacre of Bloody Sunday," PhD diss., University of California, Berkeley, 1968).

A138.   Sanders, J.L. "The Moscow Uprising of December, 1905: A Background Study," PhD diss., Washington, Seattle, 1981.

A139.   Shanin, T. *The Roots of Otherness: Russia's Turn of the Century. Vol.2: Russia, 1905-07: Revolution as a Moment of Truth* (Basingstoke & London: Macmillan, 1986).

A140.   Trotsky, L. *1905* (New York: Vintage, 1971).

A141.   Ular, A. *Russia from Within* (London: Heinemann, 1905).

A142.   Verner, A.M. *The Crisis of Russian Autocracy. Nicholas II and the 1905 Revolution* (Princeton: Princeton U.P., 1990).

A143.   Von Laue, T.H. "Count Witte and the Russian Revolution of 1905," *ASEER* 17 (1958), no.1, pp.25-46.

A144.   Weinberg, R. *The Revolution of 1905 in Odessa: Blood on the Steps* (Bloomington: Indiana U.P., 1993).

A145.   Wolfe, B.D. "Gapon and Zubatov: An Experiment in "Police Socialism"," *RR* 7 (1947-48), no.2, pp.53-61.

A146.   Wood, A. "Russia 1905: Dress Rehearsal for Revolution," *HT* 31 (August 1981), pp.28-33.

The February Revolution:

A147.   Anin, D. "The February Revolution: A Note on the Causes of its Defeat," *SS* 18 (1967), no.3, pp.265-266.

A148.   Ashworth, T. "Soldiers Not Peasants: The Moral Basis of the February Revolution of 1917," *Sociology* 26 (1992), no.3, pp.455-470.

A149.   Burdzhalov, E.N. "Revolution in Moscow," *SSH* 26 (1987-88), no.1.

A150.   Burdzhalov, E.N. *Russia's Second Revolution: The February 1917 Uprising in Petrograd*, trans. and edited by D.J.Raleigh (Bloomington & Indianapolis: Indiana U.P., 1987).

A151.   Burdzhalov, E.N. "The Second Russian Revolution: the Uprising in Petrograd," *SSH* 18 (1979-80), no.1, pp.11-107.

A152.   Chamberlin, W.H. "The First Russian Revolution," *RR* 26 (1967), no.1, pp.4-12.

A153.   Diakin, V.S. "The Leadership Crisis in Russia on the Eve of the February Revolution," *SSH* 23 (1984-85), no.1, pp.10-38.

A154.   Ferro, M. *The Russian Revolution of February 1917*, trans.by J.L.Richards (Englewood Cliffs, N.J.: Prentice-Hall, 1972).

A155.   Glindin, I.F. "Problems in the History of the February Revolution and its Socioeconomic Preconditions," *SSH* 7 (1968-69), no.3, pp.3-25.

A156.   Hasegawa, T. "Rodzianko and the Grand Dukes' Manifesto of 1 March 1917," *CSP* 18 (1976), no.2, pp.154-167.

A157.   Hasegawa, T. "The February Revolution of 1917 in Russia," PhD diss., Washington, Seattle, 1969.

A158.   Hasegawa, T. *The February Revolution: Petrograd 1917* (Seattle: University of Washington Press, 1981).

A159.   Hasegawa, T. "The Problem of Power in the February Revolution of 1917 in Russia," *CSP* 14 (1972), no.4, pp.611-632.

A160.   Johnston, R.H. "In Defence of the Defeated: *Sovremennye zapiski* and the February Revolution," *CSP* 24 (1982), no.1, pp.11-24.

A161.   Katkov, G. *Russia 1917: The February Revolution* (London: Longmans, Green & Co., 1967).

A162. Kerensky, A. "Why the Russian Monarchy Fell," *SEER* 8 (1929-30), pp.496-513.

A163. Longley, D.A. "Iakovlev's Question, or the Historiography of the Problem of Spontaneity and Leadership in the Russian Revolution of February 1917," in: E.R.Frankel et al (eds.) *Revolution in Russia: Reassessments of 1917* (Cambridge: Cambridge U.P., 1992), pp.365-387.

A164. Longley, D.A. "The Mezhraionka, the Bolsheviks and International Women's Day: In Response to Michael Melancon," *SS* 41 (1989), no.4, pp.625-645.

A165. Melancon, M. "International Women's Day, the Finland Station Proclamation, and the February Revolution: A Reply to Longley and White," *SS* 42 (1990), no.3, pp.583-589.

A166. Melancon, M. "Who Wrote What and When?: Proclamations of the February Revolution in Petrograd, 23 February - 1 March 1917," *SS* 40 (1988), no.3, pp.479-500.

A167. Norton, B.T. "Russian Political Masonry and the February Revolution of 1917," *IRSH* 28 (1983), pp.240-258.

A168. Norton, B.T. "Russian Political Masonry, 1917, and Historians," *RH* 11 (1984), no.1, pp.83-100.

A169. Schakovskoy, Z. "The February Revolution as Seen by a Child," *RR* 26 (1967), no.1, pp.68-73.

A170. White, J.D. "The February Revolution and the Bolshevik Vyborg District Committee (In Response to Michael Melancon)," *SS* 41 (1989), no.4, pp.602-624.

A171. White, J.D. "The Sormovo-Nikolaev *Zemlyachestvo* in the February Revolution," *SS* 31 (1979), no.4, pp.475-504.

The October Revolution:

A172. Buldakov, V.P. "At the Sources of Soviet History: the Road to October," *SSH* 29 (1990-91), no.4, pp.34-59.

A173. Bunyan, J. & Fisher, H.H. (eds.) *The Bolshevik Revolution 1917-8, Documents and Materials* (Stanford: Stanford U.P., 1934 [reprinted 1961, 1965]).

A174. Daniels, R. *Red October: The Bolshevik Revolution of 1917* (New York: Scribner's, 1967).

A175. Daniels, R.V. "The Bolshevik Gamble," *RR* 26 (1967), no.4, pp.331-340.

A176. Ferro, M. *October 1917. A Social History of the Russian Revolution* (London: Routledge & Kegan Paul, 1980).

A177. Jackson, G.D. "Spontaneity and the Legitimacy of the October Revolution: The Moscow Insurrection as a Case Study," in: R.C.Elwood (ed.) *Reconsiderations on the Russian Revolution* (Cambridge, Mass.: Slavica, 1976), pp.42-80.

A178. Laverychev, V.Ia. "On the Question of the Material Preconditions of the Great October Revolution," *SSH* 27 (1988-89), no.1, pp.38-61.

A179. Lobanov-Rostovsky, A. "Psychological Undercurrents of the Russian Revolution," *SEER* 7 (1928-29), pp.554-564.

A180. Medvedev, R.A. *The October Revolution*, trans.by G.Saunders (London: Constable, 1979).

A181. Melgunov, S.P. *Bolshevik Seizure of Power*, trans.by J.S.Beaver (Santa Barbara, California: Clio Press, 1972).

A182. Rabinowitch, A. *The Bolsheviks Come to Power: The Revolution of 1917 in Petrograd* (New York: Norton, 1976).

A183. Reed, J. *Ten Days That Shook the World* (London: Penguin, 1977 [first published in 1919]).

A184. Rogger, H. "October 1917 and the Tradition of Revolution," *RR* 27 (1968), no.4, pp.395-413.

A185. Saul, N.E. "Lenin's Decision to Seize Power: The Influence of Events in Finland," *SS* 24 (1972-73), no.4, pp.491-505.

A186. Schakovskoy, Z. "The October Revolution as Seen by a Child," *RR* 26 (1967), no.4, pp.376-390.

A187. Sobolev, P.N. (ed.) *History of the October Revolution* (Moscow: Progress, 1966).

A188. Sobolev, P.N. (ed.) *The Great October Socialist Revolution* (Moscow: Progress, 1970).

A189. Startsev, V.I. "The Question of Power in the October Days of 1917," *SSH* 27 (1988-89), no.2, pp.56-85.

A190. Trotsky, L. *Lessons of October*, trans.by J.G.Wright (London: New Park Publications, 1971).

B

HISTORIOGRAPHY

B1.   Acton, E. *Rethinking the Russian Revolution* (London: Edward Arnold, 1990).

B2.   Acton, E. "The Libertarians Vindicated? The Libertarian View of the Revolution in the Light of Recent Western Research," in: E.R.Frankel et al (eds.) *Revolution in Russia: Reassessments of 1917* (Cambridge: Cambridge U.P., 1992), pp.388-405.

B3.   Acton, E. "The Russian Revolution," *HT* 32 (July 1982), pp.48-49.

B4.   Adams, A.E. "New Books on the Revolution - Old Wine in New Bottles," *RR* 26 (1967), no.4, pp.391-398.

B5.   Anin, D.S. "The February Revolution: Was the Collapse Inevitable?," *SS* 18 (1967), no.4, pp.435-457.

B6.   Anon. "The Study of the History of the Great October Revolution," *SSH* 27 (1988-89), no.2, pp.6-45.

B7.   Ascher, A. "Soviet Historians and the Revolution of 1905," in: F. X.Coquin & C.Gervais-Francelle (eds.) *1905: La Premiere Revolution Russe* (Paris: Publications de la Sorbonne et Institut d'etudes slaves, 1986), pp.475-496.

B8.   Asher, H. "The Rise, Fall, and Resurrection of M.N. Pokrovsky," *RR* 31 (1972), no.1, pp.49-63.

B9.   Baron, S.H. "Plekhanov, Trotsky, and the Development of Soviet Historiography," *SS* 26 (1974), no.3, pp.380-395.

B10. Baron, S.H. "The Resurrection of Plekhanovism in Soviet Historiography," *RR* 33 (1974), no.4, pp.386-404.

B11. Baron, S.H. & Heer, N.W. (eds.) *Windows on the Russian Past: Essays on Soviet Historiography since Stalin* (Columbus, Ohio: AAASS, 1977).

B12. Beilmarz, P. "Trotsky as Historian," *History Workshop* 20 (1985), pp.36-55.

B13.   Bloomfield, E. "Soviet Historiography of 1905 as Reflected in Party Histories of the 1920s," PhD diss., University of Washington, 1966.

B14.   Byrnes, R.F. "Creating the Soviet Historical Profession, 1917-1934," *SR* 50 (1991), no.2, pp.297-308.

B15.   Byrnes, R.F. "Kliuchevskii and the Revolution of 1905," in: F.X.Coquin & C.Gervais-Francelle (eds.) *1905: La Premiere Revolution Russe* (Paris: Publications de la Sorbonne et Institut d'etudes slaves, 1986), pp.79-96.

B16.   Cross, T.B. "The Star Crossed Marriage: Determinism and 1917," *RR* 27 (1968), no.4, pp.414-420.

B17.   Daniels, R.V. "Soviet Historians Prepare for the Fiftieth, *SR* 26 (1967), no.1, pp.113-118.

B18.   Daniels, R.V. "The Bolshevik Gamble," *RR* 26 (1967), no.4, pp.331-340.

B19.   Dobbie-Bateman, A.F. "Michael Pokrovsky," *SEER* 11 (1932-33), pp.187-189.

B20.   Eissenstat, B.W. "M.N. Pokrovsky and Soviet Historiography," PhD diss., Kansas, 1967.

B21.   Eissenstat, B.W. "M.N. Pokrovsky and Soviet Historiography: Some Reconsiderations," *SR* 28 (1969), no.4, pp.604-618.

B22.   Enteen, G.M. "M.N. Pokrovskii and the Society of Marxist Historians," PhD diss., George Washington, 1965.

B23.   Enteen, G.M. "Soviet Historians Review Their Own Past: the Rehabilitation of M.N. Pokrovsky," *SS* 20 (1968-69), no.3, pp.306-320.

B24.   Enteen, G.M. *The Soviet Scholar-Bureaucrat: M.N. Pokrovskii and the Society of Marxist Historians* (University Park & London: Pennsylvania State U.P., 1978).

B25.   Flenley, P. "Perestroika and the History of the Revolution: A First Glimpse," *Revolutionary Russia* 1 (1988), no.2, pp.151-156.

B26.   Frankel, J. "Party Genealogy and the Soviet Historians (1920-1938)," *SR* 25 (1966), no.4, pp.563-603.

B27.   Getzler, I. "Nikolai Sukhanov's *Zapiski o revoliutsii*," *Revolutionary Russia* 7 (1994), no.1, pp.1-19.

B28.   Gorodetskii, E.N. "Some Characteristics of Contemporary Historiography of the October Revolution," *SSH* 6 (1967-68), no.4, pp.3-23.

B29.   Heer, N.W. *Politics and History in the Soviet Union* (Cambridge, Mass.: The MIT Press, 1971).

B30.   Holmes, L.E. "Soviet Historical Studies of 1917 Bolshevik Activity in Petrograd," PhD diss., Kansas, 1968.

B31.   Holmes, L.E. "Soviet Rewriting of 1917: The Case of A.G. Shliapnikov," *SR* 38 (1979), no.2, pp.224-242.

B32. Humenuk, S. "Russian Historiography in Russian Writings, 1815 to the Present: A Bibliographical Essay," PhD diss., Illinois, 1974.

B33. Inoiatov, Kh.-Sh. & Landa, L.M. "Soviet Historiography of the October Revolution in Central Asia," *SSH* 6 (1967-68), no.3, pp.3-26.

B34. Keep, J. "Lenin's Letters as a Historical Source," *RR* 30 (1971), no.1, pp.33-42.

B35. Keep, J. "The Agrarian Revolution of 1917-1918 in Soviet Historiography," *RR* 36 (1977), no.4, pp.405-423.

B36. Laqueur, W. *The Fate of the Revolution: Interpretations of Soviet History* (New York: Macmillan, 1967).

B37. Lieven, D. "Western Scholarship on the Rise and Fall of the Soviet Regime," *JCH* 29 (1994), no.2, pp.195-227.

B38. Logue, J.J. "The Political Philosophy of Edward Hallet Carr," PhD diss., Chicago, 1966.

B39. McCann, J.M. "Beyond the Bug: Soviet Historiography of the Soviet-Polish War of 1920," *SS* 36 (1984), no.4, pp.475-493.

B40. McKean, R.B. "Russia, 1855-1917," *The Historian* no.5 (1984-85), pp.12-15.

B41. McNeal, R.H. "Soviet Historiography on the October Revolution: A Review of Forty Years," *ASEER* 17 (1958), no.3, pp.269-281.

B42. Mawdsley, E. "Rewriting Russia's Revolution," *HT* 40 (June 1990), pp.48-52.

B43. Menasche, L. "Demystifying the Russian Revolution," *Radical History Review* 18 (1978), pp.142-154.

B44. Mints, I.I. "On Restructuring in the Study of the October Revolution," *SSH* 27, no.1 (1988-89), pp.26-37.

B45. Myers, R.H. "William Henry Chamberlain: His Views of the Soviet Union," PhD diss., Indiana, 1973.

B46. Oulianoff, N. "In Commemoration of S.P. Melgunov," *RR* 17 (1958), no.3, pp.193-200.

B47. Parsons, W.H. "Soviet Historians and 'Bourgeois' Interpretations of the Russian Revolution," PhD diss., Indiana, 1966.

B48. Pundeff, M. (ed.) *History in the U.S.S.R.: Selected Readings* (San Francisco: Chandler, 1967).

B49. Radzilowski, T. "Unscrambling the Jumbled Catalog: Feudalism and the Revolution of 1905 in the Writings of N.P. Pavlov-Silvanskii," in: E.H. Judge & J.Y. Simms, Jr. (eds.) *Modernization and Revolution: Dilemmas of Progress in Late Imperial Russia: Essays in Honor of Arthur P. Mendel* (New York: East European Monographs, distributed by Columbia U.P., 1992), pp.95-127.

B50. Sanders, J.T. "The Past in the Service of the Future: Russian Historians and Russian Society, 1880-1930," PhD diss., Stanford, 1989.

B51.   Seleznev, M.S. "Questions of Method in the Publication of Sources on the History of the Great October," *SSH* 7 (1968-69), no.1, pp.42-52.

B52.   Shelestov, D.K. "On Study of the Historiography of the Civil War in the USSR," *SSH* 8 (1969-70), no.1, pp.3-30.

B53.   Sherter, S.R. "The Soviet System and the Historian: E.V. Tarle (1875-1955) as a Case Study," PhD diss., Wayne State, 1968.

B54.   Sidorov, A.L. "Some Thoughts on the Work and Experience of a Historian," *SSH* 3 (1964-65), no.2, pp.47-66.

B55.   Smith, S. "Writing the History of the Russian Revolution After the Fall of Communism," *Europe-Asia Studies* 46 (1994), no.4, pp.563-578.

B56.   Sokolov, O.D. "V.I. Lenin and the Shaping of M.N. Pokrovskii's Views," *SSH* 2 (1963-64), no.3, pp.21-32.

B57.   Spring, D. "Soviet Historians in Crisis," *Revolutionary Russia* 1 (1988), no.1, pp.24-35.

B58.   Suny, R.G. "Revision and Retreat in the Historiography of 1917: Social History and Its Critics," *RR* 53 (1994), no.2, pp.165-182.

B59.   Suny, R.G. "Towards a Social History of the October Revolution," *AHR* 88 (1983), pp.31-52.

B60.   Szeftel, M. "Facts of Russian History and its Philosophy as Viewed by Bertram D.Wolfe in 'Three Who Made A Revolution'," *ASEER* 15 (1956), pp.71-85.

B61.   Szporluk, R. "M.N. Pokrovsky's Interpretation of Russian History," PhD diss., Stanford, 1965.

B62.   Szporluk, R. "Pokrovskii's View of the Russian Revolution," *SR* 26 (1967), no.1, pp.70-84.

B63.   Thurston, R.W. "New Thoughts on the Old Regime and the Revolution of 1917 in Russia: A Review of Recent Western Literature," in: E.H. Judge & J.Y. Simms, Jr. (eds.) *Modernization and Revolution: Dilemmas of Progress in Late Imperial Russia: Essays in Honor of Arthur P. Mendel* (New York: East European Monographs, distributed by Columbia U.P., 1992), pp.129-168.

B64.   Vodolagin, V.M. "Soviet Historical Literature on the October Armed Insurrection in Petrograd," *SSH* 7 (1968-69), no.1, pp.32-41.

B65.   Volobuev, P.V. "Perestroika and the October Revolution in Soviet Historiography," *RR* 51 (1992), no.4, pp.566-576.

B66.   Warth, R.D. "On the Historiography of the Russian Revolution," *SR* 26 (1967), no.2, pp.247-264.

B67.   White, J.D. "Early Soviet Historical Interpretations of the Russian Revolution 1918-24," *SS* 37 (1985), no.3, pp.330-352.

B68.   White, J.D. " M.N. Pokrovsky and the Origin of Soviet Historiography," PhD diss., Glasgow, 1972.

B69.   Wolfe, B.D. "In Defense of 'Three Who Made A Revolution'," *ASEER* 15 (1956), pp.86-102.

B70.   Wolfe, B.D. "Leon Trotsky as Historian," *SR* 20 (1961), no.3, pp.495-502.

B71.   Wood, A. (ed.) *EHQ* 22 (1992), no.4. Issue on "Rewriting Russia 1917".

C

POLITICAL STRUCTURES

Tsarist Court and Establishment:

C1.   Almedingen, E.M. *The Romanovs. Three Centuries of an Ill-Fated Dynasty* (London: Bodley Head, 1966).

C2.   Anon. "The Empress Maria Feodorovna," *SEER* 7 (1928-29), pp.410-414.

C3.   Bark, Sir P. "The Last Days of the Russian Monarchy - Nicholas II at Army Headquarters," *RR* 16 (1957), no.3, pp.35-44.

C4.   Benkendorf, Count P.K. *Last Days of Tsarskoe Selo: being the personal notes and memories of Count Paul Benckendorff, telling of the last sojourn of the Emperor & Empress of Russia at Tsarskoe Selo from March 1 to August 1, 1917,* trans.by M.Baring (London: Heinemann, 1927).

C5.   Bergamini, J.D. *The Tragic Dynasty. A History of the Romanovs* (London: Constable, 1970).

C6.   Bing, E.J. (ed.) *The Letters of Tsar Nicholas and Empress Marie. Being the Confidential Correspondence Between Nicholas II, Last of the Tsars, and His Mother, Dowager Empress Maria Feodorovna* (London: Ivor Nicholson & Watson, 1937).

C7.   Boylen, J.O. "The Tsar's 'Lecturer-General'. W.T. Snead and the Russian Revolution of 1905 with Two Unpublished Memoranda of Audiences with the Dowager Empress Marie Fedorovna and Nicholas II," *Georgia State College School of Arts and Sciences Research Papers*, no.23 (July 1969).

C8.   Cowles, V. *The Last Tsar and Tsarina* (London: Weidenfeld & Nicolson, 1977).

C9.   Cowles, V. *The Romanovs* (London: Collins, 1971).

C10.   Gilliard, P. *Thirteen Years at the Russian Court. A personal record of the last years and death of the Czar Nicholas II and his family*, trans.by F.A.Holt (London: Hutchinson, 1921).

C11.   Grey, I. *The Romanovs: the rise and fall of a Russian Dynasty* (Newton Abbot: David & Charles, 1971).

C12.   Harcave, S. *Years of the Golden Cockerel: the Last Romanov Tsars, 1814-1917* (New York: Robert Hale, 1968).

C13.   Hingley, R. *The Tsars. Russian Autocrats, 1533-1917* (London: Weidenfeld & Nicolson, 1968).

C14.   Knox, A. "The Grand Duke Nicholas," *SEER* 7 (1928-29), pp.535-539.

C15.   Kokovtsov, V.N. *Out of My Past. The Memoirs of Count Kokovtsov*, trans.by L.Matveev (Stanford: Stanford U.P., 1935).

C16.   Kulikowski, M. "Rasputin and the Fall of the Romanovs," PhD diss., SUNY, Binghampton, 1982.

C17.   Lieven, D. *Russia's Rulers Under the Old Regime* (New Haven & London: Yale U.P., 1989).

C18.   Lieven, D. "The Russian Ruling Elite under Nicholas II: Career patterns," *Cahiers du Monde Russe et Sovietique* 25 (1984), no.4, pp.429-454.

C19.   Massie, R.K. *Nicholas and Alexandra* (London: Victor Gollancz, 1968).

C20.   Mazour, A.G. *The Rise and Fall of the Romanovs* (Princeton: D.Van Nostrand, 1960).

C21.   Mosolov, A.A. *At the Court of the Last Tsar. Being the memoirs of A.A. Mossolov, head of the Court Chancellery, 1900-1916*, trans.by E.W.Dickes (London: Methuen, 1935).

C22.   Pares, B. (ed.) *Letters of the Tsaritsa to the Tsar 1914-1916* (London: Duckworth, 1923).

C23.   Pridham, Vice-Admiral Sir F. *Close of a Dynasty* (London: Allan Wingate, 1956).

C24.   Sava, G. *One Russian's Story* (London: Robert Hale, 1970).

C25.   Sworakowski, W.S. "The Authorship of the Abdication Document of Nicholas II," *RR* 30 (1971), no.3, pp.277-286.

C26.   Trewin, J.C. *Tutor to the Tsarevich: An Intimate Portrait of the Last Days of the Russian Imperial Family compiled from the papers of Charles Sydney Gibbes* (London & Basingstoke: Macmillan, 1975).

C27.   Verner, A.M. "Nicholas II and the Role of the Autocrat during the First Russian Revolution, 1904-1907," PhD diss., Columbia, 1986.

C28.   Vinogradoff, I. "The Emperor Nicholas II, Stolypin and Rasputin: A Letter of 10th October 1906," *OSP* 12 (1965), pp.114-116.

C29.   Viroubova, A. *Memories of the Russian Court* (London: Macmillan, 1923).

C30.   Vorres, I. *The Last Grand Duchess: Her Imperial Highness Grand Duchess Olga Alexandrovna* (New York: Scribner,1965).

C31.   Warth, R.D. "Before Rasputin: Piety and Occult at the Court of Nicholas II," *The Historian* 47 (1985) no.3, pp.323-337.

C32.   Witte, Count *The Memoirs of Count Witte*, trans. & edited by S.Harcave (Armonk, New York, London: M.E.Sharpe, 1990).

C33.   Wortman, R.S. "'Invisible Threads': The Historical Imagery of the Romanov Tercentenary," *RH* 16 (1989), pts.2/4, pp.389-408.

Tsar and Ministers:

C34.   Brancouan, C.E. "Grand Duke Nikolay Mikhailovich on the Ministerial and Parliamentary Crisis of March-April 1911: Five Letters to Frederic Masson," *OSP(NS)* 6 (1973), pp.66-81.

C35.   Cherniavsky, M. (ed.) *Prologue to Revolution: Notes of A.N. Iakhontov on the Secret Meetings of the Council of Ministers, 1915* (Englewood Cliffs, N.J.: Prentice-Hall, 1967).

C36.   Chmielewski, E. "Stolypin and the Ministerial Crisis of 1909," *California Slavic Studies* 4 (1967), pp.1-38.

C37.   Chmielewski, E. "Stolypin's Last Crisis," *California Slavic Studies* 3 (1964), pp.95-126.

C38.   Doctorow, G.S. "The Government Program of 17 October 1905," *RR* 34 (1975), no.2, pp.123-136.

C39.   Doctorow, G.S. "The Fundamental State Laws of 23 April 1906," *RR* 35 (1976), no.1, pp.33-52.

C40.   Edwards, J.A.D. "The Evolution of Collective Ministerial Authority in Imperial Russia: A Comparison of the Nineteenth Century Committee of Ministers and the Reformed Council of Ministers from 1906 to 1911," PhD diss., Stanford, 1979.

C41.   Gangelin, R.Sh. "On the Eve of 'Bloody Sunday' (the Royal Authorities, January 6-8, 1905)," *SSH* 20 (1981-82), no.3, pp.96-119.

C42.   Gerus, O.W. "The Reformed State Council, 1905-1917: A Phase in Russian Constitutionalism," PhD diss., Toronto, 1970.

C43.   Gurko, V.I. *Features and Figures of the Past: Government and Opinion in the Reign of Nicholas II*, trans.by L.Matveev (Stanford: Stanford U.P., 1939).

C44.   Healy, A.K.E. "The Russian Autocracy in Crisis: Tsarism and the Opposition from 1905 to 1907," PhD diss., Wisconsin, 1972.

C45.   Jones, M.E. "The Uses and Abuses of Article 87: A Study in the Development of Russian Constitutionalism, 1906-1917," PhD diss., Syracuse, 1975.

C46.   Kilcoyne, M.J. "The Political Influence of Rasputin," PhD diss., Washington, Seattle, 1961.

C47.   Kochan, L. "Sergei Witte: the Last Statesman of Imperial Russia," *HT* 18 (1968), pp.102-108.

C48.   Kokovtsov, V.N.   *Out of My Past. The Memoirs of Count Kokovtsov*, trans.by L.Matveev (Stanford: Stanford U.P., 1935).

C49.   Lieven, D. *Russia's Rulers Under the Old Regime* (New Haven & London: Yale U.P., 1989).

C50.   Lieven, D.C.B. "Stereotyping an Elite: The Appointed Members of the State Council, 1894-1914," *SEER* 63 (1985), no.2, pp.244-272.

C51.   Lieven, D.C.B. "The Russian Establishment in the Reign of Nicholas II: The Appointed Members of the Council of State, 1894-1914," PhD diss., London, 1979.

C52.   Mehlinger, H.D. "Count Sergei Iu. Witte and the Problems of Constitutionalism in Russia, 1905-1906,"   PhD diss., Kansas, 1964.

C53.   Mehlinger, H.D. & Thompson, J.J. *Count Witte and the Tsarist Government in the 1905 Revolution* (Bloomington & London: Indiana U.P., 1972).

C54.   Santoni, W.D. "P.N. Durnovo as Minister of Internal Affairs in the Witte Cabinet: A Study in Suppression," PhD diss., Kansas, 1968.

C55.   Schultz, L. "Constitutional Law in Russia," in: G.Katkov et al (eds.) *Russia Enters the Twentieth Century, 1894-1917* (London: Temple Smith, 1971), pp.34-59.

C56.   Shecket, A.D. "The Russian Imperial State Council and the Policies of P.A. Stolypin, 1906-1911: Bureaucratic and *Soslovie* Interests Versus Reform," PhD diss., Columbia, 1974.

C57.   Tager, A.B. *The Decay of Czarism: The Beiliss Trial. A contribution to the history of the political reaction during the last years of Russian Czarism* (Philadelphia: Jewish Publication Society of America, 1935).

C58.   Thomson, T.J. "Boris Sturmer and the Imperial Russian Government, February 2 - November 22, 1916," PhD diss., Duke, 1972.

C59.   Yaney, G.L. "Some Aspects of the Imperial Russian Government on the Eve of the First World War," *SEER* 43 (1964-65), pp.68-90.

Bureaucracy:

C60.   Bolsover, G.H. "Izvolsky and Reform of the Russian Ministry of Foreign Affairs," *SEER* 63 (1985), no.1, pp.21-40.

C61.   Hamburg, G.M. "Portrait of an Elite: Russian Marshals of the Nobility, 1861-1917," *SR* 40 (1981), no.4, pp.585-602.

C62.   Levin, A. "Russian Bureaucratic Opinion in the Wake of the 1905 Revolution," *JFGO* (1963), no.4, pp.1-12.

C63. Lieven, D. *Russia's Rulers Under the Old Regime* (New Haven & London: Yale U.P., 1989).

C64. Lieven, D.C.B. "Russian Senior Officialdom under Nicholas II. Careers and Mentalities," *JFGO* 32 (1984), pp.199-223.

C65. Lieven, D.C.B. "The Russian Civil Service under Nicholas II: Some Variations on the Bureaucratic Theme," *JFGO* 29 (1981), pp.366-403.

C66. McKean, R.B. "The Bureaucracy and the Labour Problem, June 1907-February 1917," in: R.B.McKean (ed.) *New Perspectives in Modern Russian History* (Basingstoke & London: Macmillan, 1992), pp.222-249.

C67. Macey, D.A.J. *Government and Peasant in Russia, 1861-1906: The Prehistory of the Stolypin Reforms* (DeKalb, Illinois: Northern Illinois U.P., 1987).

C68. Macey, D.A.J. "The Russian Bureaucracy and the 'Peasant Problem': The Pre-History of the Stolypin Reforms, 1861-1907," PhD diss., Columbia, 1976.

C69. Mosse, W.E. "Aspects of Tsarist Bureaucracy: Recruitment to the Imperial State Council, 1855-1914," *SEER* 57 (1979), no.2, pp.240-254.

C70. Mosse, W.E. "Russian Bureaucracy at the End of the *Ancien Regime*: The Imperial State Council, 1897-1915," *SR* 39 (1980), no.4, pp.616-632.

C71. Perrins, M. "The Council for State Defence, 1905-9: A Study in Russian Bureaucratic Politics," *SEER* 58 (1980), no.3, pp.370-398.

C72. Rowney, D.K. "Higher Civil Servants in the Russian Ministry of Internal Affairs: Some Demographic and Career Characteristics, 1905-1916," *SR* 31 (1972), no.1, pp. 101-110.

C73. Rowney, D.K. "Organizational Change and Social Adaptation: The Pre-Revolutionary Ministry of Internal Affairs," in: W.M.Pintner & D.K.Rowney (eds.) *Russian Officialdom: The Bureaucratization of Russian Society from the Seventeenth to the Twentieth Century* (London: Macmillan, 1980), pp.283-315.

C74. Sinel, A.A. "The Socialization of the Russian Bureaucratic Elite, 1811-1917: Life at the Tsarskoe Selo Lyceum and the School of Jurisprudence," *RH* 3 (1976), pt.1, pp.1-31.

C75. Snow, G.E. "Vladimir Nikolaevich Kokovtsov: Case Study of an Imperial Russian Bureaucrat, 1904-1906," PhD diss., Indiana, 1970.

C76. Sternheimer, S. "Administering Development and Developing Administration: Organizational Conflict and Bureaucracy, 1906-14," *CASS* 9 (1975), no.3, pp.277-301.

C77. Urussov, S.D. *Memoirs of a Russian Governor*, trans.by H.Rosenthal (London & New York: Harper, 1908).

C78. Wcislo, F.W. "Bureaucratic Reform Before World War I," *RH* 16 (1989), pts.2/4, pp.377-387.

24 *Russian Revolution*

C79.   Wcislo, F.W. "Bureaucratic Reform in Tsarist Russia: State and Local Society, 1881-1914," PhD diss., Columbia, 1984.

C80.   Wcislo, F.W. *Reforming Rural Russia: State, Local Society, and National Politics, 1855-1914* (Princeton: Princeton U.P., 1990).

C81.   Wcislo, F.W. "*Soslovie* or Class? Bureaucratic Reformers and Provincial Gentry in Conflict, 1906-1908," *RR* 47 (1988), no.1, pp.1-24.

C82.   Weissman, N.B. *Reform in Tsarist Russia: The State Bureaucracy and Local Government, 1900-1914* (New Brunswick, N.J.: Rutgers U.P., 1981).

C83.   Yaney, G. "Bureaucracy as Culture: A Comment," *SR* 41 (1982), no.1, pp.104-111.

C84.   Yaney, G.L. "Some Aspects of the Imperial Russian Government on the Eve of the First World War," *SEER* 43 (1964-65), pp.68-90.

Judiciary:

C85.   Atwell, J.W. "The Jury System and Its Role in Russia's Legal, Social, and Political Development from 1857 to 1914," PhD diss., Princeton, 1970.

C86.   Ballantine, E. "A.F. Koni and the Russian Judiciary, 1864-1917," PhD diss., Yale, 1986.

C87.   Dussel, D.C. "Russian Judicial Reforms and Counter-Reforms: 1864-1914," PhD diss., Missouri, 1981.

C88.   Kucherov, S. *Courts, Lawyers and Trials under the Last Three Tsars* (New York: Frederick A.Praeger, 1953).

C89.   Kucherov, S. "Courts, Lawyers and Trials Under the Last Three Czars," PhD diss., Columbia, 1955.

C90.   McIntire, S.W. "The Russian Judicial Reform of 1864: Its Origins and Development, 1825-1964," PhD diss., SUNY, Binghamton, 1973.

C91.   Rawson, D. "The Death Penalty in Late Tsarist Russia: An Investigation of Judicial Procedures," *RH* 11 (1984), pt.1, pp.29-52.

Police and Okhrana:

C92.   Anin, D. "Lenin and Malinovsky," *Survey* 21 (Autumn 1975), no.4, pp.145-156.

C93.   Bailey, S.D. ""Police Socialism" in Tsarist Russia," *Review of Politics* 19 (1957), pp.462-471.

C94.   Bradley, J.F.N. "The Russian Secret Service in the First World War," *SS* 20 (1968-69), no.2, pp.242-248.

C95.   Burtsev, V. "Police Provocation in Russia," *SEER* 6 (1927-28), pp.247-267.

C96.   Deacon, R. *A History of the Russian Secret Service* (London: Grafton, 1972 [revised edition 1987]).

C97.   Elwood, R.C. *Roman Malinovsky: A Life Without Cause* (Newtonville, Mass.: Oriental Research Partners, 1977).

C98.   Hingley, R. *The Russian Secret Police. Muscovite, Imperial Russian and Soviet Political Security Operations 1565-1970* (London: Hutchinson, 1970).

C99.   Johnson, R.J. "The *Okhrana* Abroad, 1885-1917: A Study in International Police Cooperation," PhD diss., Columbia, 1970.

C100.   Johnson, R.J. "Zagranichnaya agentura: the tsarist political police in Europe," *JCH* 7 (1972), no.1/2, pp.221-242.

C101.   Kaledin, Colonel V. *High Treason: Four Major Cases of the St.Petersburg Personal Court Branch* (London: Hurst & Blackett, 1936).

C102.   Kaledin, Colonel V. *K.14-O.M.66. Adventures of a Double Spy* (London: Hurst & Blackett, 1934).

C103.   Levin, A. "The Shornikova Affair," *SEER* 21 (1943), pp.1-18.

C104.   Lieven, D.C.B. "The Security Police, Civil Rights, and the Fate of the Russian Empire, 1855-1917," in: O.Crisp & L.Edmondson (eds.) *Civil Rights in Imperial Russia* (Oxford: Clarendon, 1989), pp.235-262.

C105.   Pearson, R. "The Okhrana Archives as an Historical Source," *Sbornik (SGRR)* no.1 (1975), pp.20-23.

C106.   Ruud, C.A. "A.A. Lopukhin, Police Insubordination and the Rule of Law," *RH* 20 (1993), nos.1-4, pp.147-162.

C107.   Schleifmann, I. "The Internal Agency: Linchpin of the political police in Russia," *Cahiers du Monde Russe et Sovietique* 24 (1983), nos.1-2, pp.151-177.

C108.   Schleifmann, N. "The Okhrana and Burtsev - Provocateurs and Revolutionaries," *Survey* 27 (1983), pp.22-40.

C109.   Schneiderman, J. "From the Files of the Moscow Gendarme Corps: A Lecture on Combatting Revolution," *Canadian Slavic Studies* 2 (1968), no.1, pp.86-99.

C110.   Senn, A.E. "Russian Emigre Funds in Switzerland 1916: An Okhrana Report," *IRSH* 13 (1968), pp.76-84.

C111.   Smith, E.E. & Lednicky, R. *"The Okhrana": The Russian Department of Police: A Bibliography* (Stanford: Hoover Institution,1967).

C112.   Thurston, R.W. "Police and People in Moscow, 1906-1914," *RR* 39 (1980), no.3, pp.320-338.

C113.   Ulunian, A. "The Special Branch of the Russian Police: Greece and Turkey Through Intelligence Eyes (1912-14)," *Revolutionary Russia* 5 (1992), no.2, pp.209-217.

C114. Vassilyev, A.T. *The Ochrana: the Russian Secret Police* (London: G.G.Harrap, 1930).

C115. Weissman, N. "Regular Police in Tsarist Russia, 1900-1914," *RR* 44 (1985), no.1, pp.45-68.

C116. Zuckerman, F.S. "Political Police and Revolution: The Impact of the 1905 Revolution on the Tsarist Secret Police," *JCH* 27 (1992), no.2, pp.279-300.

C117. Zuckerman, F.S. "The Russian Political Police at Home and Abroad (1880-1917): Its Structure, Functions, and Method and Its Struggle with the Organized Opposition," PhD diss., New York, 1973.

C118. Zuckerman, F.S. "Vladimir Burtsev and the Tsarist Political Police in Conflict, 1907-14," *JCH* 12 (1977), no.1, pp.193-219.

The Duma:

C119. Christian, R.F. "Alexis Aladin, Trudovik Leader in the First Russian Duma: Materials for a Biography (1873-1920)," *OSP (NS)* 21 (1988), pp.131-152.

C120. Conroy, M.S. *Petr Arkad'evich Stolypin. Practical Politics in Late Tsarist Russia* (Boulder: Westview, 1976).

C121. Coonrod, R.W. "The Duma's Attitude Toward War-time Problems of Minority Groups," *ASEER* 13 (1954), pp.29-46.

C122. Coonrod, R.W. "The Fourth Duma and the War, 1914-1917," PhD diss., Stanford, 1951.

C123. Costello, D.R. "Prime Minister Kokovtsev and the Duma: A Study in the Disintegration of the Tsarist Regime, 1911-1914," PhD diss., Virginia, 1970.

C124. Doctorow, G.S. "The Introduction of Parliamentary Institutions in Russia during the Revolution of 1905-1907," PhD diss., Columbia, 1975.

C125. Doctorow, G.S. "The Polish Electoral Law to the Russian State Duma," *RH* 2 (1975), pt.2, pp.163-175.

C126. Emmons, T. "Russia's First National Elections," in: F.X.Coquin and C.Gervais-Francelle (eds.) *1905: La Premiere Revolution Russe* (Paris: Publications de la Sorbonne et Institut d'etudes slaves, 1986), pp.31-44.

C127. Goldenweiser, E.A. "The Russian Duma," *Political Science Quarterly* 29 (1914), pp.408-422.

C128. Harper, S.N. *The New Electoral Law for the Russian Duma* (Chicago, 1908).

C129. Healy, A.E. *The Russian Autocracy in Crisis, 1905-1907* (Hamden, Conn.: Archon, 1976).

C130. Heilbronner, H. "Piotr Khristianovich von Schwanebakh and the Dissolution of the First Two Dumas," *CSP* 11 (1969), pp.31-55.

C131.   Hollingsworth, B. "The British Memorial to the Russian Duma, 1906," *SEER* 53 (1975), pp.539-557.

C132.   Hosking, G.A. "Stolypin and the Octobrist Party," *SEER* 47 (1969), pp.137-160.

C133.   Hosking, G.A. "Government and Duma in Russia (1907-14)," PhD diss., Cambridge, 1970.

C134.   Hosking, G.A. *The Russian Constitutional Experiment: Government and Duma, 1907-1914* (Cambridge: Cambridge U.P., 1973).

C135.   Keep, J.L.H. "Russian Social Democracy and the First State Duma," *SEER* 34 (1955-56), pp.180-199.

C136.   Korros, A.S. "Activist Politics in a Conservative Institution: The Formation of Factions in the Russian Imperial State Council, 1906-1907," *RR* 52 (1993), no.1, pp.1-19.

C137.   Lerner, L.W. "The Progressists in the Russian State Duma, 1907-1915," PhD diss., Washington, 1976.

C138.   Levin, A. "June 3, 1907: Action and Reaction," in: A.D.Ferguson & A.Levin (eds.) *Essays in Russian History: A Collection Dedicated to George Vernadsky* (Hamden, Conn.: Archon, 1964), pp.231-273.

C139.   Levin, A. "The Fifth Social Democratic Congress and the Duma," *JMH* 11 (1939), pp.484-508.

C140.   Levin, A. *The Third Duma, Election and Profile* (Hamden, Conn.: Archon, 1973).

C141.   Levin, A. "The Russian Voter in the Elections to the Third Duma," *SR* 21 (1962), no.4, pp.660-677.

C142.   Levin, A. *The Second Duma: A Study of the Social-Democratic Party and the Russian Constitutional Experiment* (New Haven: Yale U.P., 1940).

C143.   Levitsky, S.L. "Legislative Initiative in the Russia Duma," *ASEER* 15 (1956), pp.313-324.

C144.   Maklakov, V.A. *The First State Duma. Contemporary Reminiscences*, trans.by M.Belkin (Bloomington: Indiana U.P., 1964).

C145.   Pares, B. "Michael Rodzyanko," *SEER* 2 (1923-24), pp.604-608.

C146.   Pares, B. "Michael Stakhovich," *SEER* 2 (1923-24), pp.608-610.

C147.   Pares, B. "Nicholas Homyakov," *SEER* 4 (1925-26), no.2, pp.463-471.

C148.   Pares, B. "Sergius Shidlovsky," *SEER* 1 (1922-23), pp.445-447.

C149.   Pares, B. "The Second Duma," *SEER* 2 (1923-24), pp.36-55.

C150.   Pares, B. "Vladimir Nabokov," *SEER* 1 (1922-23), pp.443-445.

C151.   Riha, T. "Miliukov and the Progressive Bloc in 1915: a Study in Last-Chance Politics," *JMH* 32 (1960), no.1, pp.16-24.

C152.   Schaeffer, M.E. "Political Policies of P.A. Stolypin, Minister of the Interior and Chairman of the Council of Ministers in Russia, 1906-1911," PhD diss., Indiana, 1964

C153.   Smith, C.J., Jr. "The Russian Third State Duma: an Analytical Profile," *RR* 17 (1958), no.3, pp.201-210.

C154.   Snow, G.E. "The Peterhof Conference of 1905 and the Creation of the Bulygin Duma," *RH* 2 (1975), pt.2, pp.149-162.

C155.   Strakhovsky, L.I. "Stolypin and the Second Duma," *CSP* 6 (1964), pp.3-17.

C156.   Szeftel, M. *The Russian Constitution of April 23, 1906: Political Institutions of the Duma Monarchy* (Bruxelles: La Libraire Encyclopedique, 1976).

C157.   Tokmakoff, G. "P.A. Stolypin and the Second Duma," *SEER* 50 (1972), pp.49-62.

C158.   Tokmakoff, G. *P.A. Stolypin and the Third Duma: an appraisal of three major issues* (Washington: University Press of America, 1981).

C159.   Tuck, R.L. "Paul Miljukov and Negotiations for a Duma Ministry 1906," *ASEER* 10 (1951), no.2, pp.117-129.

C160.   Waldron, P. "Constitutional Change and Reform in Imperial Russia After 1905," *Sbornik (SGRR)* no.9 (1983), pp.15-40.

C161.   Walsh, W.B. "Political Parties in the Russian Dumas," *JMH* 22 (1950), no.2, pp.144-150.

C162.   Walsh, W.B. "Changing Perceptions of the State Duma: Some Personal Retrospections," *RR* 38 (1979), no.3, pp.339-347.

C163.   Walsh, W.B. "The Composition of the Dumas," *RR* 8 (1949) no.2, pp.111-116.

Zemstvo and Local Government:

C164.   Allen, S.E., Jr. "The *Zemstvo* as a Force for Social and Civic Regeneration in Russia: A Study of Selected Aspects, 1864-1905," PhD diss., Clark, 1969.

C165.   Conroy, M.S. "Stolypin's Attitude toward Local Self-Government," *SEER* 46 (1968), pp.446-461.

C166.   Dodge, R.H. "The Moscow Zemstvo and Elementary Education, 1868-1910," PhD diss., Syracuse, 1970.

C167.   Emmons, T. & Vucinich, W.S. (eds.) *The Zemstvo in Russia: An Experiment in Local Self-Government* (Cambridge: Cambridge U.P., 1982).

C168.   Fallows, T. "Politics and the War Effort in Russia: The Union of Zemstvos and the Organization of the Food Supply, 1914-1916," *SR* 37 (1978), no.1, pp.70-90.

C169.   Fallows, T.S. "Forging the *Zemstvo* Movement: Liberalism and Radicalism on the Volga, 1890-1905," PhD diss., Harvard, 1981.

C170.   Figes, O. "The Village and *Volost* Soviet Elections of 1919," *SS* 40 (1988), no.1, pp.21-45.

C171.   George, M. "Liberal Opposition in Wartime Russia: A Case Study of the Town and Zemstvo Unions, 1914-1917," *SEER* 65 (1987), no.3, pp.371-390.

C172.   George, M. "The All-Russian Zemstvo Union and the All-Russian Union of Towns. 1914-1917: A Political Study," PhD diss., London, 1986.

C173.   Gleason, W.E. "The All-Russian Union of Towns and the All-Russian Union of *Zemstvos* in World War I: 1914-1917," PhD diss., Indiana, 1972.

C174.   Hamburg, G.M. "Portrait of an Elite: Russian Marshals of the Nobility, 1861-1917," *SR* 40 (1981), no.4, pp.585-602.

C175.   Hamm, M.F. "Khar'kov's Progressive Duma, 1910-1914: A Study in Russian Municipal Reform," *SR* 40 (1981), no.1, pp.17-36.

C176.   LeDonne, J.P. "'From *Gubernia* to *Oblast*': Soviet Territorial Administrative Reforms, 1917-1923," PhD diss., Columbia, 1962.

C177.   Long, J.W. "The Volga Germans and the Zemstvos, 1865-1917," *JFGO* 30 (1982), pp.336-361.

C178.   MacNaughton, R.D. & Manning, R.T. "The Crisis of the Third of June System and Political Trends in the Zemstvos, 1907-14," in: L.H.Haimson (ed.) *The Politics of Rural Russia, 1905-1914* (Bloomington & London: Indiana U.P., 1979), pp.184-218.

C179.   Manning, R.T. "Zemstvo and Revolution: The Onset of the Gentry Reaction, 1905-1907," in: L.H.Haimson (ed.) *The Politics of Rural Russia, 1905-1914* (Bloomington & London: Indiana U.P., 1979), pp.30-66.

C180.   Orlovsky, D.T. "Reform during Revolution: Governing the Provinces in 1917," in: R.O.Crummey (ed.) *Reform in Russia and the U.S.S.R. Past and Prospects* (Urbana & Chicago: Board of Trustees of the University of Illinois, 1989), pp. 100-125.

C181.   Polner, T.J. *Russian Local Government During the War and the Union of Zemstvos* (New Haven: Yale U.P., 1930).

C182.   Porter, T.E. "The Development of Political Pluralism in Late Imperial Russia: Local Self-Government and the Movement for a National Zemstvo Union, 1864-1917," PhD diss., Washington, Seattle, 1990.

C183.   Poulsen, T.M. "The Provinces of Russia: Changing Patterns with Regional Allocation of Authority, 1708-1962," PhD diss., Wisconsin, 1963.

C184.   Renehan, T.J. "The Failure of Local Soviet Government, 1917-1918," PhD diss., SUNY, Binghampton, 1984.

C185.   Robbins, R.G. "His Excellency The Governor: The Style of Russian Provincial Governance at the Beginning of the Twentieth Century," in: E.Mendelsohn & M.S.Shatz (eds.) *Imperial Russia, 1700-1917: State, Society, Opposition. Essays in Honor of Marc Raeff* (DeKalb, Illinois: Northern Illinois Press, 1988), pp.76-92.

C186.   Robbins, R.G. *The Tsar's Viceroys: Russian Provincial Governors in the Last Years of the Empire* (Ithaca & London: Cornell U.P, 1987).

C187.   Rosenberg, W.G. "The Russian Municipal Duma Elections of 1917: A Preliminary Computation of Returns," *SS* 21 (1969-70), no.2, pp.131-163.

C188.   Timberlake, C.E. "The Birth of *Zemstvo* Liberalism in Russia: Ivan Il'ich Petrunkevich in Chernigo," PhD diss., Washington, Seattle, 1968.

C189.   Urussov, S.D. *Memoirs of a Russian Governor*, trans.by H.Rosenthal (London & New York: Harper, 1908).

C190.   Vinogradoff, P. *Self-Government in Russia* (London: Constable, 1915).

C191.   Waldron, P.R. "The Stolypin Programme of Reform, 1906-1911, with Special Reference to Local Government and Religious Affairs," PhD diss., London, 1981.

C192.   Weissman, N.B. *Reform in Tsarist Russia: The State Bureaucracy and Local Government, 1900-1914* (New Brunswick, N.J.: Rutgers U.P., 1981).

C193.   Weissman, N.B. "State, Estate and Society in Tsarist Russia: The Question of Local Government, 1900-1908," PhD diss., Princeton, 1977.

Provisional Government:

C194.   Browder, R.P. "Kerenskij Revisited," *HSS* 4 (1957), pp.421-434.

C195.   Browder, R.P. & Kerensky, A.F. (eds.) *The Russian Provisional Government of 1917: Documents*, 3 vols. (Stanford: Stanford U.P., 1961).

C196.   Dailey, K.I. "The Russian Provisional Government of 1917," PhD diss., Syracuse, 1957.

C197.   Elkin, B. "Further Notes on the Policies of the Kerensky Government," *SR* 25 (1966), no.2, pp.323-332.

C198.   Johnston, R.H. "Continuity Versus Revolution: The Russian Provisional Government and the Balkans, March-November, 1917," PhD diss., Yale, 1966.

C199.   Kerensky, A. "The Policy of the Provisional Government of 1917," *SEER* 11 (1932-33), pp.1-19.

C200.   Mau, V. "Bread, Democracy and the Bolshevik Coup," *Revolutionary Russia* 7 (1994), no.1, pp.34-37.

C201.   Melancon, M. "The Syntax of Soviet Power: the Resolutions of Local Soviets and Other Institutions, March-October 1917," *RR* 52 (1993), no.4, pp.486-505.

C202.   Morris, L.P. "The Russians, the Allies and the War, February-July 1917," *SEER* 50 (1972), no.118, pp.29-48.

C203.   Mosse, W.E. "Interlude: The Russian Provisional Government 1917," *SS* 15 (1964), no.4, pp.408-419.

C204.   Mosse, W.E. "The February Regime: Prerequisites of Success," *SS* 19 (1967), no.1, pp.100-108.

C205.   Nabokov, V.D. *V.D. Nabokov and the Russian Provisional Government, 1917* (New Haven & London: Yale U.P., 1976).

C206.   Onou, A. "The Provisional Government of Russia in 1917," *Contemporary Review* October 1933, pp.446-454.

C207.   Rocheleau, J.R. "From July Days to November Revolution: A Study of the Provisional Government of Alexander F. Kerensky," PhD diss., Idaho, 1969.

C208.   Schapiro, L. *1917. The Russian Revolutions and the Origins of Present-Day Communism* (Hounslow, Middlesex: Maurice Temple Smith, 1984).

C209.   Stojko, W. "The Attitude of the Russian Provisional Government Toward the Non-Russian Peoples of Its Empire," PhD diss., New York, 1969.

C210.   Walsh, W.B. "May-June, 1917: An Estimate of the Situation (George Kennan to Douglas W. Johnson)," *RR* 27 (1968), no.4, pp.468-470.

C211.   White, H.J. "Civil Rights and the Provisional Government," in: O.Crisp & L.Edmondson (eds.) *Civil Rights in Imperial Russia* (Oxford: Clarendon, 1989), pp.287-312.

Soviets:

C212.   Abrams, R. "Political Recruitment and Local Government: the Local Soviets of the RSFSR, 1918-21," *SS* 19 (1968), no.4, pp.573-580.

C213.   Abrams, R. "The Local Soviets of the RSFSR, 1918-21," PhD diss., Columbia, 1966.

C214.   Andreev, A.M. "Local Soviets and the State Conference," *SSH* 6 (1967-68), no.4, pp.24-58.

C215.   Andreyev, A. *The Soviets of Workers' and Soldiers' Deputies on the Eve of the October Revolution, March - October 1917*, trans.by J.Langstone (Moscow: Progress, 1971).

C216.   Anweiler, O. *The Soviets: The Russian Workers, Peasants, and Soldiers Councils, 1905-1921*, trans.by R.Hein (New York: Pantheon, 1974).

C217.   Gal'perina, B.D. "The Petrograd Soviet in September and October 1917 (New Data)," *SSH* 23 (1984-85), no.1, pp.84-103.

C218.   Garvy, G. "The Financial Manifesto of the St. Petersburg Soviet, 1905," *IRSH* 20 (1975), pp.16-32.

C219.   Getzler, I. "All power to Soviets: maximalist ideology and Kronstadt practice," in: E.Kamenka (ed.) *Community as a Social Ideal* (London: Edward Arnold, 1982), pp.82-98.

C220.   Getzler, I. *Kronstadt 1917-1921: The Fate of a Soviet Democracy* (Cambridge: Cambridge U.P., 1983).

C221.   Getzler, I. "Soviets as Agents of Democratisation," in: E.R.Frankel et al (eds.) *Revolution in Russia: Reassessments of 1917* (Cambridge: Cambridge U.P., 1992), pp.17-33.

C222.   Gimpel'son, E.G. "Literature of the Soviets During the First Years of the Dictatorship of the Proletariat (Nov.1917-1920)," *SSH* 2 (1963-64), no.4, pp.23-37.

C223.   Hall, T.R. "The Petersburg Soviet of Workmen Deputies in the Revolution of 1905," PhD diss., Chicago, 1942.

C224.   Hasegawa, T. "The Bolsheviks and the Formation of the Petrograd Soviet in the February Revolution," *SS* 29 (1977), no.1, pp.86-107.

C225.   Keep, J.L.H. (ed.) *The Debate on Soviet Power. Minutes of the All-Russian Central Executive Committee of Soviets: Second Convocation, October 1917-January 1918* (Oxford: Clarendon, 1979).

C226.   Medlin, V.D. "The Reluctant Revolutionaries: The Petrograd Soviet of Workers' and Soldiers' Deputies 1917," PhD diss., Oklahoma, 1974.

C227.   Melancon, M. "The Syntax of Soviet Power: the Resolutions of Local Soviets and Other Institutions, March-October 1917," *RR* 52 (1993), no.4, pp.486-505.

C228.   Morgan, A.D. "The St.Petersburg Soviet of Workers' Deputies: A Study of Labor Organization in the 1905 Russian Revolution," PhD diss., Indiana, 1979.

C229.   Rabinowitch, A. "The Evolution of Local Soviets in Petrograd, November 1917-June 1918: The Case of the First City District Soviet," *SR* 46 (1987), no.1, pp.20-37.

C230.   Slavin, N.F. "On the Question of the Methods to be Used in the Struggle for the Transfer of Power to the Soviets after the Rout of the Kornilov Revolt," *SSH* 23 (1984-85), no.1, pp.56-83.

C231.   Slusser, R.M. "The Forged Bolshevik Signature: A Problem in Soviet Historiography," *SR* 23 (1964), no.2, pp.294-308.

C232.   Slusser, R.M. "The Moscow Soviet of Workers' Deputies of 1905: Origin, Structure, and Policies," PhD diss., Columbia, 1963.

C233.   Sutton, K.A. "Class and Revolution in Russia: The Soviet Movement of 1905," PhD diss., Birmingham, 1987.

C234.   Von Loewe, K.F. "Challenge to Ideology: The Petrograd Soviet, February 27 - March 3, 1917," *RR* 26 (1967), no.2, pp.164-175.

C235.   Wade, R.A. "The Rajonnye Sovety of Petrograd: The Role of Local Political Bodies in the Russian Revolution," *JFGO* 20 (1972), pp.226-240.

C236.   Wade, R. "The Triumph of Siberian Zimmerwaldism: (March-May, 1917)," *Canadian Slavic Studies* 1 (1967), no.2, pp.253-270.

C237.   Wade, R.A. "Why October? The Search for Peace in 1917," *SS* 20 (1968-69), no.1, pp.36-45.

Constituent Assembly:

C238.   Dando, W.A. "A Map of the Election to the Russian Constituent Assembly of 1917," *SR* 25 (1966), no.2, pp.314-319.

C239.   Garber, A. "The Ideological Dimensions of the Historical Explanations to the Russian Constituent Assembly, January 18, 1918," PhD diss., California, Berkeley, 1958.

C240.   Kochan, L. "Kadet Policy in 1917 and the Constituent Assembly," *SEER* 45 (1967), pp.183-192.

C241.   Pipes, R. "The Bolsheviks Dissolve the Constituent Assembly," *Survey* 30 (1988), no.3, pp.148-175.

C242.   Radkey, O. *The Election to the Russian Constituent Assembly of 1917* (Cambridge, Mass.: Harvard U.P., 1950 [updated edition Ithaca: Cornell U.P., 1989]).

Construction of the Soviet State:

C243.   Akhapkin, Y. (ed.) *First Decrees of Soviet Power* (London: Lawrence & Wishart, 1970).

C244.   Basil, J.D. "Russia and the Bolshevik Revolution," *RR* 27 (1968), no.1, pp.42-53.

C245.   Bettelheim, C. *Class Struggles in the USSR: First Period: 1917-1923*, trans.by B.Pearce (Hassocks, Sussex: Harvester Press, 1977)

C246.   Brinton, M. *The Bolsheviks and Workers' Control, 1917-1921: the State and Counter-Revolution* (London: Solidarity, 1970).

C247.   Bunyan, J. *The Origin of Forced Labor in the Soviet State, 1917-1921: Documents and Materials* (Baltimore: Johns Hopkins U.P., 1967).

C248.   Duval, C. "Yakov M. Sverdlov and the All-Russian Central Executive Committee of Soviets (VTsIK). A Study in Bolshevik Consolidation of Power, October 1917 - July 1918," *SS* 31 (1979), no.1, pp.3-22.

C249.   Ferro, M. "The Birth of the Soviet Bureaucratic System," in: R.C.Elwood (ed.) *Reconsiderations on the Russian Revolution* (Cambridge, Mass.: Slavica, 1976), pp.100-132.

C250.   Helgesen, M.M. "The Origins of the Party-State Monolith in Soviet Russia: Relations Between the Soviets and Party Committees in the Central Provinces, October 1917 - March 1921," PhD diss., SUNY, Stony Brook, 1980.

C251.   Kleubort, D. "Lenin on the State: Theory and Practice after October," PhD diss., Chicago, 1977.

C252.   Koenker, D.P., Rosenberg, W.G. & Suny, R.G. (eds.) *Party, State, and Society in the Russian Civil War. Explorations in Social History* (Bloomington & Indianapolis: Indiana U.P., 1989).

C253.   Liberman, S. *Building Lenin's Russia* (Chicago: University of Chicago Press, 1945).

C254.   McCauley, M. *The Russian Revolution and the Soviet State 1917-1921. Documents* (London & Basingstoke: Macmillan, 1980).

C255.   Oppenheim, S.A. "The Supreme Economic Council 1917-21," *SS* 25 (1973), no.1, pp.3-27.

C256.   Pethybridge, R.W. "The Bolsheviks and technical disorder, 1917-1918," *SEER* 49 (1971), no.116, pp.410-424.

C257.   Rees, E.A. *State Control in Soviet Russia: The Rise and Fall of the Workers' and Peasants' Inspectorate, 1920-1934* (London: Macmillan, 1987).

C258.   Remington, T.F. *Building Socialism in Bolshevik Russia: Ideology and Industrial Organization 1917-1921* (Pittsburgh: University of Pittsburgh Press, 1984).

C259.   Remington, T.F. "Democracy and Development in Bolshevik Socialism, 1917-1921," PhD diss., Yale, 1978.

C260.   Remington, T. "Institution Building in Bolshevik Russia: The Case of "State *Kontrol*'"," SR 41 (1982), no.1, pp.91-103.

C261.   Rigby, T.H. *Lenin's Government: Sovnarkom 1917-1922* (London: Cambridge U.P., 1979).

C262.   Rigby, T.H. "Staffing USSR Incorporated: The Origins of the Nomenklatura System," *SS* 40 (1988), no.4, pp.523-537.

C263.   Rigby, T.H. "The Soviet Political Elite 1917-1922," *British Journal of Political Science* 1 (1971), part 4, pp.415-436.

C264.   Rosenberg, W.G. "Russian Labor and Bolshevik Power After October," *SR* 44 (1985), no.2, pp.205-238, followed by "Discussion" pp.239-256.

C265.   Rosenberg, W.G. "Social Mediation and State Construction(s) in Revolutionary Russia," *Social History* 19 (1994), no.2, pp.169-188.

C266.   Sakwa, R. *Soviet Communists in Power: A Study of Moscow during the Civil War, 1918-1921* (New York: St.Martin's Press, 1988).

C267.   Sakwa, R. "The Commune State in Moscow in 1918," *SR* 46 (1987), no.3/4, pp.429-449.

C268.   Schapiro, L. *The Origin of the Communist Autocracy* (New York: Praeger, 1965 [originally published in 1955]. 2nd ed. Cambridge, Mass.: Harvard U.P., 1977).

C269.   Service, R. "From Polyarchy to Hegemony: The Party's Role in the Construction of the Central Institutions of the Soviet State, 1917-1919," *Sbornik (SGRR)* no.10 (1984), pp.77-90.

C270.   Shkliarevsky, G.L. "Factory Committees and the Establishment of the Bolshevik Dictatorship," *RH* 13 (1986), pt.4, pp.399-432.

C271.   Spoerry, P.S. "The Central Rabkrin Apparatus: 1917-1925," PhD diss., Harvard, 1968.

C272.   Towster, J. "The Conception of Political Control in the U.S.S.R., 1917-1947," PhD diss., Chicago, 1948.

C273.   Wolfe, B.D. "The Influence of Early Military Decisions upon the National Structure of the Soviet Union," *ASEER* 9 (1950), no.3, pp.169-179.

Communist Party in Power:

C274.   Adelman, J.R. "The Development of the Soviet Party Apparat in the Civil War: Center, Localities and Nationality Areas," *RH* 9 (1982), pt.1, pp.86-110.

C275.   Ali, J. "Aspects of the RKP(B) Secretariat, March 1919 to April 1922," *SS* 26 (1974), no.3, pp.396-416.

C276.   Colton, T.J. "Military Councils and Military Politics in the Russian Civil War," *CSP* 18 (1976), no.1, pp.36-57.

C277.   Gregor, R. (ed.) *Resolutions and Decisions of the Communist Party of the Soviet Union. Vol.II: The Early Soviet Period, 1917-1929* (Toronto & Buffalo: University of Toronto Press, 1974).

C278.   Harding, N. "Authority, Power and the State, 1916-20," in: T.H.Rigby et al (eds.) *Authority, Power and Policy in the USSR: Essays dedicated to Leonard Schapiro* (London & Basingstoke: Macmillan, 1980), pp.32-56.

C279.   Kalynowych, W. "The Top Elite of the Communist Party of the USSR in 1919-1971: A Comparative Study," PhD diss., Indiana, 1972.

C280.   McAuley, M. "Party and Society in Petrograd during the Civil War," *Sbornik (SGRR)* no.10 (1984), pp.43-59.

C281.   Neuweld, M. "The Central Organization of the Communist Party of the Soviet Union: Its Structure, Leadership and Dynamics of Development, 1917-1930," PhD diss., Harvard, 1956.

C282.   Rigby, T.H. *Communist Party Membership in the U.S.S.R., 1917-1967* (Princeton: Princeton U.P., 1968).

C283.   Rigby, T.H. "The Soviet Political Elite 1917-1922," *British Journal of Political Science* 1 (1971), part 4, pp.415-436.

C284.   Sakwa, R. "Party and Society in Moscow during the Civil War," *Sbornik (SGRR)* no.10
        (1984), pp.60-74.

C285.   Sakwa, R.T. "The Communist Party and War Communism in Moscow, 1918-1921," PhD
        diss., Birmingham, 1984.

C286.   Schapiro, L.B. *The Communist Party of the Soviet Union*, 2nd ed. (London: Methuen,
        1970).

C287.   Service, R. "From Polyarchy to Hegemony: The Party's Role in the Construction of the
        Central Institutions of the Soviet State, 1917-1919," *Sbornik (SGRR)* no.10
        (1984), pp.77-90.

Cheka:

C288.   Andics, H. *Rule of Terror*, trans.by A.Lieven (London: Constable, 1969).

C289.   Carr, E.H. "The Origin and Status of the Cheka," *SS* 10 (1958-59), no.1, pp.1-11.

C290.   Gerson, L.D. *The Secret Police in Lenin's Russia* (Philadelphia: Temple U.P., 1976).

C291.   Gerson, L.D. "The Shield and the Sword: Felix Dzerzhinskii and the Establishment of
        the Soviet Secret Police," PhD diss., George Washington, 1973.

C292.   Heller, M. "Lenin and the Cheka: the Real Lenin," *Survey* 24 (1979), no.2, pp.175-192.

C293.   Hollis, E.V. "Development of the Soviet Police System, 1917-1946," PhD diss.,
        Columbia, 1955.

C294.   Leggett, G.H. "Lenin, Terror, and the Political Police," *Survey* 21 (1975), no.4, pp.157-
        187.

C295.   Leggett, G.H. "Lenin's Reported Destruction of the Cheka Archive," *Survey* 24 (1979),
        no.2, pp.193-199.

C296.   Leggett, G. "The Cheka and a Crisis of Communist Conscience," *Survey* 25 (1980), no.3,
        pp.122-137.

C297.   Leggett, G. *The Cheka: Lenin's Political Police. The All-Russian Extraordinary
        Commission for Combating Counter-Revolution and Sabotage (December 1917
        to February 1922)* (Oxford & New York: Oxford U.P., 1981).

C298.   Levytsky, B. *The Uses of Terror: The Soviet Secret Service 1917-1970*, trans.by
        H.A.Piehler (London: Sidgwick & Jackson, 1971).

C299.   Popov, G.K. *The Tcheka* (London: A.Philpot, 1925).

C300.   Scott, E.J. "The Cheka," *St. Anthony's Papers* 1 (Soviet Affairs no.1), (1956), pp.1-23.

C301.   Wolin, S. & Slusser, R.M. (eds.) *The Soviet Secret Police* (London: Methuen, 1957).

D

SOCIETY

General:

D1.   Bettelheim, C. *Class Struggles in the USSR: First Period: 1917-1923*, trans.by B.Pearce (Hassocks, Sussex: Harvester Press, 1977)

D2.   Chase, W. "Voluntarism, Mobilisation and Coercion: *Subbotniki* 1919-1921," *SS* 41 (1989), no.1, pp.111-128.

D3.   Fitzpatrick, S. "The Bolsheviks' Dilemma: Class, Culture, and Politics in the Early Soviet Years," *SR* 47 (1988), no.4, pp.599-613. Followed by discussion, pp.614-626.

D4.   Freeze, G.L. "The *Soslovie* (Estate) Paradigm and Russian Social History," *AHR* 91 (1986), no.1, pp.11-36.

D5.   Friedgut, T.H. *Iuzovka and Revolution. Vol.1: Life and Work in Russia's Donbass, 1869-1924* (Princeton: Princeton U.P., 1989).

D6.   Friedgut, T.H. *Iuzovka and Revolution. Vol.2: Politics and Revolution in Russia's Donbass, 1864-1924* (Princeton: Princeton U.P., 1994).

D7.   Goldman, W.Z. *Women, the State and Revolution: Soviet Family Policy and Social Life, 1917-1936* (Cambridge: Cambridge U.P., 1993).

D8.   Hagen, M. "*Obshchestvennost'*: Formative Processes in Russian Society Prior to 1914," *Sbornik (SGRR)* no.10 (1984), pp.23-36.

D9.   Haimson, L.H. "The Problem of Social Identities in Early Twentieth Century Russia," *SR* 47 (1988), no.1, pp.1-20, followed by "Discussion," pp.21-38.

D10.   Haimson, L.H. "The Problem of Social Identities in Early Twentieth Century Russia: Observations on the Commentaries by Alfred Rieber and William Rosenberg," *SR* 47 (1988), no.3, pp.512-517.

D11.   Haimson, L. "The Problem of Social Stability in Urban Russia, 1905-1917," Part I: *SR* 23 (1964), no.4, pp.619-642; Part II: *SR* 24 (1965), no.1, pp.1-22.

D12.   Johnson, C. *Revolution and the Social System* (Stanford: Hoover Institution, 1964).

D13.   Juviler, P.H. *Revolutionary Law and Order: Politics and Social Change in the USSR* (New York & London: Free Press & Collier Macmillan, 1976).

D14.   Koenker, D. "Urban Families, Working-Class Youth Groups, and the 1917 Revolution in Moscow," in: D.L.Ransel (ed.) *The Family in Imperial Russia: New Lines of Historical Research* (Urbana: University of Illinois Press, 1978), pp.280-304.

D15.   Levin, A. "More on Social Stability, 1905-1917," *SR* 25 (1966), no.1, pp.149-154.

D16.   McAuley, M. *Bread and Justice: State and Society in Petrograd, 1917-1922* (Oxford: Clarendon, 1991).

D17.   McAuley, M. "Party and Society in Petrograd during the Civil War," *Sbornik (SGRR)* no.10 (1984), pp.43-59.

D18.   Rosenberg, W.G. "Social Mediation and State Construction(s) in Revolutionary Russia," *Social History* 19 (1994), no.2, pp.169-188.

D19.   Sakwa, R. "Party and Society in Moscow during the Civil War," *Sbornik (SGRR)* no.10 (1984), pp.60-74.

D20.   Salzman, C. "Consumer Cooperative Societies in Russia, Goals V. Gains, 1900-1918," *Cahiers du Monde Russe et Sovietique* 23 (1982), nos.3-4, pp.351-369.

D21.   Service, R. (ed.) *Society and Politics in the Russian Revolution* (Basingstoke & London: Macmillan, 1992).

D22.   Siegelbaum, L.H. *The Politics of Industrial Mobilization in Russia, 1914-17: A Study of the War-Industries Committees* (London & Basingstoke: Macmillan, 1983).

D23.   Solomon, S.G. & Hutchinson, J.F. (eds.) *Health and Society in Revolutionary Russia* (Bloomington & Indianapolis: Indiana U.P., 1990).

D24.   Suny, R.G. "Towards a Social History of the October Revolution," *AHR* 88 (1983), pp.31-52.

D25.   Surh, G.D. *1905 in St.Petersburg: Labor, Society, and Revolution* (Stanford: Stanford U.P., 1989).

D26.   Von Laue, T.H. "The Chances for Liberal Constitutionalism," *SR* 24 (1965), no.1, pp.34-46.

D27.   Yaney, G.L. "Social Stability in Prerevolutionary Russia: A Critical Note," *SR* 24 (1965), no.3, pp.521-527.

Workers:

General:

D28.   Bonnell, V.E. "Radical Politics and Organized Labor in Pre-revolutionary Moscow 1905-1914," *JSH* 12 (1978-79), no.2, pp.282-300.

D29.   Bonnell, V.E. "The Politics of Labor in Pre-Revolutionary Russia: Moscow Workers' Organizations, 1905-1914," PhD diss., Harvard, 1975.

D30.   Bonnell, V.E. (ed.) *The Russian Worker: Life and Labor under the Tsarist Regime* (Berkeley: University of California Press, 1983).

D31.   Bonnell, V. *Roots of Rebellion: Workers' Politics and Organisations in St. Petersburg and Moscow, 1900-1914* (Berkeley: University of California Press, 1983).

D32.   Desjeans, M.F. "The Common Experience of the Russian Working Class: The Case of St. Petersburg, 1892-1904," PhD diss., Duke, 1979.

D33.   Flenley, P.S. "Workers' Organizations in the Russian Metal Industry, February 1917-August 1918: A Study in the History and Sociology of the Labour Movement in the Russian Revolution," PhD diss., Birmingham, 1983.

D34.   Golub, P.A., Laverychev, V.Ia. & Sobolev, P.N. "Concerning the Book: *The Russian Proletariat: Nature, Struggle, Hegemony*," *SSH* 22 (1983-84), no.3, pp.83-114.

D35.   Gordon, M. *Workers Before and After Lenin* (New York: E.P.Dutton & Co., 1941).

D36.   Haimson, L.H. & Petrusha, R. "Two Strike Waves in Imperial Russia (1905-07, 1912-14): A Quantitative Analysis," in: L.H.Haimson & C.Tilly (eds.) *Strikes, Wars, and Revolutions in an International Perspective: Strike Waves in the Late Nineteenth and Early Twentieth Centuries* (New York: Cambridge U.P., 1989).

D37.   Kir'ianov, Iu. I. "On the Nature of the Russian Working Class," *SSH* 22 (1983-84), no.3, pp.8-60.

D38.   McDaniel, T. *Autocracy, Capitalism, and Revolution in Russia* (Berkeley, Los Angeles, London: University of California Press, 1988).

D39.   McDaniel, T. "Autocratic Capitalist Industrialization, Tsarist Labor Policy, and the Labor Movement in Russia, 1861-1917," PhD diss., California, Berkeley, 1979.

D40.   McKean, R.B. *St. Petersburg Between the Revolutions: Workers and Revolutionaries, June 1907-February 1917* (New Haven & London: Yale U.P., 1990).

D41.   Meierovich, M.G. " On the Sources from which Factory and Plant Workers were Recruited in the Imperialist Era (Based on Data from Yaroslavl Gubernia)," *SSH* 19 (1980-81), no.4, pp.43-77.

D42.   Palat, M.K. "Labor Legislation and Reform in Russia, 1905-1914," PhD diss., Oxford, 1974.

D43.   Pipes, R. *Social Democracy and the St. Petersburg Labor Movement, 1885-1897* (Cambridge, Mass.: Harvard U.P., 1963).

D44.   Read, C. "Labour and Socialism in Tsarist Russia," in: D.Geary (ed.) *Labour and Socialist Movements in Europe before 1914* (Oxford, New York, Munich: Berg, 1989), pp.137-181.

D45.   Rosenberg, W.G. "Understanding Strikes in Revolutionary Russia," *RH* 16 (1989), pts.2/4, pp.263-296.

D46.   Shkliarevsky, G.L. "The Russian Revolution and Organized Labor," PhD diss., Virginia, 1985.

D47.   Smith, S.A. "Class and Gender: Women's Strikes in St Petersburg, 1895-1917 and in Shanghai, 1895-1927," *Social History* 19 (1994), no.2, pp.141-168.

D48.   Smith, S.A. "Workers and Civil Rights in Tsarist Russia, 1899-1917," in: O.Crisp & L. Edmondson (eds.) *Civil Rights in Imperial Russia* (Oxford: Clarendon, 1989), pp.145-169.

D49.   Smith, S.A. "Workers and Supervisors: St Petersburg 1906-1917 and Shanghai 1895-1927," *Past and Present* no.139 (1993), pp.131-177.

D50.   Swain, G.R. "Bolsheviks and Metal Workers on the Eve of the First World War," *JCH* 16 (1981), no.2, pp.273-291.

D51.   Volobuev, P.V. "The Proletariat - Leader of the Socialist Revolution," *SSH* 22 (1983-84), no.3, pp.61-82.

D52.   Ward, B. "Wild Socialism in Russia: The Origins," *California Slavic Studies* 3 (1964), pp.127-148.

1905-07:

D53.   Dunne, J. "The Workers' Control Movement on the Russian Railways in 1905," *Irish Slavonic Studies* 4 (1983), pp.59-72.

D54.   Engelstein, L. "Moscow in the 1905 Revolution: A Study in Class Conflict and Political Organisation," PhD diss., Stanford, 1976.

D55.   Engelstein, L. *Moscow, 1905. Working-Class Organization and Political Conflict* (Stanford: Stanford U.P., 1982).

D56.   Gard, W.G. "The Party and the Proletariat in Ivanovo-Voznesensk, 1892-1906," PhD diss., Illinois, 1967.

D57.   Gard, W.G. "The Party and the Proletariat in Ivanovo-Voznesensk, 1905," *RH* 2 (1975), pt.2, pp.101-123.

D58.   Lewis, R.D. "The Labor Movement in Russian Poland in the Revolution of 1905-1907," PhD diss., California, Berkeley, 1971.

D59.   Prevo, K. "Voronezh in 1905: Workers and Politics in a Provincial City," *RH* 12 (1985), pt.1, pp.48-70.

D60.   Prevo, K. "Worker Reaction to Bloody Sunday in Voronezh," in: F.-X.Coquin & C.Gervais-Francelle (eds.) *1905: La Premiere Revolution Russe* (Paris: Publications de la Sorbonne et Institut d'etudes slaves, 1986), pp.165-178.

D61.   Reichman, H. *Railwaymen and Revolution: Russia, 1905* (Berkeley: University of California Press, 1987).

D62.   Reichman, H.F. "Russian Railwaymen in the Revolution of 1905," PhD diss., California, Berkeley, 1977.

D63.   Rice, C. "Russian Workers and the Socialist Revolutionary Party Through the Revolution of 1905-07," *Sbornik (SGRR)* no.11 (1985), pp.84-100.

D64.   Roosa, R.A. "Russian Industrialists, Politics, and Labor Reform in 1905," *RH* 2 (1975), pt.2, pp.124-148.

D65.   Schwarz, S. *The Russian Revolution of 1905. The Workers' Movement and the Formation of Bolshevism and Menshevism*, trans.by G.Vakar (Chicago & London: University of Chicago Press, 1967).

D66.   Snow, G.E. "The Kokovtsov Commission: An Abortive Attempt at Labor Reform in Russia in 1905," *SR* 31 (1972), no.4, pp.780-796.

D67.   Steinberg, M.D. *The Culture of Class Relations in the Russian Printing Industry, 1867-1907* (Berkeley: University of California Press, 1992).

D68.   Surh, G.D. *1905 in St.Petersburg: Labor, Society, and Revolution* (Stanford: Stanford U.P., 1989).

D69.   Surh, G.D. "Petersburg Workers in 1905: Strikes, Workplace Democracy, and the Revolution," PhD diss., California, Berkeley, 1979.

D70.   Surh, G.D. "Petersburg's First Mass Labor Organization: The Assembly of Russian Workers and Father Gapon," : Part I: *RR* 40 (1981), no.3, pp.241-262; Part II: *RR* 40 (1981), no.4, pp.412-441.

D71.   Weinberg, R. "The Politicization of Labour in 1905: The Case of Odessa Salesclerks," *SR* 49 (1990), no.3, pp.427-445.

D72.   Weinberg, R.E. "Worker Organization and Politics in the Revolution of 1905 in Odessa," PhD diss., California, Berkeley, 1985.

D73.   Weinberg, R. "Workers, Pogroms and the 1905 Revolution in Odessa," *RR* 46 (1987), no.1, pp.53-75.

D74.   Wynn, C. *Workers, Strikes, and Pogroms: The Donbass-Dnepr Bend in Late Imperial Russia, 1870-1905* (Princeton: Princeton U.P., 1992).

D75.   Wynn, C.S. "Russian Labor in Revolution and Reaction: The Donbass Working Class, 1870-1905," PhD diss., Stanford, 1987.

1907-14:

D76.   Bonnell, V.E. "Radical Politics and Organized Labor in Pre-Revolutionary Moscow, 1905-1914," *JSH* 12 (1978-79), no.2, pp.282-300.

D77.   Bonnell, V.E. "The Politics of Labor in Pre-revolutionary Russia: Moscow Workers' Organizations 1905-1914," PhD diss., Harvard, 1975.

D78.   Bonnell, V.E. "Urban Working Class Life in Early Twentieth Century Russia: Some Problems and Patterns," *RH* 8 (1981), pt.3, pp.360-378.

D79.   Brym, R.J. & Economakis, E. "Peasant or Proletarian? Militant Pskov Workers in St Petersburg, 1913," *SR* 53 (1994), no.1, pp.120-139.

D80.   Ewing, S. "The Russian Social Insurance Movement, 1912-1914: An Ideological Analysis," *SR* 50 (1991), no.4, pp.914-926.

D81.   McKean, R.B. "Government, Employers and the Labour Movement in St.Petersburg on the Eve of the First World War," *Sbornik (SGRR)* no.12 (1986), pp.65-94.

D82.   Mendel, A.P. "Peasant and Worker on the Eve of the First World War," *SR* 24 (1965), no.1, pp.23-33.

D83.   Roosa, R.A. "Workers' Insurance Legislation and the Role of the Industrialists in the Period of the Third State Duma," *RR* 34 (1975), no.4, pp.410-452.

D84.   Suny, R.G. "A Journeyman for the Revolution: Stalin and the Labour Movement in Baku, June 1907-May 1908," *SS* 23 (1972), no.3, pp.373-394.

D85.   Suny, R.G. "Labor and Liquidators: Revolutionaries and the "Reaction" in Baku, May 1908-April 1912," *SR* 34 (1975), no.2, pp.319-340.

D86.   Swain, G.R. "Political Developments within the Organized Working Class: Petersburg 1906-1914," PhD diss., London, 1979.

D87.   Swain, G.R. *Russian Social Democracy and the Legal Labour Movement, 1906-1914* (London & Basingstoke: Macmillan, 1983).

D88.   Vasil'ev, B.N. "The Size, Composition and Territorial Distribution of the Factory-Plant Proletariat of European Russia and the Transcaucasus in 1913-1914," *SSH* 19 (1980-81), no.4, pp.6-42.

1914-17:

D89.   Siegelbaum, L.H. "The Workers' Groups and the War-Industries Committees: Who Used Whom?" *RR* 39 (1980), no.2, pp.150-180.

1917:

D90.   Augustine, W.R. "Russia's Railwaymen, July-October, 1917," *SR* 24 (1965), no.4, pp.666-679.

D91.   Avrich, P.H. "Russian Factory Committees in 1917," *JFGO* 11 (1963), pp.161-182.

D92.   Boll, M.M. *The Petrograd Armed Workers Movement in the February Revolution (February-July 1917): A Study in the Radicalization of the Petrograd Proletariat* (Washington D.C.: University Press of America, 1979).

D93.   Devlin, R.J. "Petrograd Workers and Workers' Factory Committees in 1917: An Aspect of the Social History of the Russian Revolution," PhD diss., SUNY, Binghampton, 1976.

D94.   Galili, Z. "Workers, Industrialists and the Menshevik Mediators: Labor Conflicts in Petrograd, 1917," *RH* 16 (1989), pts.2/4, pp.239-261.

D95.   Gill, G.J. "The Role of the Countryside in an Urban Revolution: A Short Note," *Sbornik (SGRR)* no.2 (1976), pp.44-50.

D96.   Hogan, H. "Conciliation Boards in Revolutionary Petrograd: Aspects of the Crisis of Labor-Management Relations in 1917," *RH* 9 (1982), pt.1, pp.49-66.

D97.   Husband, W.B. "Local Industry in Upheaval: The Ivanovo-Kineshma Textile Strike of 1917," *SR* 47 (1988), no.3, pp.448-463.

D98.   Kaiser, D.H. (ed.) *The Workers' Revolution in Russia, 1917. The View From Below* (Cambridge: Cambridge U.P., 1987).

D99.   Koenker, D. "Moscow, 1917: Workers' Revolution, Worker Control," in: E.H. Judge & J.Y. Simms, Jr. (eds.) *Modernization and Revolution: Dilemmas of Progress in Late Imperial Russia: Essays in Honor of Arthur P. Mendel* (New York: East European Monographs, distributed by Columbia U.P., 1992), pp.187-206.

D100.   Koenker, D. *Moscow Workers and the 1917 Revolution* (Princeton: Princeton U.P., 1981).

D101.   Koenker, D.G.P. "Moscow Workers in 1917," PhD diss., Michigan, 1976.

D102.   Koenker, D.P. & Rosenberg, W.G. "Perceptions and Reality of Labour Protest, March to October 1917," in: E.R.Frankel et al (eds.) *Revolution in Russia: Reassessments of 1917* (Cambridge: Cambridge U.P., 1992), pp.131-156.

D103.   Koenker, D. & Rosenberg, W.G. "Skilled Workers and the Strike Movement in Revolutionary Russia," *JSH* 19 (1985-86), no.4, pp.605-629.

D104.   Koenker, D.P. & Rosenberg, W.G. *Strikes and Revolution in Russia, 1917* (Princeton: Princeton U.P., 1989).

D105.   Koenker, D. "The Evolution of Party Consciousness in 1917: The Case of the Moscow Workers," *SS* 30 (1978), no.1, pp.38-62.

D106. Mandel, D. *Petrograd Workers and the Fall of the Old Regime, From the February Revolution to the July Days, 1917* (London: Macmillan, 1983).

D107. Mandel, M.D. "The Development of Revolutionary Consciousness Among the Industrial Workers of Petrograd between February and November 1917," PhD diss., Columbia, 1978.

D108. Page, S.W. "The Role of the Proletariat in March, 1917: Contradictions Within the Official Bolshevik Version," *RR* 9 (1950), no.2, pp.146-149.

D109. Rosenberg, W.G. & Koenker, D.P. "The Limits of Formal Protest: Workers' Activism and Social Polarization in Petrograd and Moscow, March to October, 1917," *AHR* 92 (1987), no.2, pp.296-326.

D110. Smith, S. "Craft Consciousness, Class Consciousness Petrograd 1917," *History Workshop* 11 (1981), pp.33-58.

1917-18:

D111. Avrich, P.H. "The Bolshevik Revolution and Workers' Control in Russian Industry," *SR* 22 (1963), no.1, pp.47-63.

D112. Berk, S.M. "The 'Class-Tragedy' of Izhevsk: Working-Class Opposition to Bolshevism in 1918," *RH* 2 (1975), pt.2, pp.176-?

D113. Flenley, P.S. "Workers' Organizations in the Russian Metal Industry, February 1917-August 1918: A Study in the History and Sociology of the Labour Movement in the Russian Revolution," PhD diss., Birmingham, 1983.

D114. Mandel, D. *The Petrograd Workers and the Soviet Seizure of Power, From the July Days 1917 to July 1918* (London: Macmillan, 1984).

D115. Rosenberg, W. "Workers and Workers' Control in the Russian Revolution," *History Workshop* 5 (1978), pp.89-97.

D116. Shkliarevsky, G. *Labor in the Russian Revolution: Factory Committees and Trade Unions, 1917-1918* (New York: St Martin's Press, 1993).

D117. Smith, S.A. *Red Petrograd: Revolution in the Factories, 1917-18* (Cambridge: Cambridge U.P., 1983).

D118. Smith, S.A. "The Russian Revolution and the Factories of Petrograd, February 1917 to June 1918," PhD diss., Birmingham, 1981.

1917-21:

D119. Aves, J. "Worker Unrest in Soviet Russia during War Communism and the Transition to the New Economic Policy, 1918-1922," PhD diss., London, 1990.

D120.   Bataeva, T.V. "An Important Source on the History of the Soviet Working Class in 1918-1920," *SSH* 10 (1971-72), no.3, pp.221-244.

D121.   Brinton, M. *The Bolsheviks and Workers' Control, 1917-1921: the State and Counter-Revolution* (London: Solidarity, 1970).

D122.   Brovkin, V. "Workers' Unrest and the Bolsheviks' Response in 1919," *SR* 49 (1990), no.3, pp.350-373.

D123.   Bunyan, J. *The Origin of Forced Labor in the Soviet State, 1917-21: Documents and Materials* (Baltimore: Johns Hopkins U.P., 1967).

D124.   Chase, W.J. "Moscow and Its Working Class, 1918-1928: A Social Analysis," PhD diss., Boston College, 1979.

D125.   Daxton, L.E. "Lenin and the Working Man," *Sbornik (SGRR)* no.1 (1975), pp.28-32.

D126.   Dewar, M. *Labour Policy in the USSR, 1917-1928* (London & New York: Royal Institute of International Affairs / Oxford U.P., 1956).

D127.   Gimpel'son, E.G. "On Workers' Control After Passage of the Decree on Nationalizing Industry in the USSR," *SSH* 23 (1984-85), no.2, pp.34-53.

D128.   Kaplan, F.I. *Bolshevik Ideology and the Ethics of Soviet Labor: 1917-1920: The Formative Years* (New York: Philosophical Library, 1969).

D129.   Kaplan, F. "Russian Labor and the Bolshevik Party, 1917-1920," PhD diss., California, Berkeley, 1957.

D130.   Koenker, D.P. et al (eds.) *Party, State, and Society in the Russian Civil War. Explorations in Social History* (Bloomington & Indianapolis: Indiana U.P., 1989).

D131.   Perrins, M. "*Rabkrin* and Workers' Control in Russia 1917-1934," *European Studies Review* 10 (1980), no.2, pp.225-246.

D132.   Rosenberg, W.G. "Russian Labor and Bolshevik Power After October," *SR* 44 (1985), no.2, pp.213-238, followed by "Discussion" pp.239-256.

D133.   Shkliarevsky, G.L. "Factory Committees and the Establishment of the Bolshevik Dictatorship," *RH* 13 (1986), pt.4, pp.399-432.

D134.   Siegelbaum, L.H. "Defining and Ignoring Labor Discipline in the Early Soviet Period: The Comrades-Disciplinary Courts, 1918-1922," *SR* 51 (1992), no.4, pp.705-730.

D135.   Siranni, C.J. "Workers' Control and Socialist Democracy: The Early Soviet Experience in Comparative Perspective," PhD diss., SUNY, Binghampton, 1979.

D136.   Siranni, C. *Workers' Control and Socialist Democracy: The Soviet Experience* (London: Verso, 1982).

D137.   Smele, J.D. "Labour Conditions and the Collapse of the Siberian Economy under Kolchak, 1918-19," *Sbornik (SGRR)* no.13 (1987), pp.31-59.

D138.   Wade, R.A. *Red Guards and Workers' Militias in the Russian Revolution* (Stanford: Stanford U.P., 1984).

Peasants:

General:

D139.   Anfimov, A.M. "On the History of the Russian Peasantry at the Beginning of the Twentieth Century," *RR* 51 (1992), no.3, pp.396-407.

D140.   Anfimov, A.M. & Zyrianov, P.N. "Elements of the Evolution of the Russian Peasant Commune in the Post-Reform Period (1861-1914)," *SSH* 21 (1982-83), no.3, pp.68-96.

D141.   Atkinson, D. *The End of the Russian Land Commune, 1905-1930* (Stanford: Stanford U.P., 1983).

D142.   Atkinson, D.G.H. "The Russian Land Commune and the Revolution," PhD diss., Stanford, 1971.

D143.   Bartlett, R. (ed.) *Land Commune and Peasant Community in Russia: Communal Forms in Imperial and Early Soviet Society* (Basingstoke & London: Macmillan, 1990).

D144.   Burds, J.P. "Patterns of Change in the Central Russian Village: Community Relations and the Market Economy, 1840-1914," PhD diss., Yale, 1990.

D145.   Chamberlin, W.H. "The Ordeal of the Russian Peasantry," *RR* 14 (1955), no.4, pp.295-300.

D146.   Confino, M. "Russian Customary Law and the Study of Peasant Mentalities," *RR* 44 (1985), no.1, pp.35-43.

D147.   Crisp, O. "Peasant Land Tenure and Civil Rights Implications before 1906," in: O.Crisp & L. Edmondson (eds.) *Civil Rights in Imperial Russia* (Oxford: Clarendon, 1989), pp.33-64.

D148.   Eklof, B. "Ways of Seeing: Recent Anglo-American Studies of the Russian Peasant (1861-1914)," *JFGO* 36 (1988), pp.57-79.

D149.   Eklof, B. & Frank, S. (eds.) *The World of the Russian Peasant: Post-Emancipation Culture and Society* (Boston: Unwin Hyman, 1990).

D150.   Ellison, H.J. "Peasant Colonization of Siberia (A Study of the Growth of Russian Rural Society in Siberia with Particular Emphasis on the Years 1890 to 1918)," PhD diss., London, 1955.

D151. Engel, B.A. "Russian Peasant Views of City Life, 1861-1914," *SR* 52 (1993), no.3, pp.446-459.

D152. Figes, O.G. "The Political Transformation of Peasant Russia: Peasant Soviets in the Middle Volga, 1912-1920," PhD diss., Cambridge, 1987.

D153. Friesen, C.F. "Peasant Participation in Russian Politics Between 1905 and 1911: The Case of the Stolypin Land Reform Program," PhD diss., Harvard, 1972.

D154. Hoch, S.L. "On Good Numbers and Bad: Malthus, Population Trends and Peasant Standard of Living in Late Imperial Russia," *SR* 53 (1994), no.1, pp.41-75.

D155. Hussain, A. & Tribe, K. *Marxism and the Agrarian Question. Vol.2: Russian Marxism and the Peasantry 1861-1930* (London & Basingstoke: Macmillan, 1981).

D156. Judge, E.H. "Peasant Resettlement and Social Control in Late Imperial Russia," in: E.H. Judge & J.Y. Simms, Jr. (eds.) *Modernization and Revolution: Dilemmas of Progress in Late Imperial Russia: Essays in Honor of Arthur P. Mendel* (New York: East European Monographs, distributed by Columbia U.P., 1992), pp.75-93.

D157. Kachorovsky, K. "The Russian Land Commune in History and Today," *SEER* 7 (1928-29), pp.565-576.

D158. Kennard, H.P. *The Russian Peasant* (London: T. Werner Laurie, 1907).

D159. Koslow, J. *The Despised and the Damned: The Russian Peasant Through the Ages* (New York: Macmillan, 1972).

D160. Lewin, M. "Customary Law and Russian Rural Society in the Post-Reform Era," *RR* 44 (1985), no.1, pp.1-19.

D161. Lewin, M. "Rural Society in Twentieth-Century Russia: an Introduction," *Social History* 9 (1984), pp.171-180.

D162. Lih, L.T. *Bread and Authority in Russia, 1914-1921* (Berkeley, Los Angeles, Oxford: University of California Press, 1990).

D163. Long, J. "Agricultural Conditions in the German Colonies of Novouzensk, Samara Province, 1861-1914," *SEER* 57 (1979), no.4, pp.531-551.

D164. Maklakov, B. "The Agrarian Problem in Russia Before the Revolution," *RR* 9 (1950), no.1, pp.3-15.

D165. Maklakov, B. "The Peasant Question and the Russian Revolution," *SEER* 2 (1923-24), pp.225-248.

D166. Maynard, J. *Russia in Flux* (New York: Macmillan, 1948).

D167. Maynard, J. *The Russian Peasant: And Other Studies* (London: Victor Gollancz, 1942).

D168. Mixter, T.R. "Migrant Agricultural Laborers in the Steppe Grainbelt of European Russia, 1830-1913," PhD diss., Michigan, 1992.

D169.   Mixter, T. "The Hiring Market as Workers' Turf: Migrant Agricultural Laborers and the Mobilization of Collective Action on the Steppe Grainbelt of European Russia, 1853-1913," in: E.Kingston-Mann & T.Mixter (eds.) *Peasant Economy, Culture, and Politics of European Russia, 1800-1921* (Princeton: Princeton U.P., 1991), pp.294-340.

D170.   Moghaddam, Y. "The Russian Peasant Movement, 1905-17," PhD diss., Keele, 1978.

D171.   Munting, R. "Outside Earnings in the Russian Peasant Farm - the Case of Tula Province 1900-1917," *Journal of Peasant Studies* 3 (1976), pp.428-447.

D172.   Ohsol, J.G. "The Recent Agrarian Movement in Russia and Its Historical Background," PhD diss., Harvard, 1914.

D173.   Owen, L.A. "The Russian Peasant Movement, 1906-17," PhD diss., London, 1933.

D174.   Perrie, M. "'A Worker in Disguise': A.V. Peshekhonov's Contribution to the Debate on the Peasant at the Turn of the Century," in: L.Edmondson & P.Waldron (eds.) *Economy and Society in Russia and the Soviet Union, 1860-1930* (Basingstoke & London: Macmillan, 1992), pp.65-84.

D175.   Perrie, M. "Folklore as Evidence of Peasant *Mentalite*: Social Attitudes and Values in Russian Popular Culture," *RR* 48 (1989), no.2, pp.119-143.

D176.   Ramer, S.C. "Traditional Healers and Peasant Culture in Russia, 1861-1917," in: E.Kingston-Mann & T.Mixter (eds.) *Peasant Economy, Culture, and Politics of European Russia, 1800-1921* (Princeton: Princeton U.P., 1991), pp.207-232.

D177.   Robinson, G.T. "Rural Russia Under the Old Regime: A History of the Landlord-Peasant World and a Prologue to the Peasant Revolution of 1917," PhD diss., Columbia, 1930.

D178.   Robinson, G.T. *Rural Russia Under the Old Regime. A History of the Landlord-Peasant World and a Prologue to the Peasant Revolution of 1917* (New York & London: Longmans, Green & Co., 1932 [reprinted in 1962]).

D179.   Russell, E.J. "Sir John Maynard and His Studies of the Russian Peasant," *SEER* 24 (1946), no.63, pp.56-65.

D180.   Salmond, W.R. "The Modernization of Folk Art in Imperial Russia: The Revival of the Kustar Art Industries, 1885-1917," PhD diss., Texas, 1989.

D181.   Seregny, S.J. "Russian Teachers and Peasant Revolution, 1895-1917," in: E.H. Judge & J.Y. Simms, Jr. (eds.) *Modernization and Revolution: Dilemmas of Progress in Late Imperial Russia: Essays in Honor of Arthur P. Mendel* (New York: East European Monographs, distributed by Columbia U.P., 1992), pp.59-74.

D182.   Shanin, T. *The Awkward Class: Political Sociology of Peasantry in a Developing Society. Russia, 1910-1925* (Oxford: Clarendon, 1972).

D183.   Shanin, T. "The Socio-Economic Mobility of the Russian Peasantry, 1910-1925, and the Political Sociology of Rural Society," PhD diss., Birmingham, 1969.

D184. Shinn, W.T., Jr. "The Law of the Russian Peasant Household," *SR* 20 (1961), no.4, pp.601-621.

D185. Tian-Shanskaia, O.S. *Village Life in Late Tsarist Russia* (edited by D.L. Ransel) (Bloomington: Indiana U.P., 1993).

D186. Treadgold, D.W. "Was Stolypin in Favor of Kulaks?" *ASEER* 14 (1955), pp.1-14.

D187. Wcislo, F.W. *Reforming Rural Russia: State, Local Society, and National Politics, 1855-1914* (Princeton: Princeton U.P., 1990).

D188. Wheatcroft, S.G. "Crises and the Condition of the Peasantry in Late Imperial Russia," in: E.Kingston-Mann & T.Mixter (eds.) *Peasant Economy, Culture, and Politics of European Russia, 1800-1921* (Princeton: Princeton U.P., 1991), pp.128-172.

D189. Wolfe, B.D. "Lenin, Stolypin, and the Russian Village," *RR* 6 (1946-47), no.2, pp.40-54.

D190. Worobec, C.D. "Reflections on Customary Law and Post-Reform Peasant Russia," *RR* 44 (1985), no.1, pp.21-25.

D191. Yaney, G. "Some Suggestions Regarding the Study of Russian Peasant Society prior to Collectivization," *RR* 44 (1985), no.1, pp.27-33.

D192. Zaitsev, C. "The Russian Agrarian Revolution," *SEER* 9 (1930-31), pp.547-566.

1905-07:

D193. Bukhovets, O.G. "The Political Consciousness of the Russian Peasantry in the Revolution of 1905-1907: Sources, Methods, and Some Results," *RR* 47 (1988), no.4, pp.357-374.

D194. Bukhovets, O.G. "Towards a Technique for Studying the Prigover Movement and Its Role in the Struggle of the Peasantry in 1905-1907 (On Materials from Samara Province)," *SSH* 20 (1981-82), no.3, pp.11-45.

D195. Edelman, R. *Proletarian Peasants: The Revolution of 1905 in Russia's Southwest* (Ithaca: Cornell U.P., 1987).

D196. Edelman, R.S. "Rural Proletarians and Peasant Disturbances: The Right Bank Ukraine in the Revolution of 1905," *JMH* 57 (1985), no.2, pp.248-277.

D197. Engel, B.A. "Women, Men, and the Languages of Peasant Resistance, 1870-1907," in: S.P.Frank & M.D.Steinberg (eds.) *Cultures in Flux: Lower-Class Values, Practices, and Resistance in Late Imperial Russia* (Princeton: Princeton U.P., 1994), pp.34-53.

D198. Jones, S.F. "Marxism and Peasant Revolt in the Russian Empire: the Case of the Gurian Republic," *SEER* 67 (1989), no.3, pp. 403-434.

D199. Kingston-Mann, E. "Lenin and the Challenge of Peasant Militance: From Bloody Sunday, 1905 to the Dissolution of the First Duma," *RR* 38 (1979), no.4, pp.434-455.

D200. Macey, D.A.J. *Government and Peasant in Russia, 1861-1906: The Prehistory of the Stolypin Reforms* (DeKalb, Illinois: Northern Illinois U.P., 1987).

D201. Macey, D.A.J. "The Russian Bureaucracy and the 'Peasant Problem': The Pre-History of the Stolypin Reforms, 1861-1907," PhD diss., Columbia, 1976.

D202. Mandel, J.I. "Paternalistic Authority in the Russian Countryside, 1856-1906," PhD diss., Columbia, 1978.

D203. Masloff, C.S. "Peasant Disorders and the Russian Moderate Left, 1905-7," PhD diss., Kent State, 1975.

D204. Mixter, T.R. "Peasant Collective Action in Saratov Province, 1902-1906," in: R.A.Wade & S.J.Seregny (eds.) *Politics and Society in Provincial Russia: Saratov, 1590-1917* (Columbus, Ohio: Ohio State U.P., 1989), pp.191-232.

D205. Perrie, M. "The Russian Peasant Movement of 1905-1907: Its Social Composition and Revolutionary Significance," *Past and Present* no.57 (1972), pp.123-155.

D206. Schneer, M. "The Markovo Republic: A Peasant Community during Russia's First Revolution, 1905-1906," *SR* 53 (1994), no.1, pp.104-119.

D207. Seregny, S.J. "A Different Type of Peasant Movement: The Peasant Unions in the Russian Revolution of 1905," *SR* 47 (1988), no.1, pp.51-67.

D208. Seregny, S.J. "Peasants and Politics: Peasant Unions during the 1905 Revolution," in: E.Kingston-Mann & T.Mixter (eds.) *Peasant Economy, Culture, and Politics of European Russia, 1800-1921* (Princeton: Princeton U.P., 1991), pp.341-377.

D209. Seregny, S.J. *Russian Teachers and Peasant Revolution. The Politics of Education in 1905* (Bloomington & Indianapolis: Indiana U.P., 1989).

D210. Watters, F.M. "Land Tenure and Financial Burdens of the Russian Peasant, 1861-1905," PhD diss., California, Berkeley, 1966.

D211. Worobec, C.D. "Family, Community, and Land in Peasant Russia, 1860-1905," PhD diss., Toronto, 1984.

1907-14:

D212. Baker, A.B. "Deterioration or Development? The Peasant Economy of Moscow Province Prior to 1914," *RH* 5 (1978), pt.1, pp.1-23.

D213. Jones, A.N. "The Peasants of Late Imperial Russia: Economy and Society in the Era of the Stolypin Land Reform," PhD diss., Harvard, 1988.

D214. Macey, D.A.J. "Government Actions and Peasant Reactions During the Stolypin Reforms," in: R.B.McKean (ed.) *New Perspectives in Modern Russian History* (Basingstoke & London: Macmillan, 1992), pp.133-173.

D215. Mendel, A.P. "Peasant and Worker on the Eve of the First World War," *SR* 24 (1965), no.1, pp.23-33.

D216. Mosse, W.E. "Stolypin's Villages," *SEER* 43 (1964-65), pp.257-274.

D217. Owen, L.A. *The Russian Peasant Movement 1906-1917* (New York: Russell & Russell, 1963 [first published in 1937]).

D218. Pallot, J. "*Khutora* and *Otruba* in Stolypin's Program of Farm Individualization," *SR* 43 (1984), no.2, pp.242-256.

D219. Pallot, J. & Shaw, D.J.B. *Landscape and Settlement in Romanov Russia, 1613-1917* (Oxford: Clarendon, 1990).

D220. Perrie, M. "The Russian Peasantry in 1907-08: A Survey by the Socialist Revolutionary Party," *History Workshop* 4 (1977), pp.171-191.

D221. Vinogradoff, E.D. "The Russian Peasantry and the Elections to the Fourth Duma: Estate Political Consciousness and Class Political Consciousness," PhD diss., Columbia, 1974.

D222. Vinogradoff, E.D. "The Russian Peasantry and the Elections to the Fourth State Duma," in: L.H.Haimson (ed.) *The Politics of Rural Russia, 1905-1914* (Bloomington and London: Indiana U.P., 1979), pp.219-260.

D223. Yaney, G.L. "The Concept of the Stolypin Land Reform," *SR* 23 (1964), no.2, pp.275-293.

D224. Yaney, G.L. "The Imperial Russian Government and the Stolypin Land Reform," PhD diss., Princeton, 1961.

1917:

D225. Bonine, R.P. "The Russian Peasant and the Failure of Rural Government, March-October, 1917," PhD diss., London, 1960.

D226. Channon, J. "The Peasantry in the Revolutions of 1917," in: E.R.Frankel et al (eds.) *Revolution in Russia: Reassessments of 1917* (Cambridge: Cambridge U.P., 1992), pp.105-130.

D227. Gill, G.J. "The Mainsprings of Peasant Action in 1917," *SS* 30 (1978), no.1, pp.63-86.

D228. Gill, G. "Peasants and Political Consciousness: A Reply," *SS* 32 (1980), no.2, pp.291-296.

D229. Gill, G.J. "The Failure of Rural Policy in Russia, Febraury-October 1917," *SR* 37 (1978), no.2, pp.241-258.

D230. Gill, G.J. "The Role of the Peasants in the Revolution in European Russian between March and November 1917," PhD diss., London, 1976.

D231. Kingston-Mann, E. "Lenin and the Beginnings of Marxist Peasant Revolution: the Burden of Political Opportunity, July-October 1917," *SEER* 50 (1972), no.121, pp.570-588.

D232. Kingston-Mann, E. "Problems of Order and Revolution: Lenin and the Peasant Question in March and April 1917," *RH* 6 (1979), pt.1, pp.39-56.

D233. Kress, J.H. "The Political Consciousness of the Russian Peasantry: A Comment on Graeme Gill's 'The Mainsprings of Peasant Action in 1917'," *SS* 31 (1979), no.4, pp.574-580.

D234. Owen, L.A. "The Russian Agrarian Revolution of 1917," *SEER* 12 (1933-34), pp.155-166 and pp.368-386.

1917-18:

D235. Channon, J. "The Bolsheviks and the Peasantry: the Land Question During the First Eight Months of Soviet Rule," *SEER* 66 (1988), no.4, pp.593-624.

D236. Gerasimenko, G.A. "Local Peasant Organizations in 1917 and the First Half of 1918," *SSH* 16 (1977-78), no.3, pp.12-129.

1917-21:

D237. Channon, J. "Land Revolution and Land Reform: The Case of the Central Black-Earth Region, 1917-24," in: L.Edmondson & P.Waldron (eds.) *Economy and Society in Russia and the Soviet Union, 1860-1930* (Basingstoke & London: Macmillan, 1992), pp.189-233.

D238. Channon, J. "'Peasant Revolution' and 'Land Reform': Land Distribution in European Russia, October 1917-1920," PhD diss., Birmingham, 1984.

D239. Figes, O. "Peasant Farmers and the Minority Groups of Rural Society: Peasant Egalitarianism and Village Social Relations during the Russian Revolution (1917-1921)," in: E.Kingston-Mann & T.Mixter (eds.) *Peasant Economy, Culture, and Politics of European Russia, 1800-1921* (Princeton: Princeton U.P., 1991), pp.378-401.

D240. Figes, O. *Peasant Russia, Civil War. The Volga Countryside in Revolution (1917-1921)* (Oxford: Clarendon, 1989).

D241. Kabanov, V.V. "The Agrarian Revolution in Russia," *SSH* 29 (1990-91), no.4, pp.60-81.

D242. Lih, L.T. "Bread and Authority in Russia: Food Supply and Revolutionary Politics, 1919-1921," PhD diss., Princeton, 1984.

D243. Pereira, N.G.O. "Lenin and the Siberian Peasant Insurrections," in: G.Diment & Y.Slezkine (eds.) *Between Heaven and Hell: The Myth of Siberia in Russian Culture* (New York: St.Martin's Press, 1993), pp.133-150.

D244. Pethybridge, R.W. "Social and Political Attitudes of the Peasantry in the Kursk guberniya at the Start of NEP," *SEER* 63 (1985), no.3, pp.372-387.

D245. Radkey, O.H. "The Socialist Revolutionaries and the Peasantry After October," *HSS* 4 (1957), pp.457-479.

Middle Classes:

D246. Clowes, E.W., Kassow, S.D. & West, J.L. (eds.) *Between Tsar and People: Educated Society and the Quest for Public Identity in Late Imperial Russia* (Princeton: Princeton U.P., 1991).

D247. Engelstein, L. *The Keys to Happiness: Sex and the Search for Modernity in Fin-de-Siecle Russia* (Ithaca, New York: Cornell U.P., 1993).

D248. Gindin, I.F. "The Russian Bourgeoisie in the Period of Capitalism," *SSH* 6 (1967-68), no.1, pp.3-50.

D249. Miller, J. "Questions on 1917," *SS* 19 (1967), no.2, pp.255-256.

D250. Owen, T.C. *Capitalism and Politics in Russia: A Social History of the Moscow Merchants, 1855-1905* (Cambridge: Cambridge U.P., 1981).

D251. Rieber, A.J. *Merchants and Entrepreneurs in Imperial Russia* (Chapel Hill: University of North Carolina Press, 1982).

D252. Siegelbaum, L.H. *The Politics of Industrial Mobilization in Russia, 1914-17: A Study of the War-Industries Committees* (London & Basingstoke: Macmillan, 1983).

D253. West, J.L. "The Rjabusinskij Circle: Russian Industrialists in Search of a Bourgeoisie, 1909-1914," *JFGO* 32 (1984), pp.358-377.

Nobility/Gentry:

D254. Becker, S. *Nobility and Privilege in Late Imperial Russia* (DeKalb: Northern Illinois U.P., 1985).

D255. Doctorow, G.S. "The Russian Gentry and the Coup d'Etat of 3 June 1907," *Cahiers du Monde Russe et Sovietique* 17 (1976), no.1, pp.43-51.

D256. Edelman, R. *Gentry Politics on the Eve of the Russian Revolution: The Nationalist Party 1907-1917* (New Brunswick, N.J.: Rutgers U.P., 1980).

D257. Emmons, T. "The Russian Landed Gentry and Politics," *RR* 33 (1974), no.3, pp.269-283.

D258.   Emmons, T. "The Russian Nobility and Party Politics before the Revolution," in I.Banac & P.Bushkovitch (eds.) *The Nobility in Russia and Eastern Europe* (New Haven: Yale Concilium on International and Area Studies, 1983), pp.177-220.

D259.   Haimson, L.H. (ed.) *The Politics of Rural Russia, 1905-1914* (Bloomington & London: Indiana U.P., 1979).

D260.   Hamburg, G.M. *Politics of the Russian Nobility, 1881-1905* (New Brunswick, N.J.: Rutgers U.P., 1984).

D261.   Hamburg, G.M. "The Russian Nobility on the Eve of the 1905 Revolution," *RR* 38 (1979), no.3, pp.323-338.

D262.   Hause, T.S. "State and Gentry in Russia, 1861-1917," PhD diss., Stanford, 1974.

D263.   Kleinmichel, Countess M. *Memories of a Shipwrecked World, Being the Memoirs of Countess Kleinmichel* (London: Brentano's, 1923).

D264.   Macey, D.A.J. "The Land Captains: A Note on their Social Composition, 1889-1913," *RH* 16 (1989), pts.2/4, pp.327-351.

D265.   Manning, R.T. *The Crisis of the Old Order in Russia. Gentry and Government* (Princeton: Princeton U.P., 1982).

D266.   Manning, R.T. "The Russian Provincial Gentry in Revolution and Counterrevolution, 1905-1907," PhD diss., Columbia, 1975.

D267.   Munting, R. "Economic Change and the Russian Gentry, 1861-1914," in: L.Edmondson & P.Waldron (eds.) *Economy and Society in Russia and the Soviet Union, 1860-1930* (Basingstoke & London: Macmillan, 1992), pp.24-43.

D268.   Simmonds, G.W. "The Congress of Representatives of the Nobles' Associations, 1906-1916: A Case Study of Russian Conservatism," PhD diss., Columbia, 1964.

Women:

General:

D269.   Atkinson, D., Dallin, A. & Lapidus, G.W. (eds.) *Women in Russia* (Hassocks, Sussex: Harvester, 1978 [originally Stanford 1977]).

D270.   Bernstein, L. "Sonya's Daughters: Prostitution and Society in Russia," PhD diss., Berkeley, 1987.

D271.   Bobroff, A. "The Bolsheviks and Working Women, 1905-20," *SS* 26 (1974), no.4, pp.540-567.

D272.   Bobroff, A.L. "Working Women, Bonding Patterns, and the Politics of Daily Life: Russia at the End of the Old Regime," PhD diss., Michigan, 1982.

D273.　Bohachevsky-Chomiak, M. *Feminists Despite Themselves: Women in Ukrainian Community Life, 1884-1939* (Edmonson: Canadian Institute of Ukrainian Studies, University of Alberta, 1988).

D274.　Clements, B.E. "Aleksandra Kollontai: Libertine or Feminist?," in: R.C.Elwood (ed.) *Reconsiderations on the Russian Revolution* (Cambridge, Mass.: Slavica, 1976), pp.241-255.

D275.　Clements, B.E. "Baba and Bolshevik: Russian Women and Revolutionary Change," *Soviet Union* 12 (1985), pt.2, pp.161-184.

D276.　Clements, B.E. "Emancipation Through Communism: The Ideology of A.M. Kollontai," *SR* 32 (1973), no.2, pp.323-338.

D277.　Clements, B.E., Engel, B.A. & Worobec, C.D. (eds.) *Russia's Women: Accommodation, Resistance, Transformation* (Berkeley, Los Angeles, Oxford: University of California Press, 1991).

D278.　Drumm, R.E. "The Bolshevik Party and the Organization and Emancipation of Working Women, 1914-1921: or a History of the Petrograd Experiment," PhD diss., Columbia, 1977.

D279.　Dudgeon, R.A. "The Forgotten Minority: Women Students in Imperial Russia, 1872-1917," *RH* 9 (1982), pt.1, pp.1-26.

D280.　Dudgeon, R.A.F. "Women and Higher Education in Russia, 1855-1905," PhD diss., George Washington, 1975.

D281.　Edmondson, L.H. "Feminism in Russia, 1900-1917," PhD diss., London, 1981.

D282.　Edmondson, L.H. *Feminism in Russia, 1900-1917* (London: Heinemann, 1984).

D283.　Edmondson, L.H. "Russian Feminists and the First All-Russian Congress of Women," *RH* 3 (1976), pt.2, pp.123-149.

D284.　Engel, B.A. *Between the Fields and the City: Women, Work, and Family in Russia, 1861-1914* (Cambridge: Cambridge U.P., 1994).

D285.　Engel, B.A. "Women, Men, and the Languages of Peasant Resistance, 1870-1907," in: S.P.Frank & M.D.Steinberg (eds.) *Cultures in Flux: Lower-Class Values, Practices, and Resistance in Late Imperial Russia* (Princeton: Princeton U.P., 1994), pp.34-53.

D286.　Engel, B.A. "Women, Work and Family in the Factories of Rural Russia," *RH* 16 (1989), pts.2/4, pp.223-237.

D287.　Engelstein, L. "Abortion and the Civic Order: The Legal and Medical Debates," in: B.E.Clements et al (eds.) *Russia's Women: Accommodation, Resistance, Transformation* (Berkeley, Los Angeles, Oxford: University of California Press, 1991), pp.185-207.

D288.　Farnsworth, B. *Aleksandra Kollontai: Socialism, Feminism, and the Bolshevik Revolution* (Stanford: Stanford U.P., 1980).

D289.   Farnsworth, B.B. "Bolshevism, the Woman Question and Aleksandra Kollontai," *AHR* 81 (1976), pp.292-316 [also printed in: M.J.Boxer & J.H.Quataert (eds.) *Socialist Women: European Socialist Feminism in the Nineteenth and Early Twentieth Centuries* (New York, Oxford, Shannon: Elsevier, 1978), pp.182-214].

D290.   Fieseler, B. "The Making of Russian Female Social Democrats, 1890-1917," *IRSH* 34 (1989), pp.193-226.

D291.   Glickman, R.L. *Russian Factory Women. Workplace and Society, 1880-1914* (Berkeley: University of California Press, 1984).

D292.   Goldberg, R.L. "The Russian Women's Movement, 1859-1917," PhD diss., Rochester, 1976.

D293.   Hutton, M.J. "Russian and Soviet Women, 1897-1939: Dreams, Struggles, and Nightmares," PhD diss., Iowa, 1986.

D294.   Ingemanson, B. "The Political Function of Domestic Objects in the Fiction of Aleksandra Kollontai," *SR* 48 (1989), no.1, pp.71-82.

D295.   Knight, A. "Female Terrorists in the Russian Socialist Revolutionary Party," *RR* 38 (1979), no.2, pp.139-159.

D296.   Knight, A.W. "The Participation of Women in the Revolutionary Movement in Russia from 1890 to 1914," PhD diss., London, 1977.

D297.   Kollontai, A. *Selected Writings*, edited by A.Holt (London: Allison & Busby, 1977).

D298.   Kollontai, A. *The Autobiography of a Sexually Emancipated Communist Woman*, trans.by S.Attanasio (New York: Herder & Herder, 1971).

D299.   Mullaney, M.M. "The Female Revolutionary, the Woman Question, and European Socialism, 1871-1921," PhD diss., Rutgers, 1980.

D300.   Norton, B.T. "The making of a female Marxist: E.D. Kuskova's conversion to Russian Social Democracy," *IRSH* 34 (1989), pp.227-247.

D301.   Perlina, N. "Primeval and Modern Mythologies in the Life of Ol'ga Mikhailovna Freidenburg," *RR* 51 (1992), no.2, pp.188-197.

D302.   Pertzoff, M.H. "'Lady in Red': A Study of the Early Career of Alexandra Mikhailovna Kollontai," PhD diss., Virginia, 1968.

D303.   Porter, C. *Alexandra Kollontai. A Biography* (London: Virago, 1980).

D304.   Price, H. *Alexandra Kollontai: Soviet Marxist and Feminist* (University of Kent at Canterbury: Women's Studies occasional papers, Paper No.19, 1990).

D305.   Ramer, S.C. "The Transformation of the Russian Feldsher, 1864-1914," in: E.Mendelsohn & M.S.Shatz (eds.) *Imperial Russia, 1700-1917: State, Society, Opposition. Essays in Honor of Marc Raeff* (DeKalb, Illinois: Northern Illinois Press, 1988), pp.136-160.

D306.   Ross, D. "The Role of the Women of Petrograd in War, Revolution and Counter-Revolution, 1914-1921," PhD diss., Rutgers, 1973.

D307.   Satina, S. *Education of Women in Pre-Revolutionary Russia*, trans.by A.F.Poustchine (New York: 1966).

D308.   Scott, M.C. "Her Brother's Keeper: The Evolution of Women Bolsheviks," PhD diss., Kansas, 1980.

D309.   Smith, S.A. "Class and Gender: Women's Strikes in St Petersburg, 1895-1917 and in Shanghai, 1895-1927," *Social History* 19 (1994), no.2, pp.141-168.

D310.   Stites, R. "Alexandra Kollontai and the Russian Revolution," in: J.Slaughter & R.Kern (eds.) *European Women on the Left: Socialism, Feminism, and the Problems Faced by Political Women, 1880 to the Present* (Westport, Conn. & London: Greenwood, 1981).

D311.   Stites, R. "Prostitute and Society in Pre-Revolutionary Russia," *JFGO* 31 (1983), pp.348-364.

D312.   Stites, R. *The Women's Liberation Movement in Russia. Feminism, Nihilism and Bolshevism, 1860-1930* (Princeton: Princeton U.P., 1978).

D313.   Wagner, W.G. "The Trojan Mare: Women's Rights and Civil Rights in Late Imperial Russia," in: O.Crisp & L. Edmondson (eds.) *Civil Rights in Imperial Russia* (Oxford: Clarendon, 1989), pp.65-84.

D314.   Zeide, A. "Larisa Reisner: Myth as Justification for Life," *RR* 51 (1992), no.2, pp.172-187.

1905:

D315.   Edmondson, L. "Feminists in the Revolution of 1905," *Sbornik (SGRR)* no.9 (1983), pp.118-126.

1914-17:

D316.   Meyer, A. "The Impact of World War I on Russian Women's Lives," in: B.E.Clements et al (eds.) *Russia's Women: Accommodation, Resistance, Transformation* (Berkeley, Los Angeles, Oxford: University of California Press, 1991), pp.208-224.

1917:

D317.   Donald, M. "Bolshevik Activity amongst the Working Women of Petrograd in 1917," *IRSH* 27 (1982), pp.129-160.

D318.   Pankhurst, E. In *Britannica*, 13 July, 16 November 1917.

1917-21:

D319.   Bonnell, V.E. "The Representation of Women in Early Soviet Political Art," *RR* 50 (1991), no.3, pp.267-288.

D320.   Clements, B.E. "The Revolution and the Revolutionary: Aleksandra Mikhailovna Kollontai, 1917-23," PhD diss., Duke, 1971.

D321.   Goldman, W.Z. *Women, the State and Revolution: Soviet Family Policy and Social Life, 1917-1936* (Cambridge: Cambridge U.P., 1993).

D322.   Hayden, C.E. "Feminism and Bolshevism: The *Zhenotdel* and the Politics of Women's Emancipation in Russia, 1917-1930," PhD diss., California, Berkeley, 1979.

D323.   Hayden, C.E. "The Zhenotdel and the Bolshevik Party," *RH* 3 (1976), pt.2, pp.150-173.

D324.   Lapidus, G.H. *Women in Soviet Society: Equality, Development, and Social Change* (Berkeley, Los Angeles, London: University of California Press, 1978).

D325.   Stavrakis, B.D. "Women and the Communist Party in the Soviet Union, 1918-1935," PhD diss., Western Reserve, 1961.

D326.   Stites, R. "Zhenotdel: Bolshevism and Russian Women, 1917-1930," *RH* 3 (1976), pt.2, pp.174-193.

D327.   Waters, E. "Childcare Posters and the Modernisation of Motherhood," *Sbornik (SGRR)* no.13 (1987), pp.65-93.

D328.   Waters, E.J. "From the Old Family to the New: Work, Marriage, and Motherhood in Urban Soviet Russia, 1917-1931," PhD diss., Birmingham, 1985.

Children:

D329.   Ball, A. *And Now My Heart is Hardened. Abandoned Children in Soviet Russia, 1918-1930* (Berkeley, Los Angeles, & London: University of California Press, 1994).

D330.   Ball, A. "State Children: Soviet Russia's *Besprizornye* and the New Socialist Generation," *RR* 52 (1993), no.2, pp.228-247.

D331.   Ball, A. "Survival in the Street World of Soviet Russia's *Besprizornye*," *JFGO* 39 (1991), pp.33-52.

D332.   Ball, A. "The Roots of *Besprizornost'* in Soviet Russia's First Decade," *SR* 51 (1992), no.2, pp.247-270.

D333.   Muckle, J. "Saving the Russian Children: Materials in the Archive of the Save the Children Fund Relating to Eastern Europe in 1920-23," *SEER* 68 (1990), no.3, pp.507-511.

D334.   Riordan, J. "The Russian Boy Scouts," *HT* 38 (1988), pp.48-52.

D335.   Stevens, J.A. "Children of the Revolution: Soviet Russia's Homeless Children (Besprizorniki) in the 1920s," *RH* 9 (1982), pts.2/3, pp.242-264.

D336.   Stolee, M.K. "Homeless Children in the USSR, 1917-1957," *SS* 40 (1988), no.1, pp.64-83.

D337.   Waters, E. "Childcare Posters and the Modernisation of Motherhood," *Sbornik (SGRR)* no.13 (1987), pp.65-93.

Demography and Urbanisation:

D338.   Bater, J.H. "Some Dimensions of Urbanization and the Response of Municipal Government: Moscow and St.Petersburg," *RH* 5 (1978), pt.1, pp.46-63.

D339.   Bater, J.H. *St.Petersburg: Industrialization and Change* (London: Edward Arnold, 1976).

D340.   Bater, J.H. "Transience, Residential Persistence, and Mobility in Moscow and St.Petersburg, 1900-1914," *SR* 39 (1980), no.2, pp.239-254.0

D341.   Bradley, J. *Muzhik and Muscovite: Urbanization in Late Imperial Russia* (Berkeley, Los Angeles, London: University of California Press, 1985).

D342.   Coale, A.J., Anderson, B.A. & Harm, E. *Human Fertility in Russia since the Nineteenth Century* (Princeton: Princeton U.P., 1979).

D343.   Corrsin, S.D. "The Changing Composition of the City of Riga, 1867-1913," *Journal of Baltic Studies* 13 (1982), pp.19-39.

D344.   Demko, G.J. *The Russian Colonization of Kazakhstan, 1896-1916* (The Hague: Mouton, 1969).

D345.   Garson, L.K. "The Centenarian Question: Old-Age Mortality in the Soviet Union, 1897-1970," PhD diss., Princeton, 1986.

D346.   Gleason, W.E. "The All-Russian Union of Towns and the Politics of Urban Reform in Tsarist Russia," *RR* 35 (1976), no.3, pp.290-302.

D347.   Hamm, M.F. (ed.) *The City in Russian History* (Lexington: University Press of Kentucky, 1976).

D348.   Hoch, S.L. "On Good Numbers and Bad: Malthus, Population Trends and Peasant Standard of Living in Late Imperial Russia," *SR* 53 (1994), no.1, pp.41-75.

D349.   Koenker, D. "Urbanization and Deurbanization in the Russian Revolution and Civil War," *JMH* 57 (1985), no.3, pp.424-450.

D350.   Koenker, D.P. et al (eds.) *Party, State, and Society in the Russian Civil War. Explorations in Social History* (Bloomington & Indianapolis: Indiana U.P., 1989).

D351.   Leasure, J.W. & Lewis, R.A. *Population Changes in Russia and the USSR: A Set of Comparable Territorial Units* (San Diego: San Diego State College Press, 1966).

D352.   Matossian, M.K. "Climate, Crops, and Natural Increase in Rural Russia, 1861-1913," *SR* 45 (1986), no.3, pp.457-469.

D353.   Murdzek, B.P. "Population Movements in the Polish Provinces of Prussia, Russia and Austria, 1870-1914: Policies and Attitudes," PhD diss., American, 1960.

D354.   Thurston, R.W. *Liberal City, Conservative State: Moscow and Russia's Urban Crisis, 1906-1914* (New York & Oxford: Oxford U.P., 1989).

D355.   Thurston, R.W. "Urban Problems and Local Government in Late Imperial Russia: Moscow, 1906-1914," PhD diss., Michigan, 1980.

D356.   Treadgold, D.W. *The Great Siberian Migration: Government and Peasant in Resettlement from Emancipation to the First World War* (Princeton: Princeton U.P., 1957).

D357.   Vorderer, S.M. "Urbanization and Industrialization in Late Imperial Russia: Ivanovo-Voznesensk, 1880-1914," PhD diss., Boston College, 1990.

D358.   Wojtun, B.S. "Demographic Transition in West Poland, 1816-1914," PhD diss., Pennsylvania, 1968.

Health and Welfare:

D359.   Bradley, J. "The Moscow Workhouse and Urban Welfare Reform in Russia," *RR* 41 (1982), no.4, pp.427-444.

D360.   Edmondson, C.M. "The Politics of Hunger: The Soviet Response to Famine, 1921," *SS* 29 (1977), no.4, pp.506-518.

D361.   Hutchinson, J.F. "Science, Politics and the Alcohol Problem in post-1905 Russia," *SEER* 58 (1980), no.2, pp.232-254.

D362.   Jahn, H.F. "The Housing Revolution in Petrograd, 1917-1920," *JFGO* 38 (1990), pp.212-227.

D363.   Lindenmeyer, A. "A Russian Experiment in Voluntarism: The Municipal Guardianships of the Poor, 1894-1914," *JFGO* 30 (1982), pp.429-451.

D364.   Lindenmeyer, A. "Public Poor Relief and Private Charity in Late Imperial Russia," PhD diss., Princeton, 1980.

D365.   Muckle, J. "Saving the Russian Children: Materials in the Archive of the Save the Children Fund Relating to Eastern Europe in 1920-23," *SEER* 68 (1990), no.3, pp.507-511.

D366.   Solomon, S.G. & Hutchinson, J.F. (eds.) *Health and Society in Revolutionary Russia* (Bloomington & Indianapolis: Indiana U.P., 1990).

D367.   Surh, G. "A Matter of Life or Death: St Petersburg's Public Health Doctors Between Disease and Government Neglect," *RH* 20 (1993), nos.1-4, pp.125-146.

D368.   Williams, C. "The 1921 Russian Famine: Centre and Periphery Responses," *Revolutionary Russia* 6 (1993), no.2, pp.277-314.

Crime:

D369.   Adams, B.F. "Criminology, Penology and Prison Administration in Russia, 1863-1917," PhD diss., Maryland, 1981.

D370.   Healey, D. "The Russian Revolution and the Decriminalisation of Homosexuality," *Revolutionary Russia* 6 (1993), no.1, pp.26-54.

D371.   Neuberger, J. "Crime and Culture: Hooliganism in St.Peterburg, 1900-1914," PhD diss., Stanford, 1985.

D372.   Neuberger, J. "Culture Besieged: Hooliganism and Futurism," in: S.P.Frank & M.D.Steinberg (eds.) *Cultures in Flux: Lower-Class Values, Practices, and Resistance in Late Imperial Russia* (Princeton: Princeton U.P., 1994), pp.185-203.

D373.   Neuberger, J. *Hooliganism: Crime, Culture, and Power in St.Petersburg, 1900-1914* (Berkeley: University of California Press, 1993).

D374.   Shelley, L.I. "Soviet Criminology: Its Birth and Demise, 1917-1936," PhD diss., Pennsylvania, 1977.

D375.   Solomon, P.H., Jr. "Criminalization and Decriminalization in Soviet Criminal Policy, 1917-1941," *Law and Society Review* 16 (1981-82), no.1, pp.9-43.

D376.   Solomon, P.H., Jr. "Soviet Penal Policy, 1917-1934: A Reinterpretation," *SR* 39 (1980), no.2, pp.195-217.

D377.   Weissman, N.B. "Rural Crime in Tsarist Russia: The Question of Hooliganism, 1905-1914," *SR* 37 (1978), no.2, pp.228-240.

E

REACTIONARIES AND REFORMISTS

Right Wing Movements:

E1.   Adams, B. "The Extraordinary Career of Vasilii Shul'gin," *Revolutionary Russia* 5 (1992), no.2, pp.193-208.

E2.   Bohn, J.W. "Reactionary Politics in Russia: 1905-1909," PhD diss., North Carolina, 1967.

E3.   Brock, J.J., Jr. "The Theory and Practice of the Russian People 1905-1907: A Case Study of 'Black-Hundred' Politics," PhD diss., Michigan, 1972.

E4.   Brock, J. "The Theory and Practice of Black Hundred Politics," PhD diss., Michigan, 1977.

E5.   Edelman, R. "Russian Nationalism and Class Consciousness: the Rise of the All-Russian Nationalist Party, 1907-1912," PhD diss., Columbia, 1974.

E6.   Edelman, R. "The Russian Nationalist Party and the Political Crisis of 1909," *RR* 34 (1975), no.1, pp.22-54.

E7.   Oberlander, E. "The role of the political parties," in: G.Katkov et al (eds.) *Russia Enters the Twentieth Century, 1894-1917* (London: Temple Smith, 1971), pp.60-84.

E8.   Rawson, D.C. "Rightist Politics in the Revolution of 1905: The Case of Tula Province," *SR* 51 (1992), no.1, pp.99-116.

E9.   Rawson, D.C. "The Union of Russian People, 1905-1907: A Study of the Radical Right," PhD diss., Washington, 1971.

E10.   Rogger, H. "The Formation of the Russian Right, 1900-1906," *California Slavic Studies* 3 (1964), pp.66-94.

E11.   Rogger, H. "Was There a Russian Fascism? The Union of Russian People," *JMH* 36 (1964), no.4, pp.398-415.

E12.   Shulgin, V.V. *Days of the Russian Revolution: Memoirs from the Right, 1905-1917*, trans.by B.F.Adams (Gulf Breeze, Fl.: Academic International Press, 1990).

E13.   Shulgin, V.V. *The Years. Memoirs of a Member of the Russian Duma, 1906-1917*, trans. by T.Davis (New York: Hippocrene, 1984).

E14.   Zimmerman, E.R. "The Right Radical Movement in Russia, 1905-1917," PhD diss., London, 1968.

Liberal Movements and Parties:

E15.   Astrakhan, Kh.M. "The History of Russia's Bourgeois and Petit-Bourgeois Parties in 1917 in the most recent Soviet literature," *SSH* 15 (1976-77), no.1, pp.3-30.

E16.   Bensman, S.J. "The Constitutional Ideas of the Russian Liberation Movement: The Struggle for Human Rights during the Revolution of 1905," PhD diss., Wisconsin, 1977.

E17.   Boll, M.M. "The Social and Political Philosophy of Semen L. Frank: A Study in Prerevolutionary Twentieth Century Russian Liberalism," PhD diss., Wisconsin, 1970.

E18.   Brainerd, M.C. "The Octobrists and the Gentry, 1905-1907: Leaders and Followers?," in: L.H.Haimson (ed.) *The Politics of Rural Russia, 1905-1914* (Bloomington & London: Indiana U.P., 1979), pp.67-93.

E19.   Brainerd, M.C. "The Octobrists and the Gentry in the Russian Social Crisis of 1913-14," *RR* 38 (1979), no.2, pp.160-179.

E20.   Brainerd, M.C. "The Union of October 17 and Russian Society, 1905-1907," PhD diss., Columbia, 1976.

E21.   Breuillard, S. "Russian Liberalism - Utopia or Realism? The Individual and the Citizen in the Political Thought of Milyukov," in: R.B.McKean (ed.) *New Perspectives in Modern Russian History* (Basingstoke & London: Macmillan, 1992), pp.99-116.

E22.   Burns, P.E. "Liberalism without Hope: The Constitutional Democratic Party in the Russian Revolution, February-July 1917," PhD diss., Indiana, 1967.

E23.   Chamberlin, W.H. "The Short Life of Russian Liberalism," *RR* 26 (1967), no.2, pp.144-152.

E24.   Clabby, J.F., Jr. "D.N. Shipov and Zemstvo Liberalism," PhD diss., Arizona, 1979.

E25.   Cockfield, J.H. "*The Union Sacree*: Tsarism and the Constitutional Democratic Party, 1914-1917," PhD diss., Virginia, 1972.

E26.   Crisp, O. "The Russian Liberals and the 1906 Anglo-French Loan to Russia," *SEER* 39 (1960-61), pp.497-511.

E27.   Duggan, W.L., Jr. "The Progressists and Russian Politics, 1914-1917," PhD diss., Columbia, 1984.

E28.   Emmons, T. "Russia's Banquet Campaign," *California Slavic Studies* 10 (1977), pp.45-86.

E29.   Emmons, T. *The Formation of Political Parties and the First National Elections in Russia* (Cambridge, Mass.: Harvard U.P., 1983).

E30.   Fischer, G. "The Russian Intelligentsia and Liberalism," *HSS* 4 (1957), pp.317-336.

E31.   Fleischhauer, I. "The Agrarian Program of the Russian Constitutional Democrats," *Cahiers du Monde Russe et Sovietique* 20 (1979), no.2, pp.173-201.

E32.   Frohlich, K. *The Emergence of Russian Constitutionalism, 1900-1904. The Relationship Between Social Mobilization and Political Group Formation in Pre-Revolutionary Russia* (The Hague: Martinus Nijhoff, 1981).

E33.   Galai, S. "The Impact of the Russo-Japanese War on the Russian Liberals 1904-5," *Government and Opposition* 1 (1965), no.1, pp.85-109.

E34.   Galai, S. "The Kadet Quest for the Masses," in: R.B.McKean (ed.) *New Perspectives in Modern Russian History* (Basingstoke & London: Macmillan, 1992), pp.80-98.

E35.   Galai, S. "The Kadets and Russia's Foreign Policy," *Sbornik (SGRR)* no.12 (1986), pp.2-24.

E36.   Galai, S. "The Role of the Union of Unions in the Revolution of 1905," *JFGO* 24 (1976), pp.512-525.

E37.   Galai, S. "The Tragic Dilemma of Russian Liberalism as Reflected in Ivan Il'ic Petrunkevic's Letters to his Son," *JFGO* 29 (1981), pp.1-29.

E38.   Geifman, A. "The Kadets and Terrorism, 1905-1907," *JFGO* 36 (1988), pp.248-267.

E39.   Gleason, W. *Alexander Guchkov and the End of the Russian Empire* (Philadelphia: American Philosophical Society Transactions vol.73, part 3, 1983).

E40.   Greicus, E.M. "Efforts of the Progressive Bloc to Influence the Conduct of the War in Russia, 1915-1917," PhD diss., Tulane, 1969.

E41.   Hamm, M.F. "Liberal Politics in Wartime Russia: An Analysis of the Progressive Bloc," *SR* 33 (1974), no.3, pp.453-468.

E42.   Hamm. M.F. "Liberalism and the Jewish Question: The Progressive Bloc," *RR* 31 (1972), no.2, pp.163-172.

E43.   Hamm, M.F. "The Progressive Bloc of Russia's Fourth State Duma," PhD diss., Indiana, 1971.

E44.   Holowinsky, Y. "Promoting Russian Liberalism in America," *RR* 49 (1990), no.2, pp.167-174.

E45.   Hutchinson, J.F. "The Octobrists and the Future of Imperial Russia as a Great Power," *SEER* 50 (1972), no.119, pp.220-237.

E46.   Hutchinson, J.F. "The Octobrists in Russian Politics, 1905-1917," PhD diss., London, 1966.

E47.   King, V. "The Liberal Movement in Russia 1904-5," *SEER* 14 (1935-36), pp.124-137.

E48.   Kochan, L. "Kadet Policy in 1917 and the Constituent Assembly," *SEER* 45 (1967), pp.183-192.

E49.   Kroner, A. "The Role of the Kadets in the Three Attempts to Form Coalition Cabinets in 1905-6," *Revolutionary Russia* 5 (1992), no.1, pp.22-45.

E50.   Lerner, L.W. "The Progressists in the Russian State Duma, 1907-1915," PhD diss., Washington, 1976.

E51.   Long, J.W. "French Attempts at Constitutional Reform in Russia," *JFGO* 23 (1975), pp.496-503.

E52.   Long, J.W. "Organized Protest Against the 1906 Russian Loan," *Cahiers du Monde Russe et Sovietique* 13 (1972), no.1, pp.24-39.

E53.   Menashe, L. "Alexander Guchkov and the Origins of the Octobrist Party: The Russian Bourgeoisie in Politics, 1905," PhD diss., New York, 1966.

E54.   Miliukov, P.N. *Political Memoirs 1905-1917*, trans.by C.Goldberg (Ann Arbor: University of Michigan Press, 1967).

E55.   Oberlander, E. "The role of the political parties," in: G.Katkov et al (eds.) *Russia Enters the Twentieth Century, 1894-1917* (London: Temple Smith, 1971), pp.60-84.

E56.   Owen, T.C. *Capitalism and Politics in Russia: A Social History of the Moscow Merchants, 1855-1905* (Cambridge: Cambridge U.P., 1981).

E57.   Pares, B. "Fedor Rodichev," *SEER* 12 (1933-34), no.34, pp.199-201.

E58.   Parker, C. "Paul Vinogradoff, the Delusions of Russian Liberalism, and the Development of Russian Studies in England," *SEER* 69 (1991), no.1, pp.40-59.

E59.   Pearson, R. "Milyukov and the Sixth Kadet Congress," *SEER* 53 (1975), no.131, pp.210-229.

E60.   Pearson, R. "The Russian Moderate Parties in the Fourth State Duma, 1912-February 1917," PhD diss., Durham, 1973.

E61.   Pearson, R. *The Russian Moderates and the Crisis of Tsarism, 1914-1917* (London: Macmillan, 1977).

E62.   Pearson, R. "The Vyborg Complex," *ISS* no.1 (1980), pp.73-91.

E63.   Pinchuk, B.-C. "The Octobrists in the Third Duma: 1907-1912," PhD diss., Washington, Seattle, 1969.

E64. Pinchuk, B.-C. *The Octobrists in the Third Duma, 1907-1912* (Seattle and London: University of Washington Press, 1974).

E65. Piotrow, F. "Paul Milyukov and the Constitutional-Democratic Party," PhD diss., Oxford, 1962.

E66. Putnam, G. "Russian Liberalism Challenged from Within: Bulgakov and Berdyayev in 1904-05," *SEER* 43 (1964-65), pp.335-353.

E67. Pyziur, E. "Constitutional Thought in Pre-Revolutionary Russia," PhD diss., Notre Dame, 1961.

E68. Raeff, M. "Some Reflections on Russian Liberalism," *RR* 18 (1959), no.3, pp.218-230.

E69. Rainey, T.B., Jr. "The Union of 17 October: An Experiment in Moderate Constitutionalism (1905-1906)," PhD diss., University of Illinois, 1966.

E70. Rhyne, G.N. "The Constitutional Democratic Party from Its Origins Through the First State Duma," PhD diss., North Carolina, 1968.

E71. Riha, T. *A Russian European: Paul Miliukov in Russian Politics* (Notre Dame & London: University of Notre Dame Press, 1969).

E72. Riha, T. "1917 - A Year of Illusions," *SS* 19 (1967), no.1, pp.115-121.

E73. Riha, T. "Paul Miliukov's Parliamentary Career, 1907-1917," PhD diss., Harvard, 1962.

E74. Rodichev, F. "The Liberal Movement in Russia, 1855-1917," *SEER* 2 (1923-24), pp.1-13 & pp.249-262.

E75. Rosenberg, W.G. "Constitutional Democracy and the Russian Civil War," PhD diss., Harvard, 1967.

E76. Rosenberg, W.G. *Liberals in the Russian Revolution: The Constitutional Democratic Party, 1917-1921* (Princeton: Princeton U.P., 1974).

E77. Rosenberg, W.G. "Russian Liberals and the Bolshevik Coup," *JMH* 40 (1968), no.3, pp.328-347.

E78. Sanders, J.E. "The Union of Unions: Political, Economic, Civil, and Human Rights Organizations in the 1905 Russian Revolution," PhD diss., Columbia, 1985.

E79. Shatsillo, K.F. "The 'Pinkening' of the Liberals at the Beginning of the First Russian Revolution," *SSH* 20 (1981-82), no.3, pp.45-73.

E80. Smith, N. "The Constitutional Democratic Movement in Russia, 1902-1906," PhD diss., Illinois, 1959.

E81. Suny, R.G. "Some Thoughts on 1917: In Lieu of a Review of William Rosenberg's *Liberals in the Russian Revolution: The Constitutional Democratic Party, 1917-1921*," *Sbornik (SGRR)* no.1 (1975), pp.24-27.

E82.   Timberlake, C.E. *Essays on Russian Liberalism* (Columbia, Missouri: University of Missouri Press, 1972).

E83.   Treadgold, D.W. "The Constitutional Democrats and the Russian Liberal Tradition," *ASEER* 10 (1951), no.2, pp.85-94.

E84.   Tyrkova-Williams, A. "Russian Liberalism," *RR* 10 (1951), no.1, pp.3-14.

E85.   Tyrkova-Williams, A. "The Cadet Party," *RR* 12 (1953), no.3, pp.173-186.

E86.   West, J.L. "The Moscow Progressists: Russian Industrialists in Liberal Politics, 1905-1914," PhD diss., Princeton, 1975.

E87.   Williams, A. "Prince Paul Dolgorukov," *SEER* 6 (1927-28), no.16, pp.200-201.

E88.   Zimmerman, J.E. "Between Revolution and Reaction: the Constitutional Democratic Party: October 1905 to June 1907," PhD diss., Columbia, 1967.

E89.   Zimmerman, J.E. "Russian Liberal Theory, 1900-17," *CASS* 14 (1980), no.1, pp.1-20.

E90.   Zimmerman, J.E. "The Political Views of the 'Vekhi' Group," *CASS* 10 (1976), no.3, p.307-327.

The Stolypin Reforms:

E91.   Chmielewski, E. "Stolypin's Last Crisis," *California Slavic Studies* 3 (1964), pp.95-126.

E92.   Conroy, M.S. *Petr Arkad'evich Stolypin. Practical Politics in Late Tsarist Russia* (Boulder: Westview, 1976).

E93.   Conroy, M.S. "Stolypin's Attitude toward Local Self-Government," *SEER* 46 (1968), pp.446-461.

E94.   Gerasimenko, G.A. "The Stolypin Agrarian Reforms in Saratov Province," in: R.A.Wade & S.J.Seregny (eds.) *Politics and Society in Provincial Russia: Saratov, 1590-1917* (Columbia, Ohio: Ohio State U.P., 1989), pp.233-254.

E95.   Hosking, G.A. "Stolypin and the Octobrist Party," *SEER* 47 (1969), pp.137-160.

E96.   Hosking, G.A. *The Russian Constitutional Experiment: Government and Duma, 1907-1914* (Cambridge: Cambridge U.P., 1973).

E97.   Jones, A.N. "The Peasants of Late Imperial Russia: Economy and Society in the Era of the Stolypin Land Reform," PhD diss., Harvard, 1988.

E98.   Macey, D.A.J. "Government Actions and Peasant Reactions During the Stolypin Reforms," in: R.B.McKean (ed.) *New Perspectives in Modern Russian History* (Basingstoke & London: Macmillan, 1992), pp.133-173.

E99.   Mosse, W.E. *Perestroika under the Tsars* (London & New York: I.B. Tauris, 1992).

E100.   Mosse, W.E. "Stolypin's Villages," *SEER* 43 (1964-65), pp.257-274.

E101.   Pallot, J. "Did the Stolypin Land Reform Destroy the Peasant Commune?" in: R.B.McKean (ed.) *New Perspectives in Modern Russian History* (Basingstoke & London: Macmillan, 1992), pp.117-132.

E102.   Pallot, J. "*Khutora* and *Otruba* in Stolypin's Program of Farm Individualization," *SR* 43 (1984), no.2, pp.242-256.

E103.   Pallot, J. & Shaw, D.J.B. *Landscape and Settlement in Romanov Russia, 1613-1917* (Oxford: Clarendon, 1990).

E104.   Schaeffer, M.E. "Political Policies of P.A. Stolypin, Minister of the Interior and Chairman of the Council of Ministers in Russia, 1906-1911," PhD diss., Indiana, 1964

E105.   Shecket, A.D. "The Russian Imperial State Council and the Policies of P.A. Stolypin, 1906-1911: Bureaucratic and *Soslovie* Interests Versus Reform," PhD diss., Columbia, 1974.

E106.   Tokmakoff, G. "P.A. Stolypin and the Second Duma," *SEER* 50 (1972), pp.49-62.

E107.   Tokmakoff, G. *P.A. Stolypin and the Third Duma: an appraisal of three major issues* (Washington: University Press of America, 1981).

E108.   Treadgold, D.W. "Was Stolypin in Favor of Kulaks?" *ASEER* 14 (1955), pp.1-14.

E109.   Waldron, P.R. "The Stolypin Programme of Reform, 1906-1911, with Special Reference to Local Government and Religious Affairs," PhD diss., London, 1981.

E110.   Yaney, G.L. "The Concept of the Stolypin Land Reform," *SR* 23 (1964), no.2, pp.275-293.

E111.   Yaney, G.L. "The Imperial Russian Government and the Stolypin Land Reform," PhD diss., Princeton, 1961.

E112.   Zenkovsky, A.V. *Stolypin: Russia's Last Great Reformer*, trans.by M.Patoski (Princeton: Kingston Press, 1986).

F

REVOLUTIONARY MOVEMENT

General:

F1.   Akashi, M. *Rakka Ryusui: Colonel Akashi's Report on his Secret Cooperation with the Russian Revolutionary Parties during the Russo-Japanese War* (Selected Chapters, trans.by I.Chiharu) (Helsinki: Finnish Historical Society, Studia Historica 31, 1988).

F2.   Baldwin, Rev. A.-J. "The Russian Revolutionary Movements from the Decembrists to the Bolsheviks (1825-1917)," PhD diss., Georgetown, 1948.

F3.   D'Agostino, A.W. "Marxism and the Russian Anarchists," PhD diss., California, L.A., 1971.

F4.   Desind, P. *Jewish and Russian Revolutionaries Exiled to Siberia, 1901-1917* (Lewiston, New York: Edwin Mellen Press, 1990).

F5.   Duncan, P.J.S. "Ivanov-Razumnik and the Russian Revolution: From Scythianism to Suffocation," *CSP* 21 (1979), no.1, pp.15-27.

F6.   Friedgut, T.H. "Professional Revolutionaries in the Donbass: The Characteristics and Limitations of the *Apparat*," *CSP* 27 (1985), no.3, pp.284-300.

F7.   Futrell, M. "Colonel Akashi and Japanese Contacts with Russian Revolutionaries in 1904-5," *St.Anthony's Papers* 20 (1967) (Far Eastern Affairs no.4), pp.7-22.

F8.   Garcia, Z.G.Y. "The Origins of Revolutionary Defensism: I.G. Tsereteli and the "Siberian Zimmerwaldists"," *SR* 41 (1982), no.3, pp.454-476.

F9.   Geifman, A. *Thou Shalt Kill: Revolutionary Terrorism in Russia, 1894-1917* (Princeton: Princeton U.P., 1993).

F10.   Geifman, A. "Political Parties and Revolutionary Terrorism in Russia, 1900-1917," PhD diss., Harvard, 1990.

F11.   Getzler, I. "Marxist Revolutionaries and the Dilemma of Power," in: A.Rabinowitch et al (eds.) *Revolution and Politics in Russia: Essays in Memory of B.I. Nicolaevsky* (Bloomington: Indiana U.P., 1972), pp.88-112.

F12.   Kerensky, A. "Catherine Breshkovsky 1844-1934," *SEER* 13 (1934-35), pp.428-431.

F13.   Kirimli, H. "The "Young Tatar" Movement in the Crimea, 1905-1909," *Cahiers du Monde Russe et Sovietique* 34 (1993), no.4, pp.529-560.

F14.   Kolonitskii, B.I. "Antibourgeois Propaganda and Anti-*'Burzhui'* Consciousness in 1917," *RR* 53 (1994), no.2, pp.183-196.

F15.   Kowalski, R.I. "The Development of 'Left Communism' Until 1921: Soviet Russia, Poland, Latvia and Lithuania," PhD diss., Glasgow, 1978.

F16.   Leont'ev, Ia. & Nimulin, M. "In Memory of Vera Figner," *Revolutionary Russia* 6 (1993), no.1, pp.145-147.

F17.   Long, J.W. "Organized Protest Against the 1906 Russian Loan," *Cahiers du Monde Russe et Sovietique* 13 (1972), no.1, pp.24-39.

F18.   McDaniel, J.F. "Political Assassination and Mass Execution: Terrorism in Revolutionary Russia, 1878-1938," PhD diss., Michigan, 1976.

F19.   McKean, R.B. *St.Petersburg Between the Revolutions: Workers and Revolutionaries, June 1907-February 1917* (New Haven & London: Yale U.P., 1990).

F20.   Markovic, J.J. "Socialization and Radicalization in Russia, 1861-1917: An Analysis of the Personal Backgrounds of Russian Revolutionaries," PhD diss., Bowling Green State, 1990.

F21.   Melancon, M. "'Marching Together!': Left Bloc Activities in the Russian Revolutionary Movement, 1900 to February 1917," *SR* 49 (1990), no.2, pp.239-252.

F22.   Miliukov, P. *Bolshevism: An International Danger. Its Doctrine and Its Practice Through War and Revolution* (London: George Allen & Unwin, 1920).

F23.   Naimark, M. "Terrorism and the Fall of Imperial Russia," *Boston University lecture pamphlet* (14th April 1986).

F24.   Naimark, N.M. "Terrorism and the Fall of Imperial Russia," *Terrorism and Political Violence* 2 (1990), no.2, pp.171-192.

F25.   Nelson, H.W. "Leon Trotsky and the Art of Insurrection, 1905-1917," PhD diss., Michigan, 1978.

F26.   Newell, D.A. "The Russian Marxist Response to Terrorism: 1878-1917," PhD diss., Stanford, 1981.

F27.   Oberlander, E. "The role of the political parties," in: G.Katkov et al (eds.) *Russia Enters the Twentieth Century, 1894-1917* (London: Temple Smith, 1971), pp.60-84.

F28.   Pearce, B. "Lenin versus Trotsky on 'Revolutionary Defeatism'," *Sbornik (SGRR)* no.13 (1987), pp.16-30.

F29. Prevost, G.F. "Marxism and Anarchism - Some Problems in the Controversy," PhD diss., Minnesota, 1977.

F30. Schapiro, L. "The Role of the Jews in the Russian Revolutionary Movement," *SEER* 40 (1961-62), pp.148-167.

F31. Senn, A.E. "The Politics of *Golos* and *Nashe Slovo*," *IRSH* 17 (1972), pp.675-704.

F32. Treadgold, D.W. *Lenin and His Rivals. The Struggle for Russia's Future, 1898-1906* (London: Methuen, 1955).

F33. Ulam, A.B. *Ideologies and Illusions: Revolutionary Thought from Herzen to Solzhenitsyn* (Cambridge, Mass. & London: Harvard U.P., 1976).

F34. Ulam, A.B. "Reflections on the Revolution," *Survey* 64 (July 1967), pp.3-13.

F35. Wade, R.A. "Irakli Tsereteli and Siberian Zimmerwaldism," *JMH* 39 (1967), pp.425-431.

F36. Wade, R. "The Triumph of Siberian Zimmerwaldism: (March-May, 1917)," *Canadian Slavic Studies* 1 (1967), no.2, pp.253-270.

F37. Wilson, E. *To the Finland Station: A Study in the Writing and Acting of History* (London: Penguin, 1991 [first published 1940]).

F38. Wolfe, B.D. "War Comes to Russia-in-Exile," *RR* 20 (1961), no.4, pp.294-311.

Social Democrats:

F39. Biggart, J. "Bogdanov and Lunacharskii in Vologda," *Sbornik (SGRR)* no.5 (1979), pp.28-40.

F40. Bonnell, V.E. *Roots of Rebellion: Workers' Politics and Organisations in St.Petersburg and Moscow, 1900-1914* (Berkeley: University of California Press, 1983).

F41. Boshyk, G.Y. "The Rise of Ukrainian Political Parties in Russia, with Special Reference to Social Democracy, 1900-1907," PhD diss., Oxford, 1981.

F42. Brym, R.J. *The Jewish Intelligentsia and Russian Marxism: A Sociological Study of Intellectual Radicalism and Ideological Divergence* (London: Macmillan, 1978).

F43. Donald, M. "Karl Kautsky and Russian Social Democracy," *Sbornik (SGRR)* no.11 (1985), pp.26-46.

F44. Donald, M. "Karl Kautsky and Russian Social Democracy, 1900-1914," PhD diss., Leeds, 1986.

F45. Donald, M. *Marxism and Revolution: Karl Kautsky and the Russian Marxists, 1900-1924* (New Haven & London: Yale U.P., 1993).

F46.　Dudden, A.P. & Von Laue, T.H. "The RSDLP and Joseph Fels: A Study in Intercultural Contact," *AHR* 61 (1955-56), no.1, pp.21-47.

F47.　Elwood, R.C. (ed.) *Resolutions and Decisions of the Communist Party of the Soviet Union. Vol.I: The Russian Social Democratic Labour Party, 1898-October 1917* (Toronto and Buffalo: University of Toronto Press, 1974).

F48.　Elwood, R.C. *Russian Social Democracy in the Underground: A Study of the RSDRP in the Ukraine, 1907-1914* (Assen: Van Goorcum, 1974).

F49.　Elwood, R.C. "The Congress That Never Was. Lenin's Attempt to Call a 'Sixth' Party Congress in 1914," *SS* 31 (1979), no.3, pp.343-363.

F50.　Elwood, R.C. "The R.S.D.R.P in Ekaterinoslav: Profile of an Underground Organization, 1907-14," *CSP* 7 (1965), pp.203-222.

F51.　Elwood, R.C. "The RSDRP in the Underground: A Study of the Russian Social Democratic Party in the Ukraine, 1907-1914," PhD diss., Columbia, 1969.

F52.　Elwood, R.C. "Trotsky's Questionnaire," *SR* 29 (1970), no.2, pp.296-301.

F53.　Ewing, S. "The Russian Social Insurance Movement, 1912-1914: An Ideological Analysis," *SR* 50 (1991), no.4, pp.914-926.

F54.　Frankel, J. (ed.) *Vladimir Akimov on the Dilemmas of Russian Marxism, 1895-1903: The Second Congress of the Russian Social Democratic Labour Party; a Short History of the Social Democratic Movement in Russia* (Cambridge: Cambridge U.P., 1969).

F55.　Haimson, L.H. "Consciousness and Spontaneity: Explorations into the Origins of Bolshevism and Menshevism," PhD diss., Harvard, 1952.

F56.　Kalnins, B. "The Social Democratic Movement in Latvia," in: A.Rabinowitch et al (eds.) *Revolution and Politics in Russia: Essays in Memory of B.I. Nicolaevsky* (Bloomington: Indiana U.P., 1972), pp.134-156.

F57.　Keep, J.L.H. "The Development of Social Democracy in Russia, 1898-1907," PhD diss., London, 1954.

F58.　Lane, D.S. *Social and organisational difference between Bolsheviks and Mensheviks, 1903 to 1907* (Discussion Papers Series Rc/C, No.1, Centre for Russian and East European Studies, University of Birmingham, 1964).

F59.　Lane, D. *The Roots of Russian Communism. A Social and Historical Study of Russian Social-Democracy, 1898-1907* (Assen: Royal Van Gorcum, 1969; London: Martin Robertson, 1975).

F60.　Lane, D. "The Russian Social Democratic Labour Party in St. Petersburg, Tver and Ashkhabad, 1903-1905," *SS* 15 (1964), no.3, pp.331-344.

F61.　Lane, D.S. "The Social Composition, Structure and Activity of Russian Social-Democratic Groups, 1898-1907," PhD diss., Oxford, 1966.

F62.   Levin, A. "The Fifth Social Democratic Congress and the Duma," *JMH* 11 (1939), pp.484-508.

F63.   Levin, A. "The Russian Social Democrats in the Second Duma," PhD diss., Yale, 1937.

F64.   Levin, A. *The Second Duma: A Study of the Social Democratic Party and the Russian Constitutional Experiment* (New Haven: Yale U.P. 1940).

F65.   Longley, D.A. "The Russian Social Democrats' Statement to the Duma on 26 July (8 August) 1914: A New Look at the Evidence," *English Historical Review* 102 (1987), pp.599-621.

F66.   Melancon, M. "Athens or Babylon? The Birth of the Socialist Revolutionary and Social Democratic Parties in Saratov, 1890-1905," in: R.A.Wade & S.J.Seregny (eds.) *Politics and Society in Provincial Russia: Saratov, 1590-1917* (Columbus, Ohio: Ohio State U.P., 1989), pp.73-112.

F67.   Nicolaysen, H.M. "Looking Backward: A Prosopography of the Russian Social Democratic Elite, 1883-1907," PhD diss., Stanford, 1991.

F68.   Pipes, R. *Social Democracy and the St. Petersburg Labor Movement, 1885-1897* (Cambridge, Mass.: Harvard U.P., 1963).

F69.   Schwarz, S. *The Russian Revolution of 1905. The Workers' Movement and the Formation of Bolshevism and Menshevism*, trans.by G.Vakar (Chicago & London: University of Chicago Press, 1967).

F70.   Suny, R.G. "Labor and Liquidators: Revolutionaries and the "Reaction" in Baku, May 1908-April 1912," *SR* 34 (1975), no.2, pp.319-340.

F71.   Swain, G. *Russian Social Democracy and the Legal Labour Movement, 1906-1914* (London & Basingstoke: Macmillan, 1983).

F72.   Wildman, A.K. *The Making of a Workers' Revolution: Russian Social Democracy, 1891-1903* (Chicago and London: University of Chicago Press, 1967).

Bolsheviks:

F73.   Anin, D. "Lenin and Malinovsky," *Survey* 21 (Autumn 1975), no.4, pp.145-156.

F74.   Anin, D.S. "Lenin, Trotsky and Parvus," *Survey* 24 (Winter 1979), no.1, pp.204-212.

F75.   Badayev, A. *The Bolsheviks in the Tsarist Duma* (London: Martin Lawrence, 1932).

F76.   Beria, L.P. *On the History of the Bolshevik Organizations in Transcaucasia. A lecture delivered at a meeting of active workers of the Tbilisi Party Organization, July 21-22, 1935*, trans. from 4th Russian ed. (London: Lawrence & Wishart, 1939).

F77.   Biggart, J. ""Anti-Leninist Bolshevism": the *Forward* Group of the RSDRP," *CSP* 23 (1981), no.2, pp.134-153.

F78.   Bobrovskaya, C. *Twenty Years in Underground Russia: Memoirs of a Rank-and-File Bolshevik* (London: Martin Lawrence, 1934).

F79.   Bowman, B. "The Moscow Bolsheviks, February-November 1917," PhD diss., Indiana, 1973.

F80.   Chase, W. & Getty, J.A. "The Moscow Bolshevik Cadres of 1917: A Prosopographic Analysis," *RH* 5 (1978), pt.1, pp.84-105.

F81.   Dan, T. *The Origins of Bolshevism*, trans.by J.Carmichael (London: Secker & Warburg, 1964).

F82.   Duval, C., Jr. "The Bolshevik Secretariat and Yakov Sverdlov: February to October 1917," *SEER* 51 (1973), no.122, pp.47-57.

F83.   Elwood, R.C. "Lenin and Grammatikov: An Unpublished and Undeserved Testimonial," *CSP* 28 (1986), no.3, pp.304-313.

F84.   Elwood, R.C. *Roman Malinovsky: A Life Without Cause* (Newtonville, Mass.: Oriental Research Partners, 1977).

F85.   Ezergailis, A. "The Bolshevization of the Latvian Social Democratic Party," *Canadian Slavic Studies* 1 (1967), no.2, pp.238-252.

F86.   Ezergailis, A. "The Thirteenth Conference of the Latvian Social Democrats, 1917: Bolshevik Strategy Victorious," in: R.C.Elwood (ed.) *Reconsiderations on the Russian Revolution* (Cambridge, Mass.: Slavica, 1976), pp.133-153.

F87.   Getzler, I. "The Bolshevik Onslaught on the Non-Party 'Political Profile' of the Petersburg Soviet of Workers' Deputies October-November 1905," *Revolutionary Russia* 5 (1992), no.2, pp.123-146.

F88.   Golub, P. *The Bolsheviks and the Armed Forces in Three Revolutions: Problems and Experience of Military Work* (Moscow: Progress, 1979).

F89.   Haimson, L.H. *The Russian Marxists and the Origins of Bolshevism* (Cambridge, Mass.: Harvard U.P., 1955).

F90.   Hasegawa, T. "The Bolsheviks and the Formation of the Petrograd Soviet in the February Revolution," *SS* 29 (1977), no.1, pp.86-107.

F91.   Hedlin, M.W. "Zinoviev's Revolutionary Tactics in 1917," *SR* 34 (1975), no.1, pp.19-43.

F92.   Johnson, J.G., Jr. "The Petrograd Military-Revolutionary Committee (October-December, 1917)," PhD diss., Emory, 1974.

F93.   Katkov, G. & Shukman, H. *Lenin's Path to Power: Bolshevism and the Destiny of Russia* (London: MacDonald, 1971).

F94.   Kaun, A. "Maxim Gorky and the Bolsheviks," *SEER* 9 (1930-31), pp.432-448.

F95.   Kennan, G.F. "The Sisson Documents," *JMH* 28 (1956), no.2, pp.130-154.

F96.   Kingston-Mann, E. "Lenin and the Beginnings of Marxist Peasant Revolution: the Burden of Political Opportunity, July-October 1917," *SEER* 50 (1972), no.121, pp.570-588.

F97.   Kowalski, R.I. *The Bolshevik Party in Conflict: The Left Communist Opposition of 1918* (Pittsburgh: University of Pittsburgh Press, 1991).

F98.   Lane, D.S. *The "Social Eidos" of the Bolsheviks in the 1905 Revolution* (Discussion Papers Series Rc/C no.2, Centre for Russian and East European Studies, University of Birmingham).

F99.   Lavender, W. "Bolshevik Tactics and Propaganda in Petrograd after the February Revolution, April-November, 1917," PhD diss., Washington, Seattle, 1969.

F100.   LeBlanc, P. *Lenin and the Revolutionary Party* (Atlantic Highlands, N.J.: Humanities Press, 1990).

F101.   Longley, D. "Some Historiographical Problems of Bolshevik Party History (The Kronstadt Bolsheviks in March 1917)," *JFGO* 22 (1974), pp.494-514.

F102.   Longley, D.A. "The Divisions in the Bolshevik Party in March 1917," *SS* 24 (1972-73), no.1, pp.61-76.

F103.   McKean, R.B. "Social Insurance in Tsarist Russia, St Petersburg, 1907-17," *Revolutionary Russia* 3 (1990), no.1, pp.55-89.

F104.   Miliukov, P. *Bolshevism: An International Danger. Its Doctrine and Its Practice Through War and Revolution* (London: George Allen & Unwin, 1920).

F105.   Milligan, S. "The Petrograd Bolsheviks and Social Insurance, 1914-17," *SS* 20 (1968-69), no.3, pp.369-374.

F106.   Mosse, W.E. "Makers of the Soviet Union," *SEER* 46 (1968), pp.141-154.

F107.   Odom, W.E. "Sverdlov: Bolshevik Party Organiser," *SEER* 44 (1966), pp.421-443.

F108.   Oppenheim, S.A. "A Bolshevik in Revolution: G.Ya. Sokolnikov, the Party and the State, 1888-1921," *Australian Slavonic and East European Studies* 4 (1990), nos.1/2, pp.109-133.

F109.   Page, S.W. "Lenin's Assumption of International Proletarian Leadership," *JMH* 26 (1954), no.3, pp.233-245.

F110.   Page, S.W. "Lenin's April Theses and the Latvian Peasant-Soldiery," in: R.C.Elwood (ed.) *Reconsiderations on the Russian Revolution* (Cambridge, Mass.: Slavica, 1976), pp.154-172.

F111.   Pearson, M. *The Sealed Train: Journey to Revolution, Lenin 1917* (London: Macmillan, 1975).

F112.   Piatnitsky, O. *Memoirs of a Bolshevik* (London: Martin Lawrence, n.d.).

F113.   Rabinowitch, A. *Prelude to Revolution. The Petrograd Bolsheviks and the July 1917 Uprising* (Bloomington: Indiana U.P., 1968).

F114.   Rabinowitch, A. "The Petrograd Bolsheviks and the June and July Demonstrations of 1917," PhD diss., Indiana, 1965.

F115.   Radziwill, C. *The Firebrand of Bolshevism: the true story of the Bolsheviks and the forces that directed them* (Boston: Small, Maynard & Co., 1919).

F116.   Rosenberg, A. *History of Bolshevism. From Marx to the first Five Years' Plan*, trans.by I.F.D.Morrow (London: Oxford U.P., 1934).

F117.   Schiebel, J. "Aziatchina: The Controversy Concerning the Nature of Russian Society and the Organization of the Bolshevik Party," PhD diss., Washington, Seattle, 1972.

F118.   Schiebel, J. *The Controversy Concerning the Nature of Russian Society and the Organisation of the Bolshevik Party* (Seattle, 1972).

F119.   Selznick, P. *The Organizational Weapon: A Study of Bolshevik Strategy and Tactics* (Glencoe, Illinois: Free Press, 1960).

F120.   Service, R. *The Bolshevik Party in Revolution: A Study in Organisational Change* (London: Macmillan, 1979).

F121.   Service, R. "The Bolsheviks on Political Campaign in 1917: a Case Study of the War Question," in: E.R.Frankel et al (eds.) *Revolution in Russia: Reassessments of 1917* (Cambridge: Cambridge U.P., 1992), pp.304-325.

F122.   Shlyapnikov, A. *On the Eve of 1917*, trans.by R.Chappell (London and New York: Allison & Busby, 1982).

F123.   Shub, D. "Kamo - the Legendary Old Bolshevik of the Caucasus," *RR* 19 (1960), no.3, pp.227-247.

F124.   Silverman, S.N. "A World to Win: A Study in the Roots and Pre-Revolutionary Development of the Bolshevik Approach to World Affairs," PhD diss., Yale, 1963.

F125.   Snow, R.E. "The Bolsheviks in Siberia, February 1917-March 1918," PhD diss., SUNY, Stony Brook, 1972.

F126.   Swain, G.R. "Bolsheviks and Metal Workers on the Eve of the First World War," *JCH* 16 (1981), no.2, pp.273-291.

F127.   Swain, G.R. "The Bolsheviks' Prague Conference Revisited," *Revolutionary Russia* 2 (1989), no.1, pp.134-141.

F128.   Thatcher, I.D. "Trotskii, Lenin and the Bolsheviks, August 1914 - February 1917," *SEER* 72 (1994), no.1, pp.72-114.

F129.   *The Bolsheviks and the October Revolution: Minutes of the Central Committee of the Russian Social-Democratic Labour Party (bolsheviks), August 1917-February 1918*, trans.by A.Bone (London: Pluto, 1974).

F130.   Ulam, A. *Lenin and the Bolsheviks: the Intellectual and Political History of the Triumph of Communism in Russia* (London: Secker & Warburg, 1966).

F131.   White, J.D. "Latvian and Lithuanian Sections in the Bolshevik Party on the Eve of the February Revolution," *Revolutionary Russia* 3 (1990), pp.90-106.

F132.   Wildman, A.K. "The Bolsheviks of the Twelfth Army and Latvian Social Democracy," in: R.C.Elwood (ed.) *Reconsiderations on the Russian Revolution* (Cambridge, Mass.: Slavica, 1976), pp.173-183.

F133.   Williams, R.C. *The Other Bolsheviks: Lenin and His Critics, 1904-1914* (Bloomington & Indianapolis: Indiana U.P., 1986).

Mensheviks:

F134.   Ascher, A. *Pavel Axelrod and the Development of Menshevism* (Cambridge, Mass.: Harvard U.P., 1972).

F135.   Ascher, A. (ed.) *The Mensheviks in the Russian Revolution* (London: Thames & Hudson, 1976).

F136.   Basil, J.D. "Political Decisions Made By the Menshevik Leaders in Petrograd During the Revolution of 1917," PhD diss., Washington, Seattle, 1966.

F137.   Basil, J.D. *The Mensheviks in the Revolution of 1917* (Columbus, Ohio: Slavica, 1984).

F138.   Broido, E. *Memoirs of a Revolutionary*, trans.by V.Broido (London: Oxford U.P., 1967).

F139.   Brovkin, V. (ed.) *Dear Comrades: Menshevik Reports on the Bolshevik Revolution and Civil War* (Stanford: Hoover Institution Press, 1991).

F140.   Brovkin, V. "The Menshevik's Political Comeback: The Elections to the Provincial City Soviets in Spring 1918," *RR* 42 (1983), no.1, pp.1-50.

F141.   Burbank, J. "Waiting for the People's Revolution: Martov and Chernov in revolutionary Russia, 1917-1923," *Cahiers du Monde Russe et Sovietique* 26 (1985), nos.3-4, pp.375-394.

F142.   Galili, Z. *The Menshevik Leaders in the Russian Revolution: Social Realities and Political Strategies* (Princeton: Princeton U.P., 1989).

F143.   Galili, Z. "Workers, Industrialists and the Menshevik Mediators: Labor Conflicts in Petrograd, 1917," *RH* 16 (1989), pts.2/4, pp.239-261.

F144.   Garcia, Z.G.Y. "The Menshevik Revolutionary Defensists and the Workers in the Russian Revolution of 1917," PhD diss., Columbia, 1980.

F145.   Garcia, Z.G.Y. "Workers, Industrialists, and Mensheviks: Labor Relations and the Question of Power in the Early Stages of the Russian Revolution," *RR* 44 (1985), no.3, pp.239-269.

F146.   Getzler, I. *Martov: A Political Biography of a Russian Social Democrat* (Cambridge: Cambridge U.P., 1967).

F147.   Getzler, I. "The Mensheviks," *Problems of Communism* (1967), no.6, pp.15-29.

F148.   Haimson, L.H. "The Mensheviks After the October Revolution," Part I: *RR* 38 (1979), no.4, pp.456-473; Part II: *RR* 39 (1980), no.2, pp.181-207; Part III: *RR* 39 (1980), no.4, pp.462-483.

F149.   Haimson, L. *The Making of Three Russian Revolutionaries: Voices from the Menshevik Past* (Cambridge: Cambridge U.P., 1987).

F150.   Sapir, B. (ed.) *Theodore Dan. Letters (1899-1946)* (Amsterdam, 1985).

F151.   Stishov, M.I. "On the Question of the So-Called SR-Menshevik Conception of the Proletarian Revolution," *SSH* 10 (1971-72), no.4, pp.299-310 [and replies, pp.311-326].

F152.   Stishov, M.I. & Tochenyi, D.S. "The Collapse of the Socialist Revolutionary and Menshevik Party Organizations along the Volga," *SSH* 13 (1974-75), no.1, pp.56-81.

Bund:

F153.   Johnpoll, B.K. *The Politics of Futility: The General Jewish Workers Bund of Poland, 1917-1943* (Ithaca: Cornell U.P., 1967).

F154.   Patkin, A.L. *The Origins of the Russian-Jewish Labour Movement* (Melbourne & London: F.W.Cheshire, 1947). ·

F155.   Portnoy, S.A. *Vladimir Medem: The Life and Soul of a Legendary Jewish Socialist* (New York: KTAV Publishing House, 1979).

F156.   Shukman, H. "The Jewish Bund and the Russian Social-Democratic Party, 1897-1903/5," PhD diss., Oxford, 1961.

F157.   Tobias, H.J. "History of the Jewish Bund in Lithuania, Poland and Russia," PhD diss., Stanford, 1957.

F158.   Tobias, H.J. "The Archives of the Jewish Bund: New Materials on the Revolutionary Movement," *ASEER* 17 (1958), no.1, pp.81-85.

F159.   Tobias, H.J. "The Bund and Lenin Until 1903," *RR* 20 (1961), no.4, pp.344-357.

F160.   Tobias, H.J. "The Bund and the First Congress of the RSDWP: An Addendum," *RR* 24 (1965), no.4, pp.393-405.

F161.   Tobias, H.J. *The Jewish Bund in Russia: From Its Origins to 1905* (Stanford: Stanford U.P., 1972).

F162.   Tobias, H.J. & Woodhouse, C.E. "Political Reaction and Revolutionary Careers: the Jewish Bundists in Defeat, 1907-1910," *Comparative Studies in History and Society* 19 (1977), pp.367-396.

F163.   Woodhouse, C.E. & Tobias, H.J. "Primordial Ties and Political Process in Pre-Revolutionary Russia: the Case of the Jewish Bund," *Comparative Studies in History and Society* 8 (1965-66), pp.331-360.

Socialists-Revolutionaries (SRs):

F164. Blakely, A. "The Socialist Revolutionary Party, 1901-1907: The Populist Response to the Industrialization of Russia," PhD diss., Berkeley, 1971.

F165. Browne, W.H. "Morning Coat, Sats, and Pistol: Boris V. Savinkov, the Terrorist as Politician and Diplomat (1917-1925)," PhD diss., George Washington, 1979.

F166. Burbank, J. "Waiting for the People's Revolution: Martov and Chernov in revolutionary Russia, 1917-1923," *Cahiers du Monde Russe et Sovietique* 26 (1985), nos.3-4, pp.375-394.

F167. Christensen, P.G. "Camus and Savinkov: Examining the Problems of Terrorism," *Scottish Slavonic Review* no.21 (1993), pp.33-51.

F168. Christensen, P.G. "The Critique of Terrorism in the Novels of Boris Savinkov," *Australian Slavonic and East European Studies* 7 (1993), no.2, pp.1-14.

F169. Cross, T.B. "Purposes of Revolution: Chernov and 1917," *RR* 26 (1967), no.4, pp.351-360.

F170. Eiter, R.H. "Organizational Growth and Revolutionary Tactics: Unity and Discord in the Socialist Revolutionary Party in Russia, 1901-1907," PhD diss., Pittsburgh, 1978.

F171. Geifman, A. "Aspects of Early Twentieth-Century Russian Terrorism: The Socialist-Revolutionary Combat Organization," *Terrorism and Political Violence* 4 (1992), no.2, pp.23-46.

F172. Hildermeier, M. "Neopopulism and Modernization: The Debate on Theory and Tactics in the Socialist Revolutionary Party, 1905-14," *RR* 34 (1975), no.4, pp.453-475.

F173. Hildermeier, M. "The Terrorist Strategies of the Socialist-Revolutionary Party in Russia, 1900-1914," in: W.J.Mommsen and G.Hirschfeld (eds.) *Social Protest, Violence and Terror in Nineteenth and Twentieth Century Europe* (London: Macmillan, 1982), pp.80-87.

F174. Jansen, M. "Government Partners of the Bolsheviks. The Russian Socialist Revolutionaries in the Far Eastern Republic, 1920-22," *IRSH* 28 (1983), pp.296-303.

F175. Melancon, M. "Athens or Babylon? The Birth of the Socialist Revolutionary and Social Democratic Parties in Saratov, 1890-1905," in: R.A.Wade & S.J.Seregny (eds.) *Politics and Society in Provincial Russia: Saratov, 1590-1917* (Columbus, Ohio: Ohio State U.P., 1989), pp.73-112.

F176. Melancon, M. ""Marching Together!": Left Bloc Activities in the Russian Revolutionary Movement, 1900-February 1917," *SR* 49 (1990), no.2, pp.239-252.

F177. Melancon, M. *The Socialist Revolutionaries and the Russian Anti-War Movement, 1914-17* (Columbus: Ohio State U.P., 1990).

F178. Melancon, M.S. "The Socialist Revolutionaries from 1902 to February 1917: A Party of the Workers, Peasants, and Soldiers," PhD diss., Indiana, 1984.

F179. Melancon, M. "The Socialist Revolutionaries from 1902 to 1907: Peasant and Workers' Party," *RH* 12 (1985), pt.1, pp.2-47.

F180. Mstislavskii, S. *Five Days Which Transformed Russia*, trans.by E.K.Zelensky (London: Hutchinson, 1988).

F181. Palmer, S.W. "A Crisis of Faith: Boris Savinkov and the Fighting Organization (1903-1912)," *Scottish Slavonic Review* no.18 (1992), pp.35-53.

F182. Perrie, M. "Political and Economic Terror in the Tactics of the Russian Socialist-Revolutionary Party before 1914," in: W.J.Mommsen and G.Hirschfeld (eds.) *Social Protest, Violence and Terror in Nineteenth and Twentieth Century Europe* (London: Macmillan, 1982), pp.63-79.

F183. Perrie, M.P. *The Agrarian Policy of the Socialist-Revolutionary Party. From its Origins through the Revolution of 1905-07* (Cambridge: Cambridge U.P., 1976).

F184. Perrie, M. "The Social Composition and Structure of the Socialist-Revolutionary Party Before 1917," *SS* 24 (1972-73), no.2, pp.223-250.

F185. Perrie, M. "The Socialist Revolutionaries on 'Permanent Revolution'," *SS* 24 (1972-73), no.3, pp.411-413.

F186. Petrov, M.N. "The Rise and Fall of the Minority Party Socialist Revolutionaries," *SSH* 23 (1984-85), no.2, pp.12-33.

F187. Radkey, O.H. "An Alternative to Bolshevism: the Program of Russian Social Revolutionism," *JMH* 25 (1953), no.1, pp.25-39.

F188. Radkey, O.H. *The Agrarian Foes of Bolshevism. Promise and Default of the Russian Socialist Revolutionaries, February to October 1917* (New York: Columbia U.P., 1958).

F189. Radkey, O.H. "The Party of the Socialist-Revolutionaries and the Russian Revolution of 1917," PhD diss., Harvard, 1939.

F190. Radkey, O.H. *The Sickle under the Hammer. The Russian Socialist Revolutionaries in the Early Months of Soviet Rule* (New York: Columbia U.P., 1963).

F191. Radkey, O.H. "The Socialist Revolutionaries and the Peasantry After October," *HSS* 4 (1957), pp.457-479.

F192. Randall, F.B. "The Major Prophets of Russian Peasant Socialism: A Study in the Social Thought of N.K. Mikhailovskii and V.M. Chernov," PhD diss., Columbia, 1961.

F193. Rice, C. "'Land and Freedom' in the Factories of Petersburg: The SRs and the Workers' Curia Elections to the Second Duma, January 1907," *SS* 36 (1984), no.1, pp.87-107.

F194. Rice, C. "Russian Workers and the Socialist Revolutionary Party Through the Revolution of 1905-07," *Sbornik (SGRR)* no.11 (1985), pp.84-100.

F195.   Rice, C. *Russian Workers and the Socialist-Revolutionary Party through the Revolution of 1905-07* (London: Macmillan, 1988).

F196.   Rice, C.J. "The Socialist-Revolutionary Party and the Urban Working Class in Russia, 1902-1914," PhD diss., Birmingham, 1984.

F197.   Savinkov, B.V. *Memoirs of a Terrorist*, trans.by J.Shaplen (New York: A. & C. Boni, 1931).

F198.   Schleifman, N. *Undercover Agents in the Russian Revolutionary Movement. The SR Party, 1902-14* (Basingstoke and London: Macmillan, 1988).

F199.   Seregny, S.J. "Revolutionary Strategies in the Russian Countryside: Rural Teachers and the Socialist Revolutionary Party on the Eve of 1905," *RR* 44 (1985), no.3, pp.221-238.

F200.   Spence, R. *Boris Savinkov, Renegade on the Left* (Boulder, Colorado: East European Monographs; distributed by Columbia U.P., 1991).

F201.   Spence, R.B. "The Terrorist and the Master Spy: the Political 'Partnership' of Boris Savinkov and Sidney Reilly, 1918-24," *Revolutionary Russia* 4 (1991), no.1, pp.111-113.

F202.   Stishov, M.I. "On the Question of the So-Called SR-Menshevik Conception of the Proletarian Revolution," *SSH* 10 (1971-72), no.4, pp.299-310 [and replies, pp.311-326].

F203.   Stishov, M.I. & Tochenyi, D.S. "The Collapse of the Socialist Revolutionary and Menshevik Party Organizations along the Volga," *SSH* 13 (1974-75), no.1, pp.56-81.

F204.   Treadgold, D.W. "The Populists Refurbished," *RR* 10 (1951), no.3, pp.185-196.

Anarchists:

F205.   Avrich, P. *Anarchist Portraits* (Princeton: Princeton U.P., 1988).

F206.   Avrich, P. "Russian Anarchists and the Civil War," RR 27 (1968), no.3, pp.296-306.

F207.   Avrich, P. "The Anarchists in the Russian Revolution," *RR* 26 (1967), no.4, pp.341-350.

F208.   Avrich, P. (ed.) *The Anarchists in the Russian Revolution* (London: Thames and Hudson, 1973).

F209.   Avrich, P. "The Legacy of Bakunin," *RR* 29 (1970), no.2, pp.129-142.

F210.   Avrich, P. *The Russian Anarchists* (Princeton: Princeton U.P., 1967).

F211.   Avrich, P. "V.M. Eikhenbaum (Volin): Portrait of a Russian Anarchist," in: E.Mendelsohn & M.S.Shatz (eds.) *Imperial Russia, 1700-1917: State, Society, Opposition. Essays in Honor of Marc Raeff* (DeKalb, Illinois: Northern Illinois Press, 1988), pp.278-288.

F212. Gooderham, P. "The Anarchist Movement in Russia, 1905-1917," PhD diss., Bristol, 1981.

F213. Hartog, S.R. "The State of Anarchy: The Political Philosophy of Peter Kropotkin," PhD diss., London, 1963.

F214. Kropotkin, P. *Memoirs of a Revolutionist* (London: Swan Sonnenschein, 1906).

F215. Straus, R. "The Anarchist Argument: An Analysis of Three Justifications of Anarchism," PhD diss., Columbia, 1973.

F216. Wenzer, K. "An Anarchist Image of the Russian Revolution," *Revolutionary Russia* 6 (1993), no.1, pp.121-144.

F217. Yaroslavsky, E. *History of Anarchism in Russia* (London: Lawrence & Wishart, n.d.).

Intelligentsia:

F218. Bedford, C.H. "Dmitry Merezhkovsky, the Intelligentsia, and the Revolution of 1905," *CSP* 3 (1958), pp.27-42.

F219. Bohachevsky-Chomiak, M. & Rosenthal, B.G. (eds.) *A Revolution of the Spirit: Crisis of Value in Russia, 1890-1918*, trans.by M.Schwartz (Newtonville, Mass.: Oriental Research Partners, 1982).

F220. Brooks, J. "Vekhi and the Vekhi Dispute," *Survey* 19 (Winter 1973), no.1, pp.21-50.

F221. Chamberlin, W.H. "The Tragedy of the Russian Intelligentsia," *RR* 18 (1959), no.2, pp.89-95.

F222. Daniels, R.V. "Intellectuals and the Russian Revolution," *SR* 20 (1961), no.2, pp.270-278.

F223. Fischer, G. "The Russian Intelligentsia and Liberalism," *HSS* 4 (1957), pp.317-336.

F224. Kelly, A.M. "Attitudes to the Individual in Russian Thought and Literature, with Special Reference to the *Vekhi* Controversy," PhD diss., Oxford, 1970.

F225. Kelly, A. "Self-Censorship and the Russian Intelligentsia, 1905-1914," *SR* 46 (1987), no.2, pp.193-213.

F226. Levin, A. "M.O. Gershenzon and *Vekhi*," *Canadian Slavic Studies* 4 (1970), no.1, pp.60-73.

F227. Lowrie, D.A. *Rebellious Prophet: A Life of Nicolai Berdyaev* (New York: Harper & Bros., 1960).

F228. Nahirny, V.C. *The Russian Intelligentsia: From Torment to Silence* (New Brunswick & London: Transaction Books, 1983).

F229. Pachmuss, T. (ed.) *Intellect and Ideas in Action: Selected Correspondence of Zinaida Hippius* (Munich: Wilhelm Fink, 1972).

F230.	Pipes, R. (ed.) *The Russian Intelligentsia* (New York & London: Columbia U.P., 1961).

F231.	Poltoratzky, N.P. "The *Vekhi* Dispute and the Significance of *Vekhi*," *CSP* 9 (1967), no.1, pp.86-106.

F232.	Poltoratzky, N.P. "Lev Tolstoy and Vekhi," *SEER* 42 (1963-64), pp.332-352.

F233.	Pomper, P. *The Russian Revolutionary Intelligentsia* (New York: Thomas Y. Crowell, 1970; second edition, Arlington Heights, Illinois: Harlan Davidson, 1993).

F234.	Putnam, G.F. "The Russian Non-Revolutionary Intelligentsia Evaluates Its Relation to the Russian Folk, 1900-1910," PhD diss., Harvard, 1962.

F235.	Read, C. *Religion, Revolution and the Russian Intelligentsia 1900-1912. The Vekhi Debate and its Intellectual Background* (London: Macmillan, 1979).

F236.	Read, C. "Russian Intelligentsia and the Bolshevik Revolution," *HT* 34 (October 1984), pp.38-44.

F237.	Read, C.J. "Religion and Revolution in the Thought of the Russian Intelligentsia from 1900 to 1912: The VEKHI Debate and Its Intellectual Background," PhD diss., London, 1975.

F238.	Read, C.J. "The 1905 Revolution and the Russian Intelligentsia," in: F.-X.Coquin & C.Gervais-Francelle (eds.) *1905: La Premiere Revolution Russe* (Paris: Publications de la Sorbonne et Institut d'etudes slaves, 1986), pp.385-396.

F239.	Schapiro, L. "The 'Vekhi' Group and the Mystique of Revolution," *SEER* 34 (1955-56), pp.56-76.

F240.	Shatz, M.S. "The Makhaevists and the Russian Revolutionary Movement," *IRSH* 15 (1970), pp.235-265.

F241.	Shatz, M. & Zimmerman, J. (translators & editors) "Vekhi (Signposts): A Collection of Articles on the Russian Intelligentsia," Part I *Canadian Slavic Studies* 2 (1968), no.2, pp.151-174; Part II *Canadian Slavic Studies* 2 (1968), no.3, pp.291-310; Part II concluded *Canadian Slavic Studies* 2 (1968), no.4, pp.447-463; Part III *Canadian Slavic Studies* 3 (1969), no.1, pp.1-21; Part IV *Canadian Slavic Studies* 3 (1969), no.3, pp.494-515; Part V *Canadian Slavic Studies* 4 (1970), no.1, pp.36-59; Part VI *Canadian Slavic Studies* 4 (1970), no.2, pp.183-198; Part VII *Canadian Slavic Studies* 5 (1971), no.3, pp.327-361.

F242.	Shragin, B. & Todd, A. (eds.) *Landmarks: A Collection of Essays on the Russian Intelligentsia, 1909: Berdyaev, Bulgakov, Gershenzon, Izgoev, Kistyakovsky, Struve, Frank*, trans.by M.Schwartz (New York: Karz Howard, 1977).

F243.	Stepun, F. "The Russian Intelligentsia and Bolshevism," *RR* 17 (1958), no.4, pp.263-277.

F244.	Tompkins, S.R. *The Russian Intelligentsia: Makers of the Revolutionary State* (Norman: University of Oklahoma Press, 1957).

F245.	Tompkins, S.R. "*Vekhi* and the Russian Intelligentsia," *CSP* 2 (1957), pp.11-25.

F246.   Znamenskii, O.N. "The Petrograd Intelligentsia during the February Revolution," *SSH* 23 (1984-85), no.1, pp.39-55.

Intelligentsia After October 1917:

F247.   Burbank, J. *Intelligentsia and Revolution: Russian Views of Bolshevism, 1917-1922* (Oxford & New York: Oxford U.P., 1986).

F248.   Burbank, J.R. "Russian Social Thought and the Bolshevik Revolution, 1917-1922," PhD diss., Harvard, 1981.

F249.   Fedyukin, S. *The Great October Revolution and the Intelligentsia. How the Old Intelligentsia Was Drawn into the Building of Socialism* (Moscow: Progress, 1975).

F250.   Koenker, D.P. et al (eds.) *Party, State, and Society in the Russian Civil War. Explorations in Social History* (Bloomington & Indianapolis: Indiana U.P., 1989).

Students and Youth:

F251.   Burch, R.J. "Social Unrest in Imperial Russia: The Student Movement at Moscow University, 1887-1905," PhD diss., Washington, Seattle, 1972.

F252.   Cornell, R. *Revolutionary Vanguard: The Early Years of the Communist Youth International, 1914-1924* (Toronto: University of Toronto Press, 1982).

F253.   Cornell, R. "The Origins and Development of the Communist Youth International: 1914-1924," PhD diss., Columbia, 1965.

F254.   Cornell, R. *Youth and Communism: An Historical Analysis of International Communist Youth Movements* (New York: Walker, 1965).

F255.   Fisher, R.T., Jr. "The Soviet Pattern for Youth as Revealed in the Proceedings of the Congresses of the Komsomol, 1918-1949," PhD diss., Columbia, 1952.

F256.   Kheraskov, I. "Reminiscences of the Moscow Students' Movement," *RR* 11 (1952), no.4, pp.223-232.

F257.   Koenker, D. "Urban Families, Working-Class Youth Groups, and the 1917 Revolution in Moscow," in: D.L.Ransel (ed.) *The Family in Imperial Russia: New Lines of Historical Research* (Urbana, Chicago, London: University of Illinois Press, 1978), pp.280-304.

F258.   Morison, J.D. "Political Characteristics of the Student Movement in the Russian Revolution of 1905," in: F.-X.Coquin & C.Gervais-Francelle (eds.) *1905: La Premiere Revolution Russe* (Paris: Publications de la Sorbonne et Institut d'etudes slaves, 1986), pp.63-75.

F259. Ploss, S.T. "The Organization of Soviet Youth: A History of the All-Union Leninist Communist League of Youth (Komsomol)," PhD diss., London, 1957.

F260. Tirado, I.A. "The Revolution, Young Peasants, and the Komsomol's Anti-Religious Campaigns (1920-28)," *CASS* 26 (1992), nos.1-4, pp.97-118.

F261. Tirado, I.A. "The Socialist Youth Movement in Revolutionary Petrograd," *RR* 46 (1987), no.2, pp.135-156.

F262. Tirado, I.A. *Young Guard!: The Communist Youth League, Petrograd 1917-1920* (Westport, Conn., New York, & London: Greenwood, 1988).

F263. Tirado, I. "Youth in Revolution: The Petrograd Komsomol Organization, 1917-1920," PhD diss., California, Berkeley, 1985.

International Aspects:

F264. Augursky, M. *The Third Rome: National Bolshevism in the USSR* (Boulder & London: Westview Press, 1987).

F265. Baron, S.H. "Plekhanov, International Socialism, and the Revolution of 1905," in: F.-X.Coquin & C.Gervais-Francelle (eds.) *1905: La Premiere Revolution Russe* (Paris: Publications de la Sorbonne et Institut d'etudes slaves, 1986), pp.101-120.

F266. Breit, F.J. "The Bolshevization of the Comintern, 1919-1924," PhD diss., Duke, 1972.

F267. Debo, R.K. "The 14 November 1918 Teleprinter Conversation of Hugo Hasse with Georgii Chicherin and Karl Radek: Document and Commentary," *CASS* 14 (1980), no.4, pp.513-534.

F268. Debo, R.K. "The Making of a Bolshevik: Georgii Chicherin in England 1914-1918," *SR* 25 (1966), no.4, pp.651-662.

F269. Elwood, R.C. "Lenin and the Brussels "Unity" Conference of July 1914," *RR* 39 (1980), no.1, pp.32-49.

F270. Fabsic, J. "Lenin and the European Revolution, 1917-1920: A Re-Interpretation," PhD diss., Manitoba, 1974.

F271. Futrell, M. *Northern Underground. Episodes of Russian revolutionary transport and communications through Scandinavia and Finland, 1863-1917* (London: Faber and Faber, 1963).

F272. Gankin, O.H. "The Bolsheviks and the Founding of the Third International," *SEER* 20 (1941), pp.88-101.

F273. Gankin, O.H. & Fisher, H.H. *The Bolsheviks and the World War: The Origin of the Third International* (Stanford: Stanford U.P., 1940).

F274. Good, J.E. "America and the Russian Revolutionary Movement, 1888-1905," *RR* 41 (1982), no.3, pp.273-287.

F275. Gvozdev, N.K. "Their Proclamation Has Gone Out Into All The Earth: Soviet Messianism and the International System," *CSP* 32 (1990), no.4, pp.431-443.

F276. Hedlin, M.W.D. "Zinoviev, the Comintern and European Revolution, 1919-1926," PhD diss., Duke, 1970.

F277. Hollingsworth, B. "The Society of Friends of Russian Freedom: English Liberals and Russian Socialists, 1890-1917," *OSP (NS)* 3 (1970), pp.45-64.

F278. Hulse, J.W. "The Communist International in Its Formative Stage, 1919-1920," PhD diss., Stanford, 1962.

F279. Kahan, V. "The Communist International, 1919-1943: the Personnel of its Highest Bodies," *IRSH* 21 (1976), pp.151-185.

F280. Kirby, D. *War, Peace and Revolution: International Socialism at the Crossroads, 1914-1918* (Aldershot: Gower, 1986).

F281. Lazitch, B. & Drachkovitch, M.M. *Lenin and the Comintern* (Stanford: Hoover Institution Press, 1972).

F282. Lindemann, A.S. "Entering the Comintern: Negotiations Between the Bolsheviks and Western Socialists at the Second Congress of the Communist International, 1920," *RH* 1 (1971), pt.2, pp.136-167.

F283. Miliukov, P. *Bolshevism: An International Danger. Its Doctrine and Its Practice Through War and Revolution* (London: George Allen & Unwin, 1920).

F284. Nation, R.C. "The Zimmerwald Left: The Roots of International Communism in the First World War," PhD diss., Duke, 1975.

F285. Nicoll, G.D. "Russian Participation in the Second International, 1889-1914," PhD diss., Boston, 1961.

F286. Pearce, B. (translator) *Congress of the Peoples of the East: Baku, September 1920. Stenographic Report* (London: New Park, 1977).

F287. Resis, A. "Comintern Policy Toward the World Trade-Union Movement: The First Year," in: J.S.Curtiss (ed.) *Essays in Russian and Soviet History* (Leiden: E.J.Brill, 1963), pp.237-252.

F288. Richards, E.B. "The Shaping of the Comintern," *ASEER* 18 (1959), pp.197-204.

F289. Riddell, J. (ed.) *Workers of the World and Oppressed Peoples, Unite! Proceedings and Documents of the Second Congress of the Communist International, 1920,* 2 vols. (New York: Pathfinder, 1992).

F290. Schlesinger, R. "Lenin as a Member of the International Socialist Bureau," *SS* 16 (1965), no.4, pp.448-458.

F291. Senn, A.E. "Russian Emigre Funds in Switzerland 1916: An Okhrana Report," *IRSH* 13 (1968), pp.76-84.

F292. Senn, A.E. "The Bolshevik Conference in Bern, 1915," *SR* 25 (1966), no.4, pp.676-678.

F293.   Senn, A.E. "The Myth of German Money During the First World War," *SS* 28 (1976), no.1, pp.83-90.

F294.   Senn, A.E. "The Politics of *Golos* and *Nashe Slovo*," *IRSH* 17 (1972), pp.675-704.

F295.   Senn, A.E. *The Russian Revolution in Switzerland, 1914-1917* (Madison, Milwaukee & London: University of Wisconsin Press, 1971).

F296.   Stone, H.M. "Another Look at the Sisson Forgeries and Their Background," *SS* 37 (1985), no.1, pp.90-102.

F297.   Wade, R.A. "Argonauts of Peace: The Soviet Delegation to Western Europe in the Summer of 1917," *SR* 26 (1967), no.3, pp.453-467.

F298.   White, J.D. "Early Encounters Between the Revolutionary Movements of Russia and China (1903-1911)," *Scottish Slavonic Review* no.1 (1983), pp.5-36.

F299.   White, S. "Communism and the East: The Baku Congress, 1920," *SR* 33 (1974), no.3, pp.492-514.

F300.   Wolfe, B.D. "French Socialism, German Theory, and the Flaw in the Foundation of the Socialist Internationals," in: J.S.Curtiss (ed.) *Essays in Russian and Soviet History* (Leiden: E.J.Brill, 1963), pp.177-197.

F301.   Zeman, Z.A.B. (ed.) *Germany and the Revolution in Russia, 1915-1918: Documents from the Archives of the German Foreign Ministry* (London: Oxford U.P., 1958).

F302.   Zeman, Z.A.B. & Scharlau, W.B. *The Merchant of Revolution: The Life of Alexander Israel Helphand (Parvus), 1867-1924* (London: Oxford U.P., 1965).

G

CIVIL WAR

General:

G1.   Argenbright, R. "Bolsheviks, Baggers and Railroaders: Political Power and Social Space, 1917-1921," *RR* 52 (1993), no.4, pp.506-527.

G2.   Azovtsev, N.N. & Naumov, V.P. "Study of the History of the Military Intervention and Civil War in the USSR," *SSH* 10 (1971-72), no.4, pp.327-360.

G3.   Bradley, J.F.N. *Civil War in Russia 1917-1920* (London and Sydney: B.T.Batsford, 1975).

G4.   Brovkin, V. *Behind the Front Lines of the Civil War: Political Parties and Social Movements in Russia, 1918-1922* (Princeton: Princeton U.P., 1994).

G5.   Brovkin, V. (ed.) *Dear Comrades: Menshevik Reports on the Bolshevik Revolution and Civil War* (Stanford: Hoover Institution Press, 1991).

G6.   Brovkin, V. "Identity, Allegiance and Participation in the Russian Civil War," *EHQ* 22 (1992), no.4, pp.541-567.

G7.   Bulygin, P. "In Prison at Ekaterinburg: An Account of an Attempt to Rescue the Imperial Family," *SEER* 7 (1928-29), pp.55-66.

G8.   Bunyan, J. (ed.) *Intervention, Civil War, and Communism in Russia, April-December 1918: Documents and Materials* (Baltimore: Johns Hopkins Press, 1936).

G9.   Chamberlin, W.H. "Russian and American Civil Wars," *RR* 11 (1952), no.4, pp.203-210.

G10.   Chamberlin, W.H. *The Russian Revolution, 1917-1921*, 2 vols. (London and New York: Macmillan, 1935 [republished by Princeton U.P., 1987]).

G11.   Colton, T.J. "Military Councils and Military Politics in the Russian Civil War," *CSP* 18 (1976), no.1, pp.36-57.

G12.   Footman, D. *Civil War in Russia* (London: Faber, 1961).

G13.   Footman, D. *Siberian Partisans in the Civil War* (Oxford: Oxford U.P., 1954).

G14.   Gordon, A.G. *Russian Civil War* (London: Cassell, 1937).

G15.   Gorky, M., Molotov, V., Voroshilov, V., Kirov, S., Zhdanov, A. & Stalin, J. (eds.) *The History of the Civil War in the USSR*, 2 vols. (New York: International Publishers, 1938-1947).

G16.   Kenez, P. *Civil War in South Russia, 1918. The First Year of the Volunteer Army* (Berkeley: University of California Press, 1971).

G17.   Kenez, P. *Civil War in South Russia, 1919-1920. The Defeat of the Whites* (Berkeley: University of California Press, 1977).

G18.   Kotsonis, Y. "Arkhangel'sk, 1918: Regionalism and Populism in the Russian Civil War," *RR* 51 (1992), no.4, pp.526-544.

G19.   Lincoln, W.B. *Red Victory: A History of the Russian Civil War* (New York: Simon & Schuster, 1989).

G20.   Long, J. "General Sir Alfred Knox and the Russian Civil War: A Brief Commentary," *Sbornik (SGRR)* no.9 (1983), pp.54-64.

G21.   McAuley, M. *Bread and Justice: State and Society in Petrograd, 1917-1922* (Oxford: Clarendon, 1991).

G22.   McAuley, M. "Party and Society in Petrograd during the Civil War," *Sbornik (SGRR)* no.10 (1984), pp.43-59.

G23.   Mawdsley, E. *The Russian Civil War* (Boston: Unwin Hyman, 1987).

G24.   Murphy, B. "The Don Rebellion March-June 1919," *Revolutionary Russia* 6 (1993), no.2, pp.315-350.

G25.   Pereira, N.G.O. "Soviet Historiography of the Civil War in Siberia," *Revolutionary Russia* 4 (1991), no.1, pp.38-51.

G26.   Pereira, N.G.O. "The Partisan Movement in Western Siberia, 1918-1920," *JFGO* 38 (1990), pp.87-97.

G27.   Pipes, R. *Russia under the Bolshevik Regime, 1919-1924* (London: Harvill/Harper Collins, 1994).

G28.   Price, M.P. *The Soviet, the Terror and Intervention* (Brooklyn: Socialist Publication Society, 1918).

G29.   Raleigh, D.J. (ed.) *A Russian Civil War Diary: Alexis Babine in Saratov, 1917-1922* (Durham, N.C. & London: Duke U.P., 1988).

G30.   Sakwa, R. "Party and Society in Moscow during the Civil War," *Sbornik (SGRR)* no.10 (1984), pp.60-74.

G31.   Starikov, S. & Medvedev, R. *Philip Mironov and the Russian Civil War*, trans.by G.Daniels (New York: Alfred A. Knopf, 1978).

G32.   Steinberg, I.N. *In the Workshop of the Revolution* (London: Victor Gollancz, 1955).

G33.   Strod, I.J. *Civil War in the Taiga: a Story of Guerilla Warfare in the Forests of Eastern Siberia* (Moscow: Cooperative Publishing Society of Foreign Workers in the USSR; New York: International Publishers, 1933; London: Modern Books, 1935).

G34.   "The Civil War in Russia: A Rountable Discussion," *Russian Studies in History* 32 (1993-94), no.4, pp.73-95.

G35.   Wise, R.B.A. *The Bolshevik Revolution: From Ascendancy to Consolidation* (London: Veritas Foundation Publication Centre, 1991).

Kornilov Affair:

G36.   Ascher, A. "The Kornilov Affair," *RR* 12 (1953), no.4, pp.235-252.

G37.   Asher, H. "The Kornilov Affair: A History and Interpretation," PhD diss., Indiana, 1971.

G38.   Asher, H. "The Kornilov Affair: A Reinterpretation," *RR* 29 (1970), no.3, pp.286-300.

G39.   Dailey, K.I. "General Kornilov's Abortive Coup," *Topic* 27 (Spring 1974), pp.5-17.

G40.   Katkov, G. *Russia 1917. The Kornilov Affair. Kerensky and the break-up of the Russian army* (London & New York: Longman, 1980).

G41.   Kerensky, A.F. *The Prelude to Bolshevism: The Kornilov Rebellion* (New York: Haskell House, 1972).

G42.   Munck, J.L. *The Kornilov Revolt: A Critical Examination of the Sources Research* (Aarhus: Aarhus U.P., 1987).

G43.   Saul, N.E. "British Involvement in the Kornilov Affair," *Rocky Mountain Social Science Journal* 10 (January 1973), pp.43-50.

G44.   Strakhovsky, L.I. "Was There a Kornilov Rebellion? - A Reappraisal of the Evidence," *SEER* 33 (1954-55), pp.372-395.

G45.   White, J.D. "A Document on the Kornilov Affair," *SS* 25 (1973), no.2, pp.283-298.

G46.   White, J.D. "The Kornilov Affair - A Study in Counter-Revolution," *SS* 20 (1968-69), no.2, pp.187-205.

G47.   Wildman, A. "Officers of the General Staff and the Kornilov Movement," in: E.R.Frankel et al (eds.) *Revolution in Russia: Reassessments of 1917* (Cambridge: Cambridge U.P., 1992), pp.76-101.

Whites:

G48.   Ainsworth, J. "The Blackwood Report on the Volunteer Army: A Missing Chapter in the Resumption of Anglo-White Relations in South Russia in November 1918," *SEER* 69 (1991), no.4, pp.621-646.

G49.   Anon. *The Supreme Ruler Admiral of the Russian Nation A.V. Kolchak* (Tokyo: Russian Press Bureau Magazine, no.1, 1919).

G50.   Arslanian, A.H. & Nichols, R.L. "Nationalism and the Russian Civil War: The Case of Volunteer Army-Armenian Relations, 1918-20," *SS* 31 (1979), no.4, pp.559-573.

G51.   Bechhofer-Roberts, C.E. *In Denikin's Russia and the Caucasus, 1919-1920* (London: W.Collins, 1931).

G52.   Berk, S.M. "The Coup d'Etat of Admiral Kolchak: The Counter-Revolution in Siberia and East Russia, 1917-1918," PhD diss., Columbia, 1971.

G53.   Borman, A. "My Meetings with White Russian Generals," *RR* 27 (1968), no.2, pp.215-224.

G54.   Bortnevski, V.G. "White Administration and White Terror (The Denikin Period)," *RR* 52 (1993), no.3, pp.354-366.

G55.   Collins, D.N. and Smele, J. (eds.) *Kolchak i Sibir: dokumenty i issledovaniia, 1919-1926 (Kolchak and Siberia: documents and studies, 1919-1926)* 2 vols. (White Plains, New York: Krans International, 1988) [introduction in English].

G56.   Connaughton, R.M. *The Republic of Ushakovka. Admiral Kolchak and the Allied Intervention in Siberia, 1918-1920* (London and New York: Routledge, 1990).

G57.   Dacy, D.A. "The White Russian Movement: A Study of the Failure of Counter-Revolution, 1917-1920," PhD diss., Texas, 1972.

G58.   Denikin, A.I. *The Russian Turmoil: Memoirs: Military, Social, and Political* (London: Hutchinson, n.d.).

G59.   Denikin, A.I. *The White Army*, trans.by C.Zvegintzov (London: Jonathan Cape, 1930).

G60.   Drujina, G. "The History of the North-West Army of General Yudenich," PhD diss., Stanford, 1950.

G61.   Fleming, P. *The Fate of Admiral Kolchak* (New York: Harcourt, Brace and World, 1936).

G62.   Footman, D. *The Last Days of Kolchak* (Oxford: Oxford U.P., 1953).

G63.   Hodgson, J. *With Denikin's Armies* (London: Lincoln Williams, 1932).

G64.   Kenez, P. "Pogroms and White ideology in the Russian Civil War," in: J.D.Klier & S.Lambroza (eds.) *Pogroms: Anti-Jewish Violence in Modern Russian History* (Cambridge: Cambridge U.P., 1992), pp.293-313.

G65.   Kenez, P. "The First Year of the Volunteer Army: Civil War in South Russia, 1918,"
        PhD diss., Harvard, 1967.

G66.   Kenez, P. "The Ideology of the White Movement," *SS* 32 (1980), no.1, pp.58-83.

G67.   Kenez, P. "The Relations Between the Volunteer Army and Georgia, 1918-1920," *SEER*
        48 (1970), no.112, pp.403-424.

G68.   Kolz, A.W.F. "British Foreign Policy and the Kolchak Government, November 1918-
        February 1920," PhD diss., Boston, 1965.

G69.   Kukk, H. "The Failure of Iudenich's Northwestern Army in 1919: A Dissenting White-
        Russian View," *Journal of Baltic Studies* 12 (1981), pp.362-383.

G70.   Lazarski, C. "White Propaganda Efforts in the South during the Russian Civil War,
        1918-19 (the Alekseev-Denikin Period)," *SEER* 70 (1992), no.4, pp.688-707.

G71.   Lehovich, D.V. "Denikin's Offensive," *RR* 32 (1973), no.2, pp.173-186.

G72.   Luckett, R. *The White Generals. An Account of the White Movement in the Russian Civil
        War* (New York: Viking, 1971).

G73.   Muniandy, T. "The Collapse of the Anti-Bolshevik Movement in South Russia, 1917-
        1920," PhD diss., Washington, Seattle, 1975.

G74.   Pereira, N.G.O. "White Power during the Civil War in Siberia (1918-1920): Dilemmas
        of Kolchak's 'War Anti-Communism'," *CSP* 29 (1987), no.1, pp.45-62.

G75.   Procyk, A.M. "Nationality Policy of the White Movement: Relations Between the
        Volunteer Army and the Ukraine," PhD diss., Columbia, 1973.

G76.   Smele, J.D. "Labour Conditions and the Collapse of the Siberian Economy under
        Kolchak, 1918-19," *Sbornik (SGRR)* no.13 (1987), pp.31-59.

G77.   Smele, J.D. "'What Kolchak Wants': Military versus Polity in White Siberia, 1918-20,"
        Revolutionary Russia 4 (1991), no.1, pp.52-110.

G78.   Smele, J.D. "White Siberia: the Anti-Bolshevik Government of Admiral Kolchak, 1918-
        1920," PhD diss., Wales, Cardiff, 1992.

G79.   Smirnov, M.I. "Admiral Kolchak," *SEER* 11 (1932-33), pp.373-387.

G80.   Stewart, G. *The White Armies of Russia: a Chronicle of Counter-Revolution and Allied
        Intervention* (New York: Macmillan, 1933; reprinted New York: Russell and
        Russell, 1970).

G81.   Thambirajah, M. "The Collapse of the Anti-Bolshevik Movement in South Russia, 1917-
        1920," PhD diss., Washington, Seattle, 1975.

G82.   Treadgold, D.W. "The Ideology of the White Movement: Wrangel's 'Leftist Policy From
        Rightist Hands'," *HSS* 4 (1957), pp.481-497.

G83.   Varneck, E. & Fisher, H.H. (eds.) *The Testimony of Kolchak and Other Siberian
        Materials* (Stanford: Stanford U.P., 1935).

G84.   Volkonskii, Prince P.N. *The Volunteer Army of Alexiev and Denikin* (London: Russian Liberation Committee Publication No.7, Avenue Press, 1919).

G85.   Volunteer Army *The Volunteer Army as a National Factor in the Renaissance of Great Russia, One and Indivisible* (Ekaterinodar: Volunteer Army, 1919 [Hoover Library]).

Gatchina Campaign:

G86.   Woytinsky, W. "The Gatchina Campaign (For the anniversary of the Bolshevik coup)," *SS* 32 (1980), no.2, pp.260-279.

G87.   Zubov, Count V. "Gatchina - October 1917. Reminiscences," *RR* 28 (1969), no.3, pp.289-302.

Czech Revolt:

G88.   Baerlein, H.P.B. *The March of the 70,000* (London: Leonard Parsons, 1926 [reprinted New York: Arno, 1971).

G89.   Becvar, G. *The Lost Legion: A Czechoslovakian Epic* (London: Stanley Paul, 1939).

G90.   Bradley, J.F.N. "The Allies and the Czech Revolt against the Bolsheviks in 1918," *SEER* 43 (1964-65), pp.275-292.

G91.   Bradley, J.F.N. *The Czechoslovak Legion in Russia, 1914-1920* (New York: Columbia, 1991).

G92.   Bradley, J.F.N. "The Czechoslovak Revolt Against the Bolsheviks," *SS* 15 (1963), no.2, pp.124-151.

G93.   Dupuy, R.E. *Perish by the Sword: The Czechoslovakian Anabasis and Our Supporting Campaign in North Russia and Siberia, 1918-1920* (Harrisburg: Military Service Publishing Co., 1939).

G94.   Fic, V.M. "The Origins of the Conflict Between the Czechoslovak Legion and the Bolsheviks: March-May 1918," PhD diss., Columbia, 1968.

G95.   Fic, V.M. *The Bolsheviks and the Czechoslovak Legion: The Origin of Their Armed Conflict, March-May 1918* (New Dehli: Abhinav, 1978).

G96.   Kennan, G.F. "The Czechoslovak Legion," Part I: *RR* 16 (1957), no.4, pp.3-16; Part II: *RR* 17 (1958), no.1, pp.11-28.

G97.   Pearce, B. *How Haig Saved Lenin* (Basingstoke & London: Macmillan, 1987).

G98.   Unterberger, B.M. *The United States, Revolutionary Russia, and the Rise of Czechoslovakia* (Chapel Hill & London: University of North Carolina Press, 1989).

G99.   Williams, R.A. "The Czech Legion Revisited," *East-Central Europe* 6 (1979), no.1, pp.20-39.

Intervention:

G100.   Ackerman, C.W. *Trailing the Bolsheviks. 12,000 miles with the allies in Siberia* (New York: Scribner's, 1919).

G101.   Ainsworth, J. "The Blackwood Report on the Volunteer Army: A Missing Chapter in the Resumption of Anglo-White Relations in South Russia in November 1918," *SEER* 69 (1991), no.4, pp.621-646.

G102.   Arslanian, A.H. "The British Military Involvement in Transcaucasia, 1917-1919," PhD diss., California, L.A., 1974.

G103.   Aten, M. & Orrmont, A. *Last Train Over Rostov Bridge* (London: Cassell, 1961).

G104.   Bell, J.M. *Sidelights on the Siberian Campaign* (Toronto: Ryerson, 1923).

G105.   Bennett, G. *Cowan's War: The Story of British Naval Operations in the Baltic, 1918-1920* (London: Collins, 1964).

G106.   Bock, B. "The Origins of the Inter-Allied Intervention in Eastern Asia, 1918-1920," PhD diss., Stanford, 1941.

G107.   Bradley, J. *Allied Intervention in Russia* (London: Weidenfeld & Nicolson, 1968).

G108.   Brandenburg, W.A., Jr. "The Origins of American Military Intervention in Russia, 1918-1920," PhD diss., Colorado, 1957.

G109.   Brinkley, G.A., Jr. "Allied Intervention and the Volunteer Army in South Russia, 1917-1921," PhD diss., Columbia, 1964.

G110.   Brinkley, G.A. *The Volunteer Army and Allied Intervention in South Russia, 1917-1921* (Notre Dame: University of Notre Dame Press, 1966).

G111.   Bullen, J.R. "The Royal Navy in the Baltic, 1918-1920," PhD diss., London, 1983.

G112.   Carley, M.J. *Revolution and Intervention: The French Government and the Russian Civil War, 1917-1919* (Kingston & Montreal: McGill-Queen's U.P., 1983).

G113.   Carley, M.J. "The French Intervention in the Russian Civil War, November 1917-April 1919," PhD diss., Queen's (Canada), 1976.

G114.   Carley, M.J. "The Origins of the French Intervention in the Russian Civil War, January - May 1918: A Reappraisal," *JMH* 48 (1976), no.3, pp.413-439.

G115.   Coates, W.P. & Zelda, K. *Armed Intervention in Russia, 1918-1922* (London: Victor Gollancz, 1935).

G116.   Coleman, F.A. *Japan Moves North: the Inside Story of the Struggle for Siberia* (London & New York: Cassell, 1918).

G117.   De Basily, L.M. "A Footnote to History - The Conference at Spa in 1920," *RR* 32 (1973), no.1, pp.72-76.

G118.   Debo, R.K. "Prelude to Negotiations: The Problem of British Prisoners in Soviet Russia, November 1918 - July 1919," *SEER* 58 (1980), no.1, pp.58-75.

G119.   Donohoe, M.H. *With the Persian Expedition* (London: Edward Arnold, 1919).

G120.   Dunsterville, L.C. *The Adventures of Dunsterforce* (London: Edward Arnold, 1920).

G121.   Eitler, W.J. "Diplomacy of the Graves Mission to Siberia," PhD diss., Georgetown, 1953.

G122.   Ellis, C.H. "Operations in Transcaspia 1918-19 and the 26 Commissars Case," *St. Anthony's Papers* no.6 (*Soviet Affairs* no.2) (1959), pp.129-153.

G123.   Ellis, C.H. *The British "Intervention" in Transcaspia, 1918-1919* (Berkeley: University of California Press, 1963).

G124.   Ewalt, D. "The Fight for Oil: Britain in Persia, 1919," *HT* 31 (September 1981), pp.11-16.

G125.   Fletcher, W.A. "The British Navy in the Baltic, 1918-20: Its Contribution to the Independence of the Baltic Nations," *Journal of Baltic Studies* 7 (1976), pp.134-144.

G126.   Gaworek, N.H. "Allied Economic Warfare Against Soviet Russia from November 1917 to March 1921," PhD diss., Wisconsin, 1970.

G127.   Gaworek, N.H. "From Blockade to Trade: Allied Economic Warfare Against Soviet Russia, June 1919 to January 1920," *JFGO* 23 (1975), pp.30-69.

G128.   Goldhurst, R. *The Midnight War: The American Intervention in Russia, 1918-1920* (New York: McGraw-Hill, 1978).

G129.   Graves, W.S. *America's Siberian Adventure, 1918-1920* (New York: Peter Smith, 1931 [reprinted 1976]).

G130.   Guins, G.C. "The Siberian Intervention, 1918-1919," *RR* 28 (1969), no.4, pp.428-440.

G131.   Halliday, E.M. *The Ignorant Armies: the Anglo-American Archangel Expedition, 1918-1919* (London: Weidenfeld & Nicolson, 1961).

G132.   Hodges, A.P. *Britmis. A great adventure of the war, being an account of Allied intervention in Siberia and of an escape across the Gobi to Peking* (London: Jonathan Cape, 1931).

G133.   Ironside, E. *Archangel 1918-1919* (London: Constable, 1953).

G134.   Jackson, R. *At War With the Bolsheviks* (London: Tandem, 1974).

G135.   Jansen, M. "International Class Solidarity or Foreign Intervention? Internationalists and Latvian Rifles in the Russian Revolution and the Civil War," *IRSH* 31 (1986), pp.68-79.

G136. Kennan, G.F. "Soviet Historiography and America's Role in the Intervention," *AHR* 65 (1959-60), pp.302-322.

G137. Kettle, M. *Russia and the Allies 1917-1920. Vol.2: The Road to Intervention, March-November 1918* (London & New York: Routledge, 1988).

G138. Kettle, M. *Russia and the Allies 1917-1920. Vol.3: Churchill and the Archangel Fiasco* (London & New York: Routledge, 1992).

G139. Kindall, S.G. *American Soldiers in Siberia* (New York: Richard R. Smith, 1945).

G140. Knollys, Lt.-Col. D.E. "Military Operations in Transcaspia, 1918-1919," *Journal of the Central Asian Society* 13 (1926), no.2, pp.89-110.

G141. Knox, A. "James M. Blair," *SEER* 4 (1925-26), pp.482-484

G142. Kolz, A.W.F. "British Economic Interests in Siberia during the Russian Civil War, 1918-1920," *JMH* 48 (1976), no.3, pp.483-491.

G143. Long, J.W. "American Intervention in Russia: The North Russian Expedition 1918-19," *Diplomatic History* 6, no.1, pp.45-67.

G144. Long, J.W. "Civil War and Intervention in North Russia, 1918-1920," PhD diss., Columbia, 1972.

G145. McNeal, R.H. "The Conference of Jassy: An Early Fiasco of the Anti-Bolshevik Movement," in: J.S.Curtiss (ed.) *Essays in Russian and Soviet History* (London: E.J.Brill, 1963), pp.221-236.

G146. MacFarlen, L.J. "Hands Off Russia: British Labour and the Russo-Polish War, 1920," *Past and Present* no.38 (1967), pp.126-152.

G147. MacLaren, R. *Canadians in Russia, 1918-1919* (Toronto: Macmillan of Canada, 1975).

G148. Maddox, R.J. *The Unknown War With Russia: Wilson's Siberian Intervention* (San Rafael, California: Presidio Press, 1977).

G149. Mannerheim, C. *The Memoirs of Marshal Mannerheim*, trans.by C.E.Lawenhaupt (London: Cassell, 1953).

G150. Maynard, C.C.M. *The Murmansk Venture, 1918-1919* (London: Hodder & Stoughton, 1928).

G151. Morley, J.W. "Samurai in Siberia: The Origins of Japan's Siberian Expedition, 1918-1922: A Case Study in the Formation of Japan's Foreign Policy," PhD diss., Columbia, 1955.

G152. Morley, J.W. *The Japanese Thrust into Siberia, 1918* (New York: Columbia U.P., 1957).

G153. Morris, L.P. "British Secret Missions in Turkestan, 1918-19," *JCH* 12 (1977), no.2, pp.363-379.

G154. Munholland, J.K. "The French Army and Intervention in Southern Russia, 1918-1919," *Cahiers du Monde Russe et Sovietique* 22 (1981), no.1, pp.43-66.

G155. Murby, R.N. "Canadian Economic Commission to Siberia, 1918-19," *CSP* 11 (1969), no.3, pp.374-393.

G156. Norris, Capt. D. "Caspian Naval Expedition, 1918-1919," *Journal of the Central Asian Society* 10 (1923), no.3, pp.216-240.

G157. O'Connor, R. "Yanks in Siberia," *American Heritage* 25 (August 1974), no.5, pp.10-17 and 80-83.

G158. Olszewski, G. "Allied Intervention in North Russia, 1918-1919," PhD diss., Georgetown, 1958.

G159. Pares, B. "John Ward," *SEER* 13 (1934-35), pp.680-683.

G160. Peake, T.R. "Jacques Sadoul and the Russian Intervention Question, 1919," *RR* 32 (1973), no.1, pp.54-63.

G161. Pearce, B. "The 26 Commissars," *Sbornik (SGRR)* nos.6-7 (1981), pp.54-66 & pp.83-95. And see *Sbornik (SGRR)* no.9 (1983), pp.83-85.

G162. Pelzel, S.R. "American Intervention in Siberia," PhD diss., Pennsylvania, 1943.

G163. Price, M.P. *The Truth About the Intervention of the Allies in Russia* (Belp: Promachos, 1918).

G164. Priest, L.W. "The *Cordon Sanitaire* Against Russia, 1918-1922," PhD diss., Stanford, 1955.

G165. Rawlinson, Lt.-Col. A. *Adventures in the Near East, 1918-1922* (London & New York: Andrew Melrose, 1923).

G166. St.John, J.D. "John F. Stevens: American Assistance to Russian and Siberian Railroads, 1917-1922," PhD diss., Oklahoma, 1969.

G167. Silverlight, J. *The Visitors' Dilemma: Allied Intervention in the Russian Civil War* (London: Barrie & Jenkins, 1970).

G168. Smart, T.L. "The French Intervention in the Ukraine, 1918-1919," PhD diss., Kansas, 1968.

G169. Smith, G. "Canada and the Siberian Intervention, 1918-1919," *AHR* 64 (1958-59), no.4, pp.866-877.

G170. Soutar, A. *With Ironside in North Russia* (London & Melbourne: Hutchinson, 1940).

G171. Strakhovsky, L.I. "The Canadian Artillery Brigade in North Russia 1918-1919," *Canadian Historical Review* 39 (1958), pp.125-146.

G172. Strakhovsky, L.I. "The Allies and the Supreme Administration of the Northern Region, August 2 - October 7, 1918," *SEER* 20 (1941), pp.102-123.

G173. Strakhovsky, L.I. *Intervention at Archangel. The story of Allied intervention and Russian counter-revolution in North Russia, 1918-1920* (Princeton: Princeton U.P., 1944)

G174.   Strakhovsky, L.I. "The Liquidation of the Murmansk Regional Soviet," *SEER* 21 (1943), part 2, pp.19-30.

G175.   Strakhovsky, L.I. *The Origins of American Intervention in North Russia* (Princeton: Princeton U.P., 1937).

G176.   Swain, G.R. "Maugham, Masaryk and the 'Mensheviks'," *Revolutionary Russia* 7 (1994), no.1, pp.78-97.

G177.   Swettenham, J. *Allied Intervention in Russia, 1918-1919: and the part played by Canada* (London: Allen & Unwin, 1967).

G178.   Sworakowski, W.S. "A Churchill Letter in Support of the Anti-Bolshevik Forces in Russia in 1919," *RR* 28 (1969), no.1, pp.77-82.

G179.   Thompson, J.M. "Lenin's Analysis of Intervention," *ASEER* 17 (1958), no.2, pp.151-160.

G180.   Trani, E.P. "Woodrow Wilson and the Decision to Intervene in Russia: A Reconsideration," *JMH* 48 (1976), no.3, pp.440-461.

G181.   Ullman, R.H. "British Intervention in Russia, November 1917 to February 1920: A Study in the Making of Foreign Policy," PhD diss., Oxford, 1960.

G182.   Unterberger, B.M. "America's Siberian Expedition, 1918-1920: A Study of National Policy," PhD diss., Duke, 1950.

G183.   Unterberger, B.M. *America's Siberian Expedition, 1918-1920: a Study of National Policy* (Durham, N.C.: Duke U.P., 1956).

G184.   Unterberger, B.M. "President Wilson and the Decision to Send American Troops to Siberia," *Pacific Historical Review* 24 (1955), pp.63-74.

G185.   Unterberger, B.M. "The Russian Revolution and Wilson's Far-Eastern Policy," *RR* 16 (1957), no.2, pp.35-46.

G186.   Ward, J. *With the "die-hards" in Siberia* (London: Cassell, 1920).

G187.   White, J.A. *Siberian Intervention* (Stanford: Stanford U.P., 1947).

G188.   White, J.A. "Siberian Intervention: the Allied Phase," PhD diss., Stanford, 1948.

G189.   White, J.A. "The American Role in the Siberian Intervention," *RR* 10 (1951), no.1, pp.26-36.

G190.   White, S. "Labour's Council of Action 1920," *JCH* 19 (1974), no.4, pp.99-122.

G191.   Wilgress, L.D. "From Siberia to Kuibyshev: Refelections on Russia, 1919-43," *International Journal (Toronto)* 22 (1967), no.3, pp.364-375.

G192.   Williamson, H.N.H. *Farewell to the Don: The Russian Revolution in the Journals of Brigadier H.N.H. Williamson* (New York: John Day, 1971).

G193.   Woodward, D.R. "The British Government and Japanese Intervention in Russia during World War I," *JMH* 46 (1974), no.4, pp.663-685.

Terror:

G194.   Andics, H. *Rule of Terror*, trans.by A.Lieven (London: Constable, 1969).

G195.   Bortnevski, V.G. "White Administration and White Terror (The Denikin Period)," *RR* 52 (1993), no.3, pp.354-366.

G196.   Buluigin, P.P. *The Murder of the Romanoffs. The Authentic Account...Including The Road to Tragedy, by Alexander Kerensky*, trans.by G.Kerensky (London: Hutchinson, 1935).

G197.   Leggett, G.H. "Lenin, Terror, and the Political Police," *Survey* 21 (Autumn 1975), no.4, pp.157-187.

G198.   Maximoff, G.P. *The Guillotine At Work. Vol.1: The Leninist Counter-Revolution* (Sanday, Orkney: Cienfuegos Press, 1979).

G199.   Melgounov, S.P. *The Red Terror in Russia* (London & Toronto: J.M.Dent, 1925).

Green Movement:

G200.   Brovkin, V.N. "On the Internal Front: The Bolsheviks and the Greens," *JFGO* 37 (1989), pp.541-568.

G201.   Radkey, O.H. *The Unknown Civil War in Soviet Russia: A Study of the Green Movement in the Tambov Region 1920-21* (Stanford: Hoover Institution Press, 1976).

G202.   Singleton, S. "The Tambov Revolt (1920-1921)," *SR* 25 (1966), no.3, pp.497-512.

Makhno and the Makhnovshchina:

G203.   Arshinov, P. *History of the Makhnovist Movement*, trans.by L. & F. Perlman (Detroit: Black & Red / Chicago: Solidarity, 1974).

G204.   Dahlmann, D. "Anarchism and the Makhno Movement," *Sbornik (SGRR)* no.11 (1985), pp.4-25.

G205.   Footman, D. "Nestor Makhno," *St. Anthony's Papers* no.6 (*Soviet Affairs* no.2) (1959), pp.75-128.

G206.   Malet, M.G. "Nestor Makhno in the Russian Civil War, 1917-1921," PhD diss., London, 1975.

G207.   Malet, M. *Nestor Makhno in the Russian Civil War* (London: Macmillan, 1982).

G208.   Palij, M. *The Anarchism of Nestor Makhno, 1918-1921. An Aspect of the Ukrainian Revolution* (Seattle & London: University of Washington Press, 1976).

G209.   Palij, M. "The Peasant Partisan Movement of the Anarchist Nestor Makhno, 1918-1921: An Aspect of the Ukrainian Revolution," PhD diss., Kansas, 1971.

Atamanshchina in the Far East:

G210.   Smith, C.F. "*Atamanshchina* in the Russian far East," *RH* 6 (1979), pt.1, pp.57-67.

G211.   Smith, C.F. "The Ungernovscina - How and Why?" *JFGO* 28 (1980), pp.590-595.

Polish War:

G212.   Bryant, F.R. "Lord D'Abernon, the Anglo-French Mission, and the Battle of Warsaw, 1920." *JFGO* 38 (1990), pp.526-547.

G213.   Dabrowski, S. "The Peace Treaty of Riga, 1921," PhD diss., Kent State, 1968.

G214.   Davies, N. "August 1920," *European Studies Review* 3 (1973), no.3, pp.269-281.

G215.   Davies, N. "The Genesis of the Polish-Soviet War, 1919-1920," *European Studies Review* 5 (1975), no.1, pp.47-67.

G216.   Davies, N. "The Missing Revolutionary War. The Polish Campaigns and the Retreat from Revolution in Soviet Russia, 1919-21," *SS* 27 (1975), no.2, pp.178-195.

G217.   Davies, N. "The Soviet Command and the Battle of Warsaw," *SS* 23 (1972), no.4, pp.573-585.

G218.   Davies, N. *White Eagle, Red Star. The Polish Soviet War, 1919-1920* (London: Macdonald, 1972).

G219.   Fiddick, T.C. "Soviet Policy and the Battle of Warsaw, 1920," PhD diss., Indiana, 1974.

G220.   Fiddick, T. "The 'Miracle of the Vistula': Soviet Policy versus Red Army Strategy," *JMH* 45 (1973), no.4, pp.626-643.

G221.   Gasiorowski, Z.J. "Joseph Pilsudski in the Light of American Reports 1919-1920," *SEER* 49 (1971), no.116, pp.425-436.

G222.   Gasiorowski, Z.J. "Pilsudski in the Light of British Reports," *SEER* 50 (1972), no.121, pp.558-569.

G223.   Kukiel, M. "The Polish-Soviet Campaign of 1920," *SEER* 8 (1929-30), pp.48-65.

G224.   Laserson, M.M. *The Curzon Line* (New York: Carnegie Endowment for International Peace, 1944).

G225.   Lerner, W. "Attempting a Revolution from Without: Poland in 1920," *Studies on the Soviet Union* 11 (1971), no.4, pp.94-106. [Also in: T.T.Hammond (ed.) *The Anatomy of Communist Takeovers* (New Haven & London: Yale U.P., 1975)].

G226.   Musialik, Rev.Z. "General Maxime Weygand and the Battle of the Vistula, 1920," PhD diss., St.John's, 1973.

G227.   Pilsudski, J. *Year 1920 and Its Climax: The Battle of Warsaw during the Polish-Soviet War, 1919-1920. With the Addition of Marshal Tukhachevski's March Beyond the Vistula* (London & New York: Pilsudski Institute of London and Pilsudski Institute of America, 1972).

G228.   Shewchuk, S.M. "The Russo-Polish War of 1920," PhD diss., Maryland, 1966.

G229.   Westoby, A. & Blick, R. "Early Soviet Designs on Poland," *Survey* 26 (1982), no.4, pp.110-126.

H

REVOLUTION IN THE PROVINCES

H1.   A Correspondent "The Revolt in Transcaspia, 1918-1919," *Central Asian Review* 7 (1959), pp.117-130.

H2.   Dotsenko, P. *The Struggle for a Democracy in Siberia, 1917-1920: Eyewitness Account of a Contemporary* (Stanford: Hoover Institution Press, 1983).

H3.   Kazemzadeh, F. "The Struggle for Transcaucasia, 1917-1921," PhD diss., Harvard, 1951.

H4.   Kazemzadeh, F. *The Struggle for Transcaucasia, 1917-1921* (New York: Philosophical Library, 1951).

H5.   King, R.D. "Sergei Kirov and the Struggle for Soviet Power in the Terek Region, 1917-1918." PhD diss., Illinois, 1983.

H6.   Kirimli, S.H. "National Movements and National Identity among the Crimean Tatars (1905-1916)," PhD diss., Wisconsin, 1990.

H7.   Mandel, D. "October in the Ivanovo-Kineshma Industrial Region," in E.R.Frankel et al (eds.) *Revolution in Russia: Reassessments of 1917* (Cambridge: Cambridge U.P., 1992), 157-187.

H8.   Morley, J.W. "The Russian Revolution in the Amur Basin," *ASEER* 16 (1957), pp.450-472.

H9.   Mosse, W.E. "Revolution in Saratov, (October-November 1917)," *SEER* 49 (1971), no.117, pp.586-602.

H10.   Pearson, R. "*Nashe Pravitel'stvo*? The Crimean Regional Government of 1918-19," *Revolutionary Russia* 2 (1989), no.2, pp.14-30.

H11.   Pethybridge, R.W. *The Spread of the Russian Revolution: Essays on 1917* (London: Macmillan, 1972).

H12.   Power, R. *Under Cossack and Bolshevik* (London: Methuen, 1919).

H13.   Price, M.P. *War and Revolution in Asiatic Russia* (London: G.Allen & Unwin, 1918).

H14.   Raleigh, D.J. "Political Power in the Russian Revolution: a Case Study of Saratov," in: E.R.Frankel et al (eds.) *Revolution in Russia: Reassessments of 1917* (Cambridge: Cambridge U.P., 1992), pp.34-53.

H15.   Raleigh, D.J. *Revolution on the Volga. 1917 in Saratov* (Ithaca and London: Cornell U.P., 1986).

H16.   Raleigh, D.J. "Revolutionary Politics in Provincial Russia: The Tsaritsyn "Republic" in 1917," *SR* 40 (1981), no.2, pp.194-209.

H17.   Raleigh, D.J. "The Impact of World War I on Saratov and Its Revolutionary Movement," in: R.A.Wade & S.J.Seregny (eds.) *Politics and Society in Provincial Russia: Saratov, 1590-1917* (Columbus, Ohio: Ohio State U.P., 1989), pp.255-276.

H18.   Raleigh, D.J. "The Revolution of 1917 and the Establishment of Soviet Power in Saratov," in: R.A.Wade & S.J.Seregny (eds.) *Politics and Society in Provincial Russia: Saratov, 1590-1917* (Columbus, Ohio: Ohio State U.P., 1989), pp.277-306.

H19.   Raleigh, D.J. "The Russian Revolutions of 1917 in Saratov," PhD diss., Indiana, 1979.

H20.   Sanders, J. "Lessons from the Periphery: Saratov, January 1905," *SR* 46 (1987), no.2, pp.229-244.

H21.   Sinel, A.A. "Ekaterinoslav in Revolution: Excerpts from the Diary of Princess Urusov," *RR* 29 (1970), no.2, pp.192-208.

H22.   Smith, C.F. "Vladivostok Under Red and White Rule, 1920-1922," PhD diss., Virginia, 1972.

H23.   Smith, C.F. *Vladivostok under Red and White Rule: Revolution and Counterrevolution in the Russian Far East, 1920-1922* (Seattle & London: University of Washington Press, 1975).

H24.   Snow, R.E. *The Bolsheviks in Siberia, 1917-1918* (Madison, N.J.: Fairleigh Dickinson U.P., 1975 and London: Associated University Presses, 1977).

H25.   Snow, R.E. "The Russian Revolution of 1917-18 in Transbaikalia," *SS* 23 (1971), no.2, pp.201-215.

H26.   Spence, R.B. "White Against Red in Uriankhai: Revolution and Civil War on Russia's Asiatic Frontier, 1918-1921," *Revolutionary Russia* 6 (1993), no.1, pp.97-120.

H27.   Strakhovsky, L.I. "The Liquidation of the Murmansk Regional Soviet," *SEER* 21 (1943), part 2, pp.19-30.

H28.   Usherwood, S. "Rostov-on Don, 1917-1918," *HT* 17 (1967), pp.444-452.

H29.   Varneck, E. "Siberian Native Peoples after the February Revolution," *SEER* 21 (1942-44), pp.70-88.

H30.   Wade, R.A. "The Revolution in the Provinces: Khar'kov and the Varieties of Response to the October Revolution," *Revolutionary Russia* 4 (1991), no.1, pp.132-142.

H31.   Wade, R.A. & Seregny, S.J. (eds.) *Politics and Society in Provincial Russia: Saratov, 1590-1917* (Columbus, Ohio: Ohio State U.P., 1989).

I

OPPOSITION AFTER OCTOBER 1917

General:

I1.   Daniels, R.V. *The Conscience of the Revolution: Communist Opposition in Soviet Russia* (London: Oxford U.P., 1960 [also New York: Clarion Books, 1969]).

I2.   Debo, R.K. "Lockhart Plot or Dzerzhinskii Plot?" *JMH* 43 (1971), no.3, pp.413-439.

I3.   Farber, S. *Before Stalinism: The Rise and Fall of Soviet Democracy* (Cambridge: Polity Press, 1990).

I4.   Fischer, R. "Background of the New Economic Policy," *RR* 7 (1947-48), no.2, pp.15-33.

I5.   Germanis, U. "Some Observations on the Yaroslav Revolt, 1918," *Journal of Baltic Studies* 4 (1973), no.3, pp.236-243.

I6.   Goldberg, H.J. "The Anarchists View the Bolshevik Regime, 1918-1922," PhD diss., Wisconsin, 1973.

I7.   Gorky, M. *Untimely Thoughts. Essays on Revolution, Culture and the Bolsheviks, 1917-1918*, trans.by H.Ermolaev (London: Garnstone, 1970).

I8.   Schapiro, L. *The Origin of the Communist Autocracy: Political Opposition in the Soviet State 1917-1922*, 2nd edition (Cambridge, Mass.: Harvard U.P., 1977 [originally published 1955]).

I9.   Shub, D. "The Trial of the SRs," *RR* 23 (1964), no.4, pp.362-369.

I10.   Spirin, L.M. "Historiography of the Struggle of the RKP(B) with the Petty-Bourgeois Parties in 1917-1920," *SSH* 5 (1966-67), no.4, pp.3-12.

I11.   Williams, R.C. "Childhood Diseases: Lenin on 'Left' Bolshevism," *Sbornik (SGRR)* no.8 (1982), pp.38-48.

Attempt on Lenin's Life:

112.   Lyandres, S. "The 1918 Attempt on the Life of Lenin: A New Look at the Evidence," *SR* 48 (1989), no.3, pp.432-448.

"July Uprising" 1918:

113.   Hafner, L. "The Assassination of Count Mirbach and the 'July Uprising' of the Left Socialist Revolutionaries in Moscow, 1918," *RR* 50 (1991), no.3, pp.324-344.

114.   Senn, A.E. & Goldberg, H.J. "The Assassination of Count Mirbach," *CSP* 21 (1979), no.4, pp.438-445.

Left Communists:

115.   Bagaev, B.F. "The Struggle Against the 'Left Communists' in the Local Party Organisations on the Eve of the 7th Party Congress," *SSH* 1 (1962-63), no.2, pp.31-42.

116.   Biggart, J. "Alexander Bogdanov, Left Bolshevism and the Proletkult, 1904-32," PhD diss., East Anglia, 1989.

117.   Daniels, R.V. "The Left Opposition in the Russian Communist Party to 1924," PhD diss., Harvard, 1951.

118.   Felshtinsky, Y. "The Bolsheviki and the Left SRs, October 1917-July 1918: Toward a Single-Party Dictatorship," PhD diss., Rutgers, 1988.

119.   Kowalski, R.I. *The Bolshevik Party in Conflict: The Left Communist Opposition of 1918* (Pittsburgh: University of Pittsburgh Press, 1991).

120.   Kowalski, R.I. "The Development of 'Left Communism' until 1921: Soviet Russia, Poland, Latvia and Lithuania," PhD diss., Glasgow, 1978.

121.   Kowalski, R.I. "The Left Communism Movement of 1918: A Preliminary Analysis of its Regional Strength," *Sbornik (SGRR)* no.12 (1986), pp.27-63.

Mensheviks:

122.   Broido, V. *Lenin and the Mensheviks. The Persecution of Socialists under Bolshevism* (Aldershot: Gower, 1987).

123.   Brovkin, V. (ed.) *Dear Comrades: Menshevik Reports on the Bolshevik Revolution and Civil War* (Stanford: Hoover Institution Press, 1991).

124.   Brovkin, V.N. "The Menshevik Opposition to the Bolshevik Regime and the Dilemma of Soviet Power, October 1917-January 1919," PhD diss., Princeton, 1984.

125.   Brovkin, V.N. *The Mensheviks After October: Socialist Opposition and Rise of the Bolshevik Dictatorship* (Ithaca: Cornell U.P., 1987).

126.   Brovkin, V. "The Mensheviks' political comeback: the elections to the provincial city soviets in spring 1918," *RR* 42 (1983), pp.1-50.

127.   Brovkin, V.N. "The Mensheviks Under Attack. The Transformation of Soviet Politics, June-September 1918," *JFGO* 32 (1984), pp.378-391.

128.   Haimson, L.H. (ed.) *The Mensheviks: From the Revolution of 1917 to the Second World War*, trans.by G.Vakar (Chicago & London: University of Chicago Press, 1974).

129.   Kenez, P. "The Relations Between the Volunteer Army and Georgia, 1918-1920," *SEER* 48 (1970), no.112, pp.403-424.

130.   Liebich, A. "Diverging Paths: Menshevik Itineraries in the Aftermath of Revolution," *Revolutionary Russia* 4 (1991), no.1, pp.28-37.

131.   Shafir, I.M. (ed.) *Secrets of Menshevik Georgia: the Plot Against Soviet Russia Unmasked: Documents* (London: Communist Party of Great Britain, 1922).

Workers' Opposition:

132.   Avrich, P. "Bolshevik Opposition to Lenin: G.T. Miasnikov and the Workers' Group," *RR* 43 (1984), no.1, pp.1-29.

133.   Clements, B. "Kollontai's Contribution to the Workers' Opposition," *RH* 2 (1975), no.2, pp.191-206.

134.   Kollontay, A. *The Workers' Opposition in Russia* (London: Dreadnought, 1923).

Kronstadt Rebellion:

135.   Avrich, P. *Kronstadt 1921* (Princeton: Princeton U.P., 1970).

136.   Berkman, A. *The Kronstadt Rebellion* (Berlin, 1922).

137.   Ciliga, A. *The Kronstadt Revolt* (London: Freedom Press, 1942).

138.   Daniels, R.V. "The Kronstadt Revolt of 1921: A Study in the Dynamics of Revolution," *ASEER* 10 (1951), no.4, pp.241-254.

139.   Getzler, I. "All power to Soviets: maximalist ideology and Kronstadt practice," in: E.Kamenka (ed.) *Community as a Social Ideal* (London: Edward Arnold, 1982), pp.82-98.

140.   Getzler, I. *Kronstadt 1917-1921: The Fate of a Soviet Democracy* (Cambridge: Cambridge U.P., 1983).

141.   Katkov, G. "The Kronstadt Rising," *St. Anthony's Papers* No.6 (*Soviet Affairs* no.2) (1959), pp.9-74.

142.   Lenin, V.I. & Trotsky, L. *Kronstadt* (New York: Monad Press, 1979).

143.   Mawdsley, E. "The Baltic Fleet and the Kronstadt Mutiny," *SS* 24 (1972-73), no.4, pp.506-521.

144.   Mett, I. *The Kronstadt Commune* (Solidarity Pamphlet no.27, 1967).

145.   Neumann, J. "A Note on the Winter of the Kronstadt Sailors' Uprising in 1921," *SS* 44 (1992), no.1, pp.153-154.

146.   Petrov-Skitaletz, E. *The Kronstadt Thesis for a Free Russian Government: "All Power to the Soviets - but to Free Democratic-Socialist, Non-Communist-Dominated Soviets!"* trans.by J.F.O'Conor (New York: Robert Speller, 1964).

147.   Voline *The Unknown Revolution: (Kronstadt 1921. Ukraine 1918-21),* trans.by H.Cantine (London: Freedom, 1955).

J

MILITARY

General:

J1.   Bushnell, J. "Peasants in Uniform: The Tsarist Army as Peasant Society," *JSH* 13 (1980), no.4, pp.565-576.

J2.   Cyril, H.I.H. the Grand Duke *My Life in Russia's Service - Then and Now* (London: Selwyn & Blount, 1939).

J3.   Denikin, A.I. *The Russian Turmoil: Memoirs: Military, Social, and Political* (London: Hutchinson, n.d.).

J4.   Fuller, W.C., Jr. "Civil-Military Conflict in Imperial Russia, 1881-1914," PhD diss., Harvard, 1980.

J5.   Fuller, W.C., Jr. *Civil-Military Conflict in Imperial Russia, 1881-1914* (Princeton: Princeton U.P., 1985).

J6.   Garthoff, R.L. "The Military in Russia, 1861-1965," in: J.Van Doorn (ed.) *Armed Forces and Society. Sociological Essays* (The Hague: Mouton, 1968).

J7.   Gatrell, P. "Defence Industries in Tsarist Russia, 1908-13: Production, Employment and Military Procurement," in: L.Edmondson & P.Waldron (eds.) *Economy and Society in Russia and the Soviet Union, 1860-1930* (Basingstoke & London: Macmillan, 1992), pp.131-151.

J8.   Gatrell, P. *Government, industry and rearmament in Russia, 1900-1914: the last argument of tsarism* (Cambridge: Cambridge U.P., 1994).

J9.   Golden, R. "The Chief of Staff in Diplomacy: A Study of the Conferences Between the Chiefs of Staffs of the French and Russian Armies, 1892-1914," PhD diss., Pennsylvania, 1940.

J10.   Goldstein, E.R. "Military Aspects of Russian Industrialization: The Defence Industries, 1890-1817," PhD diss., Case Western Reserve, 1971.

J11.   Golub, P. *The Bolsheviks and the Armed Forces in Three Revolutions: Problems and Experience of Military Work* (Moscow: Progress, 1979).

J12.   Gorbatov, A.V. *Years Off My Life. The Memoirs of General of the Soviet Army*, trans.by G.Clough & A.Cash (London: Constable, 1964).

J13.   Kenez, P. "A Profile of the Prerevolutionary Officer Corps," *California Slavic Studies* 7 (1973), pp.121-158.

J14.   Knox, A. "General A.A. Brusilov," *SEER* 5 (1926-27), pp.146-148.

J15.   Knox, A. "General V.A. Sukhomlinov," SEER 5 (1926-27), pp.148-152.

J16.   Laney, F.M. "The Military Implementation of the Franco-Russian Alliance (1890-1914)," PhD diss., Virginia, 1954.

J17.   Mayzel, M. "The Formation of the Russian General Staff, 1880-1917: A Social Study," *Cahier du Monde Russe et Sovietique* 16 (1975), nos.3-4, pp.297-321.

J18.   Mayzel, M. "The Russian General Staff During the Revolution," PhD diss., Rochester, 1975.

J19.   Mayzel, M. *Generals and Revolutionaries. The Russian General Staff During the Revolution: A Study in the Transformation of the Military Elite* (Osnabruck: Biblio Verlag, 1979).

J20.   Menning, B.W. *Bayonets Before Bullets: The Imperial Russian Army, 1861-1914* (Bloomington: Indiana U.P., 1992).

J21.   Milsom, J. *Russian Tanks, 1900-1970: The Complete Illustrated History of Soviet Armoured Theory and Design* (Harrisburg: Stackpole Books, 1971).

J22.   Perkins, M. "The Russian Military 1904-1917 and Its Role in Russian Political Affairs," PhD diss., London, 1980.

J23.   Pintner, W.M. "The Burden of Defense in Imperial Russia, 1725-1914," *RR* 43 (1984), no.3, pp.231-259.

J24.   Polovtsoff, P.A. (Polovtsov) *Glory and Downfall: Reminiscences of a Russian General Staff Officer* (London: G.Bell, 1935).

J25.   Rostunov, I.I. *General Brusilov* (Moscow, 1964).

J26.   Screen, J.E.O. "The Entry of Finnish Officers into Russian Military Service, 1809-1917," PhD diss., London, 1976.

J27.   Seton-Watson, G.H.N. "Russia. Army and Autocracy," in: M.Howard (ed.) *Soldiers and Governments. Nine Studies in Civil-Military Relations* (London: Eyre & Spottiswoode, 1957).

J28.   Smith, A.L. "The German General Staff and Russia, 1919-1926," *SS* 8 (1956-57), no.2, pp.125-133.

J29.   Snyder, J.L. "Defending the Offensive: Biases in French, German, and Russian War Planning, 1870-1914," PhD diss., Columbia, 1981.

J30.   Steinberg, J.W. "The Education and Training of the Russian General Staff: A History of the Imperial Nicholas Military Academy, 1832-1914," PhD diss., Ohio State, 1990.

J31.   Steveni, W.B. *The Russian Army from Within*, 2nd ed. (London: Hodder & Stoughton, 1914).

J32.   The Ex-Grand Duke Alexander of Russia [A.Mihailovitch] *Once a Grand Duke* (London: Cassell, 1932).

J33.   Van Dyke, C. *Russian Imperial Military Doctrine and Education, 1832-1914* (New York, Westport, Connecticut, and London: Greenwood Press, 1990).

J34.   Walz, J.D. "State Defense and Russian Politics under the Last Tsar," PhD diss., Syracuse, 1967.

Russo-Japanese War:

J35.   Akashi, M. *Rakka Ryusui: Colonel Akashi's Report on his Secret Cooperation with the Russian Revolutionary Parties during the Russo-Japanese War* (Selected Chapters, trans.by I.Chiharu) (Helsinki: Finnish Historical Society, Studia Historica 31, 1988)

J36.   Asakawa, K. *The Russo-Japanese Conflict. Its Causes and Issues* (Haymarket: Archibald Constable, 1904).

J37.   Brooke, L. *An Eye-Witness in Manchuria* (London: Eveleigh Nash, 1905).

J38.   Chasseur *A Study of the Russo-Japanese War* (Edinburgh & London: William Blackwood, 1905).

J39.   Diedrich, E.C. "The Last Iliad: The Siege of Port Arthur in the Russo-Japanese War, 1904-1905," PhD diss., New York, 1978.

J40.   Greenwood, J.T. "The American Military Observers of the Russo-Japanese War (1904-1905)," PhD diss., Kansas State, 1971.

J41.   Hamilton, General Sir I. *A Staff Officer's Scrap-Book during the Russo-Japanese War*, 2 vols. (London: Edward Arnold, 1905 and 1907).

J42.   Hough, R. *The Fleet That Had to Die* (London: Hamish Hamilton, 1958).

J43.   Ignatyev, A.A. (Ignat'ev) *A Subaltern in Old Russia*, trans.by I.Montagu (London: Hutchinson, 1944).

J44.   Kang, S.-H. "The Impact of the Russo-Japanese War on the Northeast Asian Regional Subsystem: The War's Causes, Outcome and Aftermath," PhD diss., Northern Illinois, 1981.

J45.   Kuropatkin, A.N. *The Russian Army, and the Japanese War*, 2 vols. (London: John Murray, 1909).

J46.   McCully, N.A. *The McCully Report. The Russo-Japanese War, 1904-05* (Anapolis, Maryland: Naval Institute Press, 1977).

J47.   Nish, I. *The Origins of the Russo-Japanese War* (London & New York: Longman, 1985).

J48.   Semenoff, Captain V. *The Battle of Tsu-Shima Between the Japanese and Russian Fleets, Fought on 27th May 1905*, trans.by A.B.Lindsay (London: John Murray, 1906).

J49.   Travis, F.F. "The Kennan-Russel Anti-Tsarist Propaganda Campaign among Russian Prisoners of War in Japan, 1904-1905," *RR* 40 (1981), no.3, pp.263-277.

J50.   Tsai, W. "The Russo-Japanese Conflict in the Far East," PhD diss., Illinois, 1938.

J51.   Walder, D. *The Short Victorious War. The Russo-Japanese Conflict, 1904-5* (Newton Abbot: Readers Union/Hutchinson, 1974).

J52.   Warner, D. & P. *The Tide at Sunrise: A History of the Russo-Japanese War, 1904-1905* (London: Angus & Robertson, 1975).

J53.   Westwood, J.N. *Russia Against Japan, 1904-05: A New Look at the Russo-Japanese War* (Albany: State University of New York Press, 1986).

J54.   Westwood, J.N. *Witnesses of Tsushima* (Tokyo: Sophia University, in cooperation with The Diplomatic Press, Tallahassee, Florida, 1970).

J55.   Wiren, A.R. "The Lesson of Port Arthur," *RR* 1 (1941-42), no.2, pp.40-43.

J56.   Wrangel, Count G. *The Cavalry in the Russo-Japanese War: Lessons and Critical Considerations*, trans.by J.Montgomery (London: Hugh Rees, 1907).

1905 Revolution:

J57.   Bennett, G. "The *Potemkin* Mutiny," *United States Naval Institute Proceedings*, 1959, no.9, pp.58-66.

J58.   Bushnell, J. "Mutineers and Revolutionaries: Military Revolution in Russia, 1905-1907," PhD diss., Indiana, 1977.

J59.   Bushnell, J. *Mutiny amid Repression: Russian Soldiers in the Revolution of 1905-1906* (Bloomington: Indiana U.P., 1985).

J60.   Bushnell, J. "The Dull-Witted Muzhik in Uniform: Why Did He Smash the Revolution?," in: F.-X.Coquin & C.Gervais-Francelle (eds.) *1905: La Premiere Revolution Russe* (Paris: Publications de la Sorbonne et Institut d'etudes slaves, 1986), pp.203-223.

J61.   Bushnell, J. "The Revolution of 1905-06 in the Army: the Incidence and Impact of Mutiny," *RH* 12 (1985), pt.1, pp.71-94.

J62.   Perrins, M. "Russian Military Policy in the Far East and the 1905 Revolution in the Russian Army," *European Studies Review* 9 (1979), no.3, pp.331-349.

1905-14:

J63.   Bushnell, J. "The Tsarist Officer Corps 1881-1914: Customs, Duties, Inefficiency," *AHR* 86 (1981), no.4, pp.753-780.

J64.   Denikin, A.I. *The Career of a Tsarist Officer: Memoirs, 1872-1916*, trans.by M.Patoski (Minneapolis: University of Minnesota Press, 1975).

J65.   Kenez, P. "A Profile of the Prerevolutionary Officer Corps," *California Slavic Studies* 7 (1973), pp.121-158.

J66.   Kenez, P. "Russian Officer Corps Before the Revolution: The Military Mind," *RR* 31 (1972), no.3, pp.226-236.

J67.   Wilfong, W.T. "Rebuilding the Russian Army, 1905-14: The Question of a Comprehensive Plan for National Defense," PhD diss., Indiana, 1977.

World War I:

J68.   Adelman, J.R. *Revolution, Armies, and War: A Political History* (Boulder, Colorado: Rienner, 1985).

J69.   Alexinsky, T. *With the Russian Wounded*, trans.by G.Cannan (London: T.Fisher Unwin, 1916).

J70.   Botcharsky, S. & Pier, F. *They Knew How To Die. Being a Narrative of the Personal Experiences of a Red Cross Sister on the Russian Front* (London: Peter Davies, 1931).

J71.   Botchkareva, M. *Yaska: My Life as Peasant, Exile and Soldier* (London: Constable, 1919).

J72.   "Briedis" (trans. & annotated by D.Guild) *Revolutionary Russia* 6 (1993), no.1, pp.1-25 and no.2, pp.173-192.

J73.   Brussilov, General A.A. *A Soldier's Note-Book, 1914-1918* (London: Macmillan, 1930 [reprinted Westport, Conn.: Greenwood, 1970 and 1976]).

J74.   Churchill, W.S. *The World Crisis. The Eastern Front* (London: Thornston Butterworth, 1931).

J75.   Czernin, C.O. *In the World War* (London: Cassell, 1919).

J76.   Farmborough, F. *Nurse at the Russian Front: A Diary 1914-18* (London: Constable, 1974).

J77.   Feldman, R.S. "The Russian General Staff and the June 1917 Offensive," *SS* 19 (1968), no.4, pp.526-543.

J78.   Golovin, N. "The Russian War Plan of 1914," *SEER* 14 (1935-36), pp.564-584 and *SEER* 15 (1936-37), pp.70-90.

J79.   Golovin, N. "Brusilov's Offensive: The Galician Battle of 1916," *SEER* 13 (1934-35), pp.571-596.

J80.   Golovin, N. "The Great Battle of Galicia (1914): A Study in Strategy," *SEER* 5 (1926-27), pp.25-47.

J81.   Golovine, Lieutenant-General N.N. *The Russian Army in the World War* (New Haven: Yale U.P., 1931).

J82.   Graf, D.W. "Military Rule Behind the Russian Front, 1914-1917: The Political Ramifications," *JFGO* 22 (1974), pp.390-411.

J83.   Graf, D.W. "The Reign of the Generals: Military Government in Western Russia, 1914-1915," PhD diss., Nebraska, 1972.

J84.   Gurko, V.I. (Gourko) *Memories and Impressions of War and Revolution in Russia, 1914-1917* (London: John Murray, 1918).

J85.   Heenan, L.E. *Russian Democracy's Fatal Blunder: The Summer Offensive of 1917* (Westport, CT., New York, London: Praeger, 1987).

J86.   Heenan, L.E. "Russia's Fatal Blunder: The Summer Offensive of 1917: Diplomatic, Military, Political and Social Aspects," PhD diss., Texas, 1983.

J87.   Ironside, E. *Tannenburg. The First Thirty Days in East Prussia* (Edinburgh and London: William Blackwood, 1925).

J88.   Jahn, H.F. "Patriotic Culture in Russia during World War I," PhD diss., Georgetown, 1991.

J89.   Jones, D.R. "Nicholas II and the Supreme Command: An Investigation of Motives," *Sbornik (SGRR)* no.11 (1985), pp.47-83.

J90.   Kenez, P. "Changes in the Social Composition of the Officer Corps During World War I," *RR* 31 (1972), no.4, pp.369-375.

J91.   Kettle, M. *Russia and the Allies 1917-1920. Vol.I: The Allies and the Russian Collapse, March 1917-March 1918* (London: Andre Deutsch, 1981).

J92.   Knox, Major-General Sir Alfred *With the Russian Army 1914-1917, Being Chiefly Extracts from the Diary of a Military Attache*, 2 vols. (London: Hutchinson, 1921).

J93.   Lambert, D.W. "The Deterioration of the Imperial Russian Army in the First World War, August 1914-March 1917," PhD diss., Kentucky, 1975.

J94.   Lawrence, M. "The Serbian Divisions in Russia, 1916-17," *JCH* 6 (1971), no.4, pp.183-192.

J95.   Lebedev, V.V. "A Contribution to the Historiography of the Problem of Russia's Leaving the War on the Eve of the February Revolution," *SSH* 11 (1972-73), no.2, pp.178-192.

J96.   Lincoln, W.B. *Passage Through Armageddon. The Russians in War and Revolution 1914-1918* (New York: Simon & Schuster, 1986).

J97.   Lobanov-Rostovsky, A.A. *The Grinding Mill: Reminiscences of War and Revolution in Russia, 1913-1920* (New York: Macmillan, 1935).

J98.   Manakin, V. "The Shock-Battalions of 1917: Reminiscences," *RR* 14 (1955), no.3, pp.214-232 & *RR* 14 (1955), no.4, pp.332-344.

J99.   Morse, J. *An Englishman in the Russian Ranks: Ten Months' Fighting in Poland* (London: Duckworth, 1915).

J100.   Neilson, K. "Russian Foreign Purchasing in the Great War: A Test Case," *SEER* 60 (1980), no.4, pp.572-590.

J101.   Neilson, K.E. "Strategy and Supply: Anglo-Russian Relations 1914-1917," PhD diss., Cambridge, 1978.

J102.   Neilson, K. *Strategy and Supply. The Anglo-Russian Alliance, 1914-17* (London: George Allen & Unwin, 1984).

J103.   Pares, B. *Day by Day with the Russian Army, 1914-15* (London: Constable, 1915).

J104.   Pearce, B. *How Haig Saved Lenin* (Basingstoke & London: Macmillan, 1987).

J105.   Rutherford, W. *The Russian Army in World War I* (London: Gordon Cremonesi, 1975).

J106.   Shklovsky, V.B. "At the Front - Summer 1917," *RR* 26 (1967), no.3, pp.219-230.

J107.   Smith, C.J. "Legacy to Stalin: Russian War Aims, 1914-1917," PhD diss., Harvard, 1953.

J108.   Smith, M.D. "Britain, Russia, the Gallipoli Campaign and the Straits," PhD diss., Florida State, 1979.

J109.   Solzhenitsyn, A. *August 1914*, trans. by M.Glenny (London: Bodley Head, 1972).

J110.   Stone, N. *The Eastern Front 1914-1917* (London: Hodder & Stoughton, 1975).

J111.   Tschebotarioff, G.P. *Russia, My Native Land. A U.S. Engineer Reminisces and Looks at the Present* (New York, London, Toronto: McGraw-Hill, 1964).

J112.   Turner, L.C.F. "The Russian Mobilization in 1914," *JCH* 3 (1968), no.1, pp.65-88.

J113.   Washburn, S. *Field Notes from the Russian Front* (London: Andrew Melrose, 1915).

J114.   Washburn, S. *The Russian Campaign: April to August 1915, Being the Second Volume of "Field Notes from the Russian Front"* (London: Andrew Melrose, n.d.)

J115.   Washburn, S. *The Russian Advance: Being the Third Volume of Field Notes from the Russian Front, Embracing the Period from June 5th to September 1st, 1916* (London: Curtis Brown, 1917).

J116.   Washburn, S. *Victory in Defeat: The Agony of Warsaw and the Russian Retreat* (London: Constable, 1916).

J117.   Wild, M. *Secret Service on the Russian Front*, trans.by A.Haigh (London: Geoffrey Bles, 1932).

1917:

J118.   Boyd, J.R. "The Origins of Order No.1," *SS* 19 (1968), no.3, pp.359-372.

J119.   Feldman, R.S. "Between War and Revolution: The Russian General Staff, February-July, 1917," PhD diss., Indiana, 1967.

J120.   Ferro, M. "The Russian Soldier in 1917: Undisciplined, Patriotic, and Revolutionary," *SR* 30 (1971), no.3, pp.483-512.

J121.   Hasegawa, T. "The Formation of the Militia in the February Revolution: An Aspect of the Origins of Dual Power," *SR* 32 (1973), no.2, pp.303-322.

J122.   Jones, D.R. "The Officers and the October Revolution," *SS* 28 (1976), no.2, pp.207-223.

J123.   Mawdsley, E. "Soldiers and Sailors," in: R.Service (ed.) *Society and Politics in the Russian Revolution* (Basingstoke & London: Macmillan, 1992), pp.103-119.

J124.   Nikolaieff, A.M. "The February Revolution and the Russian Army," *RR* 6 (1946-47), no.1, pp.17-25.

J125.   Rabinowitch, A. "The Petrograd Garrison and the Bolshevik Seizure of Power," in: A.Rabinowitch et al (eds.) *Revolution and Politics in Russia: Essays in Memory of B.I. Nicolaevsky* (Bloomington: Indiana U.P., 1972), pp.172-191.

J126.   Toropov, L.N. "Soldiers Committees of Central Russia in the Spring of 1917," *SSH* 15 (1976-77), no.4, pp.63-92.

J127.   White, H. "1917 in the Rear Garrisons," in: L.Edmondson & P.Waldron (eds.) *Economy and Society in Russia and the Soviet Union, 1860-1930* (Basingstoke & London: Macmillan, 1992), pp.152-168.

J128.   Wildman, A.K. *The End of the Russian Imperial Army: The Old Army and the Soldiers' Revolt (March-April 1917)* (Princeton: Princeton U.P., 1980).

J129.   Wildman, A.K. *The End of the Russian Imperial Army: The Road to Soviet Power and Peace* (Princeton: Princeton U.P., 1987).

J130.   Wildman, A. "The February Revolution in the Russian Army," *SS* 22 (1970-71), no.1, pp.3-23.

Red Guard and Red Army:

J131.   Benvenuti, F. *The Bolsheviks and the Red Army 1918-1922*, trans.by C.Woodall (Cambridge: Cambridge U.P., 1988).

J132.   Brown, S.M. "The First Cavalry Army in the Russian Civil War, 1918-1920," PhD diss., Wollongong (Australia), 1990.

J133.   Collins, D.N. "A Note on the Numerical Strength of the Russian Red Guard in October 1917," *SS* 24 (1972-73), no.2, pp.270-280.

J134.   Collins, D.N. "The Origins, Structure and Role of the Russian Red Guard," PhD diss., Leeds, 1975.

J135.   Colton, T.J. "Military Councils and Military Politics in the Russian Civil War," *CSP* 18 (1976), no.1, pp.36-57.

J136.   Dune, E.M. *Notes of a Red Guard* (trans. & edited by D.P. Koenker & S.A. Smith) (Urbana: University of Illinois Press, 1993).

J137.   Erickson, J. *The Soviet High Command: A Military-Political History, 1918-1941* (London: Macmillan, 1962).

J138.   Fedotoff-White, D. "The Growth of the Red Army," PhD diss., Columbia, 1944.

J139.   Fedotoff-White, D. *The Growth of the Red Army* (Princeton: Princeton U.P., 1944).

J140.   Figes, O. "The Red Army and Mass Mobilization during the Russian Civil War 1918-1920," *Past and Present* no.129 (1990), pp.168-211.

J141.   Heyman, N.M. "Leon Trotsky as a Military Thinker," PhD diss., Stanford, 1972.

J142.   Jones, D.R. "The Officers and the Soviets, 1917-1920: A Study in Motives," *Sbornik (SGRR)* no.2 (1976), pp.21-33.

J143.   Liddell Hart, B.H. *The Red Army: The Red Army, 1918 to 1945; The Soviet Army, 1946 to the Present* (Gloucester, Mass.: Peter Smith, 1968).

J144.   Nove, A. "The Red Army in the Civil War: A Note on a New Source," *SS* 31 (1979), no.3, pp.443-444.

J145.   O'Ballance, E. *The Red Army* (London: Faber & Faber, 1964).

J146.   Rapoport, V. and Alexeev, Y. *High Treason. Essays on the History of the Red Army, 1918-1938* (Durham, N.C.: Duke U.P., 1985).

J147.   Trotsky, L. *The Military Writings and Speeches of Leon Trotsky: How the Revolution Armed*, 5 vols., trans. by B.Pearce (London: New Park Publications, 1979-81).

J148.   Von Hagen, M. "Civil-Military Relations and the Evolution of the Soviet Socialist State," *SR* 50 (1991), no.2, pp.268-276.

J149.   Von Hagen, M.L. "School of the Revolution: Bolsheviks and Peasants in the Red Army, 1918-1928," PhD diss., Stanford, 1985.

J150.   Von Hagen, M. *Soldiers in the Proletarian Dictatorship: The Red Army and the Soviet Socialist State, 1917-1930* (Ithaca & London: Cornell U.P., 1990).

J151.   Wade, R.A. *Red Guards and Workers' Militias in the Russian Revolution* (Stanford: Stanford U.P., 1984).

J152.   Wade, R.A. "Self-Organisation and Leadership in the Russian Revolution: The Workers' Armed Bands," *Revolutionary Russia* 1 (1988), no.1, pp.57-67.

J153.   Wade, R.A. "Spontaneity in the Formation of the Workers' Militia and Red Guards, 1917," in: R.C.Elwood (ed.) *Reconsiderations on the Russian Revolution* (Cambridge, Mass.: Slavica, 1976), pp.20-41.

J154.   Wade, R.A. "The Red Guards: Spontaneity and the October Revolution," in: E.R.Frankel et al (eds.) *Revolution in Russia: Reassessments of 1917* (Cambridge: Cambridge U.P., 1992), 53-75.

J155.   Wade, R.A. "The Saratov Red Guards," in: R.A.Wade & S.J.Seregny (eds.) *Politics and Society in Provincial Russia: Saratov, 1590-1917* (Columbia, Ohio: Ohio State U.P., 1989), pp.307-325.

J156.   Wildman, A.K. "The Bolsheviks of the Twelfth Army and Latvian Social Democracy," in: R.C.Elwood (ed.) *Reconsiderations on the Russian Revolution* (Cambridge, Mass.: Slavica, 1976), pp.173-183.

J157.   Winsbury, R. "Trotsky's War Train," *HT* 25 (1975), pp.523-531.

J158.   Wollenberg, E. *The Red Army* (London: Secker & Warburg, 1938).

Sailors and the Navy:

J159.   Bennett, G. "The *Potemkin* Mutiny," *United States Naval Institute Proceedings*, 1959, no.9, pp.58-66.

J160.   Fel'dman, K. *The Revolt of the "Potemkin"*, trans.by C.Garnett (London: Heinemann, 1908).

J161.   Hartgrove, J.D. "Red Tide: The Kronstadters in the Russian Revolutionary Movement, 1901-1917," PhD diss., North Carolina, 1975.

J162.   Hough, R.A. *The Potemkin Mutiny* (London: Hamish Hamilton, 1961).

J163.   Hucul, W.C. "The Evolution of Russian and Soviet Sea-Power, 1853-1953," PhD diss., California, 1964.

J164.   Kirby, D.G. "A Navy in Revolution: The Russian Baltic Fleet in 1917," *European Studies Review* 4 (1974), no.4, pp.345-358.

J165.   Longley, D.A. "Officers and Men. A study of the development of political attitudes among the sailors of the Baltic Fleet in 1917," *SS* 25 (1973), no.1, pp.28-50.

J166.   Mawdsley, E. "The Baltic Fleet and the Kronstadt Mutiny," *SS* 24 (1972-73), no.4, pp.506-521.

J167.   Mawdsley, E. "The Baltic Fleet in the Russian Revolution, 1917-1921," PhD diss., London, 1972.

J168.   Mawdsley, E. "The Case of Captain Shchastny," *Sbornik (SGRR)* no.3 (1977), pp.22-33.

J169.   Mawdsley, E. *The Russian Revolution and the Baltic Fleet* (London: Macmillan, 1978).

J170.   Nekrasov, G. *North of Gallipoli: The Black Sea Fleet at War, 1914-1917* (Boulder, Colorado: East European Monographs, in association with Columbia U.P., 1992).

J171.   Saul, N.E. *Sailors in Revolt. The Russian Baltic Fleet in 1917* (Lawrence: Regents Press of Kansas, 1978).

J172.   Saul, N. "The Cruiser Aurora and the Russian Revolution," *HT* 22 (1972), pp.768-776.

J173.   Ullman, H.K. "Despair and Euphoria: Perspectives of Soviet Naval Development, 1917-1973," PhD diss., Tufts-Fletcher School of Law and Diplomacy, 1975.

J174.   Vulliamy, C.E. (ed.) *The Red Archives. Russian State Papers and Other Documents relating to the Years 1915-1918*, trans.by A.L.Hynes (London: Geoffrey Bles, 1929).

J175.   Westwood, J.N. "Novikov-Priboi as Naval Historian," *SR* 28 (1969), no.2, pp.297-303.

J176.   Woodward, D. *The Russians at Sea: A History of the Russian Navy* (New York & Washington: Praeger, 1966).

Air Force:

J177.   Alexander, J. "Death or Glory," *RAF Review* 13 (1958), no.10, pp.16-19.

J178.   Alexander, J. "The Russian Section," in: B.Robertson (ed.) *Air Aces of the 1914-1918 War* (Letchworth, Herts.: Harleyford, 1959), pp.148-160.

J179.   Alexander, J. "The Squadron of Flying Ships," *RAF Review* 12 (1957), no.9, pp.20-22.

J180.   Coupar, A.R. *The Smirnoff Story* (London: Jarrolds, 1960).

J181.   Higham, R. & Kipp, J.W. (eds.) *Soviet Aviation and Air Power: An Historical View* (London: Brassey's, 1978).

J182.   Meos, E. "Schooner Below!" *RAF Review* 12 (1957), no.1, pp.44-46.

J183.   Nowarra, H.J. & Duval, G.R. *Russian Civil and Military Aircraft, 1884-1969* (London: Fountain Press, 1971).

J184.   Stariparloff, T. "The Russian Military Air Service up to the Revolution," *Air Power* 4 (December 1918), pp.324-337.

K

FOREIGN POLICY AND DIPLOMACY

General:

K1.   Buchanan, G. *My Mission to Russia and Other Diplomatic Memories*, 2 vols. (London: Cassell, 1923).

K2.   Clemens, W.C., Jr. "Lenin on Disarmament," *SR* 23 (1964), no.3, pp.504-525.

K3.   De Basily, N. *Diplomat of Imperial Russia, 1903-1917: Memoirs* (Stanford: Hoover Institution Press, 1973).

K4.   Dillon, E.J. "Two Russian Statesmen," *The Quarterly Review* 236 (1921), no.469, pp.402-417.

K5.   Dittmer, H.R.B. "The Russian Foreign Ministry under Nicholas II: 1894-1914," PhD diss., Chicago, 1977.

K6.   Galai, S. "The Kadets and Russia's Foreign Policy," *Sbornik (SGRR)* no.12 (1986), pp.2-24.

K7.   Geyer, D. *Russian Imperialism: The Interaction of Domestic and Foreign Policy 1860-1914*, trans.by B.Little (New Haven & London: Yale U.P., 1987).

K8.   Izvol'sky, A.P. *The Memoirs of Alexander Iswolsky*, trans.by C.L.Seeger (London: Hutchinson, 1920).

K9.   Jelavich, B. *A Century of Russian Foreign Policy, 1814-1914* (Philadelphia & New York: J.B.Lippincott, 1964).

K10.   Kalmykow, A.D. [Kalmykov] *Memoirs of a Russian Diplomat: Outposts of the Empire, 1893-1917* (New Haven & London: Yale U.P., 1971).

K11.   Katkov, G. & Futrell, M. "Russian foreign policy 1880-1914," in: G.Katkov et al (eds.) *Russia Enters the Twentieth Century*, 1894-1917 (London: Temple Smith, 1971), pp.9-33.

K12.   Kerner, R.J. "The Mission of Liman von Sanders," *SEER* 6 (1927-28), pp.12-27, pp.344-363, pp.543-560; *SEER* 7 (1928-29), pp.90-112.

K13.   Kucherov, S. "The Problem of Constantinople and the Straits," *RR* 8 (1949), no.3, pp.205-220.

K14.   Lensen, G.A. (ed.) *Revelations of a Russian Diplomat: The Memoirs of Dmitrii I. Abrikossow* (Seattle: University of Washington Press, 1964).

K15.   McDonald, D.M. "Aristocracy, Bureaucracy, and Change in the Formation of Russia's Foreign Policy, 1895-1914," PhD diss., Columbia, 1988.

K16.   Mosely, P.E. "Russian Policy in 1911-12 - A Review Article," *JMH* 12 (1940), pp.69-86.

K17.   Nabokoff, C. *The Ordeal of a Diplomat* (London: Duckworth, 1921).

K18.   Pares, B. "Sergius Sazonov," *SEER* 6 (1927-28), pp.668-671.

K19.   Peterson, C.B. III. "Geographical Aspects of Foreign Colonization in Pre-revolutionary New Russia," PhD diss., Washington, Seattle, 1969.

K20.   Phelps, D. "Izvolski and Russian Foreign Policy, 1906-1910," PhD diss., California, 1932.

K21.   "Pragmaticus" "The Lessons of Brest-Litovsk," *SEER* 15 (1936-37), pp.328-343.

K22.   Ragsdale, H. (ed.) *Imperial Russian Foreign Policy* (Cambridge: Cambridge U.P. & Woodrow Wilson Center Press, 1993).

K23.   Rieber, A.J. "Persistent factors in Russian foreign policy: an interpretive essay," in: H.Ragsdale (ed.) *Imperial Russian Foreign Policy* (Cambridge: Cambridge U.P. & Woodrow Wilson Center Press, 1993), pp.315-359.

K24.   Rieber, A.J. "The historiography of Imperial Russian foreign policy: a critical survey," in: H.Ragsdale (ed.) *Imperial Russian Foreign Policy* (Cambridge: Cambridge U.P. & Woodrow Wilson Center Press, 1993), pp.360-443.

K25.   Rosen, Baron *Forty Years of Diplomacy*, 2 vols. (London: George Allen & Unwin, 1922).

K26.   Savinsky, A. *Recollections of a Russian Diplomat* (London: Hutchinson, n.d.).

K27.   Sazonov, S. *Fateful Years, 1909-1916: The Reminiscences of Sergei Sazonov* (London: Jonathan Cape, 1928).

K28.   Sontag, J.P. "Tsarist Debts and Tsarist Foreign Policy," *SR* 27 (1968), no.4, pp.529-541.

K29.   Stieve, F. *Isvolsky and the World War: Based on the Documents Recently Published by the German Foreign Office*, trans.by E.Dickes (London: George Allen & Unwin, 1926).

K30.   Weeks, C.J. & Baylen, J.O. "Admiral Newton A. McCully's Mission In Russia, 1904-1921," *RR* 33 (1974), no.1, pp.63-79.

Russo-Japanese War:

K31.   Chamberlain, G.B. "Japan, France, and the Russian Baltic Fleet: A Diplomatic Sidelight on the War of 1904-1905," PhD diss., California, Berkeley, 1972.

K32.   Esthus, R.A. *Double Eagle and Rising Sun: The Russians and Japanese at Portsmouth in 1905* (Durham, N.C. & London: Duke U.P., 1988).

K33.   Esthus, R.A. "Nicholas II and the Russo-Japanese War," *RR* 40 (1981), no.4, pp.396-411.

K34.   Korostovetz, J.J. *Pre-War Diplomacy: the Russo-Japanese problem. Treaty signed at Portsmouth, U.S.A., 1905. Diary of J.J. Korostovetz* (London: British Periodicals, 1920).

K35.   Parsons, E.B. "Roosevelt's Containment of the Russo-Japanese War," *Pacific Historical Review* 38 (1969), pp.21-43.

K36.   Trani, E.P. "The Treaty of Portsmouth: An Adventure in Rooseveltian Diplomacy," PhD diss., Indiana, 1966.

K37.   Trani, E.P. *The Treaty of Portsmouth: An Adventure in American Diplomacy* (Lexington: University of Kentucky Press, 1969).

K38.   White, J.A. *The Diplomacy of the Russo-Japanese War* (Princeton: Princeton U.P., 1964).

1905-14:

K39.   Allshouse, R.H. "Aleksander Izvolskii and Russian Foreign Policy: 1910-1914," PhD diss., Case Western Reserve, 1977.

K40.   Bestuzhev, I.V. "Russian Foreign Policy February-June 1914," *JCH* 1 (1966), no.3, pp.93-112.

K41.   Dailey, K. "Alexander Isvolsky and the Buchlan Conference," *RR* 10 (1951), no.1, pp.55-63.

K42.   Heilbronner, H. "An Anti-Witte Diplomatic Conspiracy, 1905-1906: The Schwanebach Memorandum," *JFGO* (1966), no.3, pp.347-61.

K43.   Iswolsky, H. "The Fateful Years: 1906-1911," *RR* 28 (1969), no.2, pp.191-206.

K44.   Kerensky, A. "Izvolsky's Personal Diplomatic Correspondence," *SEER* 16 (1937-38), pp.386-392.

K45.   McDonald, D.M. "A lever without a fulcrum: domestic factors and Russian foreign policy, 1905-1914," in: H.Ragsdale (ed.) *Imperial Russian Foreign Policy* (Cambridge: Cambridge U.P. & Woodrow Wilson Center Press, 1993), pp.268-311.

K46.   McDonald, D.M. "A.P. Izvol'skii and Russian Foreign Policy Under 'United Government', 1906-10," in: R.B.McKean (ed.) *New Perspectives in Modern Russian History* (Basingstoke & London: Macmillan, 1992), pp.174-202.

K47.   McDonald, D.M. *United Government and Foreign Policy in Russia, 1900-1914* (Cambridge, Mass. & London: Harvard U.P., 1992).

K48.   Spring, D.W. "Russian Foreign Policy, Economic Interests and the Straits Question, 1905-14," in: R.B.McKean (ed.) *New Perspectives in Modern Russian History* (Basingstoke & London: Macmillan, 1992), pp.203-221.

World War I and Brest-Litovsk:

K49.   Aldanov, M. "P.N. Durnovo - Prophet of War and Revolution," *RR* 2 (1942-43), no.1, pp.31-45.

K50.   Bailey, S.D. "Stalin's Falsification of History: the Case of the Brest-Litovsk Treaty," *RR* 14 (1955), no.1, pp.24-35.

K51.   Barnett, R.E. "A Frustrated Partnership: Russia's Relations with Great Britain, France and the United States during World War I," PhD diss., Texas Tech, 1990.

K52.   *Brest-Litovsk Peace Conference, Proceedings of the* (Washington, D.C., 1918).

K53.   Kerner, R.J. "Russia and the Straits Question, 1915-17," *SEER* 8 (1929-30), pp.589-600.

K54.   Kerner, R.J. "Russia, the Straits and Constantinople, 1914-15," *JMH* 1 (1929), pp.400-415.

K55.   Lieven, D. "Russia and the Origins of the First World War," *Sbornik (SGRR)* no.10 (1984), pp.13-22.

K56.   Lieven, D.C.B. *Russia and the Origins of the First World War* (London: Macmillan, 1983).

K57.   Magnes, J.L. *Russia and Germany at Brest-Litovsk. A Documentary History of the Peace Negotiations* (New York: Rand School of Social Science, 1919).

K58.   Minc, M. "The Zionist Movement and the Brest-Litovsk Negotiations in January 1918," *JFGO* 28 (1980), pp.31-61.

K59.   Nekludoff, A. *Diplomatic Reminiscences Before and During the World War, 1911-1917,* 2nd ed., trans.by A.Paget (London: John Murray, 1920).

K60.   "Pragmaticus." "The Lessons of Brest-Litovsk," *SEER* 15 (1936-37), pp.328-343.

K61.   Renzi, W.A. "Great Britain, Russia and the Straits, 1914-1915," *JMH* 42 (1970), no.1, pp.1-20.

K62.   Schilling, M.F. *How the War Began in 1914. Being the Diary of the Russian Foreign Office from the 3rd to the 20th (Old Style) of July, 1914* (London: George Allen & Unwin, 1925).

K63.   Smith, C.J. "Legacy to Stalin: Russian War Aims, 1914-1917," PhD diss., Harvard, 1953.

K64.   Smith, C.J., Jr. *The Russian Struggle for Power, 1914-1917: A Study of Russian Foreign Policy During the First World War* (New York: Philosophical Library, 1956).

K65.   Thomson, T.J. "Boris Sturmer and the Imperial Russian Government, February 2 - November 22, 1916," PhD diss., Duke, 1972.

K66.   Wade, R.A. *The Russian Search for Peace, February-October 1917* (Stanford: Stanford U.P., 1969).

K67.   Warth, R.D. *The Allies and the Russian Revolution. From the Fall of the Monarchy to the Peace of Brest-Litovsk* (Durham, N.C.: Duke U.P., 1954).

K68.   Wheeler-Bennett, J.W. *The Forgotten Peace: Brest Litovsk, March 1918* (London: Macmillan, 1938).

Provisional Government:

K69.   Anon. "Boris A. Bakhmeteff, 1880-1951," *RR* 10 (1951), no.4, pp.311-312.

K70.   Benjamin, A. "The Great Dilemma - The Foreign Policy of the Russian Provisional Government, March-May, 1917," PhD diss., Columbia, 1950.

K71.   Morris, L.P. "The Russians, the Allies and the War, February-July 1917," *SEER* 50 (1972), no.118, pp.29-48.

K72.   Savage, H.H. "Official Policies and Relations of the United States with the Provisional Government of Russia, March-November, 1917," PhD diss., Minnesota, 1971.

K73.   Wade, R.A. *The Russian Search for Peace, February-October 1917* (Stanford: Stanford U.P., 1969).

K74.   Wade, R.A. "War, Peace, and Foreign Policy During the Russian Provisional Government of 1917," PhD diss., Nebraska, 1963.

1917-21:

K75.   Bradley, J.F.N. "The Allies and Russia in the Light of French Archives (7 November 1917 - 15 March 1918)," *SS* 16 (1964), no.2, pp.166-185.

K76.   Buzinkai, D.I. "The Bolsheviks, the League of Nations and the Paris Peace Conference, 1919," *SS* 19 (1967), no.2, pp.257-263.

K77.   Chicherin, G.V. *Two Years of Foreign Policy: The Relations of the Russian Socialist Federal Soviet Republic with Foreign Nations from November 7, 1917, to November 7, 1919* (New York: Russian Soviet Government Bureau, 1920).

K78. Debo, R.K. "Litvinov and Kamenev - Ambassadors Extraordinary: The Problem of Soviet Representation Abroad," *SR* 34 (1975), no.3, pp.463-482.

K79. Debo, R.K. *Revolution and Survival: The Foreign Policy of Soviet Russia, 1917-18* (Toronto & Buffalo: University of Toronto Press, 1979).

K80. Debo, R.K. *Survival and Consolidation: the Foreign Policy of Soviet Russia, 1918-1921* (Burnaby, B.C.: McGill-Queen's, 1992).

K81. Degras, J. (ed.) *Soviet Documents on Foreign Policy: Vol.I: 1917-1924* (London, New York, Toronto: Oxford U.P., 1951).

K82. Dennis, A.L.P. *The Foreign Policies of Soviet Russia* (London: J.M.Dent, 1924).

K83. Eudin, X.J. & Fisher, H.H. *Soviet Russia and the West, 1920-1927. A Documentary Survey* (Stanford: Stanford U.P., 1957).

K84. Fischer, L. *The Soviets in World Affairs: A History of Relations Between the Soviet Union and the Rest of the World, 1917-1929* (London: Jonathan Cape, 1930).

K85. Florinsky, M.T. "Soviet Foreign Policy," *SEER* 12 (1933-34), pp.535-552.

K86. Gregor, R. "Lenin's Foreign Policy, 1917-1922: Ideology or National Interest?" PhD diss., London, 1966.

K87. Griffiths, F. "Origins of Peaceful Coexistence. A Historical Note," *Survey* no.50 (January 1964), pp.195-201.

K88. Kennan, G. *Russia and the West under Lenin and Stalin* (London: Hutchinson, 1961).

K89. Lahey, D.T. "Soviet Ideological Development of Coexistence," *CSP* 6 (1964), pp.80-94.

K90. Magerovsky, E.L. "The People's Commissariat for Foreign Affairs, 1917-1946," PhD diss., Columbia, 1975.

K91. Morse, W.P., Jr. "Leonid Borisovich Krasin: Soviet Diplomat, 1918-1920," PhD diss., Columbia, 1972.

K92. Shapiro, L. "The Soviet Union's Treaties and Agreements with Foreign Powers, 1917-1948," PhD diss., Georgetown, 1949.

K93. Slobin, N.L. "Soviet Disarmament Proposals, 1917-1935," PhD diss., Chicago, 1943.

K94. Ulam, A.B. *Expansion and Coexistence: The History of Soviet Foreign Policy, 1917-67* (New York & Washington: Frederick A. Praeger, 1968).

K95. Uldricks, T.J. *Diplomacy and Ideology: The Origins of Soviet Foreign Relations 1917-1930* (London & Beverly Hills, Calif.: Sage Publications, 1979).

K96. Uldricks, T.J. "The Development of the Soviet Diplomatic Corps, 1917-1930," PhD diss., Indiana, 1972.

K97. Uldricks, T.J. "The Soviet Diplomatic Corps in the Cicerin Era," *JFGO* 23 (1975), pp.213-224.

Russian Intelligence & Espionage Abroad:

K98.   Bradley, J.F.N. "The Russian Secret Service in the First World War," *SS* 20 (1968-69), no.2, pp.242-248.

K99.   Johnson, R.J. "The *Okhrana* Abroad, 1885-1917: A Study in International Police Cooperation," PhD diss., Columbia, 1970.

K100. Johnson, R.J. "Zagranichnaya agentura: the tsarist political police in Europe," *JCH* 7 (1972), no.1/2, pp.221-242.

K101. Kaledin, Colonel V. *K.14-O.M.66. Adventures of a Double Spy* (London: Hurst & Blackett, 1934).

K102. Senn, A.E. "Russian Emigre Funds in Switzerland 1916: An Okhrana Report," *IRSH* 13 (1968), pp.76-84.

K103. Smith, E.E. & Lednicky, R. *"The Okhrana": The Russian Department of Police* (Stanford: Hoover Institution,1967).

K104. Ulunian, A. "The Special Branch of the Russian Police: Greece and Turkey Through Intelligence Eyes (1912-14)," *Revolutionary Russia* 5 (1992), no.2, pp.209-217.

K105. Zuckerman, F.S. "The Russian Political Police at Home and Abroad (1880-1917): Its Structure, Functions, and Method and Its Struggle with the Organized Opposition," PhD diss., New York, 1973.

Foreign Intelligence & Espionage in Russia:

K106. Agar, Captain A. *Baltic Episode: A Classic of Secret Service in Russian Waters* (London: Hodder & Stoughton, 1963).

K107. Blair, D. & Dand, C.H. *Russian Hazard: The Adventures of a British Secret Service Agent in Russia* (London: Robert Hale, 1937).

K108. Debo, R.K. "Lockhart Plot or Dzerzhinskii Plot?" *JMH* 43 (1971), no.3, pp.413-439.

K109. Dukes, P. *Red Dusk and the Morrow: Adventures and Investigations in Red Russia* (London: William Heinemann, 1922).

K110. Dukes, Sir P. *The Story of "S.T.25." Adventure and Romance in the Secret Intelligence Service in Red Russia* (London: Cassell, 1938).

K111. Kaledin, Colonel V. *K.14-O.M.66. Adventures of a Double Spy* (London: Hurst & Blackett, 1934).

K112. Lockhart, R.H.B. *Memoirs of a British Agent, Being an Account of the Author's Early Life in Many Lands and of His Official Mission to Moscow in 1918* (London & New York: Putnam, 1932).

K113. Reilly, S. *The Adventures of Sidney Reilly, Britain's Master-Spy* (London: Elkin Mathews & Marrot, 1931).

K114.   Schurer, H. "Karl Moor: German Agent and Friend of Lenin," *JCH* 5 (1970), no.2, pp.131-152.

K115.   Spence, R.B. "The Terrorist and the Master Spy: the Political 'Partnership' of Boris Savinkov and Sidney Reilly, 1918-24," *Revolutionary Russia* 4 (1991), no.1, pp.111-113.

K116.   Van Der Rhoer, E. *Master Spy: A True Story of Allied Espionage in Bolshevik Russia* (New York: Charles Scribner's Sons, 1981).

K117.   Wild, M. *Secret Service on the Russian Front*, trans.by A.Haigh (London: Geoffrey Bles, 1932).

League of Nations:

K118.   Buzinkai, D.I. "Soviet-League Relations, 1919-1939: A Survey and Analysis," PhD diss., New York, 1964.

K119.   Mahaney, W.L., Jr. "The Soviets, the League, and Disarmament, 1917-1935," PhD diss., Pennsylvania, 1938.

Afghanistan:

K120.   Rader, R.R. "Decline of the Afghan Problem as a Crisis Factor in Russian Foreign Policy, 1892-1907," PhD diss., Syracuse, 1965.

K121.   Volodarsky, M. *The Soviet Union and Its Southern Neighbours: Iran and Afghanistan, 1917-1933* (London: Frank Cass, 1994).

Africa:

K122.   Kanet, R.E. "The Soviet Union and Sub-Saharan Africa: Communist Party Policy Toward Africa, 1917-1965," PhD diss., Princeton, 1966.

K123.   Rollins, P.J. "Russia's Ethiopian Adventure, 1888-1905." PhD diss., Syracuse. 1967.

The Allies:

K124.   Herzstein, D.S. "The Diplomacy of Allied Credit Advanced to Russia in World War I," PhD diss., New York, 1972.

K125.   Mathis, W.J. "The Problem of Russian Representation and Recognition at the Paris Peace Conference, 1919," PhD diss., North Carolina, 1947.

K126.   Mayer, A.J. "The Politics of Allied War Aims: The Soviet and Russian Impact March, 1917-January, 1918," PhD diss., Yale, 1954.

K127.   Morris, L.P. "The Russians, the Allies and the War, February-July 1917," *SEER* 50 (1972), no.118, pp.29-48.

K128.   Thompson, J.M. *Russia, Bolshevism, and the Versailles Peace* (Princeton: Princeton U.P., 1967).

K129.   Thompson, J.M. "The Russian Problem at the Paris Conference, 1919," PhD diss., Columbia, 1960.

K130.   Warth, R.D., Jr. "Allied Diplomacy and the Russian Revolution," PhD diss., Chicago, 1950.

Asia:

K131.   Anderson, G.W. "Russia in Middle Asia on the Eve of the First World War," PhD diss., Minnesota, 1946.

K132.   Becker, S. "Russia's Central Asian Empire, 1885-1917," in: M. Rywkin (ed.) *Russian Colonial Expansion to 1917* (London & New York: Mansell, 1988).

K133.   Gillard, D. *The Struggle for Asia, 1828-1914. A Study in British and Russian Imperialism* (London: Methuen, 1977).

K134.   Holdsworth, M. "Soviet Central Asia, 1917-1940: A Study in Colonial Policy," *SS* 3 (1951-52), no.3, pp.258-277.

K135.   Kapur, H. *Soviet Russia and Asia 1917-1927: A Study of Soviet Policy towards Turkey, Iran and Afghanistan* (Geneva: Michael Joseph, 1966 / New York: Humanities Press, 1967).

K136.   Klein, I.N. "British Imperialism in Conflict and Alliance: Anglo-French and Anglo-Russian Relations in Asia, 1885-1914," PhD diss., Columbia, 1968.

K137.   Lobanov-Rostovsky, A. *Russia and Asia* (Ann Arbor: George Wahr, 1951).

K138.   Lobanov-Rostovsky, A. "Russian Imperialism in Asia," *SEER* 8 (1929-30), pp.28-47.

K139.   Pierce, R.A. *Russian Central Asia, 1857-1917: A Study in Colonial Rule* (Berkeley & Los Angeles: University of California Press, 1960).

K140.   Spring, D.W. "Russian Imperialism in Asia in 1914," *Cahiers du Monde Russe et Sovietique* 20 (1979), nos.3-4, pp.305-322.

K141.   Williams, D.S. "Russian Policy in Central Asia in the Light of the Pahlen Report of 1908-1909," PhD diss., London, 1969.

Austria:

K142.   Head, J.A. "Russian Attitudes Toward Germany and Austria, 1909-1913," PhD diss., Texas, 1981.

Balkans:

K143.   Cowles, V. *The Russian Dagger: Cold War in the Days of the Czars* (New York & Evanston: Harper & Row, 1969).

K144.   Hoffman, J.W. "The Austro-Russian Rivalry in the Balkans, 1909-1912," PhD diss., Chicago, 1938.

K145.   Jelavich, B. *Russia's Balkan Entanglements, 1806-1914* (New York: Cambridge U.P., 1991).

K146.   Johnston, R.H. "Continuity Versus Revolution: The Russian Provisional Government and the Balkans, March-November, 1917," PhD diss., Yale, 1966.

K147.   Johnston, R.H. *Tradition Versus Revolution: Russia and the Balkans in 1917* (Boulder, Colorado: East European Quarterly, 1977. Distributed by Columbia U.P., New York).

K148.   Rossos, A. "Russia and the Balkans, 1909-1914," PhD diss., Stanford, 1971.

K149.   Rossos, A. *Russia and the Balkans: Inter-Balkan rivalries and Russian foreign policy, 1908-1914* (Toronto, Buffalo, London: University of Toronto Press, 1981).

K150.   Sontag, J.P. "Russian Diplomacy, the Balkans and Europe, 1908-1912," PhD diss., Harvard, 1967.

K151.   Thaden, E.C. *Russia and the Balkan Alliance of 1912* (University Park: Pennsylvania State U.P., 1965).

K152.   Wuest, J.J. "Diplomatic Relations Between the Soviet Union and the Balkan States from the Bolshevik Revolution to the Outbreak of the Russo-German War, With Special Reference to Communist Activities in the Balkans," PhD diss., California, 1949.

Britain:

K153.   Barnett, R.E. "A Frustrated Partnership: Russia's Relations with Great Britain, France and the United States during World War I," PhD diss., Texas Tech, 1990.

K154.   Becker, R.D. "Anglo-Russian Relations, 1898-1910," PhD diss., Colorado, 1972.

K155.   Beloff, M. *Lucien Wolf and the Anglo-Russian Entente, 1907-1914* (London: Jewish Historical Society of England, 1951).

K156.   Boyd, T.F. "Anglo-Russian Colonial Relations 1907-1914," PhD diss., Tennessee, 1973.

K157.   Churchill, R.P. "The Anglo-Russian Convention of 1907," PhD diss., Chicago, 1934.

K158.   Churchill, R.P. *The Anglo-Russian Convention of 1907* (Cedar Rapids: Torch Press, 1939).

K159.   Coates, W.P. & Zelda, K. *A History of Anglo-Soviet Relations* (London: Lawrence & Wishart, The Pilot Press, 1944).

K160.   Debo, R.K. "Prelude to Negotiations: The Problem of British Prisoners in Soviet Russia, November 1918 - July 1919," *SEER* 58 (1980), no.1, pp.58-75.

K161.   Feldman, E. "British Diplomats and British Diplomacy and the 1905 Pogroms in Russia," *SEER* 65 (1987), no.4, pp.579-608.

K162.   Horning, R.C., Jr. "Winston Churchill and British Policy Towards Russia, 1918-1919," PhD diss., George Washington, 1958.

K163.   Hughes, M. "British Diplomats in Russia on the Eve of War and Revolution," *EHQ* 24 (1994), no.3, pp.341-366.

K164.   Jones, D.R. (ed.) "Documents on British Relations with Russia, 1917-1918," *CASS* 7 (1973), no.2, pp.219-237; no.3, pp.350-375; no.4, pp.498-510; 8 (1974), no.4, pp.544-562; 9 (1975), no.3, pp.361-370; 13 (1979), no.3, pp.310-331.

K165.   Kendall, G.M. "Anglo-Russian Relations in the Middle East and the Entente of 1907," PhD diss., Clark, 1932.

K166.   Klein, I.N. "British Imperialism in Conflict and Alliance: Anglo-French and Anglo-Russian Relations in Asia, 1885-1914," PhD diss., Columbia, 1968.

K167.   Kolz, A.W.F. "British Foreign Policy and the Kolchak Government, November 1918-February 1920," PhD diss., Boston, 1965.

K168.   Lieven, D. (ed.) *British Documents on Foreign Affairs: Reports and Papers from the Foreign Office Confidential Print. Part I: From the Mid-Nineteenth Century to the First World War. Series A: Russia, 1859-1914*, 6 vols. (Frederick, Md.: University Publications of America, Inc., 1983).

K169.   Martin, T.S. "The Urquart Concession and Anglo-Soviet Relations 1921-1922," *JFGO* 20 (1972), pp.551-570.

K170.   Maude, G. "Finland in Anglo-Russian Diplomatic Relations, 1899-1910," *SEER* 48 (1970), no.113, pp.557-581.

K171.   Morren, D.G. "Donald Mackenzie Wallace and British Russophilism, 1870-1919," *CSP* 9 (1967), no.2, pp.170-183.

K172.   Murray, J.A. "British Public Opinion and the Anglo-Russian Entente, 1907-1914," PhD diss., Duke, 1957.

K173.   Nabokoff, C. *The Ordeal of a Diplomat* (London: Duckworth, 1921).

K174.   Neilson, K. *Strategy and Supply. The Anglo-Russian Alliance, 1914-17* (London: George Allen & Unwin, 1984).

K175.   Oswald, J.G. "British Public Opinion on France, the Entente Cordiale and the Anglo-Russian Entente, 1903-8," PhD diss., Edinburgh, 1976.

K176.   Pares, B. "Sir George Buchanan in Russia," *SEER* 3 (1924-25), pp.576-586.

K177.   Renzi, W.A. "Great Britain, Russia and the Straits, 1914-1915," *JMH* 42 (1970), no.1, pp.1-20.

K178.   Roley, P.L. "In Search of an Accommodation: Anglo-Soviet Relations 1919-1921," PhD diss., Illinois, 1966.

K179.   Rose, J.D. "British Foreign Policy in Relation to Transcaucasia, 1918-1921," PhD diss., Toronto, 1986.

K180.   Singh, B. "Anglo-Russian Relations in the Middle East Since 1907, With Special Reference to India," PhD diss., California, 1936.

K181.   Spring, D.W. "Anglo-Russian Relations in Persia, 1909-1915," PhD diss., London, 1968.

K182.   Spring, D.W. "The Trans-Persian Railway Project and Anglo-Russian Relations, 1909-1914," *SEER* 54 (1976), no.1, pp.60-82.

K183.   Sweet, D.W. "British Foreign Policy 1907-1909: the Elaboration of the Russian Connexion," PhD diss., Cambridge, 1972.

K184.   Tompkins, R.C. "Anglo-Russian Diplomatic Relations, 1907-1914," PhD diss., North Texas State, 1975.

K185.   Ullman, R.H. *Anglo-Soviet Relations, 1917-1921. Vol.I: Intervention and the War* (Princeton:Princeton U.P., 1961)

K186.   Ullman, R.H. *Anglo-Soviet Relations, 1917-1921. Vol.II: Britain and the Russian Civil War, November 1918-February 1920* (Princeton: Princeton U.P., 1968).

K187.   Ullman, R.H. *Anglo-Soviet Relations, 1917-1921. Vol.III: The Anglo-Soviet Accord* (Princeton: Princeton U.P., 1972)

K188.   Watt, D.C. (ed.) *British Documents on Foreign Affairs: Reports and Papers from the Foreign Office Confidential Prints. Part II: From the First to the Second World War. Series A: The Soviet Union, 1917-1939*, 5 vols. (Frederick, Md.: University Publications of America, Inc., 1984).

K189.   White, C. *British and American Commercial Relations with Soviet Russia, 1918-1924* (Chapel Hill, North Carolina: University of North Carolina Press, 1992).

K190.   White, S.L. "Anglo-Soviet Relations, 1917-24: A Study in the Politics of Diplomacy," PhD diss., Glasgow, 1973.

K191.   Whitney, H.N. "British Foreign Policy and the Russo-Japanese War," PhD diss., Pennsylvania, 1949.

K192.   Woodward, E.L. & Butler, R. (eds.) *Documents on British Foreign Policy, 1919-1939*, vols. II, III, VIII (London: H.M. Stationery Office, 1949).

Bulgaria:

K193.   Stokes, A.D. "Russo-Bulgarian Relations in the Twentieth Century," PhD diss., Cambridge, 1959.

Canada:

K194.   Davies, D. "The Pre-1917 Roots of Canadian-Soviet Relations," *Canadian Historical Review* 70 (1989), pp.180-205.

China:

K195.   Bakhmetev, B. "The Issue in Manchuria," *SEER* 8 (1929-30), pp.305-314.

K196.   Chang, T.S. "International Controversies Over the Chinese Eastern Railway," PhD diss., Iowa, 1935.

K197.   Ellemen, B.A. "The Iurin Mission to China: the Prelude to Sino-Soviet Diplomatic Relations," *The Soviet and Post-Soviet Review* 19 (1992), nos.1-3, pp.137-162.

K198.   Ewing, T.E. "Russia, China, and the Origins of the Mongolian People's Republic, 1918-1921: A Reappraisal," *SEER* 58 (1980), no.3, pp.399-421.

K199.   Leong, S. "The Soviets and China: Diplomacy and Revolution, 1917-1923," PhD diss., Harvard, 1969.

K200.   Lobanov-Rostovsky, A. "Russia and Mongolia," *SEER* 5 (1926-27), pp.515-522.

K201.   McQuilkin, D.K. "Soviet Attitudes Towards China, 1919-1927," PhD diss., Kent State, 1973.

K202.   Tuan, C.-K. "Russia and the Making of Modern China, 1900-1916," PhD diss., Princeton, 1983.

K203.   Weigh, K.S. *Russo-Chinese Diplomacy* (Shanghai: Commercial Press, 1928).

K204.   Whiting, A.S. "Soviet Policy in China: 1917-1924," PhD diss., Columbia, 1953.

Eastern Europe:

K205.   Dallin, A. (ed.) *Russian Diplomacy and Eastern Europe, 1914-1917* (New York: King's Crown Press, 1963).

K206.   Russian Institute Occasional Papers: *Russian Diplomacy in Eastern Europe, 1914-1917*, intro. by H.L.Roberts (New York: King's Crown Press, 1963).

Far East:

K207.   Edwards, E.W. "The Far-Eastern Agreements of 1907," *JMH* 26 (1954), no.4, pp.340-355.

K208.   Ewing, T.E. *Between the Hammer and the Anvil? Chinese and Russian Policies in Outer Mongolia, 1911-1921* (Bloomington: Research Institute for Inner Asian Studies, Indiana University, 1980).

K209.   Ewing, T.E. "Chinese and Russian Policies in Outer Mongolia, 1911 to 1921," PhD diss., Indiana, 1977.

K210.   Ignat'ev, A.V. "The foreign policy of Russia in the Far East at the turn of the nineteenth and twentieth centuries," in: H.Ragsdale (ed.) *Imperial Russian Foreign Policy* (Cambridge: Cambridge U.P. & Woodrow Wilson Center Press, 1993), pp.247-267.

K211.   Lensen, G.A. (compiler) *Russian Diplomatic and Consular Officials in East Asia* (Tokyo: Sophia University, in cooperation with The Diplomatic Press, Tallahassee, Fla., 1968).

K212.   Price, E.B. *The Russo-Japanese Treaties of 1907-1916 concerning Manchuria and Mongolia* (Baltimore: Johns Hopkins Press, 1933).

K213.   Quested, R.K.I. *"Matey" Imperialists? The Tsarist Russians in Manchuria, 1895-1917* (Hong Kong: University of Hong Kong, 1982).

K214.   Sumner, B.H. *Tsardom and Imperialism in the Far East and Middle East, 1880-1914* (London: Humphrey Milford, 1940).

K215.   Tang, P.S.H. *Russian and Soviet Policy in Manchuria and Outer Mongolia, 1911-1931* (Durham, N.C.: Duke U.P., 1959).

K216.   Tompkins, F.P. "American-Russian Relations in the Far East, 1914-1933: A Study of American Far Eastern Policy and Its Effect on Russian Interests," PhD diss., Fletcher, 1948.

K217.   Zabriskie, E.H. *American-Russian Rivalry in the Far East. A Study in Diplomacy and Power Politics, 1895-1914* (Philadelphia: University of Pennsylvania Press / London: Geoffrey Cumberlege/Oxford U.P., 1946).

France:

K218.   Barnett, R.E. "A Frustrated Partnership: Russia's Relations with Great Britain, France and the United States during World War I," PhD diss., Texas Tech, 1990.

K219.   Bovykin, V.I. "The Franco-Russian Alliance," *History* 64 (1979), pp.20-35.

K220.   Crisp, O. "The Financial Aspect of the Franco-Russian Alliance, 1894-1914," PhD diss., London, 1954.

K221. Golden, R. "The Chief of Staff in Diplomacy: A Study of the Conferences Between the Chiefs of Staffs of the French and Russian Armies, 1892-1914," PhD diss., Pennsylvania, 1940.

K222. Laney, F.M. "The Military Implementation of the Franco-Russian Alliance (1890-1914)," PhD diss., Virginia, 1954.

K223. Long, J. "Franco-Russian Relations during the Russo-Japanese War," *SEER* 52 (1974), no.127, pp.213-233.

K224. Long, J.W. "The Economics of the Franco-Russian Alliance, 1904-1906," PhD diss., Wisconsin, 1968.

K225. Mathieu, D.R. "The Role of Russia in French Foreign Policy, 1908-1914," PhD diss., Stanford, 1968.

K226. Michon, G. *The Franco-Russian Alliance, 1891-1917*, trans.by N.Thomas (London: George Allen & Unwin, 1929).

K227. Paleologue, M.P. *An Ambassador's Memoirs*, 3 vols., trans.by F.A.Holt, 2nd ed. (London: Hutchinson, 1923).

K228. Sinanoglou, I. "France Looks Eastward: Perspectives and Policies in Russia, 1914-1918," PhD diss., Columbia, 1974.

K229. Spring, D.W. "Russia and the Franco-Russian Alliance, 1905-14: Dependence or Interdependence?" *SEER* 66 (1988), no.4, pp.564-592.

K230. Wilcox, C.H. "The Franco-Russian Alliance, 1908-1911," PhD diss., Clark, 1968.

Germany:

K231. Bernstein, H. (ed.) *The Willy-Nicky Correspondence. Being the Secret and Intimate Telegrams Exchanged Between the Kaiser and the Tsar* (New York: Alfred A.Knopf, 1918).

K232. Debo, R.K. "The 14 November 1918 Teleprinter Conversation of Hugo Hasse with Georgii Chicherin and Karl Radek: Document and Commentary," *CASS* 14 (1980), no.4, pp.513-534.

K233. Freund, G. "Germany's Political and Military Relations with Soviet Russia," PhD diss., Oxford, 1955.

K234. Freund, G. *Unholy Alliance: Russian-German Relations from the Treaty of Brest-Litovsk to the Treaty of Berlin* (London: Chatto & Windus, 1957).

K235. Hallgarten, G.W.F. "General Hans von Seeckt and Russia, 1920-1922," *JMH* 21 (1949), no.1, pp.28-34.

K236. Head, J.A. "Russian Attitudes Toward Germany and Austria, 1909-1913," PhD diss., Texas, 1981.

K237.   Herwig, H.H. "German Policy and the Eastern Baltic Sea in 1918: Expansion or Anti-Bolshevik Crusade?" *SR* 32 (1973), no.2, pp.339-357.

K238.   Himmer, R. "Soviet Policy Toward Germany During the Russo-Polish War, 1920," *SR* 35 (1976), no.4, pp.665-682.

K239.   Himmer, G.R., Jr. "Soviet Russia's Economic Relations with Germany, 1918-1922," PhD diss., Johns Hopkins, 1972.

K240.   Jarausch, K.H. "Cooperation or Intervention? : Kurt Riezler and the Failure of German *Ostpolitik*, 1918," *SR* 31 (1972), no.2, pp.381-398.

K241.   Katkov, G. "The Assassination of Count Mirbach," *St Anthony's Papers* 12 (1962) (Soviet Affairs no.3), pp.53-93.

K242.   Kochan, L. "The Russian Road to Rapallo," *SS* 2 (1950-51), no.2, pp.109-122.

K243.   MacDonald, J.L. "Russo-German Relations, 1909-1914," PhD diss., Chicago, 1940.

K244.   Mueller, G.H. "The Road to Rapallo: Germany's Relations with Russia, 1919-1922," PhD diss., North Carolina, 1970.

K245.   Oppel, B.F. "Russo-German Relations, 1904-1906," PhD diss., Duke, 1966.

K246.   Rotter, S. "Soviet and Comintern Policy Toward Germany, 1919-1923: A Case Study of Strategy and Tactics," PhD diss., Columbia, 1954.

Greece:

K247.   Ulunian, A. "The Special Branch of the Russian Police: Greece and Turkey Through Intelligence Eyes (1912-14)," *Revolutionary Russia* 5 (1992), no.2, pp.209-217.

K248.   Zapantis, A.L. *Greek-Soviet Relations, 1917-1941* (Boulder, Colorado: East European Monographs, 1982).

India:

K249.   Imam, Z. "Soviet Russia's Policy Toward India and Its Effect on Anglo-Soviet Relations, 1917-1928," PhD diss., London, 1964.

Japan:

K250.   Berton, P.A. "The Secret Russo-Japanese Alliance of 1916," PhD diss., Columbia, 1956.

K251.   Lensen, G.A. "Japan and Tsarist Russia - the Changing Relationship, 1875-1917," *JFGO* 10 (1962), pp.337-348.

K252.   Price, E.B. "The Russo-Japanese Treaties of 1907-1916, Concerning Manchuria and Mongolia," PhD diss., Johns Hopkins, 1933.

Latin America:

K253.   Barylski, R.V. "A Political Analysis and a History of Soviet-Latin American Relations from 1917-1970," PhD diss., Harvard, 1972.

K254.   Cheston, S.T. "Diplomatic Sideshow: A Study of Soviet Relations with Latin America 1918-1936," PhD diss., Georgetown, 1972.

K255.   Miller, N.A. "Soviet Relations with Latin America, 1917-1934," PhD diss., Oxford, 1986.

Middle East:

K256.   Dinerstein, H.S. "Soviet Foreign Policy in the Near and Middle East, 1917-1923," PhD diss., Harvard, 1943.

K257.   Hopwood, D. *The Russian Presence in Syria and Palestine, 1843-1914. Church and Politics in the Near East* (Oxford: Clarendon, 1969).

K258.   Singh, B. "Anglo-Russian Relations in the Middle East Since 1907, With Special Reference to India," PhD diss., California, 1936.

K259.   Sumner, B.H. *Tsardom and Imperialism in the Far East and Middle East, 1880-1914* (London: Humphrey Milford, 1940).

Netherlands:

K260.   Debo, R.K. "Dutch-Soviet Relations, 1917-1924: The Role of Finance and Commerce in the Foreign Policy of Soviet Russia and the Netherlands," *CSS* 4 (1970), no.2, pp.199-217.

Palestine:

K261.   Stavrou, T.G. *Russian Interests in Palestine, 1882-1914: A Study of Religious and Educational Enterprise* (Thessaloniki: Institute for Balkan Studies, 1963).

Persia:

K262.   Blank, S. "Soviet Politics and the Iranian Revolution of 1919-1921," *Cahiers du Monde Russe et Sovietique* 21 (1980), no.2, pp.173-194.

K263.   Entner, M.L. "Russian and Persia, 1890-1912," PhD diss., Minnesota, 1963.

K264.   Gafford, F.H. "The Anglo-Russian Condominium in Persia, 1907-1912," PhD diss., Texas, 1940.

K265.   Kazemzadeh, F. *Russia and Britain in Persia, 1864-1914: A Study in Imperialism* (New Haven & London: Yale U.P., 1968).

K266.   Kazemzadeh, F. "Russian Imperialism and Persian Railways," *HSS* 4 (1957), pp.355-373.

K267.   Meister, I.W. "Soviet Policy in Iran, 1917-1950: A Study in Techniques," PhD diss., Fletcher, 1954.

K268.   Navran, A. "Russo-Iranian Relations, 1896-1917," PhD diss., Miami, 1986.

K269.   Nazem, H. "Russia and Great Britain in Iran (1900-1914)," PhD diss., Columbia, 1954.

K270.   Pierson, C.G. "Anglo-Russian Rivalry in Persia, 1878-1914," PhD diss., Wisconsin, 1933.

K271.   Rashidi, R.A. "Iran's Economic Relations with the Soviet Union, 1917-1968," PhD diss., Pennsylvania, 1968.

K272.   Simkin, J.E. "Anglo-Russian Relations in Persia, 1914-1921," PhD diss., London, 1978.

K273.   Volodarsky, M. *The Soviet Union and Its Southern Neighbours: Iran and Afghanistan, 1917-1933* (London: Frank Cass, 1994).

K274.   Zand, B.K. "British and Soviet Policies Toward Iran in the Period Between 1917 and 1927," PhD diss., Fordham, 1957.

Poland:

K275.   Coffey, J.I. "The Pattern of Soviet Imperialism: A Case History (Poland: 1919-1921)," PhD diss., Georgetown, 1954

K276.   Dabrowski, S. "The Peace Treaty of Riga, 1921," PhD diss., Kent State, 1968.

K277.   Gasiorowski, Z.J. "Poland's Policy towards Soviet Russia, 1921-1922," *SEER* 53 (1975), no.131, pp.230-247.

K278.   Korbel, J. *Poland Between East and West: Soviet and German Diplomacy Toward Poland, 1919-1933* (Princeton: Princeton U.P., 1963).

K279.   Wandycz, P.S. *Soviet-Polish Relations, 1917-1921* (Cambridge, Mass.: Harvard U.P., 1969).

Rumania:

K280.   McCoy, P.G. "Morgenthau's Concepts of Power, National Interest, and Ideology as
         Applied to Soviet-Rumanian Relations: 1917-1964," PhD diss., American,
         1970.

Sweden:

K281.   Luntinen, P. "The Aland Question During the Last Years of the Russian Empire," *SEER*
         54 (1976), no.4, pp.557-571.

Switzerland:

K282.   Senn, A.E. *Diplomacy and Revolution: The Soviet Mission to Switzerland, 1918* (Notre
         Dame: University of Notre Dame Press, 1974).

Turkey:

K283.   Currey, V.A. "Soviet-Turkish Relations, 1917-1922," PhD diss., Iowa, 1968.

K284.   Helmreich, E.C. (ed.) "A Proposed Russian-Turkish Agreement of 1908," *JMH* 12
         (1940), pp.510-514.

K285.   Karal, H.I. "Turkish Relations with Soviet Russia During the National Liberation War of
         Turkey, 1918-1922: A Study in the Diplomacy of the Kemalist Revolution,"
         PhD diss., California, 1967.

K286.   Ulunian, A. "The Special Branch of the Russian Police: Greece and Turkey Through
         Intelligence Eyes (1912-14)," *Revolutionary Russia* 5 (1992), no.2, pp.209-217.

United States:

K287.   Askew, W.C. "Efforts to Improve Russo-American Relations before the First World
         War: the John Hays Hammond Mission," *SEER* 31 (1952-53), pp.179-185.

K288.   Bacon, E.H. "Russo-American Relations, 1917-1921," PhD diss., Georgetown, 1951.

K289.   Barnett, R.E. "A Frustrated Partnership: Russia's Relations with Great Britain, France
         and the United States during World War I," PhD diss., Texas Tech, 1990.

K290.   Batzler, L.R. "The Development of Soviet Foreign Relations with the United States,
         1917-1939," PhD diss., Georgetown, 1956.

K291.   Cockfield, J.H. (ed.) *Dollars and Diplomacy: Ambassador David Rowland Francis and
         the Fall of Tsarism, 1916-1917* (Durham, N.C.: Duke U.P., 1981).

K292.   Cohen, I.S. "Congressional Attitudes Towards the Soviet Union, 1917-1941, " PhD diss., Chicago, 1955.

K293.   Cumming, C.K. & Pettit, W.W. (eds.) *Russian-American Relations. March, 1917 - March, 1920. Documents and Papers* (New York: Harcourt, Brace & Howe, 1920).

K294.   Davison, J.D. "Raymond Robins and United States Foreign Policy Toward Revolutionary Russia," PhD diss., Notre Dame, 1984.

K295.   Dennett, T. "Roosevelt and the Russo-Japanese War," PhD diss., Johns Hopkins, 1924.

K296.   Dennett, T. *Roosevelt and the Russo-Japanese War. A critical study of American policy in Eastern Asia in 1902-5, based primarily upon the private papers of Theodore Roosevelt* (Garden City, N.Y.: Doubleday, Page & Co., 1925).

K297.   Fike, C.E. "A Study of Russian-American Relations During the Ominous Years, 1917-1921," PhD diss., Illinois, 1950.

K298.   Fike, C.E. "The Influence of the Creel Committee and the American Red Cross on Russian-American Relations, 1917-1919," *JMH* 31 (1959), no.2, pp.93-109.

K299.   Finnegan, Rev.E.H. "The United States Policy Toward Russia, March 1917 to March 1918," PhD diss., Fordham, 1947.

K300.   Gillette, P.S. "Armand Hammer, Lenin, and the First American Concession in Soviet Russia," *SR* 40 (1981), no.3, pp.355-365.

K301.   Goodman, M.A. "The Diplomacy of Nonrecognition: Soviet American Relations 1917-1933," PhD diss., Indiana, 1972.

K302.   Grayson, B.L. *Russian-American Relations in World War I* (New York: Frederick Ungar, 1979).

K303.   Healy, A.E. "Tsarist Anti-Semitism and Russian-American Relations," *SR* 42 (1983), no.3, pp.408-425.

K304.   Kennan, G.F. *Soviet-American Relations, 1917-20. Vol.I: Russia Leaves the War* (London: Faber & Faber, 1956).

K305.   Kennan, G.F. *Soviet-American Relations, 1917-20. Vol.II: The Decision to Intervene* (London: Faber & Faber, 1958).

K306.   Killen, L.R. "The Search for a Democratic Russia: The Wilson Administration's Russian Policy 1917-1921," PhD diss., North Carolina, 1975.

K307.   Libbey, J.K. "Alexander Gumberg and Soviet-American Relations, 1917-1933," PhD diss., Kentucky, 1976.

K308.   Libbey, J.K. *Alexander Gumberg and Soviet American Relations, 1917-1933* (Lexington: University Press of Kentucky, 1977).

K309. McCoy, P.C. "An Analysis of the Debates on Recognition of the Union of Soviet Socialist Republics in the United States Senate, 1917-1934," PhD diss., Northwestern, 1954.

K310. McDuffee, R.W. "The State Department and the Russian Revolution, March-November, 1917," PhD diss., Georgetown, 1954.

K311. McFadden, D.W. *Alternative Paths: Soviets and Americans, 1917-1920* (New York & Oxford: Oxford U.P., 1993).

K312. McFadden, D.W. "Methods Short of Recognition: Soviets and Americans Search for a Relationship, 1917-1920," PhD diss., Berkeley, 1990.

K313. Marye, G.T. *Nearing the End in Imperial Russia* (London: Selwyn & Blount, 1929).

K314. May, E.R. "The Far Eastern Policy of the United States in the Period of the Russo-Japanese War: A Russian View," *AHR* 62 (1956-57), no.2, pp.345-351.

K315. Mayer, A.J. *Wilson vs. Lenin: Political Origins of the New Diplomacy, 1917-1918* (Cleveland: World Publishing Co., 1964).

K316. Meiburger, A.V. "Efforts of Raymond Robins Toward the Recognition of Soviet Russia and the Outlawry of War, 1917-1933," PhD diss., Catholic University of America, 1958.

K317. Minger, R.E. "William Howard Taft's Forgotten Visit to Russia," *RR* 22 (1963), no.2, pp.149-156.

K318. Parry, A. "Washington B. Vanderlip, the "Khan of Kamchatka"," *Pacific Historical Review* 17 (1948), pp.311-330.

K319. Parsons, E.B. "Roosevelt's Containment of the Russo-Japanese War," *Pacific Historical Review* 38 (1969), pp.21-43.

K320. Propas, F.L. "The State Department, Bureaucratic Politics and Soviet-American Relations, 1918-1938," PhD diss., California, 1982.

K321. Reitzes, R.S. "Marxist-Leninist Ideology and Soviet Policies Toward the United States 1919-1939," PhD diss., Georgetown, 1973.

K322. Salzman, N.V. *Reform and Revolution: the Life and Times of Raymond Robins* (Kent, Ohio, London: Kent State U.P., 1991).

K323. Schuman, F.L. "American Policy Toward Russia Since 1917," PhD diss., Chicago, 1927.

K324. Schuman, F.L. *American Policy Toward Russia Since 1917* (New York: International Publishers, 1928).

K325. Singer, D.G. "The United States Confronts the Soviet Union, 1919-1933: The Rise and Fall of the Policy of Non-recognition," PhD diss., Loyola, Chicago, 1973.

K326. Stamatopulos, S. "Woodrow Wilson's Russian Policy: A Case Study of American-Russian Relations, 1913-1921," PhD diss., Harvard, 1957.

K327. Stewart, E.I., Jr. "American Foreign Policy Incident to the Russo-Japanese War, 1904-1905," PhD diss., California, 1939.

K328. United States, Department of State *Papers Relating to the Foreign Relations of the United States, 1918, Russia*, 3 vols. (Washington: Government Printing Office, 1931-32).

K329. United States, Department of State *Papers Relating to the Foreign Relations of the United States, 1919, Russia* (Washington: Government Printing Office, 1937).

K330. United States, Department of State *Russian series, No.3. Documents Relating to the Organisation and Purpose of the Anti-Bolshevik Forces in Russia* (Washington: Government Printing Office, 1919).

K331. Unterberger, B.M. *The United States, Revolutionary Russia, and the Rise of Czechoslovakia* (Chapel Hill & London: University of North Carolina Press, 1989).

K332. Unterberger, B.M. "Woodrow Wilson and the Bolsheviks: The 'Acid Test' of Soviet-American Relations," *Diplomatic History* 11 (1987), no.2, pp.71-90.

K333. Walsh, W.J. "Secretary of State Robert Lansing and the Russian Revolutions of 1917," PhD diss., Georgetown, 1986.

K334. Weeks, C.J., Jr. *An American Naval Diplomat in Revolutionary Russia: The Life and Times of Vice Admiral Newton A. McCully* (Annapolis, MD: Naval Institute Press, 1993).

K335. White, C. *British and American Commercial Relations with Soviet Russia, 1918-1924* (Chapel Hill, North Carolina: University of North Carolina Press, 1992).

K336. Williams, W.A. "Raymond Robins and Russian-American Relations, 1917-1938," PhD diss., Wisconsin, 1951.

K337. Zabriskie, E.H. "American-Russian Rivalry in the Far East from 1895-1914," PhD diss., Chicago, 1943.

The Vatican:

K338. Hull, H.L. "The Holy Sea and Soviet Russia, 1918-1930: A Study in Full-Circle Diplomacy," Georgetown, 1970.

K339. Zatko, J.J. "The Vatican and Famine Relief in Russia," *SEER* 42 (1963-64), no.98, pp.54-63.

L

MAIN NON-RUSSIAN NATIONALITIES AND REGIONAL IDENTITIES

General:

L1.   Blank, S. "The Bolshevik Party and the Nationalities in 1917: Reflections on the Origin of the Multi-National Soviet State," *Sbornik (SGRR)* no.9 (1987), pp.9-14.

L2.   Blank, S.J. "The Unknown Commissariat: The Soviet Commissariat of Nationalities, Narkomnats, 1917-1924," PhD diss., Chicago, 1979.

L3.   Conolly, V. "The 'nationalities question' in the last phase of tsardom," in G.Katkov et al (eds.) *Russia Enters the Twentieth Century, 1894-1917* (London: Temple Smith, 1971), pp.152-181.

L4.   Eudin, X.J. "Soviet National Minority Policies 1918-1921," *SEER* 21 (1943), pp.31-55.

L5.   Ezergailis, A. "The Nationalities Question in Bolshevik Ideology," *Bulletin of Baltic Studies* 5 (1971), pp.3-19.

L6.   Great Britain. Foreign Office *Russian Poland, Lithuania and White Russia* (Handbooks Prepared Under the Direction of the Historical Section of the Foreign Office, No.44. London, 1930).

L7.   Hardy, E.N. "The Russian Soviet Federated Socialist Republic: The Role of Nationality in Its Creation, 1917-1922," PhD diss., California, 1955.

L8.   Jones, S. "The Non-Russian nationalities," in: R.Service (ed.) *Society and Politics in the Russian Revolution* (Basingstoke & London: Macmillan, 1992), pp.35-63.

L9.   Lowe, H.-D. "Russian Nationalism and Tsarist Nationalities Policies in Semi-Constitutional Russia, 1905-1914," in: R.B.McKean (ed.) *New Perspectives in Modern Russian History* (Basingstoke & London: Macmillan, 1992), pp.250-277.

L10.   Petrus, J.A. "Marxism and Marxists and the National Question," PhD diss., Texas, 1965.

L11.   Pipes, R. *The Formation of the Soviet Union: Communism and Nationalism, 1917-1923*, revised ed. (Cambridge, Mass.: Harvard U.P., 1964).

L12.   Pipes, R.E. "The Genesis of Soviet Nationality Policy," PhD diss., Harvard, 1950.

L13.   Slezkine, Y. "Russia's Small Peoples: The Policies and Attitudes towards the Native Northerners, 17th Century-1938," PhD diss., Texas, 1989.

L14.   Smith, C.J., Jr. "Miljukov and the Russian National Question," *HSS* 4 (1957), pp.395-419.

L15.   Steinberg, A.K. "The Kholm Question in the Russian Duma Period, 1906-1912: Opinion and Action," PhD diss., Kent State, 1972.

L16.   Stetten, N. "The National Question and the Russian Civil War, 1917-1921," PhD diss., Chicago, 1977.

L17.   Stojko, W. "The Attitude of the Russian Provisional Government Toward the Non-Russian Peoples of Its Empire," PhD diss., New York, 1969.

L18.   Suny, R.G. "Nationalism and Class in the Russian Revolution: a Comparative Discussion," in: E.R.Frankel et al (eds.) *Revolution in Russia: Reassessments of 1917* (Cambridge: Cambridge U.P., 1992), pp.219-246.

L19.   Usary, S.S. "From Cosmopolitanism to Nationalism: An Introspective History of Marxian Theories of Nationalism and Supranationalism," PhD diss., Tulane, 1983.

Armenia:

L20.   Arslanian, A.H. "British Wartime Pledges, 1917-18: The Armenian Case," *JCH* 13 (1978), no.3, pp.517-529.

L21.   Davison, R.H. "The Armenian Crisis, 1912-1914," *AHR* 53 (1947-48), no.3, pp.481-505.

L22.   Hovannisian, R.G. "Armenia on the Road to Independence, 1918," PhD diss., California, 1966.

L23.   Hovannisian, R.G. *Armenia on the Road to Independence, 1918* (Berkeley & Los Angeles: University of California Press, 1967).

L24.   Hovannisian, R.G. "Dimensions of Democracy and Authority in Caucasian Armenia, 1917-1920," *RR* 33 (1974), no.1, pp.37-49.

L25.   Hovannisian, R.G. "Russian Armenia. A Century of Tsarist Rule," *JFGO* 19 (1971), pp.31-48.

L26.   Hovannisian, R. "The Allies and Armenia, 1915-18," *JCH* 3 (1968), no.1, pp.145-168.

L27.   Hovannisian, R.G. *The Republic of Armenia: The First Year, 1918-1919* (Berkeley: University of California Press, 1971).

L28.   Hovannisian, R.G. *The Republic of Armenia: From Versailles to London, 1919-1920* (Berkeley: University of California Press, 1982).

L29.   Nassibian, A. "Britain and the Armenian Question, 1915-1923," PhD diss., Oxford, 1981.

L30.   Nassibian, A. *Britain and the Armenian Question, 1915-1923* (London & Sydney: Croom Helm / New York: St.Martin's Press, 1984).

L31.   Suny, R.G. *Armenia in the Twentieth Century* (Chico, California: Scholars Press, 1983).

L32.   Suny, R.G. (ed.) *Transcaucasia: Nationalism and Social Change. Essays in the History of Armenia, Azerbaijan, and Georgia* (Ann Arbor: Michigan Slavic Publications, 1983).

L33.   Terzian, M. "The Armenian Minority Problem (1914-1934)," PhD diss., Pennsylvania, 1934.

L34.   Torry, G.H. "Armenia and the Great Powers, 1919-1921," PhD diss., Oregon, 1954.

L35.   Wee, M. "Great Britain and the Armenian Question, 1878-1914," PhD diss., Wisconsin, 1939.

Azerbaidjan:

L36.   Altstadt-Mirhadi, A.L. "The Azerbaijani Turkish Community of Baku Before World War I," PhD diss., Chicago, 1983.

L37.   Suny, R.G. *The Baku Commune, 1917-1918: Class and Nationality in the Russian Revolution* (Princeton: Princeton University Press, 1972).

L38.   Suny, R.G. "The Baku Commune, 1917-1918: Political Strategy in a Social Revolution," PhD diss., Columbia, 1968.

L39.   Suny, R.G. (ed.) *Transcaucasia: Nationalism and Social Change. Essays in the History of Armenia, Azerbaijan, and Georgia* (Ann Arbor: Michigan Slavic Publications, 1983).

L40.   Swietochowski, T. *Russian Azerbaijan, 1905-1920: The Shaping of National Identity in a Muslim Community* (Cambridge: Cambridge University Press, 1985).

L41.   Swietochowski, T. "The Himmat Party: Socialism and the National Question in Russian Azerbaijan, 1904-1920," *Cahiers du Monde Russe et Sovietique* 19 (1978), nos.1-2, pp.119-142.

Baltics:

L42.   Buchan, J. (ed.) *The Baltic and Caucasian States* (Boston: Houghton-Mifflin Co., 1923).

L43.   Hiden, J. "From War to Peace: Britain, Germany and the Baltic States 1918-1921," *Journal of Baltic Studies* 19 (1988), no.4, pp.371-382.

L44.   Hiden, J. & Salmon, P. *The Baltic Nations and Europe: Estonia, Latvia and Lithuania in the Twentieth Century* (New York: Longman, 1991).

L45.   Hale, R. *The Baltic Provinces* (U.S. Senate Document No.105. 66th Congress, 1st Session. Washington D.C., 1919)

L46.   Hinkkanen-Lievonen, M.-L. *British Trade and Enterprise in the Baltic States, 1919-1925* (Helsinki: Finnish Historical Society, 1984).

L47.   Page, S.W. "Lenin, the National Question, and the Baltic States, 1917-1919," *ASEER* 7 (1948), no.1, pp.15-31.

L48.   Page, S.W. "The Formation of the Baltic States (Lithuania, Latvia, Estonia) 1917-1920," PhD diss., Harvard, 1940.

L49.   Raun, T.U. "The Revolution of 1905 in the Baltic Provinces and Finland," *SR* 43 (1984), no.3, pp.453-467.

L50.   Tarulis, A.N. *American-Baltic Relations, 1918-1922: The Struggle Over Recognition* (Washington: Catholic University of America Press, 1965).

L51.   Thaden, E.C. (ed.) *Russification in the Baltic Provinces and Finland, 1855-1914* (Princeton: Princeton U.P., 1981).

L52.   Trapans, J.A. "The West and the Recognition of the Baltic States: 1919 and 1991. A Study of the Politics of the Major Powers," *Journal of Baltic Studies* 25 (1994), no.2, pp.153-173.

L53.   Von Rauch, G. *The Baltic States: The Years of Independence: Estonia, Latvia, Lithuania, 1917-1940*, trans.by G.Onn (Berkeley and Los Angeles: University of California Press, 1974).

L54.   White, J.D. "Latvian and Lithuanian Sections in the Bolshevik Party on the Eve of the February Revolution," *Revolutionary Russia* 3 (1990), pp.90-106.

Bashkir Republic:

L55.   Pipes, R.E. "The First Experiment in Soviet National Policy: The Bashkir Republic, 1917-1920," *RR* 9 (1950), no.4, pp.309-319.

Belorussia:

L56.   Lubachko, I. "Belorussia under Soviet Rule, 1917-1939," PhD diss., Indiana, 1964.

L57.   Lubachko, I.S. *Belorussia under Soviet Rule, 1917-1957* (Lexington: University Press of Kentucky, 1972).

L58.   Vakar, N.P. *Belorussia. The Making of a Nation. A Case Study* (Cambridge, Mass.: Harvard U.P., 1956).

L59.   Zaprudnik, J. "Political Struggle for Byelorussia in the Tsarist State Dumas, 1906-1917," PhD diss., New York, 1969.

Caucasus:

L60.   Allen, W.E.D. & Muratoff, P. *Caucasian Battlefields: A History of the Wars on the Turco-Caucasian Border, 1828-1921* (Cambridge: Cambridge U.P., 1953).

L61.   Avalov, Z. "The Caucasus since 1918," *SEER* 3 (1924-25), pp.320-336.

L62.   Bennigsen, A. "The Bolshevik Conquest of the Moslem Borderlands," *Studies on the Soviet Union* 11 (1971), no.4, pp.61-70 [also printed in T.T.Hammond (ed.) *The Anatomy of Communist Takeovers* (New Haven & London: Yale U.P., 1975].

L63.   Biggart, J. "The Astrakhan Rebellion: An Episode in the Career of Sergey Mironovitch Kirov," *SEER* 54 (1976), no.2, pp.231-247.

L64.   Buchan, J. (ed.) *The Baltic and Caucasian States* (Boston: Houghton-Mifflin Co., 1923).

Central Asia:

L65.   A Correspondent "The Revolt in Transcaspia, 1918-1919," *Central Asian Review* 7 (1959), pp.117-130.

L66.   Becker, S. "Russia's Central Asian Protectorates: Bukhara and Khiva, 1865-1917," PhD diss., Harvard, 1963.

L67.   Becker, S. *Russia's Protectorates in Central Asia: Bukhara and Khiva, 1865-1924* (Cambridge, Mass.: Harvard U.P., 1968).

L68.   Bennigsen, A. "The Bolshevik Conquest of the Moslem Borderlands," *Studies on the Soviet Union* 11 (1971), no.4, pp.61-70 [also printed in T.T.Hammond (ed.) *The Anatomy of Communist Takeovers* (New Haven & London: Yale U.P., 1975].

L69.   Braker, H. "The Muslim revival in Russia," in G.Katkov et al (eds.) *Russia Enters the Twentieth Century, 1894-1917* (London: Temple Smith, 1971), pp.182-198.

L70.   D'Encausse, H.C. *Islam and the Russian Empire: Reform and Revolution in Central Asia* (Berkeley: University of California Press, 1988).

L71.   Inoiatov, Kh.-Sh. & Landa, L.M. "Soviet Historiography of the October Revolution in Central Asia," *SSH* 6 (1967-68), no.3, pp.3-26.

L72.   Park, A.G. "Soviet Nationality Policy, 1917-1921: A Study of Bolshevik Doctrine and Practice with Special Reference to Central Asia," PhD diss., Columbia, 1953.

L73.   Pierce, R.A. "Toward Soviet Power in Tashkent, February-October 1917," *CSP* 17 (1975), no.2/3, pp.261-269.

L74.   Sokol, E.D. *The Revolt of 1916 in Russian Central Asia* (Baltimore: Johns Hopkins Press, 1954).

L75.   Zenkovsky, S.A. "'Kulturkampf' in Pre-Revolutionary Central Asia," *ASEER* 14 (1955), pp.15-41.

L76.   Zenkovsky, S.A. *Pan-Turkism and Islam in Russia* (Cambridge, Mass.: Harvard U.P., 1960).

Cossacks:

L77.   Cresson, W.P. *The Cossacks. Their History and Country* (New York: Brentano's, 1919).

L78.   Efremoff, I.N. *The Cossacks of the Don* (Paris: Imp. L.Fournier, 1919).

L79.   Gehrmann, U. "Germany and the Cossack Community in the Russian Revolution, April-November 1918," *Revolutionary Russia* 5 (1992), no.2, pp.147-171.

L80.   Janke, A.E. "Don Cossacks and the February Revolution," *CSP* 10 (1968), no.2, pp.148-165.

L81.   Janke, A.E. "The Don Cossacks on the Road to Independence," *CSP* 12 (1970), no.3, pp.273-294.

L82.   Korff, S.A. *The Constitution of the Cossacks* (Paris: L.Fournier, 1919).

L83.   La Chesnais, P.G. *The Defense of the Cossacks Against Bolshevism* (Paris: L.Fournier, 1919).

L84.   Longworth, P. *The Cossacks* (London: Constable, 1969).

L85.   McNeal, R.H. *Tsar and Cossack, 1855-1914* (London: Macmillan, 1987).

L86.   Tschebotarioff, G.P. "The Cossacks and the Revolution of 1917," *RR* 20 (1961), no.3, pp.206-216.

Crimean Tatars:

L87.   Kirimli, H. "The "Young Tatar" Movement in the Crimea, 1905-1909," *Cahiers du Monde Russe et Sovietique* 34 (1993), no.4, pp.529-560.

L88.   Kirimli, S.H. "National Movements and National Identity among the Crimean Tatars (1905-1916)," PhD diss., Wisconsin, 1990.

Estonia:

L89.   Arens, O. "Revolutionary Developments in Estonia in 1917-18 and Their Ideological and Political Background," PhD diss., Columbia, 1976.

L90.   Forgus, S.P. "Estonian Nationalism and Primary Education, 1860-1905," PhD diss., Illinois, 1974.

L91.   Forgus, S.P. "Soviet Subversive Activities in Independent Estonia, 1918-1940," *Journal of Baltic Studies* 23 (1992), no.1, pp.29-46.

L92.   Lipping, I. "Land Reform Legislation in Estonia and the Disestablishment of the Baltic German Rural Elite, 1919-1939," PhD diss., Maryland, 1980.

L93.   Parming, T. "The Pattern of Participation of the Estonian Communist Party in National Politics, 1918-1940," *SEER* 59 (1981), no.3, pp.397-412.

L94.   Raun, T.U. "Estonian Emigration within the Russian Empire 1860-1917," *Journal of Baltic Studies* 17 (1986), pp.350-363.

L95.   Raun, T.U. "Finland and Estonia: Cultural and Political Relations, 1917-40," *Journal of Baltic Studies* 18 (1987), no.1, pp.5-20.

L96.   Raun, T.U. "The Estonians and the Russian Empire, 1905-1917," *Journal of Baltic Studies* 15 (1984), pp.130-140.

L97.   Raun, T.U. "The Petseri Region of the Republic of Estonia," *JFGO* 39 (1991), pp.514-532.

L98.   Raun, T.U. "The Revolution of 1905 and the Movement for Estonian National Autonomy, 1896-1907," PhD diss., Princeton, 1969.

Finland:

L99.   Alapuro, R. *State and Revolution in Finland* (Berkeley, Los Angeles, & London: University of California Press, 1988).

L100.   Borodkin, M. *Finland. Its Place in the Russian State* (St.Petersburg: J.Ehrlich, 1911).

L101.   Churchill, S. "The East Karelian Autonomy Question in Finnish-Soviet Relations, 1917-1922," PhD diss., London, 1967.

L102.   Feodoroff, E. [Fedorov] *The Finnish Revolution In Preparation, 1889-1905, as disclosed by secret documents*, trans.by G.Dobson (St Petersburg: Imprimerie Russo-Francaise, 1911).

L103.   Graham, M.W. *The Diplomatic Recognition of the Border States. Part I: Finland* (Publications of the University of California at Los Angeles in Social Sciences, vol.2, 1933).

L104.   Hamalainen, P.K. "Revolution, Civil War and Ethnic Relations: The Case of Finland," *Journal of Baltic Studies* 5 (1974), no.2, pp.117-125.

L105.   Hannula, Lt.-Colonel J.O. *Finland's War of Independence* (London: Faber, 1939).

L106.   Harmaja, L. *Effects of the War on Economic and Social Life in Finland* (New Haven: Yale U.P., 1933).

L107.   Hodgson, J.H. *Communism in Finland: A History and Interpretation* (Princeton: Princeton U.P., 1967).

L108.   Jackson, J.H. "German Intervention in Finland, 1918," *SEER* 18 (1939), no.52, pp.93-101.

L109.   Jussila, O. "Finland and the Russian Duma," *Journal of Baltic Studies* 19 (1988), no.3, pp.241-148.

L110.   Jutikkala, E. & Pirinen, K. *A History of Finland*, trans.by P.Sjoblom (London: Thames & Hudson, 1962. Revised ed. Heinemann, 1974).

L111.   Keynas, W. "Soviet Russia and Eastern Carelia," *SEER* 6 (1927-28), pp.520-528.

L112.   Kirby, D.G. (ed.) *Finland and Russia, 1808-1920: From Autonomy to Independence. A Selection of Documents* (London: Macmillan, 1975).

L113.   Kirby, D.G. *Finland in the Twentieth Century* (Minneapolis: University of Minnesota Press, 1979).

L114.   Kirby, D. "New Wine in Old Vessels? The Finnish Socialist Workers' Party, 1919-1923," *SEER* 66 (1988), no.3, pp.426-425.

L115.   Kirby, D. "Stockholm-Petrograd-Berlin: International Social Democracy and Finnish Independence, 1917," *SEER* 52 (1974), no.126, pp.63-84.

L116.   Kirby, D. "The Finnish Social Democratic Party and the Bolsheviks," *JCH* 7 (1972), no.1/2, pp.181-198 [reprinted in *JCH* 11 (1976), no.2/3, pp.99-113].

L117.   Kirby, D. ""The Workers' Cause": Rank-and-File Attitudes and Opinions in the Finnish Social Democratic Party 1905-1918," *Past and Present* no.111 (1986), pp.130-164.

L118.   Kujala, A. "Finnish Radicals and the Russian Revolutionary Movement, 1899-1907," *Revolutionary Russia* 5 (1992), no.2, pp.172-192.

L119.   Laine, E.W. "Finland's Road from Autonomy to Integration in the Russian Empire, 1808-1910," PhD diss., McGill, 1974.

L120.   Martin, W.C. "A Sociological and Analytic Study of the Development of the Finnish Revolution of 1917-1918 in Terms of Social Structures," PhD diss., Vanderbilt, 1971.

L121.   Pachmuss, T. *A Moving River of Tears: Russia's Experience in Finland* (New York, San Francisco, Bern: Peter Lang, 1992).

L122.   Puntila, L.A. *The Political History of Finland, 1809-1966*, trans.by D.Miller (London: Heinemann. 1975).

L123. Raun, T.U. "Finland and Estonia: Cultural and Political Relations, 1917-40," *Journal of Baltic Studies* 18 (1987), no.1, pp.5-20.

L124. Raun, T.U. "The Revolution of 1905 in the Baltic Provinces and Finland," *SR* 43 (1984), no.3, pp.453-467.

L125. Smith, C.J., Jr. "Russia and the Origins of the Finnish Civil War of 1918," *ASEER* 14 (1955), pp.481-502.

L126. Smith, C.J. *Finland and the Russian Revolution, 1917-1922* (Athens, Georgia: University of Georgia Press, 1958).

L127. Smith, C.J. "Soviet Russia and the Red Revolution of 1918 in Finland," *Studies on the Soviet Union* 11 (1971), no.4, pp.71-93. [Same article also published in T.T.Hammond (ed.) *The Anatomy of Communist Takeovers* (New Haven & London: Yale U.P., 1975)].

L128. Upton, A.F. *The Finnish Revolution, 1917-1918* (Minneapolis: University of Minnesota Press, 1980).

L129. Waldron, P. "Stolypin and Finland," *SEER* 63 (1985), no.1, pp.41-55.

L130. Warner, O. *Marshal Mannerheim and the Finns* (London: Weidenfeld & Nicolson, 1967).

L131. Wuorinen, J.H. *A History of Finland* (New York & London: Columbia U.P., 1965).

Georgia:

L132. Avalishvili, Z. *The Independence of Georgia in International Politics, 1918-1921* (London: Headley Brothers, 1940).

L133. Jones, S.F. "Georgian Social Democracy, 1892-1921: In Opposition and In Power," PhD diss., London, 1984.

L134. Jones, S.F. "Georgian Social Democracy in 1917," in: E.R.Frankel et al (eds.) *Revolution in Russia: Reassessments of 1917* (Cambridge: Cambridge U.P., 1992), pp.247-273.

L135. Jones, S.F. "The Beginnings of Georgian Social Democracy," *Sbornik (SGRR)* nos.6-7 (1981), pp.22-45.

L136. Kautsky, K. *Georgia, a Social-Democratic Peasant Republic*, trans.by H.J.Stenning (London: International Bookshops, 1921).

L137. Megrian, L.D. "Tiflis During the Russian Revolution of 1905," PhD diss., California, 1968.

L138. Ogden, D. "Britain and Soviet Georgia, 1921-22," *JCH* 23 (1988), no.2, pp.245-258.

L139. Parsons, J.W.R. "The Emergence and Development of the National Question in Georgia, 1801-1921," PhD diss., Glasgow, 1987.

L140. Shafir, I.M. (ed.) *Secrets of Menshevik Georgia: the Plot Against Soviet Russia Unmasked: Documents* (London: Communist Party of Great Britain, 1922).

L141. Suny, R.G. *The Making of the Georgian Nation* (Bloomington & Indianapolis: Indiana U.P., in association with Hoover Institution Press, Stanford University, 1988).

L142. Suny, R.G. (ed.) *Transcaucasia: Nationalism and Social Change. Essays in the History of Armenia, Azerbaijan, and Georgia* (Ann Arbor: Michigan Slavic Publications, 1983).

L143. Trotskii, L.D. *Between Red and White: A Study of Some Fundamental Questions of Revolution, with Particular Reference to Georgia* (London: Communist Party of Great Britain, 1922).

Germans in Russia:

L144. Fleischhauer, I. "The Ethnic Germans in the Russian Revolution," in: E.R. Frankel et al (eds.) *Revolution in Russia: Reassessments of 1917* (Cambridge: Cambridge U.P., 1992), pp.274-284.

L145. Henriksson, A. "Nationalism, Assimilation and Identity in Late Imperial Russia: The St.Petersburg Germans, 1906-1914," *RR* 52 (1993), no.3, pp.341-353.

L146. Long, J.W. "The Volga Germans and the Famine of 1921," *RR* 51 (1992), no.4, pp.510-525.

L147. Long, J.W. "The Volga Germans of Saratov Province between Reform and Revolution, 1861-1905," in: R.A.Wade & S.J.Seregny (eds.) *Politics and Society in Provincial Russia: Saratov, 1590-1917* (Columbia, Ohio: Ohio State U.P., 1989), pp.139-159.

L148. Rempel, D.G. "The Expropriation of the German Colonists in South Russia During the Great War," *JMH* 4 (1932), pp.49-67.

Jews:

L149. Abramowitz, R. "The Jews Under the Tsars and Commissars: The History and Culture of Russian Jewry," PhD diss., Miami, 1975.

L150. Abramson, H. "Jewish Representation in the Independent Ukrainian Governments of 1917-1920," *SR* 50 (1991), no.3, pp.542-549.

L151. Baron, S.W. *The Russian Jew Under Tsars and Soviets*, 2nd ed. (New York & London: Macmillan/Collier, 1976).

L152. Corrsin, S.D. "Language Use in Cultural and Political Change in Pre-1914 Warsaw: Poles, Jews and Russification," *SEER* 68 (1990), no.1, pp.69-90.

L153. Frankel, J. *Prophecy and Politics: Socialism, Nationalism, and the Russian Jews, 1862-1917* (Cambridge & New York: Cambridge U.P., 1981).

L154. Frankel, J. "Socialism and Jewish Nationalism in Russia, 1892-1907," PhD diss., Cambridge, 1962.

L155. Gitelman, Z.Y. *Jewish Nationality and Soviet Politics. The Jewish Sections of the CPSU, 1917-1930* (Princeton: Princeton U.P., 1972).

L156. Greenbaum, A.A. "Soviet Jewry During the Lenin-Stalin Period," Part I *SS* 16 (1965), no.4, pp.406-421; Part II *SS* 17 (1965), no.1, pp.84-92.

L157. Greenberg, L.S. *The Jews in Russia. The Struggle for Emancipation*, 2 vols. (New Haven: Yale U.P., 1944, 1951).

L158. Harcave, S.S. "Jewish Political Parties and Groups and the Russian State Dumas from 1905-1907," PhD diss., Chicago, 1943.

L159. Harcave, S. "The Jews and the First Russian National Election," *ASEER* 9 (1950), no.1, pp.33-41.

L160. Heifetz, E. *The Slaughter of the Jews in the Ukraine in 1919* (New York: Seltzer, 1921).

L161. Heilbronner, H. "Count Aehrenthal and Russian Jewry, 1903-1907," *JMH* 38 (1966), no.4, pp.394-406.

L162. Joubert, C. *Russia as it Really Is*, 7th ed. (London: Eveleigh Nash, 1905).

L163. Kenez, P. "Pogroms and White ideology in the Russian Civil War," in: J.D.Klier & S.Lambroza (eds.) *Pogroms: Anti-Jewish Violence in Modern Russian History* (Cambridge: Cambridge U.P., 1992), pp.293-313.

L164. Klier, J.D. "The Concept of 'Jewish Emancipation' in a Russian Context," in: O.Crisp & L.Edmondson (eds.) *Civil Rights in Imperial Russia* (Oxford: Clarendon, 1989), pp.121-144.

L165. Klier, J.D. & Lambroza, S. (eds.) *Pogroms: Anti-Jewish Violence in Modern Russian History* (Cambridge: Cambridge U.P., 1992).

L166. Kochan, L. (ed.) *The Jews in Soviet Russia since 1917* (London: Oxford U.P., 1970).

L167. Lambroza, S. "Jewish Self-Defense During the Russian Pogroms of 1903-1906," *Jewish Journal of Sociology* (1981), no.2, pp.123-134.

L168. Lambroza, S. "The Pogrom Movement in Tsarist Russia, 1903-1906," PhD diss., Rutgers, 1981.

L169. Lambroza, S. "The pogroms of 1903-1906," in: J.D.Klier & S.Lambroza (eds.) *Pogroms: Anti-Jewish Violence in Modern Russian History* (Cambridge: Cambridge U.P., 1992), pp.195-247.

L170. Leikin, E. *The Beilis Transcripts: The Anti-Semitic Trial that Shook the World* (Northvale, N.J. & London: Aronson, 1993).

L171. Lindemann, A.S. *The Jew Accused: Three Anti-Semitic Affairs (Dreyfus, Beilis, Frank), 1894-1915* (Cambridge: Cambridge U.P., 1991).

L172. Lipset, H. "Jewish Schools in the Soviet Union, 1917-1941: An Aspect of Soviet Minorities Policy," PhD diss., Columbia, 1965.

L173. Lowe, H.-D. *The Tsars and the Jews: Reform, Reaction and Anti-Semitism in Imperial Russia, 1772-1917* (Switzerland: Harwood Academic Publishers, 1993).

L174. Mendelsohn, E. *Class Struggle in the Pale: The Formative Years of the Jewish Workers' Movement in Tsarist Russia* (Cambridge: Cambridge U.P., 1970).

L175. Nedava, J. "Trotsky and the Jewish Question," PhD diss., Pennsylvania, 1970.

L176. Patkin, A.L. *The Origins of the Russian-Jewish Labour Movement* (Melbourne & London: F.W.Cheshire, 1947).

L177. Peled, Y. "Class, Nation, and Culture: The Debate Over Jewish Nationality in the Russian Revolutionary Movement, 1893-1906," PhD diss., California, 1982.

L178. Rogger, H. "Russian Ministers and the Jewish Question, 1881-1917," *California Slavic Studies* 8 (1975), pp.15-76.

L179. Rogger, H. "The Beilis Case: Anti-Semitism and Politics in the Reign of Nicholas II," *SR* 25 (1966), no.4, pp.615-629.

L180. Rogger, H. "The Jewish Policy of Late Tsarism: A Reappraisal," *Wiener Bulletin* (1971), nos.11-12, pp.42-51

L181. Samuel, M. *Blood Accusation. The Strange History of the Beiliss Case* (New York: Alfred A.Knopf, 1966).

L182. Schapiro, L. "The Role of the Jews in the Russian Revolutionary Movement," *SEER* 40 (1961-62), pp.148-167.

L183. Szajkowski, Z. *Jews, War, and Communism. Vol.1: The Attitude of American Jews to World War I, the Russian Revolutions of 1917, and Communism (1914-1945)* (New York: KTAV Publishing House, 1972).

L184. Tager, A.B. *The Decay of Czarism: The Beiliss Trial. A contribution to the history of the political reaction during the last years of Russian Czarism* (Philadelphia: Jewish Publication Society of America, 1935).

L185. Urussov, S.D. *Memoirs of a Russian Governor*, trans.by H.Rosenthal (London & New York: Harper, 1908).

L186. Weinberg, R. "The pogroms of 1905 in Odessa: a case study," in: J.D.Klier & S.Lambroza (eds.) *Pogroms: Anti-Jewish Violence in Modern Russian History* (Cambridge: Cambridge U.P., 1992), pp.248-289.

L187. Weinberg, R. "Workers, Pogroms, and the 1905 Revolution in Odessa," *RR* 46 (1987), no.1, pp.53-75.

L188. Wolf, L. (ed.) *The Legal Sufferings of the Jews in Russia. A Survey of Their Present Situation, and a Summary of Laws* (London: T.Fisher Unwin, 1912).

L189.   Yarmolinsky, A. *The Jews and Other Minor Nationalities Under the Soviets* (New York: Vanguard, 1928).

L190.   Yodfat, A. "The Jewish Question in American-Russian Relations, 1875-1917," PhD diss., American, 1963.

Kazakhstan:

L191.   Cherot, R.A. "Nativization of Government and Party Structure in Kazakhstan, 1920-1930," *ASEER* 14 (1955), pp.42-58.

L192.   Demko, G.J. "The Russian Colonization of Kazakhstan, 1896-1916," PhD diss., Pennsylvania State, 1964.

L193.   Demko, G.J. *The Russian Colonization of Kazakhstan, 1896-1916* (The Hague: Mouton, 1969).

L194.   Lane, D. "Ethnic and Class Stratification in Soviet Kazakhstan, 1917-39," *Comparative Studies in Society and History* 17 (1975), pp.165-189.

Latvia:

L195.   Bilmanis, A. *A History of Latvia* (Princeton: Princeton U.P., 1951).

L196.   Butkus, Z. "Great Britain's Mediation in Establishing the Lithuanian-Latvian Frontier, 1920-21," *Journal of Baltic Studies* 24 (1993), no.4, pp.359-368.

L197.   Champonnois, S. "Colonel Emmanuel du Parquet's Mission in Latvia 1919-1920," *Journal of Baltic Studies* 23 (1992), no.4, pp.325-340.

L198.   Ezergailis, A. "1917 in Latvia: The Bolshevik Year," *Canadian Slavic Studies* 3 (1969), no.4, pp.646-662.

L199.   Ezergailis, A. "The Bolshevik Revolution in Latvia, March to August 1917," PhD diss., New York, 1968.

L200.   Ezergailis, A. "The Bolshevization of the Latvian Social Democratic Party," *Canadian Slavic Studies* 1 (1967), no.2, pp.238-252.

L201.   Ezergailis, A. "The Latvian 'Autonomy' Conference of 30th July 1917," *Journal of Baltic Studies* 8 (1977), pp.162-171.

L202.   Ezergailis, A. *The Latvian Impact on the Bolshevik Revolution. The First Phase: September 1917 to April 1918* (New York: Columbia U.P., 1983).

L203.   Ezergailis, A. *The 1917 Revolution in Latvia* (New York & London: Columbia U.P., 1974).

L204.   Ezergailis, A. "The October Insurrection in Latvia: a Chronology," *Journal of Baltic Studies* 3 (1972), no.3-4, pp.218-228.

L205.   Ezergailis, A. "The Thirteenth Conference of the Latvian Social Democrats, 1917: Bolshevik Strategy Victorious," in: R.C.Elwood (ed.) *Reconsiderations on the Russian Revolution* (Cambridge, Mass.: Slavica, 1976), pp.133-153.

L206.   Germanis, U. "The Idea of Independent Latvia and Its Development in 1917," in: A.Sprudzs & A.Rusis (eds.) *Res Baltica: A Collection of Essays in Honor of the Memory of Dr. Alfred Bilmanis (1887-1948)* (Leyden: A.W.Sijthoff, 1968), pp.27-87.

L207.   Hamm, M.F. "Riga's 1913 City Election: A Study in Baltic Urban Politics," *RR* 39 (1980), no.4, pp.442-461.

L208.   Henriksson, A. "The Riga German Community: Social Change and the Nationality Question, 1860-1905," PhD diss., Toronto, 1978.

L209.   Henriksson, A. *The Tsar's Loyal Germans. The Riga Community: Social Change and the Nationality Question, 1855-1905* (Boulder, Colorado: *East European Quarterly*, 1983).

L210.   Hiden, J. "Baltic Gold and Latvian Privatisation," *Journal of Baltic Studies* 23 (1992), no.1, pp.63-72.

L211.   Jansen, M. "International Class Solidarity or Foreign Intervention? Internationalists and Latvian Rifles in the Russian Revolution and the Civil War," *IRSH* 31 (1986), pp.68-79.

L212.   Kalnins, B. "The Social Democratic Movement in Latvia," in: A.Rabinowitch et al (eds.) *Revolution and Politics in Russia: Essays in Memory of B.I.Nicolaevsky* (Bloomington: Indiana U.P., 1972), pp.134-156.

L213.   Page, S.W. "Lenin and Peasant 'Bolshevism' in Latvia, 1903-1915," *Journal of Baltic Studies* 3 (1972), no.2, pp.95-112.

L214.   Page, S.W. "Lenin's April Theses and the Latvian Peasant-Soldiery," in: R.C.Elwood (ed.) *Reconsiderations on the Russian Revolution* (Cambridge, Mass.: Slavica, 1976), pp.154-172.

L215.   Page, S.W. "Social and National Currents in Latvia, 1860-1917," *ASEER* 8 (1949), no.1, pp.25-36.

L216.   Page, S.W. & Ezergailis, A. "The Lenin-Latvian Axis in the November Seizure of Power," *CSP* 19 (1977), no.1, pp.32-49.

L217.   Rodgers, H.I. "The Search for Security in the Baltic: Dilemmas of Latvian Diplomacy, 1919-1934," PhD diss., Texas, 1968.

L218.   Sedricks, A. "The Metamorphosis of the Antins Character in Latvian Drama: 1909-1973," PhD diss., Southern Illinois, 1977.

L219.   Watson, H.A.G. *The Latvian Republic: The Struggle for Freedom* (New York: Hillary House, 1965).

L220. Wildman, A.K. "The Bolsheviks of the Twelfth Army and Latvian Social Democracy," in:R.C.Elwood *Reconsiderations on the Russian Revolution* (Cambridge, Mass.: Slavica, 1976), pp.173-183.

L221. Zile, Z.L. "Legal Thought and the Formation of Law and Legal Institutions in the Socialist Republic of Latvia 1917-20," *Journal of Baltic Studies* 8 (1977), no.3, pp.195-204.

Lithuania:

L222. Aleksandravicius, E. "Political Goals of Lithuanians, 1863-1918," *Journal of Baltic Studies* 23 (1992), no.3, pp.227-238.

L223. Bielskis, J.J. (ed.) *Lithuania: Facts Supporting Her Claims for Reestablishment as an Independent Nation* (Washington D.C., 1918).

L224. Butkus, Z. "Great Britain's Mediation in Establishing the Lithuanian-Latvian Frontier, 1920-21," *Journal of Baltic Studies* 24 (1993), no.4, pp.359-368.

L225. Cadzow, J.F. "The Lithuanian Question in the Third State Duma," PhD diss., Kent State, 1972.

L226. Demm, E. "The Propaganda of Juozas Gabrys for Lithuania before 1914," *Journal of Baltic Studies* 21 (1990), no.2, pp.121-130.

L227. Lopata, R. "Lithuanian-Polish Cooperation in 1918: The Ronikier-Voldemaras Treaty," *Journal of Baltic Studies* 24 (1993), no.4, pp.349-358.

L228. Meyer-Benedictsen, A. *Lithuania: "The Awakening of a Nation"* (Copenhagen: E.H.Petersen, 1924).

L229. Senn, A.E. "Comparing the Circumstances of Lithuanian Independence, 1918-1922 and 1988-1992," *Journal of Baltic Studies* 25 (1994), no.2, pp.123-130.

L230. Senn, A.E. "Garlawa: A Study in Emigre Intrigue, 1915-1917," *SEER* 45 (1966), pp.411-424.

L231. Senn, A.E. *Jonas Basanavicius: The Patriarch of the Lithuanian National Resistance* (Newtonville, Mass.: Oriental Research Partners, 1980).

L232. Senn, A.E. "On the State of Central Lithuania," *JFGO* 12 (1964), pp.366-374.

L233. Senn, A.E. *The Emergence of Modern Lithuania* (New York: Columbia U.P., 1959).

L234. Senn, A.E. "The Foreign Relations of the Provisional Government of Lithuania, 1918-1920," PhD diss., Columbia, 1957.

L235. Stukas, J.J. "The Rise of Modern Lithuanian Nationalism," PhD diss., New York, 1965.

L236. Urbaniak, G. "Lithomania versus Panpolonism: The Roots of the Polish-Lithuanian Conflict before 1914," *CSP* 31 (1989), no.2, pp.107-127.

L237.   White, J.D. "The Revolution in Lithuania 1918-19," *SS* 23 (1971), no.2, pp.186-200.

Outer Mongolia:

L238.   Hammond, T.T. "The Communist Takeover of Outer Mongolia: Model for Eastern Europe?" *Studies on the Soviet Union* 11 (1971), no.4, pp.107-144 [same article also in: T.T.Hammond (ed.) *The Anatomy of Communist Takeovers* (New Haven & London: Yale U.P., 1975)].

L239.   Isono, F. "Soviet Russia and the Mongolian Revolution of 1921," *Past and Present* no.83 (1979), pp.116-140.

Poland:

L240.   Biskupski, M.B. "The Poles, the Root Mission and the Russian Provisional Government 1917," *SEER* 63 (1985), no.1, pp.56-68.

L241.   Biskupski, M.B. "Paderewski, Polish Politics, and the Battle of Warsaw, 1920," *SR* 46 (1987), no.3/4, pp.503-512.

L242.   Bryant, F.R. "Britain and the Polish Settlement, 1919," PhD diss., Oxford, 1969.

L243.   Chmielewski, E. *The Polish Question in the Russian State Duma* (Knoxville: University of Tennessee Press, 1970).

L244.   Corrsin, S.D. "Language Use in Cultural and Political Change in Pre-1914 Warsaw: Poles, Jews and Russification," *SEER* 68 (1990), no.1, pp.69-90.

L245.   Cottam, K.J. "Boleslaw Limanowski, a Polish Theoretician of Agrarian Socialism," *SEER* 51 (1973), no.122, pp.58-74.

L246.   Cottam, K.J. *Boleslaw Limanowski (1835-1935): A Study in Socialism and Nationalism* (Boulder: East European Quarterly / Columbia U.P., 1978).

L247.   Davies, N. "Great Britain and the Polish Jews, 1918-20," *JCH* 8 (1973), no.2, pp.119-142.

L248.   Davies, N. "Lloyd George and Poland 1919-20," *JCH* 6 (1971), no.3, pp.132-154.

L249.   Davies, N. "The Poles in Great Britain 1914-1919," *SEER* 50 (1972), no.118, pp.63-89.

L250.   Dziewanowski, M.K. "World War I and the Marxist Movement of Poland," *ASEER* 12 (1953), no.1, pp.72-92.

L251.   Dziewanowski, M.K. *Joseph Pilsudski: A European Federalist, 1918-1922* (Stanford: Hoover Institution Press, 1969).

L252.   Dziewanowski, M.K. "The Making of a Federalist," *JFGO* 11 (1963), pp.543-560.

L253.   Dziewanowski, M.K. "The Polish Revolutionary Movement and Russia, 1904-1907," *HSS* 4 (1957), pp.375-394.

L254.   Fountain, A.M., II. "Roman Dmowski: Party, Tactics, Ideology, 1895-1907," PhD diss., Columbia, 1976.

L255.   Groth, A.J. "Dmowski, Pilsudski and Ethnic Conflict in Pre-1939 Poland," *Canadian Slavic Studies* 3 (1969), no.1, pp.69-91.

L256.   Iivonen, J.K. "Independence or Incorporation? The Idea of Poland's National Self-Determination and Independence within the Russian and Soviet Socialism from the 1870s to the 1920s," PhD diss., Helsingen Yliopisto (Finland), 1990.

L257.   Janus, G.A. "The Polish Kolo, the Russian Duma, and the Question of Polish Autonomy," PhD diss., Ohio State, 1971

L258.   Jasienica, P. "The Polish Experience," *JCH* 13 (1968), no.4, pp.73-88.

L259.   Kapica, Rev.W.J. "Major Socio-Political Movements and Catholicism in Partitioned Poland, 1885-1914," PhD diss., Catholic, 1968.

L260.   Kar, A.L. "The Response of the People to the Use of Formal Education in the Attempted Denationalization of Poland, 1795-1914," PhD diss., Michigan, 1955.

L261.   Kutrzeba, S. "Political and Economic Progress in Poland," *SEER* 1 (1922-23), pp.277-294.

L262.   Latawski, P. (ed.) *The Reconstruction of Poland, 1914-23* (Basingstoke & London: Macmillan, 1992).

L263.   Lerner, W. "Attempting a Revolution from Without: Poland in 1920," *Studies on the Soviet Union* 11 (1971), no.4, pp.94-106.

L264.   Lewis, R.D. "The Labor Movement in Russian Poland in the Revolution of 1905-1907," PhD diss., California, Berkeley, 1971.

L265.   Lopata, R. "Lithuanian-Polish Cooperation in 1918: The Ronikier-Voldemaras Treaty," *Journal of Baltic Studies* 24 (1993), no.4, pp.349-358.

L266.   McKercher, B.J.C. "The Paths of Reason and Peace: Esme Howard's Unpublished Manuscript on 'Paderewski. Musician - Patriot - Statesman'," *JFGO* 41 (1993), pp.81-100.

L267.   Michaels, A.J. "Neoslavism and Its Attempt at Russo-Polish Rapprochement, 1908-1910," PhD diss., American, 1956.

L268.   Mueller, L.A. "The Triumph of Polish Nationalism and the Re-establishment of the Polish State with Special Emphasis on Posnania and Pomerania," PhD diss., Western Reserve, 1960.

L269.   Murdzek, B.P. "Population Movements in the Polish Provinces of Prussia, Russia and Austria, 1870-1914: Policies and Attitudes," PhD diss., American, 1960.

L270.   Narkiewicz, O.A. *The Green Flag. Polish Populist Politics, 1867-1970* (London: Croom Helm, 1976).

L271.   Penson, J.H. "Labour Conditions in Modern Poland," *SEER* 1 (1922-23), pp.572-583.

L272.   Pidhaini, O.S. *The Ukrainian-Polish Problem in the Dissolution of the Russian Empire, 1914-1917* (Toronto & New York: New Review Books, 1962).

L273.   Piltz, E. (ed.) *Poland. Her People, History, Industries, Finance, Science, Literature, Art, and Social Development* (London: Herbert Jenkins, 1909).

L274.   Poliakov, V. "Pilsudski," *SEER* 14 (1935-36), pp.44-52.

L275.   Rose, W.J. "Paderewski - A Tribute," *SEER* 24 (1946), no.63, pp.66-80.

L276.   Rose, W.J. "Wincenty Witos," *SEER* 25 (1946-47), no.64, pp.39-54.

L277.   Senn, A.E. "The Entente and the Polish Question, 1914-1916," *JFGO* 25 (1977), pp.21-33.

L278.   Skirmunt, C. "Poland," *SEER* 1 (1922-23), pp.273-276.

L279.   Slomka, J. *From Serfdom to Self-Government: Memoirs of a Polish Village Mayor, 1842-1927*, trans.by W.J.Rose (London: Minerva, 1941).

L280.   Steinberg, A.K. "The Kholm Question in the Russian Duma Period, 1906-1912: Opinion and Action," PhD diss., Kent State, 1972.

L281.   Stone, B.B. "Nationalist and International Currents in Polish Socialism: the PPS and SDKPIL, 1893-1921," PhD diss., Chicago, 1965.

L282.   Urbaniak, G. "Lithomania versus Panpolonism: The Roots of the Polish-Lithuanian Conflict before 1914," *CSP* 31 (1989), no.2, pp.107-127.

L283.   Wandycz, P.S. "Secret Soviet-Polish Peace Talks in 1919," *SR* 24 (1965), no.3, pp.425-449.

L284.   Wandycz, P.S. *Soviet-Polish Relations, 1917-1921* (Cambridge, Mass.: Harvard U.P., 1969).

L285.   Wandycz, P.S. *The Lands of Partitioned Poland, 1795-1918* (Seattle & London: University of Washington Press).

L286.   Weeks, T.R. "Defining Us and Them: Poles and Russians in the 'Western Provinces', 1863-1914," *SR* 53 (1994), no.1, pp.26-40.

L287.   Weeks, T.R. "Nationality and Municipality: Reforming City Government in the Kingdom of Poland, 1904-1915," *RH* 21 (1994), no.1, pp.23-47.

L288.   Wojtun, B.S. "Demographic Transition in West Poland, 1816-1914," PhD diss., Pennsylvania, 1968.

L289.   Zarnowska, A. "Religion and Politics: Polish Workers c.1900," *Social History* 16 (1991), no.3, pp.299-316.

Siberia:

L290.   Baikalov, A.V. "Siberia Since 1894," *SEER* 11 (1932-33), pp.328-340.

L291.   Baranov, E.A. "The Trans-Siberian and Urban Change in Siberia in a Time-Space Framework: 1885-1913," PhD diss., Kansas, 1987.

L292.   Collins, D.N. "Kabinet, Forest and Revolution in the Siberian Altai to May 1918," *Revolutionary Russia* 4 (1991), no.1, pp.1-27.

L293.   Nansen, F. *Through Siberia, the Land of the Future*, trans.by A.G.Chater (London: Heinemann, 1914).

L294.   Pereira, N.G.O. "Lenin and the Siberian Peasant Insurrections," in: G.Diment & Y.Slezkine (eds.) *Between Heaven and Hell: The Myth of Siberia in Russian Culture* (New York: St.Martin's Press, 1993), pp.133-150.

L295.   Pereira, N.G.O. "Regional Consciousness in Siberia before and after October 1917," *CSP* 30 (1988), no.1, pp.112-133.

L296.   Pereira, N.G.O. "The Idea of Siberian Regionalism in Late Imperial and Revolutionary Russia," *RH* 20 (1993), nos.1-4, pp.163-178.

L297.   Poppe, N. "The economic and cultural development of Siberia," in G.Katkov et al (eds.) *Russia Enters the Twentieth Century, 1894-1917* (London: Temple Smith, 1971), pp.138-151.

L298.   Treadgold, D.W. *The Great Siberian Migration: Government and Peasant in Resettlement from Emancipation to the First World War* (Princeton: Princeton U.P., 1957).

L299.   Varneck, E. "Siberian Native Peoples after the February Revolution," *SEER* 21 (1942-44), pp.70-88.

L300.   Watrous, S. "The Regionalist Conception of Siberia, 1860-1920," in: G.Diment & Y.Slezkine (eds.) *Between Heaven and Hell: The Myth of Siberia in Russian Culture* (New York: St.Martin's Press, 1993), pp.113-132.

L301.   Wright, R.L. & Digby, B. *Through Siberia: An Empire in the Making* (London: Hurst & Blackett, 1913).

Turkestan:

L302.   Allworth, E. "The Search for Group Identity in Turkistan, March 1917-September 1922," *CASS* 17 (1983), no.4, pp.487-502.

L303.   MacKenzie, D. "Turkestan's Significance to Russia (1850-1917)," *RR* 33 (1974), no.2, pp.167-188.

L304.   Olcott, M.B. "The Basmachi or Freemen's Revolt in Turkestan 1918-24," *SS* 33 (1981), no.3, pp.352-369.

L305.   Park, A.G. *Bolshevism in Turkistan, 1917-1927* (New York: Columbia U.P., 1957).

L306.   Skallerup, T.M. "Artisans between Guilds and Cooperatives: A History of Social and Economic Change in Russian Turkestan and Soviet Central Asia, 1865-1928," PhD diss., Indiana, 1990.

L307.   Yaroshevski, D. "Russian regionalism in Turkestan," *SEER* 65 (1987), no.1, pp.77-100.

Ukraine:

L308.   Abramson, H. "Jewish Representation in the Independent Ukrainian Governments of 1917-1920," *SR* 50 (1991), no.3, pp.542-549.

L309.   Adams, A.E. "The Awakening of the Ukraine," *SR* 22 (1963), no.2, pp.217-223.

L310.   Adams, A.E. "The Bolsheviks and the Ukrainian Front in 1918-19," *SEER* 36 (1957-58), pp.396-417.

L311.   Adams, A. *The Bolsheviks in the Ukraine: the Second Campaign, 1918-1919* (New Haven: Yale U.P., 1963).

L312.   Bociurkiw, B.R. "The Rise of the Ukrainian Autocephalous Church, 1919-22," in: G.A. Hosking (ed.) *Church, Nation and State in Russia and Ukraine* (Basingstoke & London, 1991), pp.228-249.

L313.   Bojcun, J.M. "The Working Class and the National Question in Ukraine, 1880-1920," PhD diss., York, 1985.

L314.   Borys, J. *The Sovietization of Ukraine, 1917-1923: The Communist Doctrine and Practice of National Self-Determination* (Edmonton: Canadian Institute of Ukrainian Studies, 1980).

L315.   Borys, J. "Who Ruled the Soviet Ukraine in Stalin's Time? (1917-1939)," *CSP* (1972), no.2, pp.213-233.

L316.   Boshyk, G.Y. "The Rise of Ukrainian Political Parties in Russia, with Special Reference to Social Democracy, 1900-1907," PhD diss., Oxford, 1981.

L317.   Chirovsky, Fr.N.L. *An Introduction to Ukrainian History, vol.III: Nineteenth and Twentieth Century Ukraine* (New York: Philosophical Library, 1986).

L318.   Dmytryshijn, B. "Moscow and the Ukraine, 1918-1953: A Study of Russian Bolshevik Nationality Policy," PhD diss., California, 1955.

L319.   Dnistrianskii, S. *Ukraine and the Peace Conference* (Berlin: Ukrainian Delegation, 1919).

L320.   Doroshenko, D. *The Ukrainian Hetman State of 1918* (Winnipeg, 1973).

L321.   Edelman, R.S. "Rural Proletarians and Peasant Disturbances: The Right Bank Ukraine in the Revolution of 1905," *JMH* 57 (1985), no.2, pp.248-277.

L322.   Eudin, X.J. "The German Occupation of the Ukraine in 1918: A documentary account," *RR* 1 (1941-42), no.1, pp.90-105.

L323.   Fedyshyn, O.S. "German Plans and Policies in the Ukraine and the Crimea, 1917-1918," PhD diss., Columbia, 1962.

L324.   Fedyshyn, O.S. *Germany's Drive to the East and the Ukrainian Revolution, 1917-1918* (New Brunswick, N.J.: Rutgers U.P., 1971).

L325. Guthier, S.L. "The Popular Base of Ukrainian Nationalism in 1917," *SR* 38 (1979), no.1, pp.30-47.

L326. Guthier, S.L. "The Roots of Popular Ukrainian Nationalism: A Demographic, Social and Political Study of the Ukrainian Nationality to 1917," PhD diss., Michigan, 1990.

L327. Hoffman, J.H. "The Ukraine Adventure of the Central Powers, 1914-1918," PhD diss., Pittsburgh, 1967.

L328. Hoffman, J.H. "V.Stepankovsky, Ukrainian Nationalist and German Agent," *SEER* 50 (1972), no.121, pp.594-602.

L329. Hunczak, T. (ed.) *The Ukraine, 1917-1921: A Study in Revolution* (Cambridge, Mass.: Harvard U.P., 1977).

L330. Kappeler, A. "The Ukrainians of the Russian Empire, 1860-1914," in: A.Kappeler (ed.) *The Formation of National Elites* (Aldershot: Dartmouth; New York: New York U.P., 1992), pp.105-132.

L331. Krawchenko, B. *Social Change and National Consciousness in Twentieth-Century Ukraine* (London: Macmillan / St.Anthony's College, Oxford, 1985).

L332. Kulchycky, G.P. "The Ukrainian Insurgent Movement, 1919 to 1926," PhD diss., Georgetown, 1970.

L333. Lukasz, E. "Ukraine at the Paris Peace Conference, 1919," PhD diss., Chicago, 1963.

L334. Luther, M.M. "The Birth of Soviet Ukraine," PhD diss., Columbia, 1962.

L335. Mace, J.E. "Communism and the Dilemma of National Liberation: National Communism in Soviet Ukraine, 1918-1933," PhD diss., Michigan, 1981.

L336. Mace, J.E. *Communism and the Dilemmas of National Liberation: National Communism in Soviet Ukraine, 1918-1933* (Cambridge, Mass.: Harvard Ukrainian Research Institute, 1983).

L337. Mazlakh, S. & Shakhrai, V. *On the Current Situation in the Ukraine*, trans.by P.J.Potichnyj (Ann Arbor: University of Michigan Press, 1970 [originally published in 1919]).

L338. Meyer, M.C. "Germans in the Ukraine, 1918," *ASEER* 9 (1950), no.2, pp.105-115.

L339. Motyl, A.J. "Viacheslav Lypyns'kyi and the Ideology and Politics of Ukrainian Monarchism," *CSP* 27 (1985), no.1, pp.31-48.

L340. Paneyko, B. "The Conditions of Ukrainian Independence, *SEER* 2 (1923-24), pp.336-345.

L341. Pidhainy, A.S. "The Formation of the Communist Party (Bolsheviks) of Ukraine," PhD diss., McGill, 1978.

L342. Pidhainy, O.S. "The Formation of the Ukrainian Republic in the First World War, 1917-1918," PhD diss., McGill, 1966.

L343.   Pidhainy, O.S. *The Formation of the Ukrainian Republic* (Toronto: New Review Books, 1966).

L344.   Pidhaini, O.S. *The Ukrainian-Polish Problem in the Dissolution of the Russian Empire, 1914-1917* (Toronto & New York: New Review Books, 1962).

L345.   Prociuk, S.G. "Russian Intervention in Early Ukrainian Economic Planning," *SS* 15 (1964), no.4, pp.443-458.

L346.   Rakowsky, J. "Franco-British Policy Toward the Ukrainian Revolution, March, 1917 to February, 1918," PhD diss., Case Western Reserve, 1974.

L347.   Reshetar, J.S. "Ukrainian Nationalism and the Orthodox Church," *ASEER* 10 (1951), no.1, pp.38-49.

L348.   Reshetar, J. *The Ukrainian Revolution, 1917-1920: A Study in Nationalism* (Princeton: Princeton U.P., 1952).

L349.   Reshetar, J.S., Jr. "The Ukrainian Revolution in Retrospect," *CSP* 10 (1968), no.2, pp.116-132.

L350.   Reshetar, J.S. "Ukraine and Revolution (1917-1920)," PhD diss., Harvard, 1950.

L351.   Saunders, D. "Britain and the Ukrainian Question (1912-1920)," *English Historical Review* 103 (1988), pp.40-68.

L352.   Shulgin, A. "Mykhailo Hrushevsky (1866-1934)," *SEER* 14 (1935-36), pp.176-181.

L353.   Solchanyk, R. "The Comintern and the Communist Party of Western Ukraine, 1919-1928," *CSP* 23 (1981), no.2, pp.181-197.

L354.   Solchanyk, R. "The Communist Party of Western Ukraine, 1919-1938," PhD diss., Michigan, 1973.

L355.   Stachiw, M., Stercho, P.G., Chirovskyy, N.L.F., Yuzyk, P. & Stachiw, J.L. *Ukraine and the European Turmoil, 1917-1919*, 2 vols. (New York: Shevchenko Scientific Society, 1973).

L356.   Stotsky, R.S. "Simon Petlyura," *SEER* 5 (1926-27), no.13, pp.154-156.

L357.   Sullivant, R.S. *Soviet Politics and the Ukraine, 1917-1957* (New York & London: Columbia U.P., 1962).

L358.   Sullivant, R.S. "Soviet Politics in the Ukraine, 1917-1957," PhD diss., Chicago, 1958.

L359.   Voskobiynyk, M.H. "The Nationalities Question in Russia in 1905-1907: A Study in the Origin of Nationalism, with Special Reference to the Ukrainians," PhD diss., Pennsylvania, 1972.

L360.   West Ukrainian People's Republic *The Book of Bloody Cruelties: Returns Concerning the Invasion of the Poles into the Ukrainian Territory of Galicia in 1918-1919* (Vienna: H.Engel, 1919 [Hoover Library]).

M

ECONOMIC

General:

M1.   Anon. "Economic Notes," *SEER* 1 (1922-23), pp.241-243.

M2.   Anon. "Economic Notes - Notes on Russian Industry," *SEER* 1 (1922-23), pp.659-663.

M3.   Bailes, K.E. "Alexei Gastev and the Soviet Controversy Over Taylorism, 1918-24," *SS* 29 (1977), no.3, pp.373-394.

M4.   Balzer, H.D. "Educating Engineers: Economic Politics and Technical Training in Tsarist Russia," PhD diss., Pennsylvania, 1980.

M5.   Blackwell, W.L. *The Industrialization of Russia: An Historical Perspective* (New York: Thomas Y. Crowell, 1970).

M6.   Borovoi, S.Ia. "On the Economic Ties Between the Top Capitalists and Tsarism in the Imperial Period," *SSH* 11 (1970-71), no.4, pp.300-321.

M7.   Bowman, L. "Russia's First Income Taxes: The Effects of Modernized Taxes on Commerce and Industry, 1885-1914," *SR* 52 (1993), no.2, pp.256-282.

M8.   Carson, G.B. "The State and Economic Development: Russia, 1890-1939," in: H.Aitken (ed.) *The State and Economic Growth* (New York: Social Science Research Council, 1959), pp.115-147.

M9.   Crisp, O. *Studies in the Russian Economy before 1914* (London: Macmillan, 1976).

M10.   Davenport, R.W. "Soviet Economic Relations with Iran, 1917-1930," PhD diss., Columbia, 1954.

M11.   Davies, R.W. (ed.) *From Tsarism to the New Economic Policy: Continuity and Change in the Economy of the USSR* (Basingstoke & London: Macmillan, 1990).

M12.   Davies, R.W., Harrison, M., & Wheatcroft, S.G. (eds.) *The Economic Transformation of the Soviet Union, 1913-1945* (Cambridge: Cambridge U.P., 1994).

M13.   Edmondson, L. & Waldron, P. (eds.) *Economy and Society in Russia and the Soviet Union, 1860-1930* (Basingstoke & London: Macmillan, 1992).

M14.   Gatrell, P.W. *Government, industry, and rearmament in Russia, 1900-1914: the last argument of tsarism* (Cambridge: Cambridge U.P., 1994).

M15.   Gatrell, P.W. "Russian Heavy Industry and State Defence 1908-1918: Pre-War Expansion and Wartime Mobilization," PhD diss., Cambridge, 1979.

M16.   Gatrell, P. *The Tsarist Economy, 1850-1917* (New York: St.Martin's Press, 1986).

M17.   Gerschenkron, A. *Continuity in History and Other Essays* (Cambridge, Mass.: Belknap Press of Harvard U.P., 1968).

M18.   Gohstand, R. "The Internal Geography of Trade in Moscow from the Mid-Nineteenth Century to the First World War," PhD diss., California, Berkeley, 1973.

M19.   Goldsmith, R.W. "The Economic Growth of Tsarist Russia 1860-1913," *Economic Development and Cultural Change* 9 (1961), no.3, pp.441-475.

M20.   Gregory, P. "Economic Growth and Structural Change in Tsarist Russia: A Case of Modern Economic Growth?" *SS* 23 (1972), no.3, pp.418-434.

M21.   Gregory, P.R. *Before Command: An Economic History of Russia from Emancipation to the First Five Year Plan* (Princeton: Princeton U.P., 1994).

M22.   Gregory, P.R. "1913 Russian National Income - Some Insights into Russian Economic Development," *Quarterly Journal of Economics* 90 (August 1976), no.3, pp.445-459.

M23.   Gulley, H.E. "Railways and the Seaborne Grain Export Trade in Tsarist Russia, 1861-1914," PhD diss., London, 1988.

M24.   Guroff, G. & Carstensen, F.V. (eds.) *Entrepreneurship in Imperial Russia and the Soviet Union* (Princeton: Princeton U.P., 1983).

M25.   Himmer, G.R., Jr. "Soviet Russia's Economic Relations with Germany, 1918-1922," PhD diss., Johns Hopkins, 1972.

M26.   Jones, R.H. "Taylorism and the Scientific Organization of Work in Russia, 1910-1925," PhD diss., Sussex, 1988.

M27.   Kohlenberg, G.C. "Russian-American Economic Relations, 1906-1917," PhD diss., Illinois, 1951.

M28.   Kohn, S. *The Cost of the War to Russia* (New Haven: Yale U.P., 1932).

M29.   Kowal, L.M. "The Economic Doctrines of M.I. Tugan-Baranovsky," PhD diss., Illinois, 1965.

M30.   Krypton, C. *The Northern Sea Route: Its Place in Russian Economic History before 1917* (New York: Research Program on the U.S.S.R., 1953).

M31. Lyashchenko, P.I. *History of the National Economy of Russia to the 1917 Revolution*, trans.by L.M.Herman (New York: Macmillan, 1949).

M32. McCaffray, S.P. "The New Work and the Old Regime Workers, Managers and the State in the Coal and Steel Industry of Ekaterinoslav Province, 1905-1914," PhD diss., Duke, 1983

M33. Mavor, J. *An Economic History of Russia*, 2 vols., 2nd ed. (New York: Russell & Russell, 1965).

M34. Miller, M.S. "The Economic Development of Russia, 1905-14," PhD diss., London, 1925.

M35. Miller, M.S. *The Economic Development of Russia, 1905-1914, with Special Reference to Trade, Industry, and Finance* (London: P.S.King, 1926).

M36. Nolde, Baron B.E. *Russia in the Economic War* (New Haven: Yale U.P., 1928).

M37. Nove, A. *An Economic History of the U.S.S.R.* (Baltimore: Penguin, 1969).

M38. Owen, T.C. *The Corporation under Russian Law, 1800-1917: A Study in Tsarist Economic Policy* (Cambridge & New York: Cambridge U.P., 1992).

M39. Owen, T.C. "The Population Ecology of Corporations in the Russian Empire, 1700-1914," *SR* 50 (1991), no.4, pp.807-826.

M40. Pratt, J.K. "The Russian Free Economic Society, 1765-1915," PhD diss., Missouri, 1983.

M41. Rashidi, R.A. "Iran's Economic Relations with the Soviet Union, 1917-1968," PhD diss., Pennsylvania, 1968.

M42. Rogger, H. "*Amerikanizm* and the Economic Development of Russia," *Comparative Studies in Society and History* 23 (1981), pp.382-420.

M43. Shoemaker, M.W. "Russo-German Economic Relations, 1850-1914," PhD diss., Syracuse, 1979.

M44. Skallerup, T.M. "Artisans between Guilds and Cooperatives: A History of Social and Economic Change in Russian Turkestan and Soviet Central Asia, 1865-1928," PhD diss., Indiana, 1990.

M45. Sontag, J.P. & Gregory, P.R. "Foreign Trade and Tsarist Policy Before World War I: An Exchange," *SR* 40 (1981), no.2, pp.264-268.

M46. Thalheim, K.C. "Russia's economic development," in: G.Katkov et al (eds.) *Russia Enters the Twentieth Century, 1894-1917* (London: Temple Smith, 1971), pp.85-110.

M47. Thiede, R.L. "Town and Function in Tsarist Russia: A Geographical Analysis of Trade and Industry in the Towns of New Russia, 1860-1910," PhD diss., Washington, Seattle, 1970.

M48. Tuve, J.E. "Changing Directions in Russian-American Economic Relations, 1912-1917," *SR* 31 (1972), no.1, pp.52-70.

General 1917-21:

M49.   Beable, W.H. *Commercial Russia* (London: Constable, 1918).

M50.   Buchanan, H.R. "Soviet Economic Policy for the Transition Period: The Supreme Council of the National Economy, 1917-1920," PhD diss., Indiana, 1972.

M51.   Canadian Department of Trade and Commerce *Report of the Canadian Economic Commission (Siberia)* (Ottawa: King's Printer, 1919).

M52.   Chossudowsky, E.M. "Soviet Trade and Distribution, 1917-1937: the Growth of a Planned Consumption," PhD diss., Edinburgh, 1940.

M53.   Cohen, S.F. "In Praise of War Communism: Bukharin's "The Economics of the Transition Period"," in: A.Rabinowitch et al (eds.) *Revolution and Politics in Russia: Essays in Memory of B.I.Nicolaevsky* (Bloomington: Indiana U.P., 1972), pp.192-203.

M54.   Dewar, M. *Labour Policy in the USSR, 1917-1928* (London & New York: Royal Institute of International Affairs / Oxford U.P., 1956).

M55.   Dobb, M. *Russian Economic Development Since the Revolution* (London: George Routledge, 1928).

M56.   Dobb, M. *Soviet Economic Development Since 1917* (London: Routledge & Kegan Paul, 1948).

M57.   Draper, F.D. "The 'Crisis in Capitalism' and Soviet/Bloc Commercial Relations with the Industrialized West, 1917-1967," PhD diss., Catholic, 1970.

M58.   Fallenbuchl, Z.M. "Economic Policy of the Period of Transition from Capitalism to Socialism," *CSP* 9 (1967), no.2, pp.245-269.

M59.   Fithian, F.J. "Soviet-American Economic Relations 1918-1933: American Business in Russia During the Period of Nonrecognition," PhD diss., Nebraska, 1964.

M60.   Gillette, P.S. "The Political Origins of American Soviet Trade, 1917-1924," PhD diss., Harvard, 1969.

M61.   Glenny, M.V. "The Anglo-Soviet Trade Agreement, March 1921," *JCH* 5 (1970), no.2, pp.63-82.

M62.   Heywood, A. "The Armstrong Affair and the Making of the Anglo-Soviet Trade Agreement, 1920-1921," *Revolutionary Russia* 5 (1992), no.1, pp.53-91.

M63.   Mieczkowski, Z. "The Economic Regionalization of the Soviet Union in the Lenin and Stalin Period," *CSP* 8 (1966), pp.89-124.

M64.   Miller, M.S. "Taxation in Soviet Russia," *SEER* 4 (1925-26), pp.124-137 & pp.418-432.

M65.   Reitzer, L.F. "United States-Russian Economic Relations, 1917-1920," PhD diss., Chicago, 1950.

M66. Smele, J.D. "Labour Conditions and the Collapse of the Siberian Economy under Kolchak, 1918-19," *Sbornik (SGRR)* no.13 (1987), pp.31-59.

M67. White, C.A. "Prelude to Trade: A Re-assessment of Anglo-American Trade and Commercial Relations with Soviet Russia, 1918-1924," PhD diss., Cambridge, 1988.

Agriculture:

M68. Antsiferov, A.N. *Russian Agriculture During the War* (New Haven: Yale U.P., 1930).

M69. Atkinson, D. *The End of the Russian Land Commune, 1905-1930* (Stanford: Stanford U.P., 1983).

M70. Atkinson, D.G.H. "The Russian Land Commune and the Revolution," PhD diss., Stanford, 1971.

M71. Atkinson, D. "The Statistics on the Russian Land Commune, 1905-1917," *SR* 32 (1973), no.4, pp.773-787.

M72. Baker, A.B. "Deterioration or Development?: The Peasant Economy of Moscow Province Prior to 1914," *RH* 5 (1978), no.1, pp.1-23.

M73. Bartlett, R. (ed.) *Land Commune and Peasant Community in Russia: Communal Forms in Imperial and Early Soviet Society* (Basingstoke & London: Macmillan, 1990).

M74. Baykalov, A. "A Brief Outline of the Russian Co-operative Movement," *SEER* 1 (1922-23), pp.130-143.

M75. Blanc, E.T. *The Cooperative Movement in Russia* (New York: Macmillan, 1924).

M76. Bubnov, J.V. *The Cooperative Movement in Russia. Its History, Significance, and Character* (Manchester: Cooperative Printing Society, 1917).

M77. Channon, J. "Land Revolution and Land Reform: The Case of the Central Black-Earth Region, 1917-24," in: L.Edmondson & P.Waldon (eds.) *Economy and Society in Russia and the Soviet Union, 1860-1930* (Basingstoke & London: Macmillan, 1992), pp.189-233.

M78. Ezergailis, A. "Prices in the Peasant Market: Valka During 1917," *Bulletin of Baltic Studies* 8 (1971), pp.24-25.

M79. Fisher, J.R. "The Witte Conference on the Needs of Agriculture in Russia: 1902-1905," PhD diss., Toronto, 1978.

M80. Gerasimenko, G.A. "The Stolypin Agrarian Reforms in Saratov Province," in: R.A.Wade & S.J.Seregny (eds.) *Politics and Society in Provincial Russia: Saratov, 1590-1917* (Columbia, Ohio: Ohio State U.P., 1989), pp.233-254.

M81. Gill, G.J. *Peasants and Government in the Russian Revolution* (London: Macmillan, 1979).

M82.   Hennessy, R. *The Agrarian Question in Russia 1905-1907: The Inception of the Stolypin Reform* (Giessen: Wilhelm Schmitz Verlag, 1977).

M83.   Kayden, E.M. *The Cooperative Movement in Russia During the War* (New Haven: Yale U.P., 1929).

M84.   Kazmer, D.R. "The Agricultural Development of Siberia, 1890-1917," PhD diss., Massachusetts Institute of Technology, 1973.

M85.   Lih, L.T. "Bread and Authority in Russia: Food Supply and Revolutionary Politics, 1919-1921," PhD diss., Princeton, 1984.

M86.   Lih, L.T. *Bread and Authority in Russia, 1914-1921* (Berkeley, Los Angeles, Oxford: University of California Press, 1990).

M87.   Long, J. "Agricultural Conditions in the German Colonies of Novouzensk, Samara Province, 1861-1914," *SEER* 57 (1979), no.4, pp.531-551.

M88.   Macey, D.A.J. "Revolution in Tsarist Agrarian Policy, 1891-1916," PhD diss., Columbia, 1977.

M89.   Munting, R.D. "Improvements in the Peasant Farm Economy in Early Twentieth Century Russia - Tula Guberniya," PhD diss., Birmingham, 1974-75.

M90.   Nutsch, J.G. "Bolshevik Agrarian Policies, 1917-1921," PhD diss., Kansas, 1968.

M91.   Ohsol, J.G. "The Recent Agrarian Movement in Russia and Its Historical Background," PhD diss., Harvard, 1914.

M92.   Pallot, J. "*Khutora* and *Otruba* in Stolypin's Program of Farm Individualization," *SR* 43 (1984), no.2, pp.242-256.

M93.   Pallot, J. "The Geography of Enclosure in Pre-Revolutionary European Russia - Tver, Tula and Samara Provinces," PhD diss., London, 1977.

M94.   Pavlovsky, G. *Agricultural Russia on the Eve of the Revolution* (London: G.Routledge, 1930 & New York: Howard Fertig, 1968).

M95.   Pavlovsky, G.A. "The Economics of Russian Farming, with Particular Reference to the Years 1900-1916," PhD diss., London, 1929.

M96.   Perrins, M. "The Politics of Russian Grain Procurement during the First World War," *SEER* 61 (1983), no.3, pp.388-410.

M97.   Petersen, A.B. "The Development of Cooperative Credit in Rural Russia, 1871-1914," PhD diss., Cornell, 1973.

M98.   Queen, G.S. "The McCormick Harvesting Machine Company in Russia," *RR* 23 (1964), no.2, pp.164-181.

M99.   Selunskaia, N.B. "Levels of Technology and the Use of Hired Labor in the Peasant and Manorial Economy of European Russia in 1917," *RR* 47 (1988), no.4, pp.409-423.

M100. Service, R. "Lenin and Agrarian Economics in 1917," in: L.Edmondson & P.Waldon (eds.) *Economy and Society in Russia and the Soviet Union, 1860-1930* (Basingstoke & London: Macmillan, 1992), pp.169-188.

M101. Shanin, T. "Socio-Economic Mobility and the Rural History of Russia 1905-30," *SS* 23 (1971), no.2, pp.222-235.

M102. Shanin, T. *The Awkward Class: Political Sociology of Peasantry in a Developing Society. Russia, 1910-1925* (Oxford: Clarendon, 1972).

M103. Shanin, T. "The Socio-Economic Mobility of the Russian Peasantry, 1910-1925, and the Political Sociology of Rural Society," PhD diss., Birmingham, 1969.

M104. Sheldon, R.C. "Socio Economic Development in a Karelian Village. History of Development of Social Organization (Principally Family) in Village (1848-1940) in Relation to Change from a Subsistence Farming Economy to a Timber Selling (Money) Economy," PhD diss., Harvard, 1953.

M105. Struve, P.B. *Food Supply in Russia During the World War* (New Haven: Yale U.P., 1930).

M106. Tokmakoff, G. "Stolypin's Agrarian Reform: An Appraisal," *RR* 30 (1971), no.2, pp.124-138.

M107. Volin, L. *A Century of Russian Agriculture* (Cambridge, Mass.: Harvard U.P., 1970).

M108. Wheatcroft, S.G. "Crises and the Condition of the Peasantry in Late Imperial Russia," in: E.Kingston-Mann & T.Mixter (eds.) *Peasant Economy, Culture, and Politics of European Russia, 1800-1921* (Princeton: Princeton U.P., 1991), pp.128-172.

M109. Wheatcroft, S.G. "The Reliability of Russian Prewar Grain Output Statistics," *SS* 26 (1974), no.2, pp.157-180.

M110. Willetts, H.T. "The agrarian problem," in: G.Katkov et al (eds.) *Russia Enters the Twentieth Century, 1894-1917* (London: Temple Smith, 1971), pp.111-137.

M111. Yaney, G. *The Urge to Mobilize: Agrarian Reform in Russia, 1861-1930* (Urbana, Chicago, London: University of Illinois Press, 1982).

M112. Zelenin, E.I. "State Farms in the First Decade of Soviet Power," *SSH* 9 (1970-71), no.1, pp.71-102.

Electrification Programme:

M113. Coopersmith, J. *The Electrification of Russia, 1880-1926* (Ithaca: Cornell U.P., 1992).

M114. Cummins, A.G. "The Road to NEP, the State Commission for the Electrification of Russia (GOELRO): A Study in Technology, Mobilization, and Economic Planning," PhD diss., Maryland, 1988.

Finance:

M115. Bowman, L.J. "The Business Tax in Imperial Russia, 1775-1917," PhD diss., California, Los Angeles, 1982.

M116. Crisp, O. "The Financial Aspect of the Franco-Russian Alliance, 1894-1914," PhD diss., London, 1954.

M117. Davies, R.W. "The Development of the Soviet Budgetary System, 1914-1941," PhD diss., Birmingham, 1955.

M118. DeMaris, E.J. "Lenin and the Soviet "Control by the Ruble" System," *SR* 22 (1963), no.3, pp.523-529.

M119. Gorlin, R.H. "Problems of Tax Reform in Imperial Russia," *JMH* 49 (1977), no.2, pp.246-265.

M120. Gorlin, R.H. "State Politics and the Imperial Russian Budget, 1905-1912," PhD diss., Michigan, 1973.

M121. Gregory, P.R. *Russian National Income; 1885-1913* (Cambridge: Cambridge U.P., 1982).

M122. Israelsen, L.D. "The Determinants of Russian State Income, 1800-1914: An Econometric Analysis," PhD diss., Massachusetts Institute of Technology, 1979.

M123. Iurkov, I.A. "Financial Policies of the Soviet Government and Monetary Trade Relations During the Civil War (1918-20)," *SSH* 23 (1984-85), no.2, pp.62-89.

M124. Michelson, A.M. *Russian Public Finance During the War* (New Haven: Yale U.P., 1928).

M125. Pares, B. "Sir Peter Bark," *SEER* 16 (1937-38), no.46, pp.189-193.

M126. Pickersgill, J.E. "Soviet Monetary Policy and the Demand for Money 1914-1937," PhD diss., Washington, Seattle, 1967.

M127. Reading, P.R. "Cooperative Banking in Rural Russia, 1865-1917," PhD diss., Birmingham, 1983.

M128. Sontag, J.P. "Tsarist Debts and Tsarist Foreign Policy," *SR* 27 (1968), no.4, pp.529-541.

Foreign Investment:

M129. Carstensen, F.V. *American Enterprise in Foreign Markets: Studies of Singer and International Harvester in Imperial Russia* (Chapel Hill & London: University of North Carolina Press, 1984).

M130. Crisp, O. "Some Problems of French Investment in Russian Joint-Stock Companies 1894-1914," *SEER* 35 (1956-57), pp.223-240.

M131. Fisher, R.B. "American Investments in Pre-Soviet Russia," *ASEER* 8 (1949), no.2, pp.90-105.

M132. Holzer, G.S. "The German Electrical Industry in Russia: From Economic Entrepreneurship to Political Activism, 1890-1918," PhD diss., Nebraska, 1970.

M133. Kirchner, W. "Siemens and A.E.G. and the Electrification of Russia, 1890-1914," *JFGO* 30 (1982), pp.399-428.

M134. Long, J.W. "Organized Protest Against the 1906 Russian Loan," *Cahiers du Monde Russe et Sovietique* 13 (1972), no.1, pp.24-39.

M135. McKay, J.P. "Foreign Entrepreneurs and Russian Industrialization, 1885-1913," PhD diss., California, Berkeley, 1968.

M136. McKay, J.P. *Pioneers for Profit: Foreign Entrepreneurship and Russian Industrialization, 1885-1913* (Chicago & London: University of Chicago Press, 1970).

M137. Ol', P.V. *Foreign Capital in Russia*, trans.by G.Jones & G.Gerenstein (New York: Garland, 1983).

M138. O'Neill, T.J. "Business, Investment and Revolution in Russia: Case Studies of American Companies, 1880s-1920s," PhD diss., McGill, 1987.

M139. Pickering, E.C. "The International Harvester Company in Russia: A Case Study of a Foreign Corporation in Russia from the 1860s to the 1930s," PhD diss., Princeton, 1974.

M140. Queen, G.S. "An American Employer and Russian Labour in 1905," *JMH* 15 (1943), no.2, pp.120-126.

M141. Queen, G.S. "The McCormick Harvesting Machine Company in Russia," *RR* 23 (1964), no.2, pp.164-181.

M142. Thompstone, S. "British Merchant Houses in Russia before 1914," in: L.Edmondson & P.Waldron (eds.) *Economy and Society in Russia and the Soviet Union, 1860-1930* (Basingstoke & London: Macmillan, 1992), pp.107-130.

M143. Tolf, R.W. *The Russian Rockefellers: The Saga of the Nobel Family and the Russian Oil Industry* (Stanford: Hoover Institution Press, 1976).

M144. Watson, D.R. "The Rise and Fall of the Russo-Asiatic Bank. Problems of a Russian Enterprise with French Shareholders, 1910-26," *EHQ* 23 (1993), no.1, pp.39-49.

M145. White, C. *British and American Commercial Relations with Soviet Russia, 1918-1924* (Chapel Hill, North Carolina: University of North Carolina Press, 1992).

Industry:

M146.   Avrich, P.H. "The Russian Revolution and the Factory Committees," PhD diss., Columbia, 1961.

M147.   Bater, J.H. *St.Petersburg: Industrialization and Change* (London: Edward Arnold, 1976).

M148.   Bater, J.H. "The Industrial Geography of St.Petersburg: 1850-1914," PhD diss., London, 1969.

M149.   Burstein, A.C. "The Iron and Steel Industry in Pre-Revolutionary Russia, 1861-1913," PhD diss., New School for Social Research, 1963.

M150.   Cooper, J.M. "The Development of the Soviet Machine Tool Industry, 1917-1941," PhD diss., Birmingham, 1975-76.

M151.   Ellis, S.C. "Management in the Industrialization of Russia, 1861-1917," PhD diss., Duke, 1981.

M152.   Falkus, M.E. *The Industrialisation of Russia, 1700-1914* (London: Macmillan, 1972).

M153.   Fenin, A.I. *Coal and Politics in Late Imperial Russia: Memoirs of a Russian Mining Engineer*, trans.by A.Fediaevsky (DeKalb: Northern Illinois U.P., 1990).

M154.   Flenley, P. "Industrial Relations and the Economic Crisis of 1917," *Revolutionary Russia* 4 (1991), no.2, pp.184-209.

M155.   Galili, Z. "Commercial-Industrial Circles in Revolution: the Failure of 'Industrial Progressivism'," in: E.R.Frankel et al (eds.) *Revolution in Russia: Reassessments of 1917* (Cambridge: Cambridge U.P., 1992), pp.188-216.

M156.   Gately, M.O. "The Development of the Russian Cotton Textile Industry in the Pre-Revolutionary Years, 1861-1913," PhD diss., Kansas, 1968.

M157.   Gatrell, P. "Defence Industries in Tsarist Russia, 1908-1913: Production, Employment and Military Procurement," in: L.Edmondson & P.Waldon (eds.) *Economy and Society in Russia and the Soviet Union, 1860-1930* (Basingstoke & London: Macmillan, 1992), pp.131-151.

M158.   Gatrell, P.W. *Government, industry, and rearmament in Russia, 1900-1914: the last argument of tsarism* (Cambridge: Cambridge U.P., 1994).

M159.   Gatrell, P.W. "Russian Heavy Industry and State Defence 1908-1918: Pre-War Expansion and Wartime Mobilization," PhD diss., Cambridge, 1979.

M160.   Goldberg, C.A. "The Association of Industry and Trade, 1906-1917: The Successes and Failures of Russia's Organized Businessmen," PhD diss., Michigan, 1974.

M161.   Goldstein, E.R. "Military Aspects of Russian Industrialization: The Defense Industries, 1890-1917," PhD diss., Case Western Reserve, 1971.

M162.   Gregory, P.R. "Russian Industrialization and Economic Growth: Results and Perspectives of Western Research," *JFGO* 25 (1977), pp.200-218.

M163. Guroff, G. "The State and Industrialization in Russian Economic Thought 1909-1914," PhD diss., Princeton, 1970.

M164. Harris, E.E. "Studies in the Industrial History of the Occupied Territories of Russian Poland During the First World War, 1914-18," PhD diss., Edinburgh, 1979.

M165. Hogan, H. "Industrial Rationalization and the Roots of Labor Militance in the St.Petersburg Metalworking Industry, 1901-1914," *RR* 42 (1983), no.2, pp.163-190.

M166. Hogan, H.J. "Labor and Management in Conflict: The St.Petersburg Metal-Working Industry, 1900-1914," PhD diss., Michigan, 1981.

M167. Husband, W.B. "Local Industry in Upheaval: The Ivanovo-Kineshma Textile Strike of 1917," *SR* 47 (1988), no.3, pp.448-463.

M168. Husband, W.B. *Revolution in the Factory: The Birth of the Soviet Textile Industry, 1917-1920* (Oxford: Oxford U.P., 1990).

M169. Husband, W.B. "The Nationalization of the Textile Industry of Soviet Russia, 1917-1920: Industrial Administration and the Workers During the Russian Civil War," PhD diss., Princeton, 1984.

M170. Joffe, M. "Regional Rivalry and Economic Nationalism: The Central Industrial Region Industrialists' Strategy for the Development of the Russian Economy 1880s-1914," *RH* 11 (1984), no.4, pp.389-421.

M171. Kuenssberg, J. "J. & P. Coates in Russia," *Scottish Slavonic Review* no.19 (1992), pp.71-88.

M172. McCaffray, S.P. "The Association of Southern Coal and Steel Producers and the Problems of Industrial Progress in Tsarist Russia," *SR* 47 (1988), no.3, pp.464-482.

M173. Madgwick, T.G. "Memories of Mining in Russia, 1903-1910," *Revolutionary Russia* 1 (1988), no.2, pp.157-202.

M174. Menashe, L. "Industrialists in Politics: Russia in 1905," *Government and Opposition* 3 (1968), no.3, pp.352-368.

M175. Miller, M.S. "The Trade Balance in Russia," *SEER* 1 (1922-23), pp.401-418.

M176. Mote, V.L. "The Cheliabinsk Grain Tariff and the Rise of the Siberian Butter Industry," *SR* 35 (1976), no.2, pp.304-317.

M177. Plaggenborg, S. "Who Paid for the Industrialisation of Tsarist Russia?" *Revolutionary Russia* 3 (1990), no.2, pp.183-210.

M178. Portal, R. "Muscovite Industrialists: The Cotton Sector (1861-1914)," in: W.L.Blackwell (ed.) *Russian Economic Development from Peter the Great to Stalin* (New York: New Viewpoints, 1974), pp.161-196.

M179. Roosa, R.A. "Russian Industrialists and 'State Socialism', 1906-17," *SS* 23 (1972), no.3, pp.395-417.

M180.   Roosa, R.A. "Russian Industrialists Look to the Future: Thoughts on Economic Development, 1906-17," in: J.S.Curtiss (ed.) *Essays in Russian and Soviet History* (Leiden: E.J.Brill, 1963), pp.198-218.

M181.   Roosa, R.A. "Russian Industrialists, Politics, and Labor Reform in 1905," *RH* 2 (1975), no.2, pp.124-148.

M182.   Roosa, R.A. "The Association of Industry and Trade, 1906-1914: An Examination of the Economic Views of Organized Industrialists in Prerevolutionary Russia," PhD diss., Columbia, 1967.

M183.   Roosa, R.A. "'United' Russian Industry," *SS* 24 (1972-73), no.3, pp.421-425.

M184.   Siegelbaum, L.H. "Moscow Industrialists and the War-Industries Committees During World War I," *RH* 5 (1978), no.1, pp.64-83.

M185.   Siegelbaum, L.H. *The Politics of Industrial Mobilization in Russia: A Study of the War-Industries Committees* (London & Basingstoke: Macmillan, 1983).

M186.   Siegelbaum, L.H. "The War-Industries Committees and the Politics of Industrial Mobility in Russia 1915-1917," PhD diss., Oxford, 1975.

M187.   Smolinski, L. "Grinevetskii and Soviet Industrialisation," *Survey* no.67 (April 1968), pp.100-115. [Comment by A.Nove and rejoinder by L.Smolinski in *Survey* no.70/71 (Winter/Spring 1969), pp.169-177].

M188.   Stackenwalt, F.M. "The Thought and Work of Dmitrii Ivanovich Mendeleev on the Industrialization of Russia, 1867-1907," PhD diss., Illinois, 1976.

M189.   Steinberg, M.D. "Consciousness and Conflict in Russian Industry: The Printers of St.Petersburg and Moscow, 1885-1905," PhD diss., California, Berkeley, 1987.

M190.   Vorderer, S.M. "Urbanization and Industrialization in Late Imperial Russia: Ivanovo-Voznesensk, 1880-1914," PhD diss., Boston College, 1990.

M191.   White, J.D. "Moscow, Petersburg and the Russian Industrialists: In Reply to Ruth Amende Roosa," *SS* 24 (1972-73), no.3, pp.414-420.

M192.   Zagorsky, S.O. *State Control of Industry in Russia During the War* (New Haven: Yale U.P., 1928).

Merchants:

M193.   Pak, B.I. "Savva Timofeevich Morozov," *SSH* 20 (1981-82), no.3, pp.74-95.

M194.   Rieber, A. *Merchants and Entrepreneurs in Imperial Russia* (Chapel Hill: University of North Carolina Press, 1982).

M195.   Roosa, R.A. "Workers' Insurance Legislation and the Role of the Industrialists in the Period of the Third State Duma," *RR* 34 (1975), no.4, pp.410-452.

M196. Thompstone, S. "British Merchant Houses in Russia before 1914," in: L.Edmondson & P.Waldron (eds.) *Economy and Society in Russia and the Soviet Union, 1860-1930* (Basingstoke & London: Macmillan, 1992), pp.107-130.

M197. Watstein, J. "Ivan Sytin - An Old Russia Success Story," *RR* 30 (1971), no.1, pp.43-53.

Trade Unions:

M198. Aves, J. "The Demise of Non-Bolshevik Trade Unionism in Moscow: 1920-21," *Revolutionary Russia* 2 (1989), no.1, pp.101-133.

M199. Borshchenko, I.L. *The Russian Trade Unions in 1907-1917* (Moscow: Profizdat, 1961).

M200. Bunyan, J. *The Origin of Forced Labor in the Soviet State, 1917-21: Documents and Materials* (Baltimore: Johns Hopkins U.P., 1967).

M201. Galai, S. "The Role of the Union of Unions in the Revolution of 1905," *JFGO* 24 (1976), pp.512-525.

M202. Kaplan, F.I. *Bolshevik Ideology and the Ethics of Soviet Labor, 1917-1920: the Formative Years* (New York: Philosophical Library, 1968).

M203. Rice, C. "Party Rivalry in the Caucasus: SRs, Armenians and the Baku Union of Oil Workers, 1907-1908," *SEER* 67 (1989), no.2, pp.228-243.

M204. Sablinsky, W. "The All-Russian Railroad Union and the Beginning of the General Strike in October, 1905," in: A.Rabinowitch et al (eds.) *Revolution and Politics in Russia: Essays in Memory of B.I. Nicolaevsky* (Bloomington: Indiana U.P., 1972), pp.113-133.

M205. Shkliarevsky, G. *Labor in the Russian Revolution: Factory Committees and Trade Unions, 1917-1918* (New York: St Martin's Press, 1993).

M206. Sorenson, J.B. "The Dilemma of Soviet Trade Unions during the First Period of Industrial Transformation: 1917-1928," PhD diss., Columbia, 1963.

M207. Sorenson, J.B. *The Life and Death of Soviet Trade Unionism 1917-1928* (New York: Atherton Press, 1969).

M208. Swain, G. "Freedom of Association and the Trade Unions, 1906-14," in: O.Crisp & L.Edmondson (eds.) *Civil Rights in Imperial Russia* (Oxford: Clarendon, 1989), pp.171-190.

M209. Tsuji, Y. "The Debate on the Trade Unions, 1920-21," *Revolutionary Russia* 2 (1989), no.1, pp.31-100.

Transport and Communications:

M210. Collins, D.N. "The Franco-Russian Alliance and Russian Railways, 1891-1914," *Historical Journal* 16 (December 1973), no.4, pp.747-788.

M211.   Dunne, J. "The Workers' Control Movement on the Russian Railways in 1905," *Irish Slavonic Studies* 4 (1983), pp.59-72.

M212.   Gulley, H.E. "Railways and the Seaborne Grain Export Trade in Tsarist Russia, 1861-1914," PhD diss., London, 1988.

M213.   Heywood, A. "The Armstrong Affair and the Making of the Anglo-Soviet Trade Agreement, 1920-1921," *Revolutionary Russia* 5 (1992), no.1, pp.53-91.

M214.   Higham, R. & Kipp, J.W. (eds.) *Soviet Aviation and Air Power: An Historical View* (London: Brassey's, 1978).

M215.   Hurt, B.E. "Russian Economic Development, 1881-1914, with Special Reference to the Railways and the Role of Government," PhD diss., London, 1963.

M216.   Kazemzadeh, F. "Russian Imperialism and Persian Railways," *HSS* 4 (1957), pp.355-373.

M217.   Le Fleming, H.M. & Price, J.H. *Russian Steam Locomotives* (New York: Augustus M.Kelley, 1969).

M218.   Marks, S.G. *Road to Power: The Trans-Siberian Railroad and the Colonization of Asian Russia, 1850-1917* (Ithaca, New York & London: Cornell U.P., 1991).

M219.   Marks, S.G. "The Trans-Siberian Railroad: State Enterprise and Economic Development in Imperial Russia," PhD diss., Harvard, 1988.

M220.   North, R.N. *Transport in Western Siberia: Tsarist and Soviet Development* (Vancouver: University of British Columbia Press & The Centre for Transportation Studies, 1979).

M221.   Nowarra, H.J. & Duval, G.R. *Russian Civil and Military Aircraft, 1884-1969* (London: Fountain Press, 1971).

M222.   Pethybridge, R. "The Significance of Communications in 1917," *SS* 19 (1967), no.1, pp.109-114.

M223.   Pethybridge, R.W. *The Spread of the Russian Revolution: Essays on 1917* (London: Macmillan, 1972).

M224.   Reichman, H. *Railwaymen and Revolution: Russia, 1905* (Berkeley: University of California Press, 1987).

M225.   Reichman, H.F. "Russian Railwaymen and the Revolution of 1905," PhD diss., California, Berkeley, 1977.

M226.   Reichman, H. "The 1905 Revolution on the Siberian Railroad," *RR* 47 (1988), no.1, pp.25-48.

M227.   Reichman, H. "Tsarist Labor Policy and the Railroads, 1885-1914," *RR* 42 (1983), no.1, pp.51-72.

M228.   Rosenberg, W.G. "The Democratization of Russia's Railroads in 1917," *AHR* 86 (1981), pp.983-1008.

M229.   Sablinsky, W. "The All-Russian Railroad Union and the Beginning of the General Strike in October, 1905," in: A.Rabinowitch et al (eds.) *Revolution and Politics in Russia: Essays in Memory of B.I. Nicolaevsky* (Bloomington: Indiana U.P., 1972), pp.113-133.

M230.   Solnick, S.L. "Revolution, Reform and the Soviet Telephone System, 1917-1927," *SS* 43 (1991), no.1, pp.157-176.

M231.   Spring, D. "Railways and Economic Development in Turkestan before 1917," in: L.Symons & C.White (eds.) *Russian Transport: An Historical and Geographical Survey* (London: G.Bell, 1975), pp.46-74.

M232.   Taylor, P.R. "The Trans-Siberian Railroad and the Russian Revolution of 1905," PhD diss., Tennessee, 1969.

M233.   Walsh, W.B. "The Bublikov-Rodzyanko Telegram," *RR* 30 (1971), no.1, pp.69-70.

M234.   Wei, C. "Foreign Railroad Interests in Manchuria: An Irritant in Chinese-Japanese Relations (1903-1937)," PhD diss., St.John's, 1980 [Russia 1903-11].

M235.   Westwood, J.N. *A History of Russian Railways* (London: George Allen & Unwin, 1964).

M236.   Westwood, J.N. "The Railway Flying Squads of 1914," *SEER* 55 (1977), no.2, pp.227-229.

War Communism and the Transition to the N.E.P.:

M237.   Anon. "Economic Notes," *SEER* 2 (1923-24), pp.436-438.

M238.   Ashin, P. "Wage Policy in the Transition to NEP," *RR* 47 (1988), no.3, pp.293-313.

M239.   Aves, J.J. "Worker Unrest in Soviet Russia during War Communism and the Transition to the New Economic Policy, 1918-22," PhD diss., London, 1990.

M240.   Berkin, I.B. "So Just What is "War Communism"," *Russian Studies in History* 33 (1994), no.1, pp.8-26.

M241.   Boettke, P.J. "The Political Economy of Soviet Socialism, 1918-1928," PhD diss., George Mason, 1989.

M242.   Buldakov, V.P. & Kabanov, V.V. ""War Communism": Ideology and Social Development," *Russian Studies in History* 33 (1994), no.1, pp.27-51.

M243.   Cohen, S.F. "In Praise of War Communism: Bukharin's *The Economics of the Transition Period*," in: A. & J.Rabinowitch (eds.) *Revolution and Politics in Russia: Essays in Memory of B.I. Nicolaevsky* (Bloomington & London: Indiana U.P., 1972), pp.192-203.

M244.   Cummins, A.G. "The Road to NEP, the State Commission for the Electrification of Russia (GOELRO): A Study in Technology, Mobilization, and Economic Planning," PhD diss., Maryland, 1988.

M245. Day, R.B. "Preobrazhensky and the Theory of the Transition Period," *SS* 27 (1975), no.2, pp.196-219.

M246. Holman, G.P., Jr. "'War Communism' or the Besieger Besieged: A Study of Lenin's Social and Political Objectives from 1918 to 1921," PhD diss., Georgetown, 1973.

M247. Lih, L.T. "Bolshevik *Razverstka* and War Communism," *SR* 45 (1986), no.4, pp.673-688.

M248. Malle, S. *The Economic Organisation of War Communism 1918-1921* (Cambridge: Cambridge U.P., 1985).

M249. Malle, S. "The War Communism Economic Organisation, 1918-1921," PhD diss., California, Berkeley, 1979.

M250. Patenaude, B.M. "Bolshevism in Retreat: The Transition to the New Economic Policy, 1920-1922," PhD diss., Stanford, 1987.

M251. Pliutto, P.A. "Aleksandr Bogdanov on the Period of 'War Communism'," *Revolutionary Russia* 5 (1992), no.1, pp.46-52.

M252. Roberts, P.C. ""War Communism": A Re-examination," *SR* 29 (1970), no.2, pp.238-261.

M253. Ronimois, H.E. "Soviet Experiment with Communist Economy, 1918-20," *CSP* 2 (1957), pp.70-85.

M254. Sokolov, N.G. "The Use of Barter During the Transition to NEP," *SSH* 23 (1984-85), no.2, pp.54-61.

M255. Suvorova, L.N. "Behind the Facade of "War Communism": Political Power and the Market Economy," *Russian Studies in History* 33 (1994), no.1, pp.72-88.

M256. Valentinov, N. "Non-Party Specialists and the Coming of the NEP," *RR* 30 (1971), no.2, pp.154-163.

M257. Veselov, S.V. "The Cooperative Movement and Soviet Rule: The Period of "War Communism"," *Russian Studies in History* 33 (1994), no.1, pp.52-71.

N

CULTURE AND EDUCATION

General:

N1.   Basso-Luca, G. "The Russian Cultural Revival, 1890-1917, Its Relevance to Russian Society," PhD diss., Georgetown, 1975.

N2.   Billington, J.H. *The Icon and the Axe: An Interpretive History of Russian Culture* (New York: Alfred A.Knopf, 1966).

N3.   Brooks, J.P. "Liberalism, Literature, and the Idea of Culture: Russia, 1905-1914," PhD diss., Stanford, 1972.

N4.   Brooks, J. *When Russia Learned to Read: Literacy and Popular Literature, 1861-1917* (Princeton: Princeton U.P., 1985).

N5.   Duncan, P.J.S. "Ivanov-Razumnik and the Russian Revolution: From Scythianism to Suffocation," *CSP* 21 (1979), no.1, pp.15-27.

N6.   Evtuhov, C. "On Neo-Romanticism and Christianity: Some 'Spots of Time' in the Russian Silver Age," *RH* 20 (1993), nos.1-4, pp.197-212.

N7.   Frank, S.P. & Steinberg, M.D. (eds.) *Cultures in Flux: Lower-Class Values, Practices, and Resistance in Late Imperial Russia* (Princeton: Princeton U.P., 1994).

N8.   Fulop-Miller, R. *The Mind and Face of Bolshevism: An Examination of Cultural Life in Soviet Russia* (New York: Harper & Row, 1965 [originally published 1926]).

N9.   Glade, S.A. "A Heritage Rediscovered Anew: Russia's Reevaluation of Pre-Petrine Icons in the Late Tsarist and Early Soviet Periods," *CASS* 26 (1992), nos.1-4, pp.145-196.

N10.   Gleason, A., Kenez, P & Stites, R. (eds.) *Bolshevik Culture. Experiment and Order in the Russian Revolution* (Bloomington: Indiana U.P., 1985).

N11.   Gorky, M. *Untimely Thoughts. Essays on Revolution, Culture and the Bolsheviks, 1917-1918*, trans.by H.Ermolaev (London: Garnstone Press, 1970).

N12.   Hilton, A.L. "Remaking Folk Art: from Russian Revival to Proletcult," in: J.O. Norman (ed.) *New Perspectives on Russian and Soviet Artistic Culture* (New York: St.Martin's Press; Basingstoke & London: Macmillan, 1994), pp.80-94.

N13.   Jahn, H.F. "For Tsar and Fatherland? Russian Popular Culture and the First World War," in: S.P.Frank & M.D.Steinberg (eds.) *Cultures in Flux: Lower-Class Values, Practices, and Resistance in Late Imperial Russia* (Princeton: Princeton U.P., 1994), pp.131-146.

N14.   Jahn, H.F. "Patriotic Culture in Russia during World War I," PhD diss., Georgetown, 1991.

N15.   Kolonitskii, B.I. "'Revolutionary Names': Russian Personal Names and Political Consciousness in the 1920s and 1930s," *Revolutionary Russia* 6 (1993), no.2, pp.210-228.

N16.   Mally, L. "Blueprint for a New Culture: A Social History of the Proletkul't, 1917-1922," PhD diss., Berkeley, 1985.

N17.   Mally, L. *Culture of the Future: the Proletkult Movement in Revolutionary Russia, 1917-1932* (Berkeley: University of California Press, 1990).

N18.   Proffer, C. & E. (eds.) *The Silver Age of Russian Culture: An Anthology* (Ann Arbor: Ardis, 1975).

N19.   Rosenberg, W. (ed.) *Bolshevik Visions: First Phase of the Cultural Revolution in Soviet Russia* (Ann Arbor: Ardis, 1984).

N20.   Salzman, C. "Consumer Cooperative Societies in Russia, Goals V. Gains, 1900-1918," *Cahiers du Monde Russe et Sovietique* 23 (1982), nos.3-4, pp.351-369.

N21.   Stites, R. "Adorning the Revolution: The Primary Symbols of Bolshevism, 1917-1918," *Sbornik (SGRR)* no.10 (1984), pp.39-42.

N22.   Stites, R. *Revolutionary Dreams: Utopian Vision and Experimental Life in the Russian Revolution* (New York & Oxford: Oxford U.P., 1989).

N23.   Stites, R. "Utopias in the Air and on the Ground: Futuristic Dreams in the Russian Revolution," *RH* 11 (1984), pts.2/3, pp.236-257.

Education and Literacy:

N24.   Alston, P.L. *Education and the State in Tsarist Russia* (Stanford: Stanford U.P., 1969).

N25.   Alston, P.L. "State Education and Social Change in the Russian Empire, 1871-1914," PhD diss., California, Berkeley, 1962.

N26.   Anon. "The Present Position of Russian Universities," *SEER* 2 (1923-24), pp.138-144.

N27.   Anweiler, O. "Russian schools," in: G.Katkov et al (eds.) *Russia Enters the Twentieth Century, 1894-1917* (London: Temple Smith, 1971), pp.287-313.

N28.   Beeman, A.E. "The American Image of Soviet Education, 1917-1935," PhD diss., Wisconsin, 1965.

N29.   Bowen, J.E. "Anton Makarenko and the Development of Soviet Education," PhD diss., Illinois, 1960.

N30.   Brooks, J. "Readers and Reading at the End of the Tsarist Era," in: W.M.Todd (ed.) *Literature and Society in Imperial Russia, 1800-1914* (Stanford: Stanford U.P., 1978), pp.98-150.

N31.   Brooks, J. *When Russia Learned to Read: Literacy and Popular Literature, 1861-1917* (Princeton: Princeton U.P., 1985).

N32.   Bruce, S.M. "The Commissariat of Education under Lunacharsky, 1917-1921," PhD diss., Oxford, 1969.

N33.   Dodge, R.H. "The Moscow Zemstvo and Elementary Education, 1868-1910," PhD diss., Syracuse, 1970.

N34.   Dorotich, D. "History in the Soviet School (1917-1937): Changing Policy and Practice," PhD diss., McGill, 1964.

N35.   Eklof, B. "Kindertempel or Shack? The School Building in Late Imperial Russia (A Case Study of Backwardness)," *RR* 47 (1988), no.2, pp.117-143.

N36.   Eklof, B. *Russian Peasant Schools. Officialdom, Village Culture, and Popular Pedagogy, 1861-1914* (Berkeley: University of California Press, 1986).

N37.   Eklof, A.B. "Spreading the Word: Primary Education and the Zemstvo in Moscow Province, 1864-1910," PhD diss., Princeton, 1977.

N38.   Eklof, B. "Worlds in Conflict: Patriarchal Authority, Discipline and the Russian School, 1861-1914," *SR* 50 (1991), no.4, pp.792-806.

N39.   Fitzpatrick, S. *The Commissariat of Enlightenment: Soviet Organization of Education and the Arts under Lunacharsky, October 1917-1921* (Cambridge: Cambridge U.P., 1970).

N40.   Forgus, S.P. "Estonian Nationalism and Primary Education, 1860-1905," PhD diss., Illinois, 1974.

N41.   Guroff, G. "The Legacy of Pre-Revolutionary Economic Education: St.Petersburg Polytechnic Institute," *RR* 31 (1972), no.3, pp.272-281.

N42.   Guroff, G. & Starr, S.F. "A Note on Urban Literacy in Russia, 1890-1914," *JFGO* 19 (1971), pp.520-531.

N43.   Hans, N.A. *A History of Russian Educational Policy, 1701-1917* (London: P.S.King & Son, 1931).

N44.   Hans, N. "Russian Educational Policy, 1801-1917," PhD diss., London, 1926.

N45.   Hans, N. *The Russian Tradition in Education* (London: Routledge & Kegan Paul, 1963).

N46.   Hayashida, R.H. "Lenin and the Third Front," *SR* 28 (1969), no.2, pp.314-324.

N47.   Hayashida, R.H. "The Third Front: The Politics of Soviet Mass Education, 1917-1918," PhD diss., Columbia, 1973.

N48.   Hinshaw, C.R. "The Soul of the Schools: The Professionalization of Urban Schoolteachers in St.Petersburg and Moscow, 1890-1907," PhD diss., California, Berkeley, 1986.

N49.   Holmes, L.E. *The Kremlin and the Schoolhouse: Reforming Education in Soviet Russia, 1917-1931* (Bloomington: Indiana U.P., 1991).

N50.   Ignatiev, Count P.N. *Russian Schools and Universities in the World War* (New Haven: Yale U.P., 1929).

N51.   Jahn, H.R. "The Development of Soviet Educational Policy during 1917-1936: A Case Study of Mathematics Education at the Elementary and Secondary Levels," PhD diss., Michigan, 1968.

N52.   Johnson, W.H.E. "Russia's Educational Heritage: Teacher Education in the Russian Empire, 1600-1917," PhD diss., Columbia, 1951.

N53.   Johnson, W.H.E. *Russia's Educational Heritage: Teacher Education in the Russian Empire, 1600-1917* (Pittsburgh: Carnegie Press, 1950).

N54.   Kabanov, P.I. "Pages from the Life of a Teacher of History," *SSH* 9 (1970-71), no.1, pp.3-42.

N55.   Kar, A.L. "The Response of the People to the Use of Formal Education in the Attempted Denationalization of Poland, 1795-1914," PhD diss., Michigan, 1955.

N56.   Kassow, S.D. "The Russian University in Crisis, 1899-1911," PhD diss., Princeton, 1976.

N57.   Kenez, P. "Liquidating Illiteracy in Revolutionary Russia," *RH* 9 (1982), pts.2/3, pp.173-186.

N58.   King, B. "Soviet Education: Its Phases and Purpose," *SEER* 17 (1938-39), pp.135-150.

N59.   Kreusler, A. "Foreign Language Teaching in Prerevolutionary Russia," *SR* 20 (1961), no.1, pp.109-113.

N60.   Krupskaya, N.K. *On Education* (Moscow: Foreign Languages Publishing House, 1957).

N61.   Kuzin, N.P. *Education in the USSR*, 2nd ed., trans.by F.Glagoleva (Moscow: Progress, 1977).

N62.   Leary, D.B. "Education and Autocracy in Russia from the Origins to the Bolsheviki," PhD diss., Columbia, 1919.

N63.   Leary, D.B. *Education and Autocracy in Russia from the Origins to the Bolsheviks* (Buffalo: University of Buffalo, 1919).

N64.   Lehrman, S.M. "The Pedagogical Ideas of Anton Semenovich Makarenko," PhD diss., Pittsburgh, 1972.

N65.   Lilge, F. "Lenin and the Politics of Education," *SR* 27 (1968), no.2, pp.230-257.

N66.   Lipset, H. "Jewish Schools in the Soviet Union, 1917-1941: An Aspect of Soviet Minorities Policy," PhD diss., Columbia, 1965.

N67.   McClelland, J.C. *Autocrats and Academics. Education, Culture, and Society in Tsarist Russia* (Chicago & London: University of Chicago Press, 1979).

N68.   McClelland, J.C. "Bolshevik Approaches to Higher Education, 1917-1921," *SR* 30 (1971), no.4, pp.818-831.

N69.   McClelland, J.C. "Bolsheviks, Professors, and the Reform of Higher Education in Soviet Russia, 1917-1921," PhD diss., Princeton, 1970.

N70.   Mironov, B.N. "Literacy in Russia, 1797-1917," *SSH* 25 (1986-87), no.3, pp.89-117.

N71.   Morison, J. "Education and the 1905 Revolution," *Revolutionary Russia* 1 (1988), no.1, pp.5-19.

N72.   Morison, J.D. "The Church Schools and Seminaries in the Russian Revolution of 1905-06," in: G.A. Hosking (ed.) *Church, Nation and State in Russia and Ukraine* (Basingstoke and London: Macmillan, 1991), pp.193-209.

N73.   Pape, C. "The 'Peasant Zemstva': Popular Education in Vjatka Gubernija, 1867-1905," *JFGO* 27 (1979), pp.498-519.

N74.   Pethybridge, R. "Spontaneity and Illiteracy in 1917," in: R.C.Elwood (ed.) *Reconsiderations on the Russian Revolution* (Cambridge, Mass.: Slavica, 1976), pp.81-99.

N75.   Pilch, J. "The Heder Metukan (The Modern Hebrew School in Russia of Pre-World War I)," PhD diss., Dropsie, 1952.

N76.   Rader, I.A. "Krupskaya: Pioneer Soviet Educator of the Masses," PhD diss., Southern Illinois, 1974.

N77.   Ramer, S.C. "The Transformation of the Russian Feldsher, 1864-1914," in: E.Mendelsohn & M.S.Shatz (eds.) *Imperial Russia, 1700-1917: State, Society, Opposition. Essays in Honor of Marc Raeff* (DeKalb, Illinois: Northern Illinois Press, 1988), pp.136-160.

N78.   Ruane, C. "The Vestal Virgins of St.Petersburg: Schoolteachers and the 1897 Marriage Ban," *RR* 50 (1991), no.2, pp.163-182.

N79.   Russell, S.J. "The Philosophy of Education of Anatolii Vasil'evich Lunacharsky, Commissioner of Education, 1917-1929," PhD diss., Indiana, 1970.

N80.   Santa Maria, P. "The Question of Elementary Education in the Third State Duma, 1907-1912," PhD diss., Kent State, 1977.

N81.   Satina, S. *Education of Women in Pre-Revolutionary Russia*, trans.by A.F.Poustchine (New York: 1966).

N82.   Schulman, E. "The Yiddish School in the Soviet Union 1818-1948," PhD diss., Dropsie, 1965.

N83.   Seregny, S.J. "Revolutionary Strategies in the Russian Countryside: Rural Teachers and the Socialist Revolutionary Party on the Eve of 1905," *RR* 44 (1985), no.3, pp.221-238.

N84.   Seregny, S.J. "Russian Teachers and Peasant Revolution, 1895-1917," in: E.H. Judge & J.Y. Simms, Jr. (eds.) *Modernization and Revolution: Dilemmas of Progress in Late Imperial Russia: Essays in Honor of Arthur P. Mendel* (New York: East European Monographs, distributed by Columbia U.P., 1992), pp.59-74.

N85.   Seregny, S.J. *Russian Teachers and Peasant Revolution. The Politics of Education in 1905* (Bloomington & Indianapolis: Indiana U.P., 1989).

N86.   Seregny, S.J. "Zemstvo Rabbits, Antichrists, and Revolutionaries: Rural Teachers in Saratov Province, 1890-1907," in: R.A.Wade & S.J.Seregny (eds.) *Politics and Society in Provincial Russia: Saratov, 1590-1917* (Columbia, Ohio: Ohio State U.P., 1989), pp.113-138.

N87.   Shimoniak, W. *Communist Education: Its History, Philosophy and Politics* (Chicago: Rand McNally, 1970).

N88.   Shore, M.J. *Soviet Education. Its Psychology and Philosophy* (New York: Philosophical Library, 1947).

N89.   Shorish, M.M. "Education in the Tajik Soviet Socialist Republic: 1917-1967," PhD diss., Chicago, 1972.

N90.   Smith, P.C. "The Soviet State and Education, 1917-1918," PhD diss., North Carolina, 1974.

N91.   Strakhovsky, L.I. "Count P.N. Ignat'yev, Reformer of Russian Education," *SEER* 36 (1957-58), pp.1-26.

N92.   Thurston, R. "Developing Education in Late Imperial Russia: The Concerns of State, 'Society', and People in Moscow, 1906-1914," *RH* 11 (1984), no.1, pp.53-82.

N93.   Timasheff, N.S. "Overcoming Illiteracy: Public Education in Russia, 1880-1940," *RR* 2 (1942-43), no.1, pp.80-88.

N94.   Uzureau, L.F. "The Educational Thought of M.I. Kalinin," PhD diss., Emory, 1981.

N95.   Widmayer, R.C. "The Communist Party and the Soviet Schools, 1917-1937," PhD diss., Radcliffe, 1953.

N96.   Zepper, J.T. "A Study of N.K. Krupskaya's Educational Philosophy," PhD diss., Missouri, 1960.

Ideology:

General:

N97.   Putnam, G.F. *Russian Alternatives to Marxism: Christian Socialism and Idealistic Liberalism in Twentieth-Century Russia* (Knoxville: University of Tennessee Press, 1977).

N98.   Ulam, A.B. *Ideologies and Illusions: Revolutionary Thought from Herzen to Solzhenitsyn* (Cambridge, Mass. & London: Harvard U.P., 1976).

Bolshevism:

N99.   Buchanan, H.R. "Lenin and Bukharin on the Transition from Capitalism to Socialism: the Meshchersky Controversy, 1918," *SS* 28 (1976), no.1, pp.66-82.

N100.   Cohen, S.F. "Bukharin, Lenin and the Theoretical Foundations of Bolshevism," *SS* 21 (1969-70), no.4, pp.436-457.

N101.   Costello, D.P. "Voluntarism and Determinism in Bolshevist Doctrine," *SS* 12 (1961), no.4, pp.394-403.

N102.   Kelly, A. "Empiriocriticism: A Bolshevik Philosophy?" *Cahiers du Monde Russe et Sovietique* 22 (1981), no.1, pp.89-118.

N103.   Leites, N. *A Study of Bolshevism* (Glencoe, Illinois: Free Press, 1953).

N104.   Marot, J.E. "Politics and Philosophy in Russian Social Democracy: Alexander Bogdanov and the Sociotheoretical Foundations of *Vpered*," *CSP* 33 (1991), nos.3-4, pp.263-284.

N105.   Mattick, P. *Anti-Bolshevik Communism* (London: Merlin, 1978).

N106.   Miliukov, P. *Bolshevism: An International Danger. Its Doctrine and Its Practice Through War and Revolution* (London: George Allen & Unwin, 1920).

N107.   Pethybridge, R. "Concern for Bolshevik Ideological Predominance at the Start of NEP," *RR* 41 (1982), no.4, pp.445-453.

N108.   Russell, B. *The Practice and Theory of Bolshevism*, 2nd ed. (London: George Allen & Unwin, 1949 [first published in 1920]).

N109.   Utechin, S.V. "Bolsheviks and their Allies after 1917: the Ideological Pattern," *SS* 10 (1958-59), no.2, pp.113-135.

Leninism:

N110.   Althusser, L. *Lenin and Philosophy and other essays*, trans.by B.Brewster (London: NLB, 1971).

N111.   Anderson, K.B. "The Dialectical Sociology of Social Change: A Study of Lenin and Hegel," PhD diss., CUNY, 1983.

N112.   Barfield, R. "Lenin's Utopianism: *State and Revolution*," *SR* 30 (1971), no.1, pp.45-56.

N113.   Besancon, A. *The Intellectual Origins of Leninism*, trans.by S.Matthews (Oxford: Basil Blackwell, 1981).

N114.   Bryner, C. "Lenin and the Search for an Elite," *CSP* 2 (1957), pp.47-56.

N115.   Carlsnaes, W.E. "The Concept of Ideology and Political Analysis: A Critical Examination of Its Usage by Marx, Lenin and Maunheim," PhD diss., Oxford, 1977.

N116.   Cassidy, F.P. "Revolutionary Politics and Normal Politics: Rousseau, Marx, and Lenin," PhD diss., Stanford, 1973.

N117.   Cohen-Almagor, R. "Foundations of Violence, Terror and War in the Writings of Marx, Engels and Lenin," *Terrorism and Political Violence* 3 (1991), no.2, pp.1-24.

N118.   Daniels, R.V. "Lenin and the Russian Revolutionary Tradition," *HSS* 4 (1957), pp.339-353.

N119.   Daniels, R.V. "The State and Revolution: a Case Study in the Genesis and Transformation of Communist Ideology," *ASEER* 12 (1953), no.1, pp.22-43.

N120.   Davis, D.E. "Lenin's Theory of War," PhD diss., Indiana, 1969.

N121.   Daxton, L.E. "Lenin and the New Economic Policy," PhD diss., Colorado, 1971.

N122.   Deborin, A.M. "Lenin as Philosopher," *Journal of World History* Special Number: Studies on Russian History (1958), pp.310-335.

N123.   Desai, M. (ed.) *Lenin's Economic Writings* (Atlantic Highlands, N.J.: Humanities Press International, 1989).

N124.   Dobrin, S. "Lenin on Equality and the Webbs on Lenin (Some Notes for the History of Ideas)," *SS* 8 (1956-57), no.4, pp.337-357.

N125.   Eissenstat, B.W. (ed.) *Lenin and Leninism. State, Law, and Society* (Lexington, Mass.: Lexington Books / D.C. Heath, 1971).

N126.   Evans, A.B. "Rereading Lenin's *State and Revolution*," *SR* 46 (1987), no.1, pp.1-19.

N127.   Frankel, J. "Lenin's Doctrinal Revolution of April 1917," *JCH* 4 (1969), no.2, pp.117-142.

N128.   Hammond, T.T. *Lenin on Trade Unions and Revolution, 1893-1917* (New York: Columbia U.P., 1957).

N129.   Hammond, T.T. "Revolutionism and Vanguardism: Lenin on Trade Unions Under Capitalism, 1893-1917," PhD diss., Columbia, 1953.

N130. Harding, N. *Lenin's Political Thought, vol.1: Theory and Practice in the Democratic Revolution* (New York: St.Martin's Press, 1978).

N131. Harding, N. *Lenin's Political Thought, vol.2: Theory and Practice in the Socialist Revolution* (New York: St.Martin's Press, 1981).

N132. Harding, N. "Lenin, Socialism and the State in 1917," in: E.R.Frankel et al (eds.) *Revolution in Russia: Reassessments of 1917* (Cambridge: Cambridge U.P., 1992), pp.287-303.

N133. Harvey, M.K.M. "The Political Views of Lenin and Nasser on State and Trans-State Politics: A Comparative Analysis," PhD diss., Southern Mississippi, 1973.

N134. Henry, M.D. "The Development of Civil Theologies in the Philosophies of Hobbes, Rousseau, Saint-Simon, Comte, and Lenin," PhD diss., Notre Dame, 1974.

N135. Hill, E. & Mudie, D. (eds.) *The Letters of Lenin*, trans.by eds. (London: Chapman & Hall, 1937).

N136. Holman, G.P., Jr. "'War Communism' or the Besieger Besieged: A Study of Lenin's Social and Political Objectives from 1918 to 1921," PhD diss., Georgetown, 1973.

N137. Jordan, Z.A. "The Dialectical Materialism of Lenin," *SR* 25 (1966), no.2, pp.259-286.

N138. Kingston, E.R. "Lenin: The Beginnings of Marxist Peasant Revolution, 1893-1917," PhD diss., Johns Hopkins, 1970.

N139. Kingston-Mann, E. "Lenin and the Beginnings of Marxist Peasant Revolution: the Burden of Political Opportunity, July-October 1917," *SEER* 50 (1972), no.121, pp.570-588.

N140. Kingston-Mann, E. *Lenin and the Problem of Marxist Peasant Revolution* (New York & Oxford: Oxford U.P., 1983).

N141. Kingston-Mann, E. "Problems of Order and Revolution: Lenin and the Peasant Question in March and April, 1917," *RH* 6 (1979), pt.1, pp.39-56.

N142. Kingston-Mann, E. "Proletarian Theory and Peasant Practice: Lenin 1901-04," *SS* 26 (1974), no.4, pp.522-539.

N143. Kleubort, D. "Lenin on the State: Theory and Practice after October," PhD diss., Chicago, 1977.

N144. Kreindler, I. "A Neglected Source of Lenin's Nationality Policy," *SR* 36 (1977), no.1, pp.86-100.

N145. Krupskaya, N.K. *How Lenin studied Marx* (London: Labour Monthly Pamphlets no.2, published at 7 John Street, Theobald's Road, London WC1, 1934).

N146. Kubalkova, V. "Marxism-Leninism and Theory of International Relations," PhD diss., Lancaster, 1975.

N147.   Lane, D. *Leninism: A Sociological Interpretation* (Cambridge & New York: Cambridge U.P., 1981).

N148.   LeBlanc, P. *Lenin and the Revolutionary Party* (Atlantic Highlands, N.J.: Humanities Press, 1990).

N149.   Lefebvre, Rev. R.R. "Lenin's Materialism: An Evaluation of the Philosophical Basis of Russian Communism," PhD diss., St.Louis, 1936.

N150.   Lenin, V.I. *Against Imperialist War. Articles and Speeches* (Moscow: Progress, 1974).

N151.   Lenin, V.I. *Collected Works*, 47 vols. (Moscow: Foreign Languages Publishing House, 1960-1963; also Progress Publishers, 1964-1980).

N152.   Lenin, V.I. *On the International Working-Class and Communist Movement* (Moscow: Foreign Languages Publishing House, n.d.).

N153.   Lenin, V.I. *Religion* (London: Martin Lawrence, n.d.).

N154.   Lenin, V.I. *Selected Works* (London: Lawrence & Wishart, 1968).

N155.   Lenin, V.I. *The Collected Works of V.I. Lenin*, 7 vols., numbered IV; XIII; XVIII-XXI; XXIII (London: Martin Lawrence, 1930, 1927-46).

N156.   Lenin, V.I. *The Revolution of 1917* (New York: International Publishers, 1932) [vol.20 of *Works*].

N157.   Lenin, V.I. *The State and Revolution* (Moscow: Progress, 1969) [various other editions].

N158.   Lenin, V.I. *The Suppressed Testament of Lenin* (New York: Pioneer Publishers, n.d.).

N159.   Lenin, V.I. *Towards the Seizure of Power* (New York: International Publishers, 1932 [vol.21 of *Works*].

N160.   Lenin, V.I. *What Is To Be Done?*, trans.by S.V. & P.Utechin (Oxford: Clarendon, 1963).

N161.   Lieberstein, S. "Leninism: A Study in the Sociology of Political Alienation," PhD diss., Berkeley, 1967.

N162.   Liebman, M. *Leninism Under Lenin*, trans.by B.Pearce (London: Jonathan Cape, 1975).

N163.   Low, A.D. *Lenin on the Question of Nationality* (New York: Bookman Associates, 1958).

N164.   Lukacs, G. *Lenin: A Study on the Unity of His Thought* (London: NLB, 1970).

N165.   Luxemburg, R. *The Russian Revolution and Leninism or Marxism?*, intro.by B.D.Wolfe (Ann Arbor: University of Michigan Press, 1961).

N166.   McKenzie, K.E. "Lenin's "Revolutionary Democratic Dictatorship of the Proletariat and Peasantry"," in: J.S.Curtiss (ed.) *Essays in Russian and Soviet History* (Leiden: E.J.Brill, 1963), pp.149-163.

N167. McKown, D.B. *The Classical Marxist Critiques of Religion: Marx, Engels, Lenin, Kautsky* (The Hague: Martinus Nijhoff, 1975).

N168. Melograni, P. *Lenin and the Myth of World Revolution: Ideology and Reasons of State, 1917-1920* (Atlantic Highlands, N.J.: Humanities Press, 1989).

N169. Meyer, A. *Leninism* (Cambridge, Mass.: Harvard U.P., 1957).

N170. Meyer, A.G. "Lenin's Theory of Revolution," PhD diss., Harvard, 1950.

N171. Padgett, S. "A Study of Marx's Method in the Work of V.I. Lenin and Rosa Luxemburg," PhD diss., Kent, 1981.

N172. Page, S.W. "The Russian Proletariat and World Revolution: Lenin's Views to 1914," *ASEER* 10 (1951), no.1, pp.1-13.

N173. Page, S.W. "Lenin and Self-Determination," *SEER* 28 (1949-50), pp.342-358.

N174. Page, S.W. *Lenin and World Revolution* (Washington Square, New York: New York U.P., 1959).

N175. Page, S.W. "Lenin: Prophet of World Revolution from the East," *RR* 11 (1952), no.2, pp.67-77.

N176. Page, S.W. *The Geopolitics of Leninism* (Boulder, Colorado: *East European Quarterly*, 1982).

N177. Pannekoek, A. *Lenin as Philosopher. A Critical Examination of the Philosophical Basis of Leninism* (London: Merlin Press, 1975).

N178. Polan, A.J. *Lenin and the End of Politics* (Berkeley: University of California Press, 1984).

N179. Rajiva, V. "Marx, Lenin, and the Problem of Revolution," PhD diss., Concordia, 1988.

N180. Roberts, J.W. "Lenin's Theory of Imperialism in Soviet Usage," *SS* 29 (1977), no.3, pp.353-372.

N181. Sawoski, M.M. "The Strategy and Tactics of Leninism with Emphasis on the Tactical Role of Compromise," PhD diss., Fletcher School of Law and Diplomacy, Tufts, 1987.

N182. Schurer, H. "Anton Pannekoek and the Origins of Leninism," *SEER* 41 (1962-63), pp.327-344.

N183. Shandro, A.M. "Orthodox Marxism and the Emergence of Lenin's Conception of Revolutionary Hegemony: On the Relation of Theory and Practice," PhD diss., Manchester, 1982.

N184. Silvermaster, N.G. "Lenin's Contributions to Economic Thought Prior to the Bolshevik Revolution," PhD diss., California, 1933.

N185. Slatter, J. "Lenin and the Commune-State: *The State and Revolution* in Context," *Irish Slavonic Studies* no.2 (1981), pp.47-68.

N186.   Smith, D.G. "The Political Theory of V.I. Lenin: Some Fundamental Concepts as the Basis for a Systematic Critique," PhD diss., Johns Hopkins, 1953.

N187.   Stalin, J.S. *Problems of Leninism* (Moscow: Foreign Languages Publishing House, 1947).

N188.   Sweezy, P.M. & Magdoff, H. (eds.) *Lenin Today. Eight Essays on the Hundredth Anniversary of Lenin's Birth* (New York & London: Monthly Review Press, 1970).

N189.   Thompson, R.B. "Lenin's Notebook on the State, 1916-1917," PhD diss., Chicago, 1955.

N190.   Topper, H.C. "From the Commune to the Cultural Revolution: A Discussion of Party Leadership and Democracy in Lenin and Mao," PhD diss., Johns Hopkins, 1991.

N191.   Tucker, R.C. (ed.) *The Lenin Anthology* (New York: Norton, 1975).

N192.   Ulam, A. *Lenin and the Bolsheviks: The Intellectual and Political History of the Triumph of Communism in Russia* (London: Secker & Warburg, 1966).

N193.   Varhall, G. "The Development of V.I. Lenin's Theory of the Dictatorship of the Proletariat," PhD diss., Notre Dame, 1982.

N194.   Witte, J. "Violence in Lenin's Thought and Practice: The Spark and the Conflagration," *Terrorism and Political Violence* 5 (1993), no.3, pp.135-203.

N195.   Wolfe, B.D. "Lenin Has Trouble with Engels: A Heretofore Unanalyzed Source of Lenin's Theory of Imperialism," *RR* 15 (1956), no.3, pp.196-209.

N196.   Wolfe, B.D. *Revolution and Reality: Essays on the Origin and Fate of the Soviet System* (Chapel Hill: University of North Carolina Press, 1981).

Panslavism:

N197.   Kohn, H. *Panslavism. Its History and Ideology* (Notre Dame, Indiana: University of Notre Dame Press, 1953).

Permanent Revolution:

N198.   Donald, M. "Karl Kautsky and Russian Social Democracy," *Sbornik (SGRR)* no.11 (1985), pp.26-46.

N199.   Donald, M. "Karl Kautsky and Russian Social Democracy, 1900-1914," PhD diss., Leeds, 1986.

N200.   Donald, M. *Marxism and Revolution: Karl Kautsky and the Russian Marxists, 1900-1924* (New Haven & London: Yale U.P., 1993).

N201.   Knapheis, B. "The Social and Political Thought of Leon Trotsky," PhD diss., Oxford, 1974.

N202.   Knei-Paz, B. *The Social and Political Thought of Leon Trotsky* (Oxford: Clarendon Press, 1978).

N203.   Limberg, W.P. "Permanent Revolution: Materials on the Origins and Meaning of the Theory and Its Influence on Marxist-Leninist Thought," PhD diss., Georgetown, 1974.

N204.   Molyneux, J. *Leon Trotsky's Theory of Revolution* (New York: St.Martin's Press, 1981).

N205.   Perrie, M. "The Socialist Revolutionaries on 'Permanent Revolution'," *SS* 24 (1972-73), no.3, pp.411-413.

N206.   Schurer, H. "The Permanent Revolution. Metamorphosis of an Idea," *Soviet Survey* no.32 (April-June 1960), pp.68-73.

N207.   Skilling, H.G. "Permanent or Uninterrupted Revolution: Lenin, Trotsky, and Their Successors on the Transition to Socialism," *CSP* 5 (1961), pp.3-30.

N208.   Stokes, C. "On the Evolution of Trotzky's Theory of Revolution," PhD diss., Michigan, 1978.

N209.   Stokes, C. *The Evolution of Trotsky's Theory of Revolution* (Washington, D.C.: University Press of America, 1982).

Russian Marxism:

N210.   Baron, S.H. "Plekhanov and the Revolution of 1905," in: J.S.Curtiss (ed.) *Essays in Russian and Soviet History* (Leiden: E.J.Brill, 1963), pp.133-148.

N211.   Belfer, E. "*Zemlya* vs. *Volya* - From *Narodnichestvo* to Marxism," *SS* 30 (1978), no.3, pp.297-312.

N212.   Bergman, J. "The Image of Jesus in the Russian Revolutionary Movement: the Case of Russian Marxism," *IRSH* 35 (1990), pp.220-248.

N213.   Bergman, J. "The Political Thought of Vera Zasulich," *SR* 38 (1979), no.2, pp.243-258.

N214.   Brown, I.C. "Plekhanov and the Iron Law of History," *HT* 31 (December 1981), pp.37-41.

N215.   Harding, N. "Authority, Power and the State, 1916-20," in: T.H.Rigby et al (eds.) *Authority, Power and Policy in the USSR: Essays dedicated to Leonard Schapiro* (London & Basingstoke: Macmillan, 1980), pp.32-56.

N216.   Hussain, A. & Tribe, K. *Marxism and the Agrarian Question. Vol.2: Russian Marxism and the Peasantry 1861-1930* (London & Basingstoke: Macmillan, 1981).

N217.   Kindersley, R. *The First Russian Revisionists. A Study of 'Legal Marxism' in Russia* (Oxford: Clarendon Press, 1962).

N218.   Knei-Paz, B. "Russian Marxism: Theory, Action and Outcome," in: E.R.Frankel et al (eds.) *Revolution in Russia: Reassessments of 1917* (Cambridge: Cambridge U.P., 1992), pp.406-420.

N219.   Knei-Paz, B. *The Social and Political Thought of Leon Trotsky* (Oxford: Clarendon Press, 1978).

N220.   Larsson, R. *Theories of Revolution: From Marx to the First Russian Revolution* (Stockholm: Almqvist & Wiksell, 1970).

N221.   Luxemburg, R. *The Russian Revolution and Leninism or Marxism?*, intro.by B.D.Wolfe (Ann Arbor: University of Michigan Press, 1961).

N222.   Matossian, M. "Two Marxist Approaches to Nationalism," *ASEER* 16 (1957), pp.489-500.

N223.   Mendel, A.P. *Dilemmas of Progress in Tsarist Russia. Legal Marxism and Legal Populism* (Cambridge, Mass.: Harvard U.P., 1961).

N224.   Theen, R.H.W. "The Idea of the Revolutionary State: Tkachev, Trotsky, and Lenin," *RR* 31 (1972), no.4, pp.383-397.

N225.   Tompkins, S.R. *The Triumph of Bolshevism: Revolution or Reaction?* (Norman: University of Oklahoma Press, 1967).

N226.   Ulam, A.B. "Reflections on the Revolution," *Survey* no.64 (July 1967), pp.3-13.

N227.   Williams, R.C. *The Other Bolsheviks: Lenin and His Critics, 1904-1914* (Bloomington & Indianapolis: Indiana U.P., 1986).

World Revolution:

N228.   Heitman, S. "Nikolai Bukharin's Theory of World Revolution," PhD diss., Columbia, 1963.

N229.   Korey, W. "Zinoviev on the Problem of World Revolution, 1919-1927," PhD diss., Columbia, 1960.

Law:

N230.   Frierson, C.A. "Rural Justice in Popular Opinion: The Volost' Court Debate, 1861-1912," *SEER* 64 (1986), no.4, pp.526-545.

N231.   Guins, G.C. "Law and Morality: The Legal Philosophy of Lev Petrazhitsky," *RR* 16 (1957), no.4, pp.27-36.

N232.   Hazard, J.N. "Law and Tradition in the New Russia," *OSP* 4 (1953), pp.132-150.

N233. Hazard, J.N. "Soviet Law: The Bridge Years, 1917-1920," in: W.E.Butler (ed.) *Russian Law: Historical and Political Perspectives* (Leyden: A.W.Sijthoff, 1977), pp.235-257.

N234. Huskey, E. *Russian Lawyers and the Soviet State: The Origins and Development of the Soviet Bar, 1917-1939* (Princeton: Princeton U.P., 1986).

N235. Huskey, E. "The Russian Bar and the Consolidation of Soviet Power," *RR* 43 (1984), no.2, pp.115-144.

N236. Jansen, M. "The Bar During the First Years of the Soviet Regime: N.K. Murav'ev," *Revolutionary Russia* 3 (1990), no.2, pp.211-223.

N237. Levin-Stankevich, B.L. "*Sudebnaia Praktika* and Russian Legal Development, 1864-1917," PhD diss., SUNY, Buffalo, 1981.

N238. Levin-Stankevich, B. "Cassation, Judicial Interpretation, and the Development of Civil and Criminal Law in Russia, 1864-1917: The Institutional Consequences of the 1864 Court Reform," PhD diss., SUNY, Buffalo, 1984.

N239. Rawson, D. "The Death Penalty in Late Tsarist Russia: An Investigation of Judicial Procedures," *RH* 11 (1984), no.1, pp.29-52.

N240. Timasheff, N.S. "The Impact of the Penal Law of Imperial Russia in Soviet Penal Law," *ASEER* 12 (1953), pp.441-462.

Philosophy:

N241. Blakeley, T.J. *Soviet Theory of Knowledge* (Dordrecht: D.Reidel, 1964).

N242. Bohachevsky-Chomiak, M. & Rosenthal, B.G. (eds.) *A Revolution of the Spirit: Crisis of Value in Russia, 1890-1918*, trans.by M.Schwartz (Newtonville, Mass.: Oriental Research Partners, 1982).

N243. Boll, M.M. "From Empiriocriticism to Empiriomonism: the Marxist Phenomenology of Aleksandr Bogdanov," *SEER* 59 (1981), no.1, pp.41-58.

N244. Carlson, M. *"No Religion Higher Than Truth": a History of the Theosophical Movement in Russia, 1875-1922* (Princeton: Princeton U.P., 1993).

N245. Compton, R.J. "The Intuitivism of N.O. Lossky," PhD diss., Yale, 1939.

N246. Copleston, F.C. *Philosophy in Russia: From Herzen to Lenin and Berdyaev* (Tunbridge Wells: Search Press; Notre Dame, Indiana: University of Notre Dame Press, 1986).

N247. Dahm, H. "The outlook for philosophy and the fate of the Slavophil Utopia," in: G.Katkov et al (eds.) *Russia Enters the Twentieth Century, 1894-1917* (London: Temple Smith, 1971), pp.236-262.

N248. Edie, J.M., Scanlan, J.P., Zeldin, M.B. & Kline, G.L. (eds.) *Russian Philosophy*, 3 vols. (Chicago: Quadrangle Books, 1965).

N249.   Hecker, J.F. *Russian Sociology. A contribution to the history of sociological thought and theory*, revised ed. (London: Chapman & Hall, 1934 ; New York: Augustus M.Kelley, 1969 [reprint of 1915 ed.]).

N250.   Hetko, A. "Educational Implications in the Philosophy of N.O.Lossky," PhD diss., Ohio State, 1958.

N251.   Jensen, K.M. "Beyond Marx and Mach: A.A. Bogdanov's *Philosophy of Living Experience*," PhD diss., Colorado, 1975.

N252.   Jensen, K.M. *Beyond Marx and Mach: Aleksandr Bogdanov's "Philosophy of Living Experience"* (Dordrecht & Boston: D.Reidel, 1978).

N253.   Kamenka, E. "Philosophy: The Bolshevik Period," *Survey* no.64 (July 1967), pp.80-98.

N254.   Kohanski, A.S. "Nicolai Ovufrievich Lossky's Theory of Knowledge," PhD diss., Vanderbilt, 1936.

N255.   Lane, A.M. "Nietzsche in Russian Thought 1890-1917," PhD diss., Wisconsin, 1976.

N256.   Lossky, N.O. *History of Russian Philosophy* (London: Allen & Unwin, 1952).

N257.   Marot, J.E. "Alexander Bogdanov: Political Theory and History," PhD diss., California, Los Angeles, 1987.

N258.   Navickas, J.-L. "The Moral Philosophy of Lossky," PhD diss., Fordham, 1958.

N259.   Putnam, G.F. "Vasilii V. Rozanov: Sex, Marriage and Christianity," *Canadian Slavic Studies* 5 (1971), no.3, pp.301-326.

N260.   Raeff, M. *Russian Intellectual History: an anthology* (New York: Harcourt, Brace and World, 1966).

N261.   Rosenthal, B.G. (ed.) *Nietzsche in Russia* (Princeton: Princeton U.P., 1986).

N262.   Simmons, E.J. (ed.) *Continuity and Change in Russian and Soviet Thought* (Cambridge, Mass.: Harvard U.P., 1955).

N263.   Vucinich, A. *Social Thought in Tsarist Russia: The Quest for a General Science of Society, 1861-1917* (Chicago: University of Chicago Press, 1976).

N264.   Walicki, A. *A History of Russian Thought from the Enlightenment to Marxism* (Oxford: Clarendon, 1980).

N265.   Walter, P.M. "The Development of the Political and Religious Philosophy of Sergei Bulgakov, 1895-1922: A Struggle for Transcendence," PhD diss., London, 1977.

N266.   Williams, R.D. "The Theology of Vladimir Lossky: An Exposition and Critique," PhD diss., Oxford, 1975.

N267.   Zenkovsky, V.V. *A History of Russian Philosophy*, 2 vols. (London: Routledge & Kegan Paul, 1953).

The Proletarian Culture Debate:

N268.   Biggart, J. "Alexander Bogdanov, Left Bolshevism and the Proletkult, 1904-32," PhD diss., East Anglia, 1989.

N269.   Biggart, J. "Bukharin and the Origins of the 'Proletarian Culture' Debate," *SS* 39 (1987), no.2, pp.229-246.

N270.   Bogdanov, A.A. "What have We Overthrown?" *Scottish Slavonic Review* no.4 (1985), pp.107-118.

N271.   Crouch, G.E., Jr. "The Theory and Practice of A.A. Bogdanov's *Proletcult*," PhD diss., North Carolina, 1973.

N272.   Gorzka, G. "Proletarian Cultural Revolution: The Conception of Aleksandr A. Bogdanov," *Sbornik (SGRR)* no.9 (1983), pp.67-82.

N273.   McClelland, J.C. "Utopianism versus Revolutionary Heroism in Bolshevik Policy: The Proletarian Culture Debate," *SR* 39 (1980), no.3, pp.403-425.

N274.   Mally, L. "Blueprint for a New Culture: A Social History of the Proletkul't, 1917-1922," PhD diss., Berkeley, 1985.

N275.   Mally, L. *Culture of the Future: the Proletkult Movement in Revolutionary Russia, 1917-1932* (Berkeley: University of California Press, 1990).

N276.   Rowley, D.G. "Millenarian Bolshevism: Empiriomonism, God-Building, Proletarian Culture," PhD diss., Michigan, 1982.

N277.   Scheibert, P. "Lenin, Bogdanov, and the Concept of Proletarian Culture," in: B.W.Eissenstat (ed.) *Lenin and Leninism. State, Law, and Society* (Lexington, Mass.: Lexington Books / D.C. Heath, 1971), pp.43-57.

N278.   Sochor, Z.A. "Modernization and Socialist Transformation: Leninist and Bogdanovite Alternatives of the Cultural Revolution," PhD diss., Columbia, 1977.

N279.   Sochor, Z.A. *Revolution and Culture: The Bogdanov-Lenin Controversy* (Ithaca & London: Cornell U.P., 1988).

N280.   Williams, R.C. "Collective Immortality: The Syndicalist Origins of Proletarian Culture, 1905-1910," *SR* 39 (1980), no.3, pp.389-402.

Religion:

General:

N281.   Basil, J.D. "Alexander Kireev and Theological Controversy in the Russian Orthodox Church, 1890-1910," in: G.A. Hosking (ed.) *Church, Nation and State in Russia and Ukraine* (Basingstoke and London: Macmillan, 1991), pp.131-147.

N282.   Bedford, C.H. "Dmitry Merezhkovsky, the Third Testament and the Third Humanity," *SEER* 42 (1963-64), no.98, pp.144-160.

N283.   Berdyaev, N. *The Russian Revolution* (Ann Arbor: University of Michigan Press, 1961).

N284.   Berg, W.P. "Choral Festivals and Choral Workshops among the Mennonites of Manitoba and Saskatchewan, 1900-1960, with an Account of Early Developments in Russia," PhD diss., Washington, Seattle, 1979.

N285.   Bergman, J. "The Image of Jesus in the Russian Revolutionary Movement: the case of Russian Marxism," *IRSH* 35 (1990), pp.220-248.

N286.   Blane, A.Q. "The Relations Between the Russian Protestant Sects and the State, 1900-1921," PhD diss., Duke, 1965.

N287.   Bulgakov, S. "The Guardian of the House of the Lord," *SEER* 4 (1925-26), pp.156-164.

N288.   Bulgakov, S. "The Old and the New: A Study in Russian Religion," *SEER* 2 (1923-24), pp.487-513.

N289.   Carlson, M. *"No Religion Higher Than Truth": a History of the Theosophical Movement in Russia, 1875-1922* (Princeton: Princeton U.P., 1993).

N290.   Christensen, P.G. "Religion and Revolution in Merezhkovskii's Russian Trilogy," *CASS* 26 (1992), nos.1-4, pp.63-76.

N291.   Cunningham, J.W. "The Russian Patriarchate and the Attempt to Recover "Symphoniia"," *CASS* 26 (1992), nos.1-4, pp.267-292.

N292.   Curtiss, J.S. "Church and State in Russia - The Last Years of the Empire (1900-1917)," PhD diss., Columbia, 1940.

N293.   Curtiss, J.S. *Church and State in Russia. The Last Years of the Empire, 1900-1917* (New York: Octagon, 1940).

N294.   Dixon, S. "The Church's Social Role in St Petersburg, 1880-1914," in: G.A. Hosking (ed.) *Church, Nation and State in Russia and Ukraine* (Basingstoke and London: Macmillan, 1991), pp.167-192.

N295.   Geekie, J.H.M. "Church and Politics in Russia, 1905-1917: A Study of the Political Behaviour of the Russian Orthodox Clergy in the Reign of Nicholas II," PhD diss., East Anglia, 1976.

N296.   Lenin, V.I. *Religion* (London: Martin Lawrence, n.d.).

N297.   McKown, D.B. "The Classical Marxist Critiques of Religion: Marx, Engels, Lenin, Kautsky," PhD diss., Florida State, 1972.

N298.   Mailleux, P. *Exarch Leonid Feodorov: Bridgebuilder Between Rome and Moscow* (New York: P.J.Kenedy, 1964).

N299.   Meerson, M.A. "The Renovationist Schism in the Russian Orthodox Church," *CASS* 26 (1992), nos.1-4, pp.293-314.

N300.   Miliukov, P. *Outlines of Russian Culture. Part I: Religion and the Church*, trans.by V.Ughet & E.Davis (Philadelphia: University of Pennsylvania Press, 1943).

N301. Nesdoly, S.J. "Evangelical Sectarianism in Russia: A Study of the Stundists, Baptists, Pashkovites and Evangelical Christians, 1855-1917," PhD diss., Queen's (Canada), 1972.

N302. Pares, B. "Father Petrov," *SEER* 5 (1926-27), pp.152-154.

N303. Read, C. "Early Twentieth Century Russia: Church and State," *Religion in Communist Lands* 4 (1976), no.1, pp.35-38.

N304. Read, C. *Religion, Revolution and the Russian Intelligentsia, 1900-1912: the Vekhi debate and its intellectual background* (London: Macmillan, 1979).

N305. Rempel, D.G. "The Mennonite Colonies in New Russia: A Study of Their Settlement and Economic Development from 1789-1914," PhD diss., Stanford, 1934.

N306. Reyburn, H.Y. *The Story of the Russian Church* (London & New York: Andrew Melrose, 1924).

N307. Robson, R.R. "Liturgy and Community Among Old Believers, 1905-1917," *SR* 52 (1993), no.4, pp.713-724.

N308. Sapiets, M. "One Hundred Years of Adventism in Russia and the Soviet Union," *Religion in Communist Lands* 12 (1984), no.3, pp.256-273.

N309. Simon, G. "Church, state and society," in: G.Katkov et al (eds.) *Russia Enters the Twentieth Century, 1894-1917* (London: Temple Smith, 1971), pp.199-235.

N310. Spinka, M. *The Church and the Russian Revolution* (New York: Macmillan, 1927).

N311. Stavrou, T.G. "The Russian Imperial Orthodox Palestine Society, 1882-1914," PhD diss., Indiana, 1961.

N312. Traina, M.J. "Lenin, Religion and the Russian Orthodox Church: An Analysis of Theory and Practice," PhD diss., Kent State, 1970.

N313. Waldron, P. "Religious Toleration in Late Imperial Russia," in: O.Crisp & L.Edmondson (eds.) *Civil Rights in Imperial Russia* (Oxford: Clarendon, 1989), pp.103-119.

N314. West, J.L. "The Neo-Old Believers of Moscow: Religious Revival and Nationalist Myth in Late Imperial Russia," *CASS* 26 (1992), nos.1-4, pp.5-28.

N315. Zernov, N. "Metropolitan Platon," *SEER* 13 (1934-35), pp.431-433.

1905 Revolution:

N316. Bedford, C.H. "Dmitry Merezhkovsky, the Intelligentsia, and the Revolution of 1905," *CSP* 3 (1958), pp.27-42.

N317. Bird, T.E. "Religion and the Revolution of 1905: An Introductory Word," *RH* 4 (1977), pt.2, pp.101-104.

N318.   Blobaum, R. "The Revolution of 1905-1907 and the Crisis of Polish Catholicism," *SR* 47 (1988), no.4, pp.667-686.

N319.   Bohachevsky-Chomiak, M. ""Christian" vs. "Neophyte": Opposition to the Formation of a Christian Party in Russia," *RH* 4 (1977), pt.2, pp.105-121.

N320.   Camfield, G.P. "The Pavlovtsy of Khar'kov Province, 1886-1905: Harmless Sectarians or Dangerous Rebels?" *SEER* 68 (1990), no.4, pp.692-717.

N321.   Cunningham, J. *A Vanquished Hope. The Movement for Church Renewal in Russia, 1905-1906* (Crestwood, N.Y.: St.Vladimir's Seminary Press, 1981).

N322.   Cunningham, J.W. "Reform in the Russian Church, 1900-1906: The Struggle for Autonomy and the Restoration of Byzantine 'Symphonia'," PhD diss., Minnesota, 1973.

N323.   Morison, J.D. "The Church Schools and Seminaries in the Russian Revolution of 1905-06," in: G.A. Hosking (ed.) *Church, Nation and State in Russia and Ukraine* (Basingstoke and London: Macmillan, 1991), pp.193-209.

N324.   Nichols, R.L. & Stavrou, T.G. (eds.) *Russian Orthodoxy under the Old Regime* (Minneapolis: University of Minnesota Press, 1978).

N325.   Valliere, P.R. "Modes of Social Action in Russian Orthodoxy: The Case of Father Petrov's Zateinik," *RH* 4 (1977), pt.2, pp.142-158.

1905-14:

N326.   Waldron, P. "Religious Reform after 1905: Old Believers and the Orthodox Church," *OSP(NS)* 20 (1987), pp.110-139.

N327.   Waldron, P.R. "The Stolypin Programme of Reform, 1906-1911, with Special Reference to Local Government and Religious Affairs," PhD diss., London, 1981.

1917-21:

N328.   Bociurkiw, B.R. "Church-State Relations in the USSR," *Survey* no.66 (January 1968), pp.4-32.

N329.   Bociurkiw, B.R. "Soviet Religious Policy in the Ukraine in Historical Perspective," *Occasional Papers on Religion in Eastern Europe* 2 (June 1982), no.3, pp.1-21.

N330.   Bociurkiw, B.R. "Soviet Church Policy in the Ukraine, 1919-1939," PhD diss., Chicago, 1961.

N331.   Bociurkiw, B.R. "The Rise of the Ukrainian Autocephalous Church, 1919-22," in: G.A. Hosking (ed.) *Church, Nation and State in Russia and Ukraine* (Basingstoke and London: Macmillan, 1991), pp.228-249.

N332.	Curtiss, J.S. "The Russian Orthodox Church and the Provisional Government," *ASEER* 7 (1948), no.3, pp.237-250.

N333.	Curtiss, J.S. *The Russian Church and the Soviet State, 1917-1950* (Boston: Little, Brown & Co., 1953).

N334.	Evtuhov, C. "The Church in the Russian Revolution: Arguments for and against Restoring the Patriarchate at the Church Council of 1917-1918," *SR* 50 (1991), no.3, pp.497-511.

N335.	Fletcher, W.C. *The Russian Orthodox Church Underground, 1917-1970* (New York & London: Oxford U.P., 1971).

N336.	Johansen, A. "The Russian Orthodox Church as Reflected in Orthodox and Atheist Publications in the Soviet Union," *Occasional Papers on Religion in Eastern Europe* 3 (February 1983), no.2, pp.1-26.

N337.	Klepinin, N. "The War on Religion," *SEER* 8 (1929-30), pp.514-532.

N338.	Loya, J.A. "Theological Clarifications of Lay Status in the Russian Church Pertaining to the Moscow Reform Council of 1917-1918," PhD diss., Fordham, 1986.

N339.	Marshall, R.H. Jr., Bird, T.E. & Blane, A.Q. (eds.) *Aspects of Religion in the Soviet Union, 1917-1967* (Chicago & London: University of Chicago Press, 1971).

N340.	Popiw, J.J. "Soviet Church Policy: Marxism, Caesaropapism, and Constitutionalism, 1917-1930," PhD diss., Notre Dame, 1958.

N341.	Pospielovsky, D. *The Russian Church under the Soviet Regime, 1917-1982*, 2 vols. (Crestwood, N.Y.: St.Vladimir's Seminary Press, 1984).

N342.	Sheshko, P.T. "The Russian Orthodox Church Council of Moscow of 1917-1918," PhD diss., Saint Paul (Ottawa), 1972.

N343.	Steeves, P.D. "The Russian Babtist Union, 1917-1935: Evangelical Awakening in Russia," PhD diss., Kansas, 1976.

N344.	Szczesniak, B. (ed.) *The Russian Revolution and Religion: A Collection of Documents Concerning the Suppression of Religion by the Communists, 1917-1925* (Notre Dame: University of Notre Dame Press, 1959).

N345.	Wall, M.J. "Protestant Churches under Soviet Rule, 1917-1945: A Study of Soviet Relations with the Lutherans, Mennonites, Seventh-Day Adventists, and Pentecostals," PhD diss., George Washington, 1980.

N346.	Walters, P. "The Renovationist Coup: Personalities and Programmes," in: G.A. Hosking (ed.) *Church, Nation and State in Russia and Ukraine* (Basingstoke and London: Macmillan, 1991), pp.250-270.

N347.	Zatko, J.J. "Christian Democracy in Russia in 1917," *SEER* 40 (1961-62), pp.458-465.

N348.	Zatko, J.J. *Descent into Darkness: The Destruction of the Roman Catholic Church in Russia, 1917-1923* (Notre Dame: University of Notre Dame Press, 1965).

N349.   Zatko, Rev. J. "The Destruction of the Catholic Church in Russia, 1917-1923," PhD diss., Notre Dame, 1957.

N350.   Zatko, J.J. "The Roman Catholic Church and its Legal Position under the Provisional Government in Russia in 1917," *SEER* 38 (1959-60), pp.476-492.

N351.   Zernov, N. "The 1917 Council of the Russian Orthodox Church," *Religion in Communist Lands* 6 (1978), no.1, pp.17-25.

Architecture:

N352.   Bliznakov, M. "Nikolai Ladovskii: The Search for a Rational Science of Architecture," *Soviet Union* 7 (1980), pts.1-2, pp.170-196.

N353.   Bliznakov, M. "The Constructivist Movement in Architecture," *Soviet Union* 3 (1976), pt.2, pp.208-232.

N354.   Bliznakov, M.T. "The Search for a Style: Modern Architecture in the U.S.S.R., 1917-1932," PhD diss., Columbia, 1971.

N355.   Bowlt, J. "Art and Architecture in the Age of Revolution, 1860-1917," in: R.Auty & D.Obolensky (eds.) *An Introduction to Russian Art and Architecture* (Cambridge: Cambridge U.P., 1980).

N356.   Brumfield, W.C. "Neoclassical Aestheticism in Pre-revolutionary Russian Architecture," in: J.O. Norman (ed.) *New Perspectives on Russian and Soviet Artistic Culture* (New York: St.Martin's Press; Basingstoke & London: Macmillan, 1994), pp.41-53.

N357.   Brumfield, W.C. (ed.) *Reshaping Russian architecture: Western technology, utopian dreams* (Cambridge: Cambridge U.P., 1990).

N358.   Hamilton, G.H. *The Art and Architecture of Russia* (Harmondsworth: Penguin, 1954).

N359.   Harrison, G.S. "Vladimir Tatlin's Project for a Monument to the Third International: A Paradigm of Russian Revolutionary Thought," PhD diss., Columbia, 1981.

N360.   Hudson, H.D., Jr. *Blueprints and Blood: The Stalinization of Soviet Architecture, 1917-1937* (Princeton: Princeton U.P., 1994).

N361.   Hudson, H.D., Jr. "'The Social Condenser of Our Epoch': The Association of Contemporary Architects and the Creation of a New Way of Life in Revolutionary Russia," *JFGO* 34 (1986), pp.557-578.

N362.   Miliukov, P. *Outlines of Russian Culture. Part III: Architecture, Painting and Music*, trans.by V.Ugher & E.Davis (Philadelphia: University of Pennsylvania Press, 1943 [New York: Perpetua, 1960]).

N363.   Milner-Gulland, R. "Tower and Dome: Two Revolutionary Buildings," *SR* 47 (1988), no.1, pp.39-50.

N364. Ovsiannikova, E.B. "The Role of the Moscow Architectural School in the Emergence of the Russian Avant-Garde," in: J.O. Norman (ed.) *New Perspectives on Russian and Soviet Artistic Culture* (New York: St.Martin's Press; Basingstoke & London: Macmillan, 1994), pp.62-79.

N365. Senkevitch, A., Jr. "Trends in Soviet Architectural Thought, 1917-1937: The Growth and Decline of the Constructivist and Rationalist Movements," PhD diss., Cornell, 1974.

N366. Shvidkovsky, O.A. *Building in the U.S.S.R., 1917-1932* (London: Studio Vista, 1971).

Science, Technology, Exploration and Medicine:

N367. Andrews, J.T. "N.A. Rubakin and the Popularization of Science in the Post-October Period," *RH* 16 (1989), pt.1, pp.9-29.

N368. Barr, W. "Rusanov, *Gerkules*, and the Northern Sea Route," *CSP* 16 (1974), no.4, pp.569-609.

N369. Barr, W. "Sedov's Expedition to the North Pole, 1912-1914," *CSP* 15 (1973), no.4, pp.499-523.

N370. Barr, W. "South to Zemlya Frantsa Iosifa! The Cruise of *Sv.Anna* and Al'banov's Sledge Journey, 1912-14," *CSP* 17 (1975), no.4, pp.567-595.

N371. Barr, W. "The Drift and Rescue of *Solovei Budimirovich* in the Kara Sea, January-June 1920," *CSP* 20 (1978), no.4, pp.483-503.

N372. Baxter, J. & Atkins, T. *The Fire Came By. The Riddle of the Great Siberian Explosion* (London: MacDonald & Jane's, 1976).

N373. Berdyaev, N. *The Russian Revolution* (Ann Arbor: University of Michigan Press, 1961).

N374. Brown, J.V. "Revolution and Psychosis: The Mixing of Science and Politics in Russian Psychiatric Medicine, 1905-13," *RR* 46 (1987), no.3, pp.283-302.

N375. Brown, J.V. "The Professionalization of Russian Psychiatry: 1857-1911," PhD diss., Pennsylvania, 1981.

N376. Coopersmith, J.C. "The Electrification of Russia, 1880-1925," PhD diss., Oxford, 1985.

N377. Friedan, N.M. *Russian Physicians in an Era of Reform and Revolution, 1856-1905* (Princeton: Princeton U.P., 1981).

N378. Graham, L.R. *Science in Russia and the Soviet Union: A Short History* (Cambridge & New York: Cambridge U.P., 1993).

N379. Green, D.W. "Industrialization and the Engineering Ascendancy: A Comparative Study of American and Russian Engineering Elites, 1870-1920," PhD diss., Berkeley, 1972.

N380.   Hutchinson, J.F. "Society, Corporation or Union? Russian Physicians and the Struggle for Professional Unity, 1890-1913," *JFGO* 30 (1982), pp.37-53.

N381.   Johnson, R. "Malaria and Malaria Control in the USSR, 1917-1941," PhD diss., Georgetown, 1988.

N382.   Joravsky, D. *Soviet Marxism and Natural Science, 1917-1932* (New York: Columbia U.P., 1961).

N383.   Joravsky, D. "The First Stage of Michurinism," in: J.S.Curtiss (ed.) *Essays in Russian and Soviet History* (Leiden: E.J.Brill, 1963), pp.120-132.

N384.   Josephson, P.R. *Physics and Politics in Revolutionary Russia* (Berkeley: University of California Press, 1992).

N385.   Krug, P.F. "Russian Public Physicians and Revolution: The Pirogov Society, 1917-1920," PhD diss., Wisconsin, 1979.

N386.   Lebedkina, E.D. "International Contacts of Soviet Scientists During 1917-1924," *SSH* 10 (1971-72), no.3, pp.267-283.

N387.   Mikulak, M.W. "Lenin on the "Party" Nature of Science and Philosophy," in: J.S.Curtiss (ed.) *Essays in Russian and Soviet History* (Leiden: E.J.Brill, 1963), pp.164-176.

N388.   Sanders, J. "Drugs and Revolution: Moscow Pharmacists in the First Russian Revolution," *RR* 44 (1985), no.4, pp.351-377.

N389.   Solnick, S.L. "Revolution, Reform and the Soviet Telephone System, 1917-1927," *SS* 43 (1991), no.1, pp.157-176.

N390.   Starokadomskiy, L.M. *Charting the Russian Northern Sea Route: The Arctic Ocean Hydrographic Expedition 1910-1915*, trans.by W.Barr (Montreal & London: McGill-Queen's U.P., 1976).

N391.   Szanser, A.J.M. "The Work of the Astronomers of Pulkhovo, 1839-1918," PhD diss., London, 1969.

N392.   Todes, D.P. "From Radicalism to Scientific Convention: Biological Psychology in Russia from Sechenov to Pavlov," PhD diss., Pennsylvania, 1981.

N393.   Vernadsky, G. "Rise of Science in Russia 1700-1917," *RR* 28 (1969), no.1, pp.37-52.

N394.   Vucinich, A.S. *Science in Russian Culture: a history*, 2 vols. (Stanford: Stanford U.P., 1963-1970).

O

CENSORSHIP AND PROPAGANDA

O1.   Balmuth, D. *Censorship in Russia, 1865-1905* (Washington, D.C.: University Press of America, 1979).

O2.   Bassow, W. "The Pre-Revolutionary 'Pravda' and Tsarist Censorship," *ASEER* 13 (1954), pp.47-65.

O3.   De Saint-Rat, A.L. "The Revolutionary Era Through the Eyes of Russian Graphic Artists," *Sbornik (SGRR)* no.2 (1976), pp.34-43.

O4.   Edwards, D.W. "Religious Aspects of Monumental Propaganda in 1918," *CASS* 26 (1992), nos.1-4, pp.29-62.

O5.   Fosburg, N.T. [Tumarkin] "The Lenin Cult: Its Origins and Early Development," PhD diss., Harvard, 1975.

O6.   Kenez, P. *The Birth of the Propaganda State: Soviet Methods of Mass Mobilization, 1917-1929* (Cambridge: Cambridge U.P., 1985).

O7.   Kolonitskii, B.I. "Antibourgeois Propaganda and Anti-'*Burzhui*' Consciousness in 1917," *RR* 53 (1994), no.2, pp.183-196.

O8.   Lazarski, C. "White Propaganda Efforts in the South during the Russian Civil War, 1918-19 (the Alekseev-Denikin Period)," *SEER* 70 (1992), no.4, pp.688-707.

O9.   Liakhov, L. (ed.) *The Soviet Advertising Poster* (Moscow: Sovetsky Khudozhnik, 1972).

O10.   Lincoln, W.B. "Soviet Political Posters: Art and Ideas for the Masses," *HT* 26 (1976), pp.302-309.

O11.   Lodder, C. "Lenin's Plan of Monumental Propaganda," *Sbornik (SGRR)* nos.6-7 (1981), pp.67-82.

O12.   Nilsson, N.A. (ed.) *Art, Society, Revolution. Russia 1917-1921* (Stockholm: Almqvist & Wicksell International, 1979).

O13.   Pavlov, G. (ed.) *Soviet Political Posters* (Leningrad: Aurora, 1973).

O14.   Pethybridge, R.W. *The Spread of the Russian Revolution: Essays on 1917* (London: Macmillan, 1972).

O15.   Reeder, R. "The Interrelationship of Codes in Maiakovskii's ROSTA Posters," *Soviet Union* 7 (1980), pts.1-2, pp.28-52.

O16.   Rigberg, B. "The Efficacy of Tsarist Censorship Operations, 1894-1917," *JFGO* 14 (1966), pp.327-346.

O17.   Rigberg, B. "Tsarist Censorship Performance, 1894-1905," *JFGO* 17 (1969), pp.59-76.

O18.   Simmons, E.J. "The Origins of Literary Control," *Survey* no.36 (April-June 1961), pp.78-84.

O19.   Stites, R. "Adorning the Revolution: The Primary Symbols of Bolshevism, 1917-1918," *Sbornik (SGRR)* no.10 (1984), pp.39-42.

O20.   Swift, E.A. "Fighting the Germs of Disorder: The Censorship of Russian Popular Theater, 1888-1917," *RH* 18 (1991), pt.1, pp.1-49.

O21.   Taylor, R. "The Spark that became a Flame: the Bolsheviks, Propaganda and the Cinema," in: T.H.Rigby et al (eds.) *Authority, Power and Policy in the USSR: Essays dedicated to Leonard Schapiro* (London & Basingstoke: Macmillan, 1980), pp.57-76.

O22.   Tumarkin, N. *Lenin Lives! The Lenin Cult in Soviet Russia* (Cambridge, Mass.: Harvard U.P., 1983).

O23.   Tumarkin, N. "Religion, Bolshevism, and the Origins of the Lenin Cult," *RR* 40 (1981), no.1, pp.35-46.

O24.   Velychenko, S. "Tsarist Censorship and Ukrainian Historiography, 1828-1906," *CASS* 23 (1989), no.4, pp.385-408.

O25.   Walkin, J. "Government Controls Over the Press in Russia, 1905-1914," *RR* 13 (1954), no.3, pp.203-209.

O26.   White, S. *The Bolshevik Poster* (New Haven & London: Yale U.P., 1988).

O27.   White, S. "The Political Poster in Bolshevik Russia," *Sbornik (SGRR)* no.8 (1982), pp.24-37.

P

PRESS, PRINTING AND PUBLISHING

General:

P1.   Bayley, R.B. "Freedom and Regulation of the Russian Periodical Press," PhD diss.,
        Illinois, 1968.

P2.   Bokhanov, A.N. "The Bourgeois Press and the System of Paid Advertizing," *SSH* 25
        (1986-87), no.1, pp.81-106.

P3.   Dinershtein, E.A. *I.D. Sytin* (Moscow: Kniga, 1983).

P4.   Ferenczi, C. "Freedom of the Press under the Old Regime, 1905-1914," in: O.Crisp &
        L.Edmondson (eds.) *Civil Rights in Imperial Russia* (Oxford: Clarendon, 1989),
        pp.191-214.

P5.   Long, J.W. "Russian Manipulation of the French Press, 1904-1906," *SR* 31 (1972), no.2,
        pp.343-354.

P6.   McReynolds, L. "Imperial Russia's Newspaper Reporters: Profile of a Society in
        Transition, 1865-1914," *SEER* 68 (1990), no.2, pp.277-293.

P7.   McReynolds, L. "Autocratic Journalism: The Case of the St.Petersburg Telegraph
        Agency," *SR* 49 (1990), no.1, pp.48-57.

P8.   McReynolds, L. *The News Under Russia's Old Regime: The Development of a Mass-
        Circulation Press* (Princeton: Princeton U.P., 1991).

P9.   Maloney, P.G. "Viacheslav Polonskii: The Press and Revolution," PhD diss., Pittsburgh,
        1973.

P10.   Pethybridge, R.W. *The Spread of the Russian Revolution: Essays on 1917* (London:
        Macmillan, 1972).

P11.   Resis, A. "Lenin on Freedom of the Press," *RR* 36 (1977), no.3, pp.274-296.

P12.   Rigberg, B. "The Tsarist Press Law, 1894-1905," *JFGO* 13 (1965), pp.331-343.

P13.   Ruud, C.A. *Fighting Words: Imperial Censorship and the Russian Press, 1804-1906* (Toronto, Buffalo, London: University of Toronto Press, 1982).

P14.   Ruud, C.A. *Russian Entrepreneur: Publisher Ivan Sytin of Moscow, 1851-1934* (Montreal, Kingston, London, Buffalo: McGill-Queen's U.P., 1990).

P15.   Ruud, C.A. "The Printing Press as an Agent of Political Change in Early Twentieth-Century Russia," *RR* 40 (1981), no.4, pp.378-395.

P16.   Sampson, C.S. "The Formative Years of the Soviet Press: An Institutional History 1917-1924," PhD diss., Massachusetts, 1970.

P17.   Senn, A.E. *Nicholas Rubakin: A Life for Books* (Newtonville, Mass.: Oriental Research Partners, 1977).

P18.   Steinberg, M.D. *Moral Communities: The Culture of Class Relations in the Russian Printing Industry, 1867-1907* (Berkeley: University of California Press, 1992).

P19.   Walkin, J. "Government Controls Over the Press in Russia, 1905-1914," *RR* 13 (1954), no.3, pp.203-209.

Conservative Press:

P20.   Costello, D.R. "*Novoe Vremia* and the Conservative Dilemma, 1911-1914," *RR* 37 (1978), no.1, pp.30-50.

P21.   Krukones, J.H. "To the People: The Russian Government and the Newspaper *Sel'skii Vestnik* (*Village Herald*), 1881-1917," PhD diss., Wisconsin, 1983.

Liberal Press:

P22.   Dinerstein, E.A. "A Leviathan Among Newspapers," *SSH* 25 (1986-87), no.1, pp.36-80.

P23.   Hardeman, H. "A "Bourgeois" Newspaper in the Russian Revolution. "Utro Rossii", Moscow 1917-1918," *Rossiia/Russia* 6 (1988), pp.61-80.

P24.   McReynolds, L.L. "News and Society: *Russkoe Slovo* and the Development of a Mass-Circulation Press in Late Imperial Russia," PhD diss., Chicago, 1984.

P25.   Riha, T. "*Riech'*: A Portrait of a Russian Newspaper," *SR* 22 (1963), no.4, pp.663-682.

Revolutionary Press:

P26.   Bassow, W. "The Pre-Revolutionary 'Pravda' and Tsarist Censorship," *ASEER* 13 (1954), pp.47-65.

P27.   Corney, F. "Trotskii and the Vienna *Pravda*, 1908-1912," *CSP* 27 (1985), no.3, pp.248-268.

P28.   Elwood, R.C. "Lenin and *Pravda*, 1912-1914," *SR* 31 (1972), no.2, pp.355-380.

P29.   Frank, P. & Kirkham, B.C. "The Revival of *Pravda* in 1917," *SS* 20 (1968-69), no.3, pp.366-368.

P30.   White, J.D. "The First *Pravda* and the Russian Marxist Tradition," *SS* 26 (1974), no.2, pp.181-204.

Foreign Press and Foreign Correspondents in Russia:

P31.   Harrison, W. "The British Press and the Russian Revolution of 1905-7," *OSP(NS)* 7 (1974), pp.75-95.

P32.   Homberger, E. *John Reed* (Manchester & New York: Manchester U.P., 1990).

P33.   Homberger, E. & Biggart, J. (eds.) *John Reed and the Russian Revolution. Uncollected Articles, Letters and Speeches on Russia, 1917-1920* (New York: St.Martin's Press, 1992).

P34.   The Moscow Correspondent - A Symposium in: *Survey* no.68 (July 1968) [in particular: M.Philips Price "Before and During the Revolution," pp.122-125 and W.H.Chamberlin "Under Lenin and Stalin," pp.125-131].

P35.   Von Mohrenschildt, D. "The Early American Observers of the Russian Revolution, 1917-1921," *RR* 3 (1943-44), no.1, pp.64-74.

P36.   Wysong, R.L. "The German Newspapers and the Russian Revolutions of 1917," PhD diss., Stanford, 1951.

Q
PERSONALITIES

General:

Q1.   Coolidge, O. *Makers of the Red Revolution* (Boston: Houghton Mifflin, 1963).

Q2.   Haupt, G. & Marie, J.-J. *Makers of the Russian Revolution: Biographies of Bolshevik Leaders*, trans.by C.I.P.Ferdinand & D.M.Bellos (London: George Allen & Unwin, 1974).

Q3.   Lunacharsky, A.V. *Revolutionary Silhouettes*, trans.by M.Glenny (New York: Hill & Wang, 1968).

Alexandra (Tsarina):

Q4.   Almedingen, E.M. *The Empress Alexandra, 1872-1918. A Study* (London: Hutchinson, 1961).

Q5.   Buxhoeveden, S. *The Life and Tragedy of Alexandra Fedorovna, Empress of Russia: a biography* (London: Longman, 1928).

Q6.   Dehn, L. *The Real Tsaritsa* (London: Thornton Butterworth, 1922).

Q7.   Massie, R.K. *Nicholas and Alexandra* (London: Victor Gollancz, 1968).

Q8.   Radziwill, C. *The Intimate Life of the Last Tsarina* (London: Cassell, 1929).

Armand, I.F. (Bolshevik):

Q9.   Elwood, R.C. *Inessa Armand: Revolutionary and Feminist* (New York & Cambridge: Cambridge U.P., 1992).

Q10.   Wolfe, B.D. "Lenin and Inessa Armand," *SR* 22 (1963), no.1, pp.96-114.

Asev, E.F. (police spy & SR):

Q11.   Nikolajewsky, B. (Nikolaevskii) *Aseff The Spy. Russian Terrorist and Police Stool*, trans.by G.Reavey (Garden City, N.Y.: Doubleday, Doran & Co., 1934 [Kraus Reprint Co., N.Y., 1970]).

Axelrod, P.B. (Menshevik leader):

Q12.   Ascher, A. "Axelrod and Kautsky," *SR* 26 (1967), no.1, pp.94-112.

Q13.   Ascher, A. "Pavel Axelrod: A Conflict Between Jewish Loyalty and Revolutionary Dedication," *RR* 24 (1965), no.3, pp.249-265.

Balabanova, A.I. (Zimmerwaldist):

Q14.   Balabanoff, A. *My Life as a Rebel*, 3rd ed. (New York: Greenwood, 1968 [first published in 1938 by Harper & Bros]).

Breshko-Breshkovskaia, E.K. (SR):

Q15.   Blackwell, A.S. (ed.) *The Little Grandmother of the Russian Revolution. Reminiscences and Letters of Catherine Breshkovsky* (Boston: Little, Brown & Co., 1917).

Q16.   Breshkovskaia, K. *Hidden Springs of the Russian Revolution. Personal Memoirs of Katerina Breshkovskaia*, edited by L.Hutchinson (Stanford: Stanford U.P., 1931).

Bukharin, N.I. (Bolshevik):

Q17.   Cohen, S.F. "Bukharin and Russian Bolshevism, 1888-1927," PhD diss., Columbia, 1967.

Q18.   Cohen, S.F. *Bukharin and the Bolshevik Revolution: A Political Biography, 1888-1938* (London: Wildwood House, 1974).

Q19.   Flaherty, J.E. "The Political Career of Nicholas Bukharin to 1929," PhD diss., New York, 1954.

Q20.   Gluckstein, D. *The Tragedy of Bukharin* (London & Boulder, Colorado: Pluto Press, 1994).

Q21.   Holmes, C. "Bukharin in England," *SS* 24 (1972-73), no.1, pp.86-90.

Q22.   Kemp-Welch, A. (ed.) *The Ideas of Nikolai Bukharin* (Oxford: Clarendon, 1992).

Q23.   Kozlov, N.N. & Weitz, E.D. (eds.) *Nikolai Ivanovich Bukharin. A Centenary Appraisal* (Westport, Conn., New York, London: Praeger, 1990).

Q24.   Slatter, J. "Bukharin in Britain," *Sbornik (SGRR)* no.5 (1979), pp.41-47.

Chapaev, V.I. (Civil War partisan):

Q25.   Furmanov, D.A. *Chapayev*, trans.by G. & J.Kittell (Moscow: Foreign Languages Publishing House, 1956).

Chernov, V.M. (SR leader):

Q26.   Cross, T.B. "Purposes of Revolution: Chernov and 1917," *RR* 26 (1967), no.4, pp.351-360.

Q27.   Cross, T.B. "Viktor Chernov: Reason and Will in a Morality for Revolution," PhD diss., Indiana, 1968.

Chicherin, G.V. (Bolshevik & diplomat):

Q28.   Debo, R.K. "George Chicherin: Soviet Russia's Second Foreign Commissar," PhD diss., Nebraska, 1964.

Q29.   Debo, R.K. "The Making of a Bolshevik: Georgii Chicherin in England, 1914-1918," *SR* 25 (1966), no.4, pp.651-662.

Q30.   Hodgson, R.M. "George Chicherin," *SEER* 15 (1936-37), pp.698-703.

Q31.   Meyendorff, Baron A. "My Cousin, Foreign Commissar Chicherin," *RR* 30 (1971), no.2, pp.173-178.

Denikin, A.I. (White leader):

Q32.   Denikin, A.I. *The Russian Turmoil: Memoirs: Military, Social, and Political* (London: Hutchinson, n.d.).

Q33.   Kenez, P. "A.I. Denikin," *RR* 33 (1974), no.2, pp.139-152.

Q34.   Lehovich, D.V. *White Against Red. The Life of General Anton Denikin* (New York: Norton, 1974).

Q35.   Patoski, M. "The Career of a Russian Officer: The Memoirs of General A.I. Denikin, an Annotated Translation from the Russian," PhD diss., Texas Christian, 1973.

Dzerzhinskii, F.E. (Cheka chief):

Q36.   Davies, R.W. "Some Soviet Economic Controllers - II," *SS* 11 (1960), no.4, pp.373-392.

Q37.   Dzerzhinsky, F. *Prison Diary and Letters* (Moscow: Foreign Languages Publishing House, 1959).

Faberge, P.C. (purveyor of eggs):

Q38.   Bainbridge, H.C. *Peter Carl Faberge, Goldsmith and Jeweller to the Russian Imperial Court and the principal Crowned Heads of Europe. An illustrated record and review of his life and work, A.D. 1846-1920* (London: B.T.Batsford, 1949).

Frunze, M.V. (Bolshevik):

Q39.   Jacobs, W.D. *Frunze: The Soviet Clausewitz, 1885-1925* (The Hague: Martinus Nijhoff, 1969).

Gapon, G.A. (priest & protester):

Q40.   Gapon, Father G. *The Story of My Life* (London: Chapman & Hall, 1905).

Q41.   Sablinsky, W. *The Road to Bloody Sunday: Father Gapon and the St.Petersburg Massacre of 1905* (Princeton: Princeton U.P., 1976).

Q42.   Sablinsky, W. "The Road to Bloody Sunday: Father Gapon, His Labor Organization, and the Massacre of Bloody Sunday," PhD diss., Berkeley, 1968).

Q43.   Wolfe, B.D. "Gapon and Zubatov: An Experiment in "Police Socialism"," *RR* 7 (1947-48), no.2, pp.53-61.

Goldman, E. (anarchist):

Q44.   Drinnon, R. *Rebel in Paradise: A Biography of Emma Goldman* (Chicago & London: University of Chicago Press, 1961).

Q45.   Goldman, E. *Living My Life*, 2 vols. (London: Duckworth, 1932).

Q46.   Wenzer, K. "An Anarchist Image of the Russian Revolution," *Revolutionary Russia* 6 (1993), no.1, pp.121-144.

Q47.   Wexler, A. *Emma Goldman in Exile: From the Russian Revolution to the Spanish Civil War* (Boston: Beacon Press, 1989).

Gorky, M. (writer):

Q48.   Hare, R. *Maxim Gorky: Romantic Realist and Conservative Revolutionary* (London: Oxford U.P., 1962).

Q49.   Kaun, A. *Maxim Gorki and his Russia* (London: Jonathan Cape, 1932).

Q50.   Kaun, A. "Maxim Gorky and the Bolsheviks," *SEER* 9 (1930-31), pp.432-448.

Q51.   Kaun, A. "Maxim Gorky in the Revolution of 1905," *SEER* 9 (1930-31), pp.133-148.

Q52.   Levin, D. "Stormy Petrel: A Study of Maxim Gorky," PhD diss., Chicago, 1965..

Q53.   Troyat, H. *Gorky: A Biography*, trans. by L.Blair (London: Allison & Busby, 1991).

Q54.   Weil, I. *Gorky: His Literary Development and Influence on Soviet Intellectual Life* (New York: Random House [1966]).

Q55.   Wolfe, B.D. *The Bridge and the Abyss: The Troubled Friendship of Maxim Gorky and V.I. Lenin* (London: Pall Mall Press, 1967).

Q56.   Yedlin, T. "Maxim Gorky: His Early Revolutionary Activity and His Involvement in the Revolution of 1905," *CSP* 17 (1975), no.1, pp.76-104.

Q57.   Yedlin, T. "The Political Career of Maxim Gorky," PhD diss., Alberta, 1969.

Guchkov, A.I. (liberal & Duma president):

Q58.   Gleason, W. *Alexander Guchkov and the End of the Russian Empire* (Philadelphia: American Philosophical Society Transactions, vol.73, part 3, 1983).

Q59.   Menashe, L. ""A Liberal With Spurs": Alexander Guchkov, A Russian Bourgeois in Politics," *RR* 26 (1967), no.1, pp.38-53.

Q60.   Pares, B. "Alexander Guchkov," *SEER* 15 (1936-37), pp.121-134.

Helphand (Parvus), A.I. (socialist):

Q61.   Schurer, H. "Alexander Helphand-Parvus - Russian Revolutionary and German Patriot," *RR* 18 (1959), no.4, pp.313-331.

Q62.   Zeman, Z.A.B. & Scharlau, W.B. *The Merchant of Revolution. The Life of Alexander Israel Helphand (Parvus) 1867-1924* (London: Oxford U.P., 1965).

Kalinin, M.I. (Bolshevik):

Q63.   Wilson, J.B. "Mikhail Ivanovich Kalinin: The Revolutionary Years, 1875-1921," PhD
        diss., Boston, 1966.

Kerensky, A.F. (politician):

Q64.   Abraham, R. *Alexander Kerensky. The First Love of the Revolution* (London: Sidgwick
        & Jackson, 1987).

Q65.   Fontenot, M.J. "Alexander F. Kerensky: The Political Career of a Russian Nationalist,"
        PhD diss., Louisiana State, 1976.

Kirov, S.M. (Bolshevik):

Q66.   Biggart, J. "Kirov Before the Revolution," *SS* 23 (1972), no.3, pp.345-372.

Kornilov, L.G. (military commander):

Q67.   Collins, D.N. "General Kornilov and the Land of Kashgar: A Note," *SS* 26 (1974), no.2,
        pp.274-275.

Krasin, L.B. (Bolshevik):

Q68.   Glenny, M. "Leonid Krasin: The Years Before 1917. An Outline," *SS* 22 (1970-71), no.2,
        pp.192-221.

Q69.   Kort, M.G. "Leonid Krasin. Engineer of Revolution, 1870-1908," PhD diss., New York,
        1973.

Q70.   Krassin, L. *Leonid Krassin: His Life and Work, by his wife* (London: Skeffington, 1929).

Q71.   Morse, W.P., Jr. "Leonid Borisovich Krasin: Soviet Diplomat, 1918-1920," PhD diss.,
        Columbia, 1972.

Q72.   O'Connor, T.E. *The Engineer of Revolution: L.B. Krasin and the Bolsheviks, 1870-1926*
        (Boulder & San Francisco: Westview Press, 1992).

Q73.   Srom, J.E. "Leonid Krasin," *SEER* 5 (1926-27), pp.439-441.

Kropotkin, P.A. (anarchist):

Q74.   Miller, M.A. *Kropotkin* (Chicago & London: University of Chicago Press, 1976).

Q75.   Shub, D. "Kropotkin and Lenin," *RR* 12 (1953), no.4, pp.227-234.

Krupskaya, N.K. (Bolshevik):

Q76.   McNeal, R.H. *Bride of the Revolution. Krupskaya and Lenin* (London: Victor Gollancz, 1973).

Q77.   Segal, L. "Nadezhda Konstantinovna Krupskaya," *SEER* 18 (1939), pp.202-204.

Q78.   Vasilieva, L. *Kremlin Wives*, trans.by C.Porter (London: Weidenfeld & Nicolson, 1994).

Lenin, V.I. (Bolshevik leader):

Q79.   Anon. *Lenin. Comrade and Man*, trans. from the Russian (Moscow: Progress, n.d.).

Q80.   Balabanoff, A. *Impressions of Lenin*, trans.by I.Cesari (Ann Arbor: University of Michigan Press, 1964).

Q81.   Baranov, I. (ed.) *The Ulyanov Family* (Moscow: Progress, 1968).

Q82.   Bobrova, R. (trans.) *Lenin in Siberia: Records, Documents and Recollections* (Moscow: Progress, 1983).

Q83.   Clark, R.W. *Lenin. The Man Behind the Mask* (London & Boston: Faber & Faber, 1988).

Q84.   Cliff, T. *Lenin*, 4 vols. (*Building the Party*; *All Power to the Soviets*; *Revolution Besieged*; *The Bolsheviks and World Communism*) (London: Pluto Press, 1975-79). Also published in 3 vols. by Bookmarks (London, Chicago, Melbourne): *Building the Party* (1986), *All Power to the Soviets* (1985), *Revolution Besieged* (1987).

Q85.   Conquest, R. *Lenin* (n.p.: Fontana, 1972).

Q86.   Deutscher, I. *Lenin's Childhood* (London: Oxford U.P., 1970).

Q87.   Deutscher, T. (ed.) *Not By Politics Alone... - the other Lenin* (London: George Allen & Unwin, 1973).

Q88.   Dobb, M. "Lenin," *SEER* 19 (1940), pp.34-54.

Q89.   Elwood, R.C. "Lenin as a Book Reviewer," *Survey* no.74/75 (1970), pp.221-224.

Q90.   Elwood, R.C. "Lenin's Correspondence with Inessa Armand," *SEER* 65 (1987), no.2, pp.218-235.

Q91.   Fischer, L. *The Life of Lenin* (London: Weidenfeld & Nicolson, 1965).

Q92.   Fotieva, L. *Pages from Lenin's Life*, trans.by O.Shartse (Moscow: Foreign Languages Publishing House, 1960).

Q93.   Fox, R. *Lenin. A Biography* (London: Victor Gollancz, 1933).

Q94.   Getzler, I. "Martov's Lenin," *Revolutionary Russia* 5 (1992), no.1, pp.92-104.

Q95.   Gourfinkel, N. [Gurfinkel'] *Lenin*, trans.by M.Thornton (London: Evergreen Books, 1961).

Q96.   Hanna, G. (ed.) *About Lenin*, trans.by J.Guralsky & O.Shartse (Moscow: Progress, 1969).

Q97.   Heller, M. "Lenin and the Cheka: the Real Lenin," *Survey* 24 (1979), no.2, pp.175-192.

Q98.   Hill, C. *Lenin and the Russian Revolution* (London: English Universities Press, 1947).

Q99.   Hill, E. & Mudie, D. (eds.) *The Letters of Lenin*, trans.by E.Hill & D.Mudie (London: Chapman & Hall, 1937).

Q100.   Hollis, C. *Lenin. Portrait of a Professional Revolutionary* (London: Longmans, 1938).

Q101.   Jackson, G.D. "Lenin and the Problems of Psychohistory," *CSP* 19 (1977), no.2, pp.207-222.

Q102.   Keep, J. "Lenin's Time Budget: the Smolny Period," in: E.R.Frankel et al (eds.) *Revolution in Russia: Reassessments of 1917* (Cambridge: Cambridge U.P., 1992), pp.326-361.

Q103.   Kenetskaya, L. *Lenin in the Kremlin. His apartment and study. The people he met. The books he read* (Moscow: Novosti Press Agency Publishing House, n.d.).

Q104.   Kerzhentsev, P. *Life of Lenin* (Moscow: Co-operative Publishing Society of Foreign Workers in the U.S.S.R., 1937).

Q105.   Kochan, L. "Lenin in London," *HT* 20 (1970), pp.229-235.

Q106.   Krasin, Y.A. (ed.) *Lenin: His Life and Work. Documents and Photographs* (Moscow: Progress, 1985).

Q107.   Kristov, L.K.D. "Reflections on Angelica Balabanoff's "Lenin"," *RR* 22 (1963), no.4, pp.369-376.

Q108.   Krupskaya, N.K. *Memories of Lenin*, 2 vols., trans.by E.Verney (London: Martin Lawrence, 1930).

Q109.   Krupskaya, N.K. *Reminiscences of Lenin* (Moscow: Foreign Languages Publishing House, 1959 / London: Lawrence & Wishart, 1960).

Q110.   Leggett, G.H. "Lenin's Reported Destruction of the Cheka Archive," *Survey* 24 (1979), no.2, pp.193-199.

Q111.   Luck, D. "A Psycholinguistic Approach to Leader Personality. Imagery of Aggression, Sex, and Death in Lenin and Stalin," *SS* 30 (1978), no.4, pp.491-515.

Q112.   [Lunacharsky] *Lenin Through the Eyes of Lunacharsky* (Moscow: Novosti Press Agency Publishing House, 1981).

Q113.   McNeal, R.H. *Bride of the Revolution. Krupskaya and Lenin* (London: Victor Gollancz, 1973).

Q114.   McNeal, R.H. "Lenin and "Lise de K...": A Fabrication," *SR* 28 (1969), no.3, pp.471-474.

Q115.   Mailloux, K.F. & H.P. *Lenin: The Exile Returns* (Princeton: Auerbach Publishers, 1971).

Q116.   Marcu, V. *Lenin*, trans.by E.W.Dickes (London: Victor Gollancz, 1928).

Q117.   Maxton, J. *Lenin* (Edinburgh: Edinburgh U.P. & London: 'Daily Express' Publications, 1932).

Q118.   Medish, V. "Lenin and Japanese Money," *RR* 24 (1965), no.2, pp.165-176.

Q119.   Mirsky, D.S. *Lenin* (London: Holme Press, 1931).

Q120.   Morgan, M.C. *Lenin* (London: Edward Arnold, 1971 / Athens: Ohio U.P., 1971).

Q121.   Muravyova, L. & Sivolap-Kaftanova, I. *Lenin in London* (Moscow: Progress, 1983).

Q122.   Myakotin, B. "Lenin," *SEER* 2 (1923-24), pp.465-487.

Q123.   Page, S.W. (ed.) *Lenin. Dedicated Marxist or Revolutionary Pragmatist* (St.Louis, Missouri: Forum Press, 1977).

Q124.   Page, S.W. "Lenin in 1917: From April to July," *HSS* 4 (1957), pp.435-455.

Q125.   Page, S.W. "Lenin, Turgenev, and the Russian Landed Gentry," *CSP* 18 (1976), no.4, pp.442-456.

Q126.   Payne, R. *The Life and Death of Lenin* (New York: Simon & Schuster, 1964).

Q127.   Pomper, P. "Necaev, Lenin and Stalin: the Psychology of Leadership," *JFGO* 26 (1978), pp.11-30.

Q128.   Pospelov, P.N. (ed.) *Vladimir Ilych Lenin: A Biography* (Moscow: Progress, 1965).

Q129.   Possony, S.T. *Lenin: The Compulsive Revolutionary* (Chicago: Henry Regnery, 1964).

Q130.   Prilezhayeva, M. *Lenin: the Story of his Life* (Moscow: Progress, 1973).

Q131.   Rothstein, A. *Lenin in Britain* (Communist Party Pamphlet, n.d.).

Q132.   Schapiro, L. "Lenin and the Russian Revolution," *HT* 20 (1970), pp.324-330.

Q133.   Schapiro, L. & Reddaway, P. (eds.) *Lenin. The Man, the Theorist, the Leader. A Reappraisal* (London: Pall Mall Press, 1967).

Q134.   Senn, A. "New Documents on Lenin's Departure from Switzerland, 1917," *IRSH* 19 (1974), pp.245-276.

Q135.   Service, R. *Lenin: A Political Life. Vol.I: The Strengths of Contradiction* (London: Macmillan, 1985).

Q136.   Service, R. *Lenin: A Political Life. Vol.II: Worlds in Collision* (London: Macmillan, 1991).

Q137.   Shub, D. *Lenin: A Biography* (Harmondsworth: Penguin, 1966).

Q138.   Shub, D. "Kropotkin and Lenin," *RR* 12 (1953), no.4, pp.227-234.

Q139.   Shub, D. "New Light on Lenin," *RR* 11 (1952), no.3, pp.131-137.

Q140.   Shukman, H. *Lenin and the Russian Revolution* (London: Batsford, 1967 [reprinted by Longman, 1977]).

Q141.   Solzhenitsyn, A. *Lenin in Zurich: Chapters*, trans.by H.T.Willets (New York: Farrar, Straus & Giroux / London: Bodley Head, 1976).

Q142.   Startsev, V.I. "Lenin in October of 1917," *SSH* 27 (1988-89), no.2, pp.86-113.

Q143.   Theen, R.H.W. *Lenin* (Princeton: Princeton U.P., 1980).

Q144.   Theen, R.H.W. *Lenin: Genesis and Development of a Revolutionary* (Philadelphia & New York: Lippincott, 1973).

Q145.   *They Knew Lenin: Reminiscences of Foreign Contemporaries*, trans.by D.Myshne (Moscow: Progress, 1968).

Q146.   Trotsky, L. *Lenin* (London: George G.Harrap, 1925).

Q147.   Trotsky, L. *On Lenin. Notes Towards a Biography*, trans.by T.Deutscher (London: George G.Harrap, 1971).

Q148.   Trotsky, L.D. *The Young Lenin*, trans.by M.Eastman (Newton Abbot, Devon: David & Charles, 1972).

Q149.   Valentinov, N. "Encounters with Lenin," *RR* 13 (1954), no.3, pp.176-185.

Q150.   Valentinov, N. [N.V. Volsky] *Encounters with Lenin*, trans.by P.Rosta & B.Pearce (London: Oxford U.P., 1968).

Q151.   Valentinov, N. [N.V. Volski] *The Early Years of Lenin*, trans.by R.H.W.Theen (Ann Arbor: University of Michigan Press, 1969).

Q152.   Various "Lenin and Solzhenitsyn," *CSP* 19 (1977), no.2, pp.123-160.

Q153.   Veale, F.J.P. *The Man from the Volga. A Life of Lenin* (London: Constable, 1932).

Q154.   Vernadsky, G. *Lenin, Red Dictator*, trans.by M.W.Davis (New Haven: Yale U.P., 1931).

Q155.   Warth, R.D. *Lenin* (New York: Twayne Publishers, 1973).

Q156.   Weber, G. & H. *Lenin: Life and Works*, trans.by M.McCauley (London & Basingstoke: Macmillan, 1980).

Q157.   White, J.D. "Lenin, the Germans and the February Revolution," *Revolutionary Russia* 5 (1992), no.1, pp.1-21.

Q158.   Wolfe, B.D. "Lenin and the Agent Provocateur Malinovsky," *RR* 5 (1945-46), no.1, pp.49-69.

Q159.   Wolfe, B.D. *Revolution and Reality: Essays on the Origin and Fate of the Soviet System* (Chapel Hill: University of North Carolina Press, 1981).

Q160.   Wolfe, B.D. *The Bridge and the Abyss: The Troubled Friendship of Maxim Gorky and V.I. Lenin* (London: Pall Mall Press, 1967).

Q161.   Wolfe, B.D. *Three Who Made a Revolution. Lenin, Trotsky and Stalin* (New York: Dial Press, 1948).

Q162.   Zetkin, C. *Reminiscences of Lenin* (London: Modern Books, 1929).

Litvinov, M.M. (Bolshevik):

Q163.   Cornwell, N. "A Bolshevik in Belfast: An Episode in the Biography of Maxim Litvinov," *Irish Slavonic Studies* 5 (1984), pp.43-47.

Q164.   Phillips, H. "From a Bolshevik to a British Subject: The Early Years of Maksim M. Litvinov," *SR* 48 (1989), no.3, pp.388-398.

Q165.   Phillips, H.D. *Between the Revolution and the West: A Political Biography of Maxim M. Litvinov* (Boulder, Colorado: Westview Press, 1992).

Q166.   Pope, A.U. *Maxim Litvinoff* (London: Secker & Warburg, 1943).

Lunacharsky, A.V. (Bolshevik):

Q167.   Fitzpatrick, S. "A.V. Lunacharsky: Recent Soviet Interpretations and Republications," *SS* 18 (1967), no.3, pp.267-289.

Q168.   O'Connor, T.E. *The Politics of Soviet Culture. Anatolii Lunacharskii* (Ann Arbor: UMI Research Press, 1983).

Q169.   Price, M.P. "Anatole Lunacharsky," *SEER* 12 (1933-34), pp.728-730.

Q170.   Tait, A.L. *Lunacharsky: Poet of the Revolution (1875-1907)* (Birmingham Slavonic Monographs no.15, Department of Russian Language and Literature, University of Birmingham, n.d.).

Q171.   Tait, A.L. "Lunacharsky, the 'Poet-Commissar'," *SEER* 52 (1974), pp.234-252.

Lvov, G.E. (zemstvo activist & Kadet):

Q172.   Onu, A. "Prince George Lvov," *SEER* 4 (1925-26), pp.168-171.

Malinovsky, R.V. (Bolshevik & police spy):

Q173.   Elwood, R.C. *Roman Malinovsky: A Life Without Cause* (Newtonville, Mass.: Oriental Research Partners, 1977).

Q174.   Elwood, R.C. "Scoundrel or Saviour? Solzhenitsyn's View of Roman Malinovskii," *CSP* 19 (1977), no.2, pp.161-166.

Mannerheim, C.G.E. (field marshal):

Q175.   Borenius, T. *Field-Marshal Mannerheim* (London & Melbourne: Hutchinson, 1940).

Q176.   Jagerskiold, S. *Mannerheim. Marshal of Finland* (Minneapolis: University of Minnesota Press, 1986).

Q177.   Screen, J.E.O. *Mannerheim: The Years of Preparation* (London: C.Hurst & Co., 1970).

Martov, L. (Menshevik leader):

Q178.   Getzler, I. "Julius Martov: His Role and Place in Russian Social Democracy," PhD diss., London, 1965.

Q179.   Getzler, I. *Martov: A Political Biography of a Russian Social Democrat* (Cambridge: Cambridge U.P., 1967).

Miliukov, P.N. (Kadet leader):

Q180.   Goldenweiser, A. "Paul Miliukov - Historian and Statesman," *RR* 16 (1957), no.2, pp.3-14.

Q181.   Morse, M. "The Political Career of Paul Nikolaevich Miliukov, 1905 to 1917," PhD diss., Wisconsin, 1950.

Q182.   Riha, T. *A Russian European: Paul Miliukov in Russian Politics* (Notre Dame & London: University of Notre Dame Press, 1969).

Q183.   Riha, T. "Paul Miliukov's Parliamentary Career, 1907-1917," PhD diss., Harvard, 1962.

Q184.   Schwartzman, J. "The Philosophy and Politics of Paul N. Miliukov (1859-1943) (To the End of the 1905 Revolution)," PhD diss., New York, 1970.

Q185.   Stockdale, M.K. "Paul N. Miliukov: An Intellectual Biography, 1859-1905," PhD diss., Harvard, 1989.

Nicholas II (Tsar):

Q186.   Bykov, P.M. *The Last Days of Tsardom*, trans.by A.Rothstein (London: Martin Lawrence, n.d.).

Q187.   Ferro, M. *Nicholas II: The Last of the Tsars*, trans.by B.Pearce (London: Penguin, 1992).

Q188.   Frankland, N. *Crown of Tragedy. Nicholas II, Last of the Tsars* (London: Kimber, 1960).

Q189.   Hanbury-Williams, J. *The Emperor Nicholas II as I Knew Him* (London: Humphreys, 1922).

Q190.   Lensen, G.A. "The Attempt on the Life of Nicholas II in Japan," *RR* 20 (1961), no.3, pp.232-253.

Q191.   Lieven, D. *Nicholas II: Emperor of all the Russias* (London: John Murray, 1993).

Q192.   Massie, R.K. *Nicholas and Alexandra* (London: Victor Gollancz, 1968).

Q193.   Oldenburg, S.S. *The Last Tsar. Nicholas II: His Reign and His Russia*, 4 vols. (Gulf Breeze, Florida, 1977).

Q194.   Radzinsky, E. *The Last Tsar: The Life and Death of Nicholas II*, trans.by M.Schwartz (London, Sydney, Auckland: Hodder & Stoughton, 1992).

Q195.   Radziwill, C. *Nicholas II: Last of the Tsars* (London: Cassell, 1931).

Q196.   Richards, G. *The Hunt for the Czar* (London: Peter Davies, 1970).

Q197.   Summers, A. & Mangold, T. *The File on the Tsar* (London: Victor Gollancz, 1976).

Q198.   Vogt, G. *Nicholas II* (New York: Chelsea House, 1987).

Pobedonostsev, K.P. (conservative):

Q199.   Byrnes, R.F. *Pobedonostsev. His Life and Thought* (Bloomington: Indiana U.P., 1968).

Q200.   Schilovsky, P.P. "Reminiscences of K.P. Pobedonostsev," *SEER* 30 (1951-52), pp.364-375.

Q201.   Shoob, L. "Konstantin Petrovich Pobedonostsev: A Study in Reaction," PhD diss., California, Berkeley, 1947.

Q202.   Sorenson, T.C. "The Thought and Politics of Konstantin P. Pobedonostsev," PhD diss., Washington, 1977.

Rakovsky, K.G. (revolutionary):

Q203.   Conte, F. *Christian Rakovski (1873-1941): A Political Biography*, trans.by A.P.M.Bradley (Boulder, Colorado: East European Monographs, 1989).

Raskolnikov, F.F. (Bolshevik):

Q204.   Saul, N.E. "Fedor Raskolnikov, a "Secondary Bolshevik"," *RR* 32 (1973), no.2, pp.131-142.

Rasputin, G.E. (favourite of Tsarina):

Q205.   De Jonge, A. *The Life and Times of Grigorii Rasputin* (n.p.: Fontana/Collins, 1982, 1983).

Q206.   Fulop-Miller, R. *Rasputin. The Holy Devil*, trans.by F.S.Flint & D.F.Tait (London: Collins, 1967).

Q207.   Kulikowski, M. "Rethinking the Origins of the Rasputin Legend," in: E.H. Judge & J.Y. Simms, Jr. (eds.) *Modernization and Revolution: Dilemmas of Progress in Late Imperial Russia: Essays in Honor of Arthur P. Mendel* (New York: East European Monographs, distributed by Columbia U.P., 1992), pp.169-186.

Q208.   Liepman, H. *The Mad Monk of Russia*, trans.by E.Fitzgerald (New York: Rolton House, 1964) [British title: *Rasputin: A New Judgment*].

Q209.   Rasputin, M. *My Father* (London: Cassell, 1934).

Q210.   Rasputin, M. & Barham, P. *Rasputin: The Man Behind the Myth, A Personal Memoir* (Englewood Cliffs, N.J.: Prentice-Hall, 1977).

Q211.   Vullaimy, C.E. (ed.) *The Red Archives. Russian State Papers and Other Documents relating to the Years 1915-1918*, trans.by A.L.Hynes (London: Geoffrey Bles, 1929).

Q212.   Wilson, C. *Rasputin and the Fall of the Romanovs* (London: Arthur Barker, 1964).

Q213.   Youssoupoff, Prince *Rasputin: His Malignant Influence and his Assassination*, trans.by O.Rayner (London: Jonathan Cape, 1934).

Rodzianko, M.V. (liberal):

Q214.   Eddy, E.M. "The Last President of the Duma: A Political Biography of M.V. Rodzianko," PhD diss., Kansas State, 1975.

Q215.   Rodzianko, M.V. *The Reign of Rasputin. An Empire's Collapse. Memoirs of M.V. Rodzianko*, trans.by C.Zvegintzoff (London: A.M.Philpot, 1927).

Rubakin, N.A. (bibliographer & writer):

Q216.   Senn, A.E. *Nicholas Rubakin: A Life for Books* (Newtonville, Mass.: Oriental Research Partners, 1977).

Rykov, A.I. (Bolshevik):

Q217.   Oppenheim, S.A. "Aleksei Ivanovich Rykov (1881-1938): A Political Biography," PhD diss., Indiana, 1972.

Q218.   Oppenheim, S.A. "The Making of a Right Communist - A.I. Rykov to 1917," *SR* 36 (1977), no.3, pp.420-440.

Shulgin, V.V. (monarchist):

Q219.   Adams, B. "The Extraordinary Career of Vasilii Shul'gin," *Revolutionary Russia* 5 (1992), no.2, pp.193-208.

Q220.   Shulgin, V.V. *Days of the Russian Revolution: Memoirs from the Right, 1905-1917,* trans.by B.F.Adams (Gulf Breeze, Fl.: Academic International Press, 1990).

Spiridonova, M.A. (terrorist & Left SR):

Q221.   Steinberg, I. *Spiridonova: Revolutionary Terrorist,* trans.by G.David & E.Mosbacher (London: Methuen, 1935).

Stalin, J.V. (Bolshevik):

Q222.   Daniels, R.V. *Trotsky, Stalin and Socialism* (Boulder, Colorado: Westview Press, 1991).

Q223.   Ellison, H.J. "Stalin and His Biographers: The Lenin-Stalin Relationship," in: R.C.Elwood (ed.) *Reconsiderations on the Russian Revolution* (Cambridge, Mass.: Slavica, 1976), pp.256-269.

Q224.   Himmer, R. "On the Origin and Significance of the Name 'Stalin'," *RR* 45 (1986), no.3, pp.269-286.

Q225.   Lee, E. "The Eremin Letter: Documentary Proof that Stalin was an Okhrana Spy?" *Revolutionary Russia* 6 (1993), no.1, pp.55-96.

Q226.   Luck, D. "A Psycholinguistic Approach to Leader Personality. Imagery of Aggression, Sex, and Death in Lenin and Stalin," *SS* 30 (1978), no.4, pp.491-515.

Q227.   McNeal, R.H. "Trotsky's Interpretation of Stalin," *CSP* 5 (1961), pp.87-97.

Q228. Pomper, P. "Necaev, Lenin and Stalin: the Psychology of Leadership," *JFGO* 26 (1978), pp.11-30.

Q229. Slusser, R.M. "On the Question of Stalin's Role in the Bolshevik Revolution," *CSP* 19 (1977), no.4, pp.405-416.

Q230. Slusser, R.M. *Stalin in October: The Man Who Missed the Revolution* (Baltimore & London: Johns Hopkins U.P., 1987).

Q231. Smith, E.E. *The Young Stalin. The early years of an elusive revolutionary* (London: Cassell, 1968).

Q232. Suny, R.G. "A Journeyman for the Revolution: Stalin and the Labour Movement in Baku, June 1907-May 1908," *SS* 23 (1972), no.3, pp.373-394.

Q233. Suny, R.G. "Beyond Psychohistory: The Young Stalin in Georgia," *SR* 50 (1991), no.1, pp.48-58.

Q234. Trotsky, L. *Stalin. An Appraisal of the Man and His Influence*, trans.by C.Malamuth (London: Hollis & Carter, 1947).

Q235. Tucker, R.C. *Stalin as Revolutionary, 1879-1929. A Study in History and Personality* (New York: W.W.Norton, 1973).

Q236. Tucker, R.C. "Stalin's Revolutionary Career Before 1917," in: A.Rabinowitch et al (eds.) *Revolution and Politics in Russia: Essays in Memory of B.I. Nicolaevsky* (Bloomington: Indiana U.P., 1972), pp.157-171.

Q237. Van Ree, E. "Stalin's Organic Theory of the Party," *RR* 52 (1993), no.1, pp.43-57.

Stolypin, P.A. (Prime Minister 1906-11):

Q238. Bock, M.S. "Stolypin in Saratov," *RR* 12 (1953), no.3, pp.187-193.

Q239. Conroy, M.S. *Petr Arkad'evich Stolypin. Practical Politics in Late Tsarist Russia* (Boulder: Westview Press, 1976).

Q240. Fallows, T. "Governor Stolypin and the Revolution of 1905 in Saratov," in: R.A.Wade & S.J.Seregny (eds.) *Politics and Society in Provincial Russia: Saratov, 1590-1917* (Columbus, Ohio: Ohio State U.P., 1989), pp.160-190.

Q241. Levin, A. "Peter Arkadevich Stolypin: a Political Reappraisal," *JMH* 37 (1965), no.4, pp.445-463.

Q242. Strakhovsky, L.I. "The Statesmanship of Peter Stolypin: A Re-appraisal," *SEER* 37 (1958-59), pp.348-370.

Q243. Tokmakoff, G.B. "A Political Evaluation of P.A. Stolypin, 1906-1911," PhD diss., London, 1963.

Q244. Tokmakoff, G. "Stolypin's Assassin," *SR* 24 (1965), no.2, pp.314-321.

Q245. Von Bock, M.P. *Reminiscences of My Father, Peter A. Stolypin*, trans.by M. Patoski (Metuchen, N.J.: Scarecrow Press, 1970).

Q246. Zenkovsky, A.V. *Stolypin: Russia's Last Great Reformer*, trans.by M.Patoski (Princeton: Kingston Press, 1986).

Struve, P.B. (journalist):

Q247. Borman, A. "Peter Struve's Escape from Soviet Russia," *RR* 12 (1953), no.1, pp.42-50.

Q248. Pipes, R. *Struve: Liberal on the Left, 1870-1905* (Cambridge, Mass.: Harvard U.P., 1970).

Q249. Pipes, R. *Struve: Liberal on the Right, 1905-1944* (Cambridge, Mass.: Harvard U.P., 1980).

Q250. Putnam, G. "P.B. Struve's View of the Russian Revolution of 1905," *SEER* 45 (1967), pp.457-473.

Q251. Williams, H. "Peter Struve," *SEER* 4 (1925-26), pp.18-22.

Sukhomlinov, V.A. (military commander):

Q252. Doumbadze, V.D. *Russia's War Minister: The Life and Work of Adjutant-General Vladimir Alexandrovitsh Soukhomlinov* (London: Simpkin Marshall, 1915).

Sverdlov, Ya.M. (Bolshevik):

Q253. Duval, C. "Iakov Mikhailovich Sverdlov: Founder of the Bolshevik Party Machine," in: R.C.Elwood (ed.) *Reconsiderations on the Russian Revolution* (Cambridge, Mass.: Slavica, 1976), pp.211-240.

Q254. Duval, C.A., Jr. "The Forgotten Bolshevik: Jacob Mikhailovich Sverdlov 1885-1917," PhD diss., Texas, 1971.

Q255. Odom, W.E. "Sverdlov: Bolshevik Party Organiser," *SEER* 44 (1966), pp.421-443.

Q256. Zelikson-Bobrovskaya, T.S. *The First President of the Republic of Labour. A Short Biographical Sketch of the Life and Work of Y.M. Sverdlov* (London: Modern Books, 1932).

Tikhon (Patriarch):

Q257. Swan, J.B. "A Biography of Patriarch Tikhon," PhD diss., Pennsylvania, 1955.

Trotsky, L.D. (revolutionary):

Q258.   Brotherstone, T. & Dukes, P. (eds.) *The Trotsky Reappraisal* (Edinburgh: Edinburgh U.P., 1992).

Q259.   Carmichael, J. *Trotsky: An Appreciation of His Life* (London: Hodder & Stoughton / New York: St.Martin's Press, 1975).

Q260.   Corney, F. "Trotskii and the Vienna *Pravda*, 1908-1912," *CSP* 27 (1985), no.3, pp.248-268.

Q261.   Cox, M. "Trotsky and His Interpreters: or, Will the Real Leon Trotsky Please Stand Up?" *RR* 51 (1992), no.1, pp. 84-102.

Q262.   Daniels, R.V. *Trotsky, Stalin and Socialism* (Boulder, Colorado: Westview Press, 1991).

Q263.   Deutscher, I. *The Prophet Armed. Trotsky: 1879-1921* (London: Oxford U.P., 1954).

Q264.   Eastman, M. *Leon Trotsky. The Portrait of a Youth* (London: Faber & Gwyer, 1926).

Q265.   Howe, I. *Leon Trotsky* (New York: Viking, 1978).

Q266.   Kern, G. "Trotsky's Autobiography," *RR* 36 (1977), no.3, pp.297-319.

Q267.   King, D. *Trotsky. A Photographic Biography* (Oxford & New York: Basil Blackwell, 1986).

Q268.   Lovell, S. (ed.) *Leon Trotsky Speaks* (New York: Pathfinder, 1972).

Q269.   McNeal, R.H. "Trotsky's Trotskyism," *Survey* 24 (1979), no.1, pp.174-177.

Q270.   Meijer, J.M. (ed.) *The Trotsky Papers, 1917-1922*, 2 vols. (London: Mouton, 1964 and 1971).

Q271.   Pantsov, A.V. "Lev Davidovich Trotskii," *SSH* 30 (1991), no.1, pp.7-43.

Q272.   Payne, R. *The Life and Death of Trotsky* (London: W.H.Allen, 1978).

Q273.   Reed, D. & Jakobson, M. "Trotsky Papers at the Hoover Institution: One Chapter of an Archival Mystery Story," *AHR* 92 (1987), no.2, pp.363-375.

Q274.   Segal, R. *The Life and Times of Leon Trotsky* (London: Hutchinson, 1979).

Q275.   Serge, V. & Trotsky, N.S. *The Life and Death of Leon Trotsky*, trans.by A.J.Pomerans (London: Wildwood House, 1975).

Q276.   Sinclair, L. *Leon Trotsky: A Bibliography* (Stanford: Hoover Institution Press, 1972).

Q277.   Thatcher, I.D. "Russian Social Patriotism in Trotskii's Paris Writings during the First World War," *Revolutionary Russia* 6 (1993), no.2, pp.229-276.

Q278.   Thatcher, I.D. "Trotsky and *Kievskaya mysl'*," *Irish Slavonic Studies* 14 (1993), pp.87-102.

Q279. Thatcher, I.D. "Trotsky and the Censor," *EHQ* 24 (1994), no.2, pp.245-258.

Q280. Trotsky, L. *My Flight from Siberia, 1907*, trans.by M.Campbell (Colombo, Sri Lanka: Young Socialist Publications, 1969).

Q281. Trotsky, L.D. *My Life: an Attempt at an Autobiography* (New York: Scribner, 1930).

Q282. Trotsky, L. *My Life: The Rise and Fall of a Dictator* (London: Thornton Butterworth, 1930).

Q283. Trotsky, L. *The Military Writings and Speeches of Leon Trotsky: How the Revolution Armed*, 5 vols., trans.by B.Pearce (London: New Park Publications, 1979-81).

Q284. Trotsky, L. *Trotsky's Diary in Exile, 1935*, trans.by E.Zarudnaya (London: Faber & Faber, 1959).

Q285. Warth, R.D. *Leon Trotsky* (Boston: Twayne Publishers, G.K.Hall & Co., 1977).

Q286. Winsbury, R. "Trotsky in 1905," *HT* 26 (1976), pp.213-222.

Q287. Wolfe, B.D. *The Bridge and the Abyss: The Troubled Friendship of Maxim Gorky and V.I. Lenin* (London: Pall Mall Press, 1967).

Tsereteli, I.G. (Menshevik):

Q288. Roobol, W.H. *Tsereteli - A Democrat in the Russian Revolution. A Political Biography*, trans.by P.Hyams & L.Richards (The Hague: Martinus Nijhoff, 1976).

Witte, S.Yu. (Tsarist statesman):

Q289. Aldanov, M. "Count Witte," *RR* 1 (1941-42), no.1, pp.56-64.

Q290. De Enden, M.N. "The Roots of Witte's Thought," *RR* 29 (1970), no.1, pp.6-24.

Q291. Dillon, E.J. "Two Russian Statesmen," *The Quarterly Review* 236 (1921), no.469, pp.402-417.

Q292. Harcave, S. "The Hessen Redaction of the Witte Memoirs," *JFGO* 36 (1988), pp.268-276.

Q293. Witte, Count *The Memoirs of Count Witte*, trans.by A.Yarmolinsky (London: William Heinemann, 1921).

Q294. Witte, Count *The Memoirs of Count Witte*, trans. & edited by S.Harcave (Armonk, New York, London: M.E.Sharpe, 1990).

Woytinsky, W.S. (Bolshevik & scholar):

Q295.   Woytinsky, E.S. (ed.) *So Much Alive: the Life and Work of Wladimir S. Woytinsky* (New York: Vanguard, 1962).

Q296.   Woytinsky, E.S. *Two Lives in One* (New York & Washington: Praeger, 1965).

Q297.   Woytinsky, W.S. *Stormy Passage: A Personal History Through Two Russian Revolutions to Democracy and Freedom: 1905-1960* (New York: Vanguard Press, 1961).

Wrangel, P.N. (White general):

Q298.   Williams, H. "General Wrangel," *SEER* 7 (1928-29), pp.198-204.

Q299.   Wrangel, A. *General Wrangel, 1878-1929: Russia's White Crusader* (London: Leo Cooper, 1990).

Q300.   Wrangel, Baron P.N. (Vrangel) *Always with Honor* (New York: Robert Speller, 1957) [published earlier as *The Memoirs of General Wrangel* (New York: Duffield, 1930)].

Yusupov, F. (Rasputin's assassin):

Q301.   Youssoupoff [Yusupov], Prince F. *Lost Splendour*, trans.by A.Green & N.Katkoff (London: Jonathan Cape, 1953).

Zasulich, V.I. (revolutionary):

Q302.   Bergman, J. *Vera Zasulich: A Biography* (Stanford: Stanford U.P., 1983).

Q303.   Bergman, J.A. "Vera Zasulich and the Politics of Revolutionary Unity," PhD diss., Yale, 1977.

Q304.   Kelly, R.M.C. "The Role of Vera Ivanovna Zasulich in the Development of the Russian Revolutionary Movement," PhD diss., Indiana, 1967.

Q305.   Meincke, E. "Vera Ivanova Zasulich: A Political Life," PhD diss., SUNY, Binghamton, 1984.

Q306.   Scepansky, A.J. "Vera Ivanovna Zasulich: From Revolutionary Terror to Scientific Marxism," PhD diss., George Washington, 1974.

Zinoviev, G.E. (Bolshevik):

Q307.   Hedlin, M.W. "Grigorii Zinoviev: The Myths of the Defeated," in: R.C.Elwood (ed.) *Reconsiderations on the Russian Revolution* (Cambridge, Mass.: Slavica, 1976), pp.184-210.

Q308.   Hedlin, M.W. "Zinoviev's Revolutionary Tactics in 1917," *SR* 34 (1975), no.1, pp.19-43.

R

DIARIES, MEMOIRS, TRAVEL AND EYEWITNESS ACCOUNTS

R1.   Alexandrian, T. *Thane: Memories of a Lost World* (Bethesda, Md.: Adder & Adder, 1988).

R2.   Almedingen, E.M. *Unbroken Unity, A Memoir of Grand-Duchess Serge of Russia, 1864-1918* (London: Bodley Head, 1964).

R3.   Andreyev, O.C. *Cold Spring in Russia*, trans.by M.Carlisle (Ann Arbor: Ardis, 1978).

R4.   Anet, C. *Through the Russian Revolution: Notes of an Eye-Witness, from 12th March - 30th May* (London: Hutchinson, 1917).

R5.   Anon. (intro.by A.Wood) *Russian Court Memoirs, 1914-1916* (Cambridge: Faulkner, 1992).

R6.   Anon. (intro.by A.Wood) *The Fall of the Romanoffs* (Cambridge: Faulkner, 1992).

R7.   Babey, A.M. "Americans in Russia 1776-1917: A Study of the American Travelers in Russia from the American Revolution to the Russian Revolution," PhD diss., Columbia, 1938.

R8.   Baring, M. *A Year in Russia* (London: Methuen, 1907).

R9.   Baring, M. *The Mainsprings of Russia* (London: T.Nelson, 1914).

R10.   Berkman, A. *The "Anti-Climax": The Concluding Chapter of My Russian Diary "The Bolshevik Myth"* (Berlin, 1925).

R11.   Berkman, A. *The Bolshevik Myth (Diary 1920-1922)* (London: Hutchinson, 1925).

R12.   Bonsal, S. *Suitors and Suppliants: The Little Nations at Versailles* (Port Washington, N.Y.: Kennikat Press, 1969 [first published in 1946]).

R13.   Botchkareva, M. *Yaska: My Life as Peasant, Exile and Soldier* (London: Constable, 1919).

R14.   Brandstrom, E. *Among Prisoners of War in Russia and Siberia*, trans.by C.M.Richmers (London: Hutchinson, 1929)

R15.   Bryant, L. *Six Red Months in Russia. An Observer's Account of Russia Before and During the Proletarian Dictatorship* (New York: Doran, 1918 & New York: Arno & The New York Times, 1970).

R16.   Buchanan, M. *Petrograd: The City of Trouble, 1914-1918* (London: Collins, 1918).

R17.   Buchanan, M. *The Dissolution of an Empire* (London: John Murray, 1932).

R18.   Bukhoeveden, S. *Left Behind: Fourteen Months in Siberia during the Revolution, December 1917-February 1919* (London: Longmans, Green, 1929).

R19.   Bulygin, P. "In Prison at Ekaterinburg: An Account of an Attempt to Rescue the Imperial Family," *SEER* 7 (1928-29), pp.55-66.

R20.   Bury, H. *Russian Life Today* (London: Mowbrays, 1915).

R21.   Cantacuzene, Princess *Revolutionary Days: Recollections of Romanoffs and Bolsheviki, 1914-1917* (London: Chapman & Hall, 1920).

R22.   Carlisle, O.A. *Voices in the Snow; Encounters with Russian Writers* (London: Weidenfeld & Nicolson, 1963).

R23.   Cockfield, J.H. "Philip Jordan and the October Revolution," *HT* 28 (1978), pp.220-227.

R24.   Colton, E.T., Sr. "With the Y.M.C.A. in Revolutionary Russia," *RR* 14 (1955), no.2, pp.128-139.

R25.   Cyril, H.I.H. the Grand Duke *My Life in Russia's Service - Then and Now* (London: Selwyn & Blount, 1939).

R26.   De Lon, R.S. "Stalin and Social Democracy: 1905-1922: The Political Diaries of David A. Sagirashvili," PhD diss., Georgetown, 1974.

R27.   Denikin, A.I. *The Russian Turmoil: Memoirs: Military, Social, and Political* (London: Hutchinson, n.d.).

R28.   De Robien, L. *The Diary of a Diplomat in Russia, 1917-1918*, trans.by C.Sykes (New York & Washington: Praeger, 1970).

R29.   De Smolianoff, O. *Russia (The Old Regime) 1903-1919: Personal Recollections* (New York, 1944).

R30.   Dukes, Sir P. *Come Hammer, Come Sickle!* (London: Cassell, 1947).

R31.   Durland, K. *The Red Reign: The True Story of an Adventurous Year in Russia* (London: Hodder & Stoughton, 1907).

R32.   Dwinger, E.E. *The Army Behind Barbed Wire: a Siberian Diary*, trans.by I.F.D.Morrow (London: George Allen & Unwin, 1930).

R33. Ehrenburg, I. *First Years of Revolution, 1918-21*, trans.by A.Bostock (London: MacGibbon & Kee, 1962).

R34. Emmons, T. & Patenaude, B. (eds.) *War, Revolution, and Peace in Russia: The Passages of Frank Golder, 1914-1927* (Stanford: Hoover Institution Press, 1992).

R35. Fedotoff-White, D. *Survival Through War and Revolution in Russia* (London: Humphrey Milford / Oxford U.P., 1939).

R36. Fenin, A.I. *Coal and Politics in Late Imperial Russia: Memoirs of a Russian Mining Engineer*, trans.by A.Fediaevsky (DeKalb: Northern Illinois U.P., 1990).

R37. Francis, D. *Russia from the American Embassy, April, 1916-November, 1918* (New York: Scribner, 1921).

R38. Fredericks, A. "Souvenir of a Petrograd Evening," *RR* 9 (1950), no.3, pp.205-208.

R39. Galton, D. & Keep, J.L.H. (eds.) "Letters from Vladivostok 1918-1923," *SEER* 45 (1967), pp.497-530.

R40. Goldman, E. *My Disillusionment in Russia* (London: C.W.Daniel, 1925).

R41. Goldman, E. *My Further Disillusionment in Russia* (Garden City, New York, 1924).

R42. Goldman. E. *The Crushing of the Russian Revolution* (London, 1922).

R43. Goode, W.T. *Bolshevism at Work* (London: George Allen & Unwin, 1920).

R44. Got'e, I.V. *Time of Troubles: The Diary of Iurii Vladimirovich Got'e, Moscow, July 8, 1917 to July 23, 1922*, trans.by T.Emmons (Princeton: Princeton U.P., 1988).

R45. Gough, H. *Soldiering On, being the Memoirs of General Sir Hubert Gough* (London: Arthur Baker, 1954).

R46. Graham, S. *Through Russian Central Asia* (London: Cassell, 1916).

R47. Gruzenberg, O.O. *Yesterday: Memoirs of a Russian-Jewish Lawyer*, trans.by D.C.Rawson & T.Tipton (Berkeley & Los Angeles: University of California Press, 1981).

R48. Guins, G.C. "The Fateful Days of 1917," *RR* 26 (1967), no.3, pp.286-295.

R49. Gukovskii, A.I. "How I Became a Historian," *SSH* 5 (1966-67), no.2, pp.3-26.

R50. Hard, W. *Raymond Robins' Own Story [of his experiences in Russia under the Bolsheviks]* (New York & London: Harper & Bros., 1920).

R51. Harper, S.N. *The Russia I Believe In* (Chicago: University of Chicago Press, 1945).

R52. Harrison, M. *Marooned in Moscow: The Story of an American Woman Imprisoned in Russia* (London: Thornton Butterworth, 1921).

R53. Heald, E.T. *Witness to Revolution: Letters from Russia, 1916-1919* (Kent, Ohio: Kent State U.P., 1972).

R54.   Hird, J.W. *Under Czar and Soviet: My Thirty Years in Russia* (London: Hurst & Blackett, 1932).

R55.   Hoare, S. *The Fourth Seal: the End of a Russian Chapter* (London: Heinemann, 1930).

R56.   Homberger, E. & Biggart, J. (eds.) *John Reed and the Russian Revolution. Uncollected Articles, Letters and Speeches on Russia, 1917-1920* (New York: St.Martin's Press, 1992).

R57.   Horsbrugh-Porter, A. (ed.) *Memories of Revolution: Russian Women Remember* (London: Routledge, 1993).

R58.   Houghteling, J.L., Jr. *A Diary of the Russian Revolution* (New York: Dodd, Mead & Co., 1918).

R59.   Il'in, A.T. (Ilyin-Zhenevsky, A.F.) *From the February Revolution to the October Revolution, 1917* (London: Modern Books, 1931).

R60.   Ilyin-Znenevsky, A.F. *The Bolsheviks in Power. Reminiscences of the Year 1918*, trans.by B.Pearce (London: New Park, 1984).

R61.   Ivanov-Razumnik, R.V. "After Twenty Years," *RR* 10 (1951), no.2, pp.146-154 and *RR* 10 (1951), no.3, pp.210-225.

R62.   Jones, S. *Russia in Revolution. Being the Experiences of an Englishman in Petrograd during the Upheaval* (London: Herbert Jenkins, 1917).

R63.   Kabanov, P.I. "Pages from the Life of a Teacher of History," *SSH* 9 (1970-71), no.1, pp.3-42.

R64.   Kerensky, A. "Russia on the Eve of World War I," *RR* 5 (1945-46), no.1, pp.10-30.

R65.   Kerensky, A.F. *The Catastrophe. Kerensky's Own Story of the Russian Revolution* (New York & London: D.Appleton, 1927).

R66.   Kerensky, A.F. *The Crucifixion of Liberty*, trans.by G.Kerensky (London: Arthur Barker, 1934).

R67.   Kerensky, A. *The Kerensky Memoirs. Russia and History's Turning Point* (London: Cassell, 1966).

R68.   Korostovetz, V. *Seed and Harvest*, trans.by D.Lumby (London: Faber & Faber, 1931).

R69.   Kroger, T. *The Forgotten Village: Four Years in Siberia* (London: Hutchinson, 1936).

R70.   Lansbury, G. *What I Saw in Russia* (London: Leonard Parsons, 1920).

R71.   Lied, J. *Return to Happiness* (London: Macmillan, 1943).

R72.   Littauer, V.S. *Russian Hussar* (London: J.A.Allen, 1965).

R73.   Lockhart, R.B. "The February Revolution of 1917," *HT* 41 (1991), pp.34-41.

R74.   Lockhart, R.B. *The Diaries of Sir Robert Bruce Lockhart, Vol.I: 1915-1938* (London: Macmillan, 1973).

R75.   Lockhart, R.H.B. *The Two Revolutions: An Eye-Witness Account of Russia, 1917* (Chester Springs, Pa.: Dufour Editions, 1967).

R76.   Loukomsky, A.S. (Lukomskii) *Memoirs of the Russian Revolution*, trans.by O.Vitali (London: T.F.Unwin, 1922).

R77.   McCullagh, F. *A Prisoner of the Reds: The Story of a British Officer Captured in Siberia* (London: John Murray, 1921).

R78.   MacDonell, R. *"...And Nothing Long"* (London: Constable & Co., 1938).

R79.   Mandel, W.M. "Arthur Ransome: Eyewitness in Russia in 1919," *SR* 27 (1968), no.2, pp.290-295.

R80.   Margolin, A.D. *From a Political Diary: Russia, the Ukraine and America, 1905-1945* (New York: Columbia U.P., 1946).

R81.   Marye, G.T. *Nearing the End in Imperial Russia* (London: Selwyn & Blount, 1929).

R82.   Miliukov, P.N. *Political Memoirs, 1905-17*, trans.by C.Goldberg (Ann Arbor: University of Michigan Press 1967)

R83.   Monkhouse, A. *Moscow, 1911-1933* (London: Victor Gollancz, 1933).

R84.   Mstislavskii, S. *Five Days Which Transformed Russia*, trans.by E.K.Zelensky (London: Hutchinson, 1988).

R85.   Nansen, F. *Through Siberia, the Land of the Future*, trans.by A.G.Chater (London: Heinemann, 1914).

R86.   Nevinson, H.W. *The Dawn in Russia, or Scenes in the Russian Revolution*, 2nd ed. (London & New York: Harper & Bros., 1906).

R87.   Nikitine, Colonel B.V. *The Fateful Years: Fresh Revelations on a Chapter of Underground History*, trans.by D.Hastie Smith (London, Edinburgh, Glasgow: William Hodge, 1938).

R88.   Noble, A. *Siberian Days: an Engineer's Record of Travel and Adventure in the Wilds of Siberia* (London: H.F. & G.Witherby, 1928).

R89.   Novomeysky, M.A. *My Siberian Life*, trans.by A.Brown (London: Max Parrish, 1956).

R90.   Ossendowski, A.F., in collaboration with L.S.Palen *Man and Mystery in Asia* (London: Edward Arnold, 1924).

R91.   Ossendowski, F. *Beasts, Men and Gods* (London: Edward Arnold, 1923).

R92.   Ouspensky, P.D. *Letters from Russia, 1919* (London: Routledge & Kegan Paul, 1978).

R93.   Pahlen, Count K.K. *Mission to Turkestan: Being the Memoirs of Count K.K. Pahlen, 1908-1909*, trans.by N.J.Couriss (London: Oxford U.P., 1964).

R94.   Paley, Princess *Memories of Russia, 1916-1919* (London: Herbert Jenkins, 1924).

R95.   Pares, B. *My Russian Memoirs* (London: Cape, 1931).

R96.   Pitcher, H. *Witnesses of the Russian Revolution* (London: John Murray, 1994).

R97.   Power, R. *Under Cossack and Bolshevik* (London: Methuen, 1919).

R98.   Price, H.T. *Boche and Bolshevik. Experiences of an Englishman in the German Army and in Russian Prisons* (London: Murray, 1919).

R99.   Price, M.P. *My Reminiscences of the Russian Revolution* (London: George Allen & Unwin, 1921).

R100.   Price, M.P. *Siberia* (London: Methuen, 1912).

R101.   Price, M.P. *War and Revolution in Asiatic Russia* (London: George Allen & Unwin, 1918).

R102.   Price, M.P. "Witnesses of the Revolution," *Survey* 41 (1962), pp.14-26.

R103.   Pridham, Vice-Admiral Sir F. *Close of a Dynasty* (London: Allan Wingate, 1956).

R104.   Pushkarev, S.G. "1917 - A Memoir," *RR* 26 (1967), no.1, pp.54-67.

R105.   Ransome, A. *Six Weeks in Russia in 1919* (London: George Allen & Unwin, 1919). [Republished - London: Redwords, 1992].

R106.   Ransome, A. *The Crisis in Russia 1920* (London: George Allen & Unwin, 1921). [Republished - London: Redwords, 1992].

R107.   Raskolnikov, F.F. *Kronstadt and Petrograd in 1917*, trans.by B.Pearce (London: New Park, 1982).

R108.   Rodzianko, M.V. *The Reign of Rasputin. An Empire's Collapse. Memoirs of M.V. Rodzianko*, trans.by C.Zvegintzoff (London: A.M.Philpot, 1927).

R109.   Rodzianko, P. (Rodzyanko, P.P.) *Tattered Banners:An Autobiography* (London: Seeley Service, 1938, 1939).

R110.   Rosmer, A. *Lenin's Moscow*, trans.by I.H.Birchall (London: Pluto, 1971 [first published 1953]).

R111.   Ross, E.A. *Russia in Upheaval* (New York: Century, 1918).

R112.   Routsky, P. "A Page from the Past," *RR* 7 (1947-48), no.2, pp.69-75.

R113.   Russell, B. *The Practice and Theory of Bolshevism*, 2nd ed. (London: George Allen & Unwin, 1949 [first published 1920]).

R114.   Serge, V. *Memoirs of a Revolutionary, 1901-1941*, trans.by P.Sedgwick (London & New York: Oxford U.P., 1963).

R115.   Shipman, C. *It had to Be Revolution: Memoirs of an American Radical* (Ithaca, New York & London: Cornell U.P., 1993).

R116.   Shklovsky, V. *A Sentimental Journey: Memoirs, 1917-1922*, trans.by R.Sheldon (Ithaca & London· Cornell U.P., 1970).

R117.   Shulgin, V. "The Months Before the Russian Revolution," *SEER* 1 (1922-23), pp.380-400.

R118.   Shulgin, V.V. *Days of the Russian Revolution: Memoirs from the Right, 1905-1917*, trans.by B.F.Adams (Gulf Breeze, Fl.: Academic International Press, 1990).

R119.   Sisson, E. *One Hundred Red Days. A Personal Chronicle of The Bolshevik Revolution (25 November 1917 - 4 March 1918)* (New Haven: Yale U.P., 1931).

R120.   Slonim, M. "An Autobiographical Fragment: the Birth of a Socialist Revolutionary," *Sbornik (SGRR)* no.4 (1978), pp.47-79.

R121.   Slonim, M. "Reminiscences on the Revolution," *Cahiers du Monde Russe et Sovietique* 18 (1977), no.4, pp.413-434.

R122.   Snowden, P. *Through Bolshevik Russia* (London: Cassell, 1920).

R123.   Sorokin, P. *Leaves from a Russian Diary* (London: Hurst & Blackett, 1925).

R124.   Stanford, D.N. *Sun and Snow: a Siberian Adventure* (London: Longmans, 1963) [American edition entitled *Siberian Odyssey* (New York: Dutton, 1964)].

R125.   Sukhanov, N.N. *The Russian Revolution 1917. A Personal Record*, trans.by J.Carmichael (London: Oxford U.P., 1955)

R126.   Sutton, F.A. *One-Arm Sutton* (New York: Viking, 1933).

R127.   Swann, H. *Home on the Neva: A Life of a British family in Tsarist St Petersburg - and after the Revolution* (London: Victor Gollancz, 1968).

R128.   Tcharykow, N.V. *Glimpses of High Politics Through War and Peace 1855-1929: The Autobiography of N.V. Tcharykow, Serfowner, Ambassador, Exile* (London: George Allen & Unwin, 1931).

R129.   Troyat, H. *Daily Life in Russia under the Last Tsar*, trans.by M.Barnes (London: Allen & Unwin, 1961 / New York: Macmillan, 1962).

R130.   Tschebotarioff, G.P. *Russia, My Native Land: A U.S. Engineer Reminisces and Looks at the Present* (New York: McGraw-Hill, 1964).

R131.   Tseretelli, I. "Reminiscences of the February Revolution. The April Crisis," Part I: *RR* 14 (1955), no.2, pp.93-108; Part II: *RR* 14 (1955), no.3, pp.184-200; Part III: *RR* 14 (1955), no.4, pp.301-321; Part IV: *RR* 15 (1956), no.1, pp.37-48.

R132.   Urussov, S.D. *Memoirs of a Russian Governor*, trans.by H.Rosenthal (London & New York: Harper, 1908).

R133.   Vandervelde, E. *Three Aspects of the Russian Revolution*, trans.by J.E.H.Findlay (London: George Allen & Unwin, 1918).

R134.   Vecchi, J. *"The Tavern is My Drum"; My Autobiography* (London: Odhams, 1948).

R135.   Vining, L.E. *Held by the Bolsheviks: the Diary of a British Officer in Russia, 1919-1920* (London: St.Catherine's Press, 1924).

R136.   Von Mohrenschildt, D. (ed.) *The Russian Revolution of 1917: Contemporary Accounts* (London: Oxford U.P., 1971).

R137.   Walling, W.E. *Russia's Message: the True World Import of the Revolution* (New York: Doubleday Page, 1908).

R138.   Walpole, H. "Denis Garsten and the Russian Revolution: A Brief Word in Memory," *SEER* 17 (1938-39), pp.587-605.

R139.   Walsh, W.B. (ed.) "Documents: Petrograd, March - July, 1917: The Letters of Edward T. Heald," *ASEER* 6 (1947), pp.116-157.

R140.   Wells, H.G. *Russia in the Shadows* (London: Hodder & Stoughton, 1920).

R141.   West, J. *The Russian Revolution and British Democracy*, Fabian Tract no.184 (London: Fabian Society, November 1917).

R142.   Williams, A.R. *Journey Into Revolution: Petrograd, 1917-1918* (Chicago: Quadrangle Books, 1969).

R143.   Williams, A.R. *Through the Russian Revolution* (New York: Boni & Liveright, 1921).

R144.   Wolkonsky, Prince S. *My Reminiscences*, 2 vols., trans.by A.E.Chamot (London: Hutchinson, n.d.).

R145.   Wolkonsky, Princess P. *The Way of Bitterness: Soviet Russia, 1920* (London: Methuen, 1931).

R146.   Woytinsky, E.S. *Two Lives in One* (New York & Washington: Praeger, 1965).

R147.   Woytinsky, W.S. *Stormy Passage: A Personal History Through Two Russian Revolutions to Democracy and Freedom: 1905-1960* (New York: Vanguard Press, 1961).

R148.   Wrangel, Baron N. *From Serfdom to Bolshevism: The Memoirs of Baron N. Wrangel, 1847-1920*, trans. by B. & B.Lunn (London: Ernest Benn, 1927).

R149.   Wright, R.L. & Digby, B. *Through Siberia, an Empire in the Making* (London: Hurst & Blackett / New York: McBride, Nast, 1913).

R150.   Yurlova, M. *Cossack Girl* (London: Cassell, 1934).

R151.   Zenzinov, V.M., with the collaboration of I.D.Levine *The Road to Oblivion* (New York: McBride, 1931).

S

PICTORIAL

S1.   Alexandrov, V. *The End of the Romanovs*, trans.by W.Sutcliffe (London: Hutchinson, 1966).

S2.   Allshouse, R.H. (ed.) *Photographs for the Tsar: The Pioneering Color Photography of Sergei Mikhailovich Prokudin-Gorskii, Commissioned by Tsar Nicholas II* (New York: Dial Press, 1980).

S3.   Astrov, W. (ed.) *An Illustrated History of the Russian Revolution*, trans.by F.Utley (London: Martin Lawrence, 1928).

S4.   Betz, M.B. "The Caricatures and Cartoons of the 1905 Russian Revolution: Images of the Opposition," PhD diss., CUNY, 1984.

S5.   Bradley, J. *The Russian Revolution* (London: Brompton/Bison, 1988).

S6.   Fitzlyon, K. & Browning, T. *Before the Revolution: A View of Russia under the Last Tsar* (London: Penguin, 1992 [first published by Allen Lane, 1977]).

S7.   Grabbe, P. & B. *The Private World of the Last Tsar. In the Photographs and Notes of General Count Alexander Grabbe* (Boston & Toronto: Little, Brown & Co., 1984 / London: Collins, 1985).

S8.   King, D. *Trotsky. A Photographic Biography* (Oxford & New York: Basil Blackwell, 1986).

S9.   King, D. & Porter, C. *Blood and Laughter. Caricatures from the 1905 Revolution* (London: Jonathan Cape, 1983).

S10.   Kochan, L. *The Russian Revolution* (London: Wayland, 1971).

S11.   Lyons, M. *Nicholas II: The Last Tsar* (New York: St.Martin's Press, 1974).

S12.   Lyons, M. *Russia in Original Photographs, 1860-1920* (London & Henley: Routledge & Kegan Paul, 1977).

S13.   Obolensky, C. *The Russian Empire: A Portrait in Photographs* (London: Jonathan Cape, 1980).

S14.   Rossif, F. & Chapsal, M. *Portrait of a Revolution: Russia, 1896-1924*, trans.by H.Kahn (Boston & Toronto: Little, Brown, & Co., 1969).

S15.   Salisbury, H.E. *Russia in Revolution, 1900-1930* (New York: Holt, Rinehart & Winston, 1978).

S16.   Sanders, J. *Russia, 1917: the Unpublished Revolution* (New York: Abberville Press, 1989).

S17.   Vyrubova, A. *The Romanov Family Album*, intro.by R.K.Massie (London: Allen Lane, 1982).

S18.   Westwood, J.N. *The Illustrated History of the Russo-Japanese War* (London: Sidgwick & Jackson, 1973).

S19.   Wyndham, F. & King, D. *Trotsky: A Documentary* (New York & Washington: Praeger, 1972).

T

THE ARTS AND AMUSEMENTS

General:

T1.   Barooshian, V.D. *Russian Cubo-Futurism, 1910-1930* (The Hague & Paris: Mouton, 1974).

T2.   Barooshian, V.D. "Russian Cubo-Futurism, 1910-1930: An Interpretation," PhD diss., Brown, 1968.

T3.   Barron, S. & Tuchman, M. *The Avant-Garde in Russia 1910-1930: New Perspectives* (Los Angeles: Los Angeles County Museum of Art, 1980).

T4.   Biggart, J. "The "Russian Academy" and the Journal *Gelios*," *Sbornik (SGRR)* no.5 (1979), pp.17-27.

T5.   Cox, W.A. "The Art World and *Mir Iskusstva*: Studies in the Development of Russian Art," PhD diss., Michigan, 1970.

T6.   Dobujinsky, M.V. "The St.Petersburg Renaissance," *RR* 2 (1942-43), no.1, pp.46-59.

T7.   Fitzpatrick, S. *The Commissariat of Enlightenment: Soviet Organization of the Arts under Lunacharsky, October 1917-1921* (Cambridge: Cambridge U.P., 1970).

T8.   Gibian, G. & Tjalsma, H.W. (eds.) *Russian Modernism: Culture and the Avant-Garde, 1900-1930* (Ithaca & London: Cornell U.P., 1976).

T9.   Grover, S.R. "The World of Art Movement in Russia," *RR* 32 (1973), no.1, pp.28-42.

T10.   Holter, H.R. "A.V. Lunacharskii and the Formulation of a Policy Toward the Arts in the RSFSR, 1921-1927," PhD diss., Wisconsin, 1967.

T11.   Holter, H.R. "The Legacy of Lunacharsky and Artistic Freedom in the USSR," *SR* 29 (1970), no.2, pp.262-282.

T12.   Howard, J. *The Union of Youth: An artists' society of the Russian avant-garde* (Manchester & New York: Manchester U.P., 1992).

T13.   Jensen, K.B. "Marinetti in Russia 1910, 1912, 1913, 1914?" *Scando-Slavica* 15 (1969), pp.21-26.

T14.   Kamensky, A. (ed.) *The World of Art Movement in Early 20th-Century Russia* (Leningrad: Aurora Art, 1991).

T15.   Kennedy, J.E. "The *Mir iskusstva* Group and Russian Art 1898-1912," PhD diss., Columbia, 1976.

T16.   Kovarsky, V. "M.V. Dobujinsky - Pictorial Poet of St.Petersburg," *RR* 19 (1960), no.1, pp.24-37.

T17.   Livshits, B. *The One and a Half-Eyed Archer*, trans.by J.E.Bowlt (Newtonville, Mass.: Oriental Research Partners, 1977).

T18.   Lodder, C. *Russian Constructivism* (New Haven & London: Yale U.P., 1983).

T19.   Markov, V. *Russian Futurism: A History* (London: MacGibbon & Kee, 1969).

T20.   Milner-Gulland, R. "Russia's Other Modernism," in: R.Bartlett (ed.) *Russian Thought and Society, 1800-1917: Essays in Honour of Eugene Lampert* (University of Keele, 1984), pp.247-259.

T21.   Nilsson, N.A. (ed.) *Art, Society, Revolution. Russia 1917-1921* (Stockholm: Almqvist & Wicksell International, 1979).

T22.   Railing, P. "Russian Avant-Garde Art and the New Society, In the Context of D.Shterenberg's 'Report of the Activities of the Section of Plastic Arts of Narkompros' of 1919," *Revolutionary Russia* 7 (1994), no.1, pp.38-77.

T23.   Reeve, F.D. "'Vesy': A Study of a Russian Magazine," *SEER* 37 (1958-59), no.88, pp.221-235.

T24.   Richardson, W. "Alexandre Benois and the Imperial Russian Past," *RH* 20 (1993), nos.1-4, pp.213-235.

T25.   Richardson, W. *"Zolotoe Runo" and Russian Modernism: 1905-1910* (Ann Arbor: Ardis, 1986).

T26.   Richardson, W.H. "*Zolotoe Runo* and Russian Modernism: 1905-1910," PhD diss., Berkeley, 1976.

T27.   Rosenthal, B.G. *Dmitri Sergeevich Merezhkovsky and the Silver Age: The Development of a Revolutionary Mentality* (The Hague: Martinus Nijhoff, 1975).

T28.   Rougle, C. "Intellectuals Organize: Gorkij's 'Culture and Freedom' Society of 1918," *Scando-Slavica* 26 (1980), pp.85-104.

T29.   Salmond, W.R. "The Modernization of Folk Art in Imperial Russia: The Revival of the Kustar Art Industries, 1885-1917," PhD diss., Texas, 1989.

T30.   Thomson, B. *The Premature Revolution: Russian Literature and Society 1917-1946* (London: Weidenfeld & Nicolson, 1972).

T31. Williams, R.C. *Artists in the Revolution: Portraits of the Russian Avant-Garde, 1905-1925* (Bloomington & London: Indiana U.P., 1977).

T32. Yablonskaya, M.N. *Women Artists of Russia's New Age, 1900-1935* (London: Thames & Hudson, 1990).

Cinema:

T33. Carter, H. *The New Theatre and Cinema of Soviet Russia* (London: Chapman & Dodd, 1924).

T34. Cohen, L.H. "The Cultural-Political Traditions and Developments of the Soviet Cinema from 1917-1972," PhD diss., Southern California, 1973.

T35. Dart, P.A. "Pudovkin's Film Theory," PhD diss., Iowa, 1965.

T36. Denyer, T. "Montage and Political Consciousness," *Soviet Union* 7 (1980), pts.1-2 (1980), pp.89-111.

T37. Lawton, A. "'Lumiere' and Darkness: The Moral Question in the Russian and Soviet Cinema," *JFGO* 38 (1990), pp.244-254.

T38. Leyda, J. *Kino: a History of the Russian and Soviet Film* (London: Allen & Unwin, 1960).

T39. Rimberg, J.D. "The Motion Picture in the Soviet Union, 1918-1952. A Sociological Analysis," PhD diss., Columbia, 1959.

T40. Stites, R. "Dusky Images of Tsarist Russia: Prerevolutionary Cinema (Video Review Essay)," *RR* 53 (1994), no.2, pp.285-295.

T41. Taylor, R. "A Medium for the Masses: Agitation in the Soviet Civil War," *SS* 22 (1970-71), no.4, pp.562-574.

T42. Taylor, R. "Soviet Cinema as Popular Culture: Or the Extraordinary Adventures of Mr Nepman in the Land of the Silver Screen," *Revolutionary Russia* 1 (1988), no.1, pp.36-56.

T43. Taylor, R.T. "The Politics of the Soviet Cinema, 1917-1929," PhD diss., London, 1977.

T44. Taylor, R. *The Politics of the Soviet Cinema, 1917-1929* (Cambridge: Cambridge U.P., 1979).

T45. Taylor, R. "The Spark that became a Flame: the Bolsheviks, Propaganda and the Cinema," in: T.H.Rigby et al (eds.) *Authority, Power and Policy in the USSR: Essays Dedicated to Leonard Schapiro* (London & Basingstoke: Macmillan, 1980), pp.57-76.

T46. Taylor, R. & Christie, I. (eds.) *The Film Factory: Russian and Soviet Cinema in Documents 1896-1939* (London: Routledge & Kegan Paul, 1988).

T47.   Taylor, R. & Christie, I. (eds.) *Inside the Film Factory. New Approaches to Russian and Soviet Cinema* (London & New York: Routledge, 1991).

T48.   Tsivian, Y. (ed.) *Silent Witness: Russian Films 1908-1919* (London: British Film Institute, 1989).

Fine Art:

T49.   Barooshian, V.D. "Vkhutemas and Constructivism," *Soviet Union* 3 (1976), pt.2, pp.197-207.

T50.   Basner, E.V. & Gusarova, A.P. (eds.) *Russian and Soviet Paintings, 1900-1930: Selections from the State Russian Museum, Leningrad* (Washington, D.C.: Smithsonian Institution, 1988).

T51.   Benois, A. *The Russian School of Painting*, trans.by A.Yarmolinsky (New York: A.A.Knopf, 1916).

T52.   Bird, A. *A History of Russian Painting* (Oxford: Phaidon, 1987).

T53.   Birnholz, A.C. "El Lissitzky (Book-Length Study of the Art of El Lissitzky, 1890-1941)," PhD diss., Yale, 1973.

T54.   Bojko, S. *New Graphic Design in Revolutionary Russia*, trans.by R.Strybel & L.Zembrzuski (New York & Washington: Praeger, 1972).

T55.   Bowlt, J. "Art and Architecture in the Age of Revolution, 1860-1917," in: R.Auty & D.Obolensky (eds.) *An Introduction to Russian Art and Architecture* (Cambridge: Cambridge U.P., 1980).

T56.   Bowlt, J.E. "From Pictures to Textile Prints," *Soviet Union* 3 (1976), pt.2, pp.311-325.

T57.   Bowlt, J.E. "From Practice to Theory: Vladimir Tatlin and Nikolai Punin," *Stanford Slavic Studies* 4 (1992), no.2, pp.50-66.

T58.   Bowlt, J.E. "Pavel Filonov: His Painting and His Theory," *RR* 34 (1975), no.3, pp.282-292.

T59.   Bowlt, J.E. "Russian Art in the Nineteen Twenties," *SS* 22 (1970-71), no.4, pp.575-594.

T60.   Bowlt, J.E. *Russian Art of the Avant-Garde. Theory and Criticism 1902-1934*, trans.by J.E.Bowlt (New York: Viking, 1976).

T61.   Bowlt, J.E. *The Silver Age: Russian Art of the Early Twentieth Century and the "World of Art" Group* (Newtonville, Mass.: Oriental Research Partners, 1979).

T62.   Bowlt, J.E. "Through the Glass Darkly: Images of Decadence in Early Twentieth-Century Russian Art," *JCH* 17 (1982), no.1, pp.93-110.

T63.   Bowlt, J.E. & Long, R.-C.W. (eds.) *The Life of Vasili Kandinsky in Russian Art: A Study of "On the Spiritual in Art"*, trans.by J.E.Bowlt (Newtonville, Mass.: Oriental Research Partners, 1980).

T64. Carson, P.H. "Russian Art in the Silver Age: The Role of *Mir Iskusstva*," PhD diss., Indiana, 1974.

T65. Cohen, R.H. "Alexandra Exter and Western Europe: An Inquiry into Russian-Western Relations in Art, Theater and Design in the Early Twentieth Century," PhD diss., New York, 1979.

T66. Compton, S.P. "Kazimir Malevich: A Study of the Paintings, 1910-1935," PhD diss., London, Courtauld Institute of Art, 1983.

T67. Compton, S.P. *The World Backwards. Russian Futurist Books 1912-16* (London: British Museum Publications, 1978).

T68. Crone, R. & Moos, D. *Kazimir Malevich: The Climax of Disclosure* (Chicago: University of Chicago Press, 1991).

T69. Curran, M.W. "Vladimir Stasov and the Development of Russian National Art, 1850-1906," PhD diss., Wisconsin, 1965.

T70. Dabrowski, M. "Constructivism in Soviet Painting," *Soviet Union* 3 (1976), pt.2, pp.152-187.

T71. De Saint-Rat, A.L. "The Revolutionary Era Through the Eyes of Russian Graphic Artists," *Sbornik (SGRR)* no.2 (1976), pp.34-43.

T72. De Saint-Rat, A.L. "Vasili Masiutin's *Der goldene Hahn*," *Soviet Union* 7 (1980), pts.1-2, pp.53-69.

T73. Douglas, C. "Suprematism: The Sensible Dimension," *RR* 34 (1975), no.3, pp.266-281.

T74. Douglas, C.C. "Swans of Other Worlds: Kazimir Malevich and the Origins of Suprematism, 1908-1915," PhD diss., Texas, 1975.

T75. Edgington, K.A. "Abstraction as a Concept in the Criticism of Gertrude Stein and Wassily Kandinsky," PhD diss., American, 1976.

T76. Elliot, D. *New Worlds. Russian Art and Society 1900-1937* (London: Thames & Hudson, 1986).

T77. Fineberg, J.D. "Kandinsky in Paris, 1906-1907," PhD diss., Harvard, 1975.

T78. Garvey, R. "The Costakis Collection: *Avant-Garde* Painting of the Revolutionary Years," *Sbornik (SGRR)* nos.6-7 (1981), pp.46-53.

T79. Gray, C. *The Great Experiment: Russian Art 1863-1922* (London: Thames & Hudson, 1962).

T80. Grover, S.R. "Savva Mamontov and the Mamontov Circle: 1870-1905 Art Patronage and the Rise of Nationalism in Russian Art," PhD diss., Wisconsin, 1971.

T81. Guerman, M. *Art of the October Revolution*, trans.by W.Freeman et al (London: Collet's, 1979).

T82. Hamilton, G.H. *The Art and Architecture of Russia* (Harmondsworth: Penguin, 1954).

T83.   Hilton, A.L. "The Art of Ilia Repin: Tradition and Innovation in Russian Realism," PhD diss., Columbia, 1979

T84.   Howlett, J. "The Origins of Socialist Realism in Soviet Visual Art," *OSP(NS)* 9 (1976), pp.91-101.

T85.   Humphreys, C.M. "Cubo-Futurism in Russia, 1912-1922: The Transformation of a Painterly Style," PhD diss., St.Andrews, 1989.

T86.   Isdebsky-Pritchard, A. *The Art of Mikhail Vrubel (1856-1910)* (Epping, Essex: Bowker, 1982).

T87.   Kamensky, A. *Martiros Saryan: Paintings, Watercolors, Drawings, Book Illustrations, Theatrical Design*, trans.by A.Mikoyan (Madison, CT: Sphinx, 1988).

T88.   Karginov, G. *Rodchenko* (London: Thames & Hudson, 1979).

T89.   Kean, B.W. *All the Empty Palaces: The Merchant Patrons of Modern Art in Pre-Revolutionary Russia* (New York: Universe Books, 1983).

T90.   Kogan, D.Z. *Sergei Iur'evich Sudeikin, 1884-1946* (Moscow: Iskusstvo, 1974).

T91.   Kristof, J. "Critic and Commissar: A.V. Lunacharskii on Art," PhD diss., Columbia, 1972.

T92.   Levin, S.G. "Wassily Kandinsky and the American Avant-Garde, 1912-1950," PhD diss., Rutgers, 1976.

T93.   Lodder, C.A. "Constructivism: From Fine Art into Design: Russia, 1913-1933," PhD diss., Sussex, 1980.

T94.   Lodder, C. "Lyubov' Popova: A Revolutionary Woman Artist," *Revolutionary Russia* 3 (1990), no.2, pp.151-182.

T95.   Long, R.-C.W. *Kandinsky: The Development of an Abstract Style* (New York: Clarendon/ Oxford U.P., 1980).

T96.   Margolin, V. "The Transformation of Vision: Art and Ideology in the Graphic Design of Alexander Rodchenko, El Lissitzky, and Laszlo Moholy-Nagy, 1917-1933," PhD diss., The Union for Experimenting Colleges and Universities, 1982.

T97.   Michaelsen, K.J. "Archipenko: A Study of the Early Works, 1908-1920," PhD diss., Columbia, 1975.

T98.   Miliukov, P. *Outlines of Russian Culture. Part III: Architecture, Painting and Music*, trans.by V.Ugher & E.Davis (Philadelphia: University of Pennsylvania Press, 1943 [New York: Perpetua, 1960]).

T99.   Milner, J. "Russian Constructivism: The First Phase: Rodchenko and Tatlin," PhD diss., London, Courtauld Institute of Art, 1979.

T100.   Milner, J. *Vladimir Tatlin and the Russian Avant-Garde* (New Haven & London: Yale U.P., 1983).

T101. Omuka, T. "A Short Note on Paul Mansouroff," *Soviet Union* 3 (1976), pt.2, pp.188-196.

T102. Parker, F. & S.J. *Russia on Canvas: Ilya Repin* (University Park: Pennsylvania State U.P., 1980).

T103. Pevitts, R.R. "Wassily Kandinsky's *The Yellow Sound*: A Synthesis of the Arts of the Stage," PhD diss., Southern Illinois, 1980.

T104. Pritchard, A.I. "The Art of Mikhail Vrubel (1856-1910)," PhD diss., New York, 1980.

T105. Rannit, A. *Invention and Tradition: Selected Works from the Julia A. Whitney Foundation and the Thomas P. Whitney Collection of Modernist Russian Art* (Charlottesville: University of Virginia Art Museum, 1980).

T106. Ross, M.C. *The Art of Karl Faberge and His Contemporaries* (Norman: University of Oklahoma Press, 1965).

T107. Rudenstine, A.Z. (ed.) *Russian Avant-Garde Art: The George Costakis Collection* (London: Thames & Hudson, 1981).

T108. Sihare, L.P. "Oriental Influences on Wassily Kandinsky and Piet Monolrian, 1909-1917," PhD diss., New York, 1967.

T109. Simmons, W.S. "Kasimir Malevich's Black Square and the Genesis of Suprematism, 1907-1915," PhD diss., Johns Hopkins, 1979.

T110. Smigocki, S.V. "An Inquiry into the Art Pedagogy of Paul Klee and Wassily Kandinsky," PhD diss., Florida State, 1974.

T111. *Soviet Union* 5 (1978), pt.2. Eight articles and one document concerning K.S.Malevich (1878-1935).

T112. Tower, B.S. *Klee and Kandinsky in Munich and at the Bauhaus* (Ann Arbor: UMI Research Press, 1981).

T113. Tower, B.S. "Wassily Kandinsky and Paul Klee in Munich and at the Bauhaus: A Comparative Study of Their Works and Theories," PhD diss., Brown, 1978.

T114. Valkenier, E.K. "Politics in Russian Art: The Case of Repin," *RR* 37 (1978), no.1, pp.14-29.

T115. Valkenier, E. *Russian Realist Art: The State and Society: The Peredvizhniki and Their Tradition* (Ann Arbor: Ardis, 1977).

T116. Vise, S.S. "Wassily Kandinsky and Arnold Schoenberg: Parallelisms in Form and Meaning," PhD diss., Washington, St.Louis, 1969.

T117. Washton, R.C. "Vasily Kandinsky, 1901-1913: Painting and Theory," PhD diss., Yale, 1968.

T118. Weiss, P. *Kandinsky in Munich: The Formative Jugendstil Years* (Princeton: Princeton U.P., 1979).

T119.   Weiss, P. "Wassily Kandinsky, the Formative Munich Years (1898-1914), from *Jugendstil* to Abstraction," PhD diss., Syracuse, 1973.

T120.   Zlobin, V. *A Difficult Soul: Zinaida Gippius* (Berkeley: University of California Press, 1980).

Literature:

T121.   Adams, M.B. "'Red Star': Another Look at Aleksandr Bogdanov," *SR* 48 (1989), no.1, pp.1-15.

T122.   Anemone, A. "Konstantin Vaginov and the Death of Nikolai Gumilev," *SR* 48 (1989), no.4, pp.631-636.

T123.   Angeloff, A. "The Revolution and Civil War in the Soviet Novel: An Ideological Interpretation," PhD diss., Syracuse, 1970.

T124.   Annenkov, G. "The Poets and the Revolution - Blok, Mayakovsky, Esenin," *RR* 26 (1967), no.2, pp.129-143.

T125.   Any, C. "Boris Eikhenbaum in OPOIAZ: Testing the Limits of the Work-Centered Poetics," *SR* 49 (1990), no.3, pp.409-426.

T126.   Aronian, S. "Remizov: Revolution and Apocalypse," *CASS* 26 (1992), nos.1-4, pp.119-140.

T127.   Barnes, C. *Boris Pasternak. A Literary Biography. Vol.I, 1890-1928* (Cambridge: Cambridge U.P., 1989).

T128.   Barratt, A. "Personal and Literary Relations of Maksim Gorky and Leonid Andreyev, 1898-1919 with Particular Reference to the Revolution of 1905," PhD diss., Durham, 1977.

T129.   Basom, A.M. "War and Revolution in the Poetry of Maksimilian Aleksandrovic Volison: 1905-1923," PhD diss., Wisconsin, 1987.

T130.   Beaujour, E.K. "Zamiatin's *We* and Modernist Architecture," *RR* 47 (1988), no.1, pp.49-60.

T131.   Bedford, C.H. *The Seeker: D.S. Merezhkovskiy* (Lawrence: University Press of Kansas, 1977).

T132.   Bernhardt, L.J. "Chapters in the Hebrew Literary Renaissance in Russia (1892-1924): Hebrew Renaissance Poetry in Russian Translations," PhD diss., Princeton, 1970.

T133.   Bethea, D.M. *Khodasevich: His Life and Art* (Princeton: Princeton U.P., 1983).

T134.   Bogdanov, A. *Red Star: The First Bolshevik Utopia*, trans.by C.Rougle (Bloomington: Indiana U.P., 1984).

T135.   Bristol, E. "Fedor Sologub's Postrevolutionary Poetry," *ASEER* 19 (1960), no.3, pp.414-422.

T136.   Bristol, E. "Idealism and Decadence in Russian Symbolist Poetry," *SR* 39 (1980), no.2, pp.269-280.

T137.   Brooks, J. "The Young Kornei Chukovsky (1905-1914). A Liberal Critic In Search of Cultural Unity," *RR* 33 (1974), no.1, pp.50-62.

T138.   Brown, C. *Mandelstam* (New York & London: Cambridge U.P., 1973).

T139.   Brown, D.B. "American Authors in Soviet Russia (1917-1941)," PhD diss., Columbia, 1951.

T140.   Brown, E.J. *Mayakovsky: A Poet in the Revolution* (Princeton: Princeton U.P., 1973).

T141.   Broyde, S. *Osip Mandel'stam and His Age: A Commentary on the Themes of War and Revolution in the Poetry 1913-1923* (Cambridge, Mass. & London: Harvard U.P., 1975).

T142.   Carden, P. "Utopia and Anti-Utopia: Aleksei Gastev and Evgeny Zamyatin," *RR* 46 (1987), no.1, pp.1-18.

T143.   Clowes, E.W. *The Revolution of Moral Consciousness: Nietzsche in Russian Literature* (De Kalb: Northern Illinois U.P., 1988).

T144.   Collins, C. *Evgenij Zamjatin: An Interpretive Study* (The Hague & Paris: Mouton, 1973).

T145.   Doherty, J.F. "Nikolai Gumilev and the Propagation of Acmeism: 'Letters on Russian Poetry'," *Irish Slavonic Studies* 13 (1992), pp.113-130.

T146.   Driver, S.N. "The Poetry of Anna Axmatova, 1912-1922," PhD diss., Columbia, 1967.

T147.   Ehre, M. "Babel's Red Cavalry: Epic and Pathos, History and Culture," *SR* 40 (1981), no.2, pp.228-240.

T148.   Feinstein, E. *A Captive Lion: The Life of Marina Tsvetaeva* (New York: E.P.Dutton, 1987).

T149.   Fetzer, L. (ed.) *Pre-Revolutionary Russian Science Fiction: An Anthology (Seven Utopias and a Dream)*, trans.by L.Fetzer (Ann Arbor: Ardis, 1982).

T150.   Fontenot, M.J. "Symbolism in Persuasion: The Influence of the Merezhkovskii Circle on the Rhetoric of Aleksandr Fedorich Kerenskii," *CASS* 26 (1992), nos.1-4, pp.241-266.

T151.   Forsyth, J. *Listening to the Wind: an introduction to Aleksandr Blok* (Oxford: William A.Meeuws, 1977).

T152.   Forsyth, J. "The beginning and the End: Blok's *The Twelve* and the Apocalypse According to Vladimir Solov'ev," *Scottish Slavonic Review* no.14 (1990), pp.117-137.

T153.   Foster, L.A. "The Revolution and the Civil War in Russian Emigre Novels," *RR* 31 (1972), no.2, pp.153-162.

T154.   Gasparov, B., Hughes, R.P. & Paperno, I. (eds.) *Cultural Mythologies of Russian Modernism: From the Golden Age to the Silver Age* (Berkeley, Los Angeles, & London: University of California Press, 1992).

T155.   Grossman, J.D. "Russian Symbolism and the Year 1905: The Case of Valery Bryusov," *SEER* 61 (1983), no.3, pp.341-362.

T156.   Gumilev, N. *On Russian Poetry*, trans.by D.Lapeza (Ann Arbor: Ardis, 1977).

T157.   Gurian, W. "The Memoirs of Bely," *RR* 3 (1943-44), no.1, pp.95-103.

T158.   Gustafson, R.F. *The Imagination of Spring: The Poetry of Afanasy Fet* (New Haven & London: Yale U.P., 1966).

T159.   Hackel, S. *The Poet and the Revolution. Alexander Blok's "The Twelve"* (London: Oxford U.P./Clarendon, 1975).

T160.   Hallett, R. *Isaac Babel* (New York: Frederick Ungar, 1973).

T161.   Henderson, E.A. "Left Front: The October Revolution in the Poetry of Vladimir Mayakovsky," PhD diss., Yale, 1975.

T162.   Hoffman, S.H. "*Scythianism*: A Cultural Vision in Revolutionary Russia," PhD diss., Columbia, 1975.

T163.   Howlett, J. "'We'll end in Hell, my passionate sisters': Russian Women Poets and World War I," in: D.Goldman (ed.) *Women and World War I: the Written Response* (Basingstoke & London: Macmillan, 1993), pp.73-91.

T164.   Ilnytzkyj, O.S. "Ukrainian Futurism, 1914-1930: History, Theory and Practice," PhD diss., Harvard, 1983.

T165.   Jangfeldt, B. *Majakovskij and Futurism: 1917-1921* (Stockholm: Almqvist & Wiksell International, 1976).

T166.   Karlinsky, S. *Marina Tsvetaeva: The Woman, Her Worlds and Her Poetry* (Cambridge: Cambridge U.P., 1985).

T167.   Kaun, A. "Russian Poetic Trends on the Eve of and the Morning After 1917," *SEER* 20 (1941), pp.55-84.

T168.   Kipa, A.A. "Gerhart Hauptmann in Russia, 1889-1917: Reception and Impact," PhD diss., Pennsylvania, 1972.

T169.   Kisch, C. *Alexander Blok. Prophet of Revolution; A Study of his Life and Work Illustrated by Translations from his Poems and other Writings* (London: Weidenfeld & Nicolson, 1960).

T170.   Kleberg, L. & Nilsson, N.A. (eds.) *Theater and Literature in Russia, 1900-1930: A Collection of Essays* (Stockholm: Almqvist & Wicksell International, 1984).

T171.   Lawton, A. *Vadim Shershenevich: From Futurism to Imaginism* (Ann Arbor: Ardis, 1981).

T172.   Lindstrom, T.S. *A Concise History of Russian Literature, vol.2: From 1900 to the Present* (New York: New York U.P., 1978).

T173.   Loe, M.L. "Maksim Gor'kii and the *Sreda* Circle: 1899-1905," *SR* 44 (1985), no.1, pp.49-66.

T174.   Lucid, D.P. "Preface to Revolution: Russian Marxist Literary Criticism, 1883-1917," PhD diss., Yale, 1972.

T175.   Luckyj, G.S.N. "Soviet Ukrainian Literature - A Study in Literary Politics (1917-1934)," PhD diss., Columbia, 1954.

T176.   Luker, N.J.L. *Aleksandr Grin: The Forgotten Visionary* (Newtonville, Mass.: Oriental Research Partners, 1980).

T177.   Luker, N.J.L. *Alexander Kuprin* (Boston: Twayne Publishers, G.K.Hall, 1978).

T178.   Luker, N. (ed.) *An Anthology of Russian Neo-Realism: The "Znanie" School of Maxim Gorky* (Ann Arbor: Ardis, 1982).

T179.   Luker, N. (ed.) *The Short Story in Russia, 1900-1917* (Nottingham: Astra Press, 1991).

T180.   Lvov-Rogachevsky, V. *A History of Russian Jewish Literature*, trans.by A.Levin (Ann Arbor: Ardis, 1979).

T181.   McLean, H. *Nikolai Leskov: The Man and His Art* (Cambridge, Mass. & London: Harvard U.P., 1977).

T182.   McVay, G. "Black and Gold: The Poetry of Ryurik Ivnev," *OSP(NS)* 4 (1971), pp.83-104.

T183.   McVay, G. *Esenin: A Life* (Ann Arbor: Ardis, 1976).

T184.   Maloney, P. "Anarchism and Bolshevism in the Works of Boris Pilnyak," *RR* 32 (1973), no.1, pp.43-53.

T185.   Markov, V. *Russian Imagism, 1919-1924*, 2 vols. (Giessen: Wilhelm Schmitz Verlag, 1980).

T186.   Marullo, T.G. (ed.) *Ivan Bunin: Russian Requiem, 1885-1920. A Portrait from Letters, Diaries, and Fiction* (Chicago: Ivan R. Dee, 1993).

T187.   Maslenikov, O. *Poetry of the Russian Symbolists* (Berkeley: University of California Press, 1958).

T188.   Maslenikov, O. *The Frenzied Poets: Andrew Biely and the Russian Symbolists* (Berkeley & Los Angeles: University of California Press, 1952).

T189.   Matich, O. *Paradox in the Religious Poetry of Zinaida Gippius* (Munich: Wilhelm Fink Verlag, 1972).

T190.   Miliukov, P. *Outlines of Russian Culture. Part II: Literature*, trans.by V.Ugher & E.Davis (Philadelphia: University of Pennsylvania Press, 1943 [New York: Perpetua, 1960]).

T191.   Mirsky, D.S. *Contemporary Russian Literature, 1881-1925* (London: George Routledge, 1926).

T192.   Mochulsky, K. *Andrei Bely: His Life and Works*, trans.by N.Szalavitz (Ann Arbor: Ardis, 1977).

T193.   Newcombe, J.M. *Leonid Andreyev* (New York: Frederick Ungar, 1973).

T194.   Ober, K.H. "Peter Emanuel Hansen and the Popularization of Scandinavian Literature in Russia, 1888-1917," PhD diss., Illinois, 1974.

T195.   Pachmuss, T. (ed.) *Between Paris and St.Petersburg: Selected Diaries of Zinaida Hippius* (Urbana: University of Illinois Press, 1975).

T196.   Pachmuss, T. *Zinaida Hippius: An Intellectual Profile* (Carbondale & Edwardsville: Southern Illinois U.P., 1971).

T197.   Peterson, R.E. (ed.) *The Russian Symbolists: An Anthology of Critical and Theoretical Writings* (Ann Arbor: Ardis, 1986).

T198.   Poggioli, R. *Rozanov* (New York: Hillary House, 1962).

T199.   Poggioli, R. "The Art of Ivan Bunin," *HSS* 1 (1953), pp.249-277.

T200.   Poggioli, R. *The Poets of Russia, 1890-1930* (Cambridge, Mass.: Harvard U.P., 1960).

T201.   Pyman, A. "Russian Poetry and the October Revolution," *Revolutionary Russia* 3 (1990), no.1, pp.5-54.

T202.   Pyman, A. *The Life of Aleksandr Blok*, 2 vols. (Oxford: Oxford U.P., 1979 and 1980).

T203.   Rayfield, D. "The Soldier's Lament: World War One Folk Poetry in the Russian Empire," *SEER* 66 (1988), no.1, pp.66-90.

T204.   Rice, M.P. *Valery Briusov and the Rise of Russian Symbolism* (Ann Arbor: Ardis, 1975).

T205.   Richards, D.J. *Zamyatin: A Soviet Heretic* (London: Bowes & Bowes, 1962).

T206.   Roberts, S.E. *Four Faces of Rozanov: Christianity, Sex, Jews and the Russian Revolution* (New York: Philosophical Library, 1978).

T207.   Rosenthal, B.G. *Dmitri Sergeevich Merezhkovsky and the Silver Age: The Development of a Revolutionary Mentality* (The Hague: Martinus Nijhoff, 1975).

T208.   Rosenthal, B.G. "Eschatology and the Appeal of Revolution: Merezhkovsky, Bely, Blok," *California Slavic Studies* 11 (1980), pp.105-139.

T209.   Rougle, C. *Three Russians Consider America: America in the Works of Maksim Gor'kij, Aleksandr Blok, and Vladimir Majakovskij* (Stockholm: Almqvist & Wicksell International, 1976).

T210.   Rusinko, E. "Acmeism, Post-symbolism, and Henri Bergson," *SR* 41 (1992), no.3, pp.494-510.

T211.   Scherr, B. "Notes on Literary Life in Petrograd, 1918-1922: A Tale of Three Houses," *SR* 36 (1977), no.2, pp.256-267.

T212.   Shane, A.M. *The Life and Works of Evgenij Zamjatin* (Berkeley & Los Angeles: University of California Press, 1968).

T213.   Shub, D. "Lenin and Vladimir Korolenko," *RR* 25 (1966), no.1, pp.46-53.

T214.   Simpson, P.A. "A Study of the Tragic Doctrine of Mystical Anarchism Within the Russian Literary Intelligentsia, 1905-1909," PhD diss., Essex, 1982.

T215.   Slonim, M. *From Chekhov to the Revolution: Russian Literature, 1900-1917* (New York: Oxford U.P./Galaxy, 1962).

T216.   Stapanian, J.R. *Mayakovsky's Cubo-Futurist Vision* (Houston, Texas: Rice U.P., 1986).

T217.   Steinberg, M.D. "Worker-Authors and the Cult of the Person," in: S.P.Frank & M.D.Steinberg (eds.) *Cultures in Flux: Lower-Class Values, Practices, and Resistance in Late Imperial Russia* (Princeton: Princeton U.P., 1994), pp.168-184.

T218.   Steinberg, M.D. "Workers on the Cross: Religious Imagination in the Writings of Russian Workers, 1910-1924," *RR* 53 (1994), no.2, pp.213-239.

T219.   Stenbock-Fermor, E. "Russian literature from 1890 to 1917," in: G.Katkov et al (eds.) *Russia Enters the Twentieth Century, 1894-1917* (London: Temple Smith, 1971), pp.263-286.

T220.   Strakhovsky, L.I. "Osip Mandelstam - the Architect of Words," *RR* 7 (1947-48), no.1, pp.61-70.

T221.   Strakhovsky, L.I. "The Silver Age of Russian Poetry: Symbolism and Acmeism," *CSP* 4 (1959), pp.61-87.

T222.   Struve, G. *Russian Literature under Lenin and Stalin, 1917-1953* (Norman: University of Oklahoma Press, 1971).

T223.   Tait, A.L. "The Literary Works of A.V. Lunacarskij (1875-1933)," PhD diss., Cambridge, 1972.

T224.   Terras, V. *Vladimir Mayakovsky* (Boston: Twayne, 1982).

T225.   Thomson, B. *The Premature Revolution: Russian Literature and Society, 1917-1946* (London: Weidenfeld & Nicolson, 1972).

T226.   Uehland, C. "Viacheslav Ivanov's 'Malicious Counter-Revolutionary Verses': Pesni Smutnogo Vremeni Reconsidered," *CASS* 26 (1992), nos.1-4, pp.77-96.

T227.   Visson, L. *Sergei Esenin: Poet of the Crossroads* (Wurzburg: Jal-Verlag, 1980).

T228.   Voronsky, A. *Stat'i: Essays on Belyi, Zamiatin, Babel' and Pil'niak* (Ann Arbor: Ardis, 1981).

T229.   West, J. *Russian Symbolism: A Study of Vyacheslav Ivanov and the Russian Symbolist Aesthetic* (London: Methuen, 1970).

T230.   Westwood, J.J. "The Red Army Man in Soviet Fiction," PhD diss., Montreal, 1961.

T231.   Winner, T.G. "Kazakh Oral Art and Literature with Special Emphasis on the Impact of the October Revolution," PhD diss., Columbia, 1950.

T232.   Zimmerman, J.F. "Leo Tolstoy and the Period of Liberation, 1894-1910," PhD diss., Harvard, 1961.

Music:

T233.   Asaf'yev, B. *A Book About Stravinsky*, trans.by R.F.French (Ann Arbor: UMI Research Press, 1982).

T234.   Ashley, P.J. "Prokofiev's Piano Music: Line, Chord and Key," PhD diss., Rochester, 1964.

T235.   Bakst, J. *A History of Russian-Soviet Music* (New York: Dodd, Mead, 1966).

T236.   Beckwith, R.S. "A.D. Kastal'skii (1856-1926) and the Quest for a Native Russian Choral Style," PhD diss., Cornell, 1969.

T237.   Blackwood, B.W. "The Music of the Ballets Russes, 1909-1919," PhD diss., Cambridge, 1972.

T238.   Brown, M.H. "The Symphonies of Sergei Prokofiev," PhD diss., Florida State, 1967.

T239.   Covatta, M.A.T. "Document: The Piano Solo Music in Smaller Forms of Nicholas Medtner (1880-1951)," PhD diss., Hahnemann Medical College, 1966.

T240.   Elmore, C.C. "Some Stylistic Considerations in the Piano Sonatas of Nikolai Medtner," PhD diss., North Carolina, 1972.

T241.   Elzinga, H. "The Sacred Choral Compositions of Paul Grigorevich Chesnokov (1872-1944)," PhD diss., Indiana, 1970.

T242.   Evans, R.K. "The Early Songs of Sergei Prokofiev and Their Relation to the Synthesis of the Arts in Russia, 1890-1922," PhD diss., Ohio State, 1971.

T243.   Froud, N. & Hanley, J. (eds.) *Chaliapin: An Autobiography as Told to Maxim Gorky*, trans.by N.Froud & J.Hanley (New York: Stein & Day, 1967).

T244.   Gordon, T.P. "Stravinsky and the New Classicism: A Critical History, 1911-1928," PhD diss., Toronto, 1983.

T245.   Keller, C.W. "The Piano Sonatas of Nicholas Medtner," Ohio State, 1972.

T246. Loftis, B.H. "The Piano Sonatas of Nikolai Medtner," PhD diss., West Virginia, 1970.

T247. Miliukov, P. *Outlines of Russian Culture. Part III: Architecture, Painting and Music*, trans.by V.Ugher & E.Davis (Philadelphia: University of Pennsylvania Press, 1943 [New York: Perpetua, 1960]).

T248. Morosan, V. *Choral Performance in Pre-Revolutionary Russia* (Ann Arbor: UMI Research Press, 1986).

T249. Morosan, W.V. "Choral Performances in Pre-Revolutionary Russia," PhD diss., Illinois, 1984.

T250. Pople, A.J.L. "Skryabin and Stravinsky 1908-1914: Studies in Analytical Method," PhD diss., Oxford, 1985.

T251. Prokofiev, S. *Prokofiev By Prokofiev: A Composer's Memoir*, trans.by G.Daniels (Garden City, N.Y.: Doubleday, 1979).

T252. Roberts, P.D. "Aspects of Modernism in Russian Piano Music, 1910-1929," PhD diss., CNAA, 1988.

T253. Robinson, H. *Sergei Prokofiev: A Biography* (London: Robert Hale, 1987).

T254. Sabaneeff, L. "A.N. Scriabin - A Memoir," *RR* 25 (1966), no.3, pp.257-267.

T255. Sahlmann, F.G. "The Piano Concertos of Sergei Prokofiev: A Stylistic Study," PhD diss., Rochester, 1967.

T256. Schwarz, B. *Music and Musical Life in Soviet Russia, 1917-1970* (New York: W.W.Norton, 1972).

T257. Seroff, V. *Sergei Prokofiev, A Soviet Tragedy: The Case of Sergei Prokofiev, His Life and Work, His Critics, and His Executioners* (New York: Funk & Wagnalls, 1968; New York: Taplinger, 1979).

T258. Staples, J.G., III "Six Lesser-Known Piano Quintets of the Twentieth Century (Nicolas Medtner)," PhD diss., Rochester, 1972.

T259. Van Den Toorn, P.C. "Stravinsky and' The Rite of Spring'," PhD diss., Berkeley, 1986.

T260. Wallace, R.K. "The Life and Times of Josef and Rosina Lhevinne: The Middle Years, 1904-1937," PhD diss., Columbia, 1972.

Porcelain:

T261. Lianda, N. "Sergei Chekhonin and the New Soviet Porcelain," *Soviet Union* 7 (1980), pts.1-2, pp.157-169.

Theatre:

T262.   Baer, N.V.N. *Theatre in Revolution: Russian Avant-Garde Stage Design, 1913-1935* (London: Thames & Hudson, 1991).

T263.   Bakshy, A. *The Path of the Modern Russian Stage and Other Essays* (London: Cecil Palmer & Hayward, 1916).

T264.   Becvar, W.J. "The Stage and Film Career of Rouben Mamoulian," PhD diss., Kansas, 1975.

T265.   Beeson, N.B. "Vsevolod Meyerhold and the Experimental Prerevolutionary Theater in Russia, 1900-1917," PhD diss., Columbia, 1960.

T266.   Benois, A. *Reminiscences of the Russian Ballet*, trans.by M.Britnieva (London: Putnam, 1941).

T267.   Black, L.C. "A Portrait of Misha: The Life and Artistic Accomplishments of Mikhail Alexandrovich Chekhov," PhD diss., Kansas, 1984.

T268.   Borovsky, V. "The Origins of Symbolist Theatre in Russia: Theory and Practice," *Irish Slavonic Studies* 14 (1993), pp.41-68.

T269.   Braun, E. "The Dramatic Theory and Practice of Vsevolod Meierkhol'd," PhD diss., Cambridge, 1970.

T270.   Buckle, R. *Nijinsky* (London: Weidenfeld & Nicolson, 1971).

T271.   Carnicke, S.M. "The Theatrical Instinct: A Study of the Work of Nikolaj Evreinov in Early Twentieth-Century Russia," PhD diss., Columbia, 1979.

T272.   Carter, H. *The New Spirit in the Russian Theatre, 1917-28. And a sketch of the Russian kinema and radio, 1919-28* (London: Brentano's, 1929).

T273.   Carter, H. *The New Theatre and Cinema of Soviet Russia* (London: Chapman & Dodd, 1924).

T274.   Chernian, L. "Lev Bakst and Vaslav Nijinsky: The 1913 Production of Jeux," *RH* 8 (1981), pts.1/2, pp.53-68.

T275.   Douglas, C. "Victory Over the Sun," *RH* 8 (1981), pts.1/2, pp.69-89.

T276.   Eaton, K.R.B. "The Theater of Meyerhold and Brecht," PhD diss., Wisconsin, 1979.

T277.   Friel, P.G. "Theater and Revolution: The Struggle for Theatrical Autonomy in Soviet Russia (1917-1920)," PhD diss., North Carolina, 1977.

T278.   Frost, M. "Marc Chagall and the Jewish State Chamber Theatre," *RH* 8 (1981), pts.1/2, pp.90-107.

T279.   Froud, N. & Hanley, J. (eds.) *Chaliapin: An Autobiography as Told to Maxim Gorky*, trans.by N.Froud & J.Hanley (New York: Stein & Day, 1967).

T280. Fulop-Miller, R. & Gregor, J. *The Russian Theatre: Its Character and History, with Especial Reference to the Revolutionary Period*, trans. by P.England (Philadelphia: J.B.Lippincott, 1929).

T281. Golub, S.J. "The Monodrama of Nikolaj Evreinov," PhD diss., Kansas, 1977.

T282. Gorchakov, N.A. *The Theater in Soviet Russia*, trans.by E.Lehrman (New York: Columbia U.P., 1957).

T283. Gordon, M.I. "Program of the Minor Leftists in the Soviet Theatre, 1919-1924," PhD diss., New York, 1981.

T284. Green, M. (ed.) *The Russian Symbolist Theatre: An Anthology of Plays and Critical Texts*, trans.by M.Green (Ann Arbor: Ardis, 1986).

T285. Hallett, R.W. "Mamont Dalsky: The Actor as Anarchist," *Scottish Slavonic Review* nos.12/13 (1989), pp.7-22.

T286. Hardy, M.C. "The Theatre Art of Richard Boleslavsky," PhD diss., Michigan, 1971.

T287. Hoover, M.L. *Meyerhold and His Set Designers* (New York: Peter Lang, 1988).

T288. Hoover, M.L. *Meyerhold: The Art of Conscious Theater* (Amherst: University of Massachusetts Press, 1974).

T289. Karsavina, T. *Theatre Street. The Reminiscences of Tamara Karsavina* (London: Dance Books, 1981).

T290. Kerensky, O. *Anna Pavlova* (London: Hamish Hamilton, 1973).

T291. Kindelan, N.A. "The Theatre of Inspiration: An Analysis of the Acting Theories of Mikhail Chekhov," PhD diss., Wisconsin, 1977.

T292. Kleberg, L. & Nilsson, N.A. (eds.) *Theater and Literature in Russia 1900-1930: A Collection of Essays* (Stockholm: Almqvist & Wiksell International, 1984).

T293. Komisarjevsky, T. [Komissarzhevskii] *Myself and the Theatre* (London: Heinemann, 1929).

T294. Kuhlke, W.L. "Vakhtangov's Legacy," PhD diss., Iowa, 1965.

T295. Leach, R. *Vsevolod Meyerhold* (Cambridge: Cambridge U.P., 1989).

T296. Legat, N. *Ballet Russe: Memoirs of Nicolas Legat*, trans.by Sir P.Dukes (London: Methuen, 1939).

T297. Levy, E. "The Theatre as an Expression of Cultural and Political Nationalism - The Habima Theatre, 1917-1968," PhD diss., Columbia, 1977.

T298. Levy, M.E.Q. "*Sakuntala*: A Reconstruction of the First Production at the Kamerny Theatre by Alexander Tairov," PhD diss., New York, 1978.

T299. Lieven, P. *The Birth of Ballets-Russes*, trans.by L.Zarine (London: George Allen & Unwin, 1936).

T300.   Lifar, S. "The Russian Ballet in Russia and in the West," *RR* 28 (1969), no.4, pp.396-402.

T301.   McReynolds, L. (ed.) *Russian Studies in History* 31 (1992-93), no.3. Issue devoted to fin-de-siecle theatre in Russia.

T302.   Marshall, H. *The Pictorial History of the Russian Theatre* (New York: Crown, 1977).

T303.   Mayer, C.S. "The Theatrical Designs of Leon Bakst," PhD diss., Columbia, 1977.

T304.   Money, K. *Anna Pavlova: Her Life and Art* (New York: Alfred A.Knopf, 1982).

T305.   Moody, C. "The Crooked Mirror," *Melbourne Slavonic Studies* no.7 (1972), pp.25-37.

T306.   Morgan, J.V. "Stanislavski's Encounter with Shakespeare: The Evolution of a Method," PhD diss., Yale, 1980.

T307.   Mudrak, M.M. "The Development of Constructivist Stage Design in Soviet Russia," *Soviet Russia* 3 (1976), pt.2, pp.253-268.

T308.   Murray, A. "A Problematical Pavilion: Alexandre Benois' First Ballet," *RH* 8 (1981), pts.1/2, pp.23-52.

T309.   Pitcher, H. *Chekhov's Leading Lady: A Portrait of the Actress Olga Knipper* (New York & London: Franklin Watts, 1980).

T310.   Proffer, E. (ed.) *Evreinov: Fotobiografiia / Evreinov: A Pictorial Biography* (Ann Arbor: Ardis, 1981).

T311.   Robinson, H. "Love for Three Operas: The Collaboration of Vsevolod Meyerhold and Sergei Prokofiev," *RR* 45 (1986), no.3, pp.287-304.

T312.   Romanovsky-Krassinsky, H.S.H. The Princess (Kschessinska) [Kshesinskaia] *Dancing in Petersburg: The Memoirs of Kschessinska*, trans.by A.Haskell (London: Victor Gollancz, 1960).

T313.   Rosenthal, B.G. "Theatre As Church: The Vision of the Mystical Anarchists," *RH* 4 (1977), pt.2, pp.122-141.

T314.   Rudnitsky, K. *Meyerhold the Director*, trans.by G.Petrov (Ann Arbor: Ardis, 1981).

T315.   Rudnitsky, K. *Russian and Soviet Theatre. Tradition and the Avant-Garde*, trans.by R.Permar (London: Thames & Hudson, 1988).

T316.   Russell, R. "People's Theatre and the October Revolution," *Irish Slavonic Studies* no.7 (1986), pp.65-84.

T317.   Russell, R. & Barratt, A. (eds.) *Russian Theatre in the Age of Modernism* (Basingstoke & London: Macmillan, 1990).

T318.   Sayler, O.M. *The Russian Theatre Under the Revolution* (Boston: Little, Brown & Co., 1920).

T319. Schmidt, P. (ed.) *Meyerhold at Work*, trans.by P.Schmidt et al (Austin, Texas: University of Texas Press, 1980).

T320. Schmidt, P.F. "The Theater of V.E. Mejerxol'd," PhD diss., Harvard, 1974.

T321. Segel, H.B. *Twentieth-Century Russian Drama: From Gorky to the Present* (New York: Columbia U.P., 1979).

T322. Senelick, L. (ed.) *Russian Dramatic Theory from Pushkin to the Symbolists* (Austin, Texas: University of Texas Press, 1981).

T323. Slonim, M. *Russian Theater: From the Empire to the Soviets* (Cleveland, Ohio: World Publishing Co., 1961).

T324. Sosin, G. "Children's Theatre and Drama in the Soviet Union, 1917-1953," PhD diss., Columbia, 1958.

T325. Stanislavski, C. *My Life in Art*, trans.by J.J.Robbins (London: Methuen, 1980).

T326. Swift, E.A. "Fighting the Germs of Disorder: The Censorship of Russian Popular Theater, 1888-1917," *RH* 18 (1991), pt.1, pp.1-49.

T327. Taschian, N.N. "Nikolai Evreinov, The Theorist of the Russian Theater," PhD diss., Berkeley, 1974.

T328. Thorpe, R.G. "The management of culture in revolutionary Russia: The Imperial theatres and the state, 1897-1928," PhD diss., Princeton, 1990.

T329. Thurston, G. "The Impact of Russian Popular Theatre, 1886-1915," *JMH* 55 (1983), no.2, pp.237-267.

T330. Torda, T.J. "Alexander Tairov and the Scenic Artists of the Moscow Kamerny Theatre 1914-1935," PhD diss., Denver, 1977.

T331. Von Geldern, J. *Bolshevik Festivals, 1917-1920* (Berkeley, Los Angeles, London: University of California Press, 1993).

T332. Von Geldern, J.R. "Festivals of the Revolution, 1917-1920: Art and Theater in the Formation of Soviet Culture," PhD diss., Brown, 1987.

T333. Weiner, J. "The Spanish Golden Age Theater in Tsarist Russia (1672-1917)," PhD diss., Indiana, 1968.

T334. Wilson, G.C. "The Dramatic Works of Vladimir Mayakovsky," PhD diss., Northwestern, 1985.

T335. Woodward, J.B. "From Brjusov to Ajkhenvald: Attitudes to the Russian Theatre, 1902-1914," *CSP* 7 (1965), pp.173-188.

T336. Yzraely, Y. "Vakhtangov Directing *The Dybbuk*," PhD diss., Carnegie-Mellon, 1971.

U

COMPARATIVE

U1.   Brinton, C. *The Anatomy of Revolutions* (New York: Vintage Books, 1965).

U2.   Chamberlin, W.H. "Russian and American Civil Wars," *RR* 11 (1952), no.4, pp.203-210.

U3.   Chamberlin, W.H. "The Jacobin Ancestry of Soviet Communism," *RR* (1958), no.4, pp.251-257.

U4.   Dukes, P. "From October 1917 to August 1991 and Beyond: Newer Thinking on the World Revolution," *EHQ* 22 (1992), no.4, pp.569-595.

U5.   Entessar, T. "Revolution and Leadership: A Study of Four Countries," PhD diss., St.Louis, 1984.

U6.   Hermassi, E. "Toward a Comparative Study of Revolutions," *Comparative Studies in Society and History* 18 (1976), no.2, pp.211-235.

U7.   Kyriakodis, H.G. "The 1991 Soviet and 1917 Bolshevik Coups Compared: Causes, Consequences and Legality," *RH* 18 (1991), pt.3, pp.317-362.

U8.   Law, D. "Trotsky and the Comparative History of Revolutions: the 'second chapter'," *Sbornik (SGRR)* no.13 (1987), pp.4-15.

U9.   LeBlanc, P.J. "Workers and Revolution: A Comparative Study of Bolshevik Russia and Sandinista Nicaragua," PhD diss., Pittsburgh, 1989.

U10.   McDaniel, T. *Autocracy, Modernization, and Revolution in Russia and Iran* (Princeton: Princeton U.P., 1993).

U11.   Skocpol, T. "France, Russia, China: A Structural Analysis of Social Revolutions," *Comparative Studies in Society and History* 18 (1976), no.2, pp.175-210.

U12.   Skocpol, T.R. "Social Revolutions in France, Russia and China: A Comparative-Historical and Structural Analysis," PhD diss., Harvard, 1975.

U13.   Skocpol, T. *States and Social Revolutions: A Comparative Analysis of France, Russia, and China* (New York & London: Cambridge U.P., 1979).

U14.   Strauss, H.J. "The Revolutionary Making Process: A Socio-Psychological Study of the Leadership of the English, American, Russian, and Irish Revolutions," PhD diss., Oregon, 1974.

V

MISCELLANEOUS

V1.   Adams, W.W. Jr. "Capital Punishment and the Russian Revolution," PhD diss., Columbia, 1968.

V2.   Aldanov, M. "P.N. Durnovo - Prophet of War and Revolution," *RR* 2 (1942-43), no.1, pp.31-45.

V3.   Best, P.J. "The Origins and Development of Insurance in Imperial and Soviet Russia," PhD diss., New York, 1965.

V4.   Blank, S. "The Origins of Soviet Language Policy, 1917-21," *RH* 15 (1988), no.1, pp.71-92.

V5.   Boobbyer, P. "The Two Democracies: Semen Frank's Interpretation of the Russian Revolutions of 1917," *Revolutionary Russia* 6 (1993), no.2, pp.193-209.

V6.   Clarke, W. *The Lost Fortune of the Tsars* (London: Weidenfeld & Nicolson, 1994).

V7.   Cross, T.B. "Geography and Arbitrariness: Factors in Russian Revolutionism," *SR* 24, (1965), no.4, pp.706-708.

V8.   Davis, D.E. & Trani, E.P. "An American in Russia: Russell M. Story and the Bolshevik Revolution, 1917-1919," *The Historian* 36 (1974), no.4, pp.704-721.

V9.   Davis, D.E. & Trani, E.P. "The American YMCA and the Russian Revolution," *SR* 33 (1974), no.3, pp.469-491.

V10.   Davis, G.H. "National Red Cross Societies and Prisoners of War in Russia, 1914-18," *JCH* 28 (1993), no.1, pp.31-52.

V11.   Engelstein, L. *The Keys to Happiness: Sex and the Search for Modernity in Fin-de-Siecle Russia* (Ithaca, New York: Cornell U.P., 1993).

V12.   Ewing, S.E. "Social Insurance in Russia and the Soviet Union, 1912-1933: A Study of Legal Form and Administrative Practice," PhD diss., Princeton, 1984.

V13.   Feuer, L.S. "Generations and the Theory of Revolution," *Survey* 18 (1972), no.3, pp.161-188.

V14.   Flaherty, P.A. "Lenin and the Russian Revolution: A Study on the Dialectics of Revolutionary and Plebian Social Mobilization," PhD diss., Harvard, 1984.

V15.   Gapochko, L.V. "Vladimir Ivanovich Nevskii," *SSH* 6 (1967-68), no.2, pp.45-50.

V16.   Goldberg, H.J. "Goldman and Berkman View the Bolshevik Regime," *SEER* 53 (1975), pp.272-276.

V17.   Hancock, R.K. "From Innocence to Boredom: Revolution in the West," PhD diss., Vanderbilt, 1975.

V18.   Harrison, W. "H.G. Wells's View of Russia," *Scottish Slavonic Review* no.7 (1986), pp.49-68.

V19.   Heilbronner, H. "Aehrenthal in Defense of Russian Autocracy," *JFGO* 17 (1969), pp.380-396.

V20.   Heuman, S.E. "Bogdan Kistiakovskii and the Problem of Human Rights in the Russian Empire, 1899-1917," PhD diss., Columbia, 1977.

V21.   Hollingsworth, B. "David Soskice in Russia in 1917," *European Studies Review* 6 (1976), no.1, pp.73-97.

V22.   Hollingsworth, B. "The Committee for Correct Information about New Russia: A Note and a Query," *Sbornik (SGRR)* no.1 (1975), pp.17-19.

V23.   Ingram, A.E. "The Root Mission to Russia, 1917," PhD diss., Louisiana State, 1970.

V24.   Iswolsky, H. "The Russian Revolution Seen from Paris," *RR* 26 (1967), no.2, pp.153-163.

V25.   Jansen, M. "L.H. Grondijs and Russia: The Acts and Opinions of a Dutch White Guard," *Revolutionary Russia* 7 (1994), no.1, pp.20-33.

V26.   Jewsbury, G.F. "Russian Students in Nancy, France, 1905-1914: A Case Study," *JFGO* 23 (1975), pp.225-228.

V27.   Kaplan, F.I. "The Origin and Function of the Subbotniks and Voskresniks," *JFGO* 13 (1965), pp.30-39.

V28.   Keep, J. "The Bolshevik Revolution: Prototype or Myth?," *Studies on the Soviet Union* 11, no.4 (1971), pp.46-60. Also in: T.T.Hammond (ed.) *The Anatomy of Communist Takeovers* (New Haven & London: Yale U.P., 1975).

V29.   Krukones, J.H. "Satan's Blood, Tsar's Ink: Rural Alcoholism in an Official 'Publication for the People,' 1881-1917," *RH* 18 (1991), pt.4, pp.435-456.

V30.   Lutskii, E.A. "Andrei Vasil'evich Shestakov," *SSH* 6 (1967-68), no.2, pp.57-64.

V31.   Meyer, H.C. "Rohrbach and His Osteuropa," *RR* 2 (1942-43), no.1, pp.60-69.

V32.   Olgin, M.J. "The Soul of the Russian Revolution," PhD diss., Columbia, 1918.

V33.   Parry, A. "Charles R. Crane, Friend of Russia," *RR* 6 (1946-47), no.2, pp.20-36.

V34.   Pearson, R. "Privileges, Rights, and Russification," in: O.Crisp & L.Edmondson (eds.) *Civil Rights in Imperial Russia* (Oxford: Clarendon, 1989), pp.85-102.

V35.   Pethybridge, R. "Political Repercussions of the Supply Problem in the Russian Revolution of 1917," *RR* 29 (1970), no.4, pp.379-402.

V36.   Poster, J.B. "A Warmth of Soul: Samuel Northrup Harper and the Russians, 1904-43," *JCH* 14 (1979), no.2, pp.235-251.

V37.   Reiman, M. "Spontaneity and Planning in the Plebian Revolution," in: R.C.Elwood (ed.) *Reconsiderations on the Russian Revolution* (Cambridge, Mass.: Slavica, 1976), pp.10-19.

V38.   Rose, M.T. "Philips Price and the Russian Revolution," PhD diss., Hull, 1988.

V39.   Rosenthal, B.G. "Lofty Ideals and Wordly Consequences: Visions of Sobornost' in Early Twentieth-Century Russia," *RH* 20 (1993), nos.1-4, pp.179-195.

V40.   Rucker, R.D. "The Making of the Russian Revolution: Revolutionaries, Workers, and the Marxian Theory of Revolution," PhD diss., Iowa, 1981.

V41.   Saunders, D. "Vladimir Burtsev and the Russian Revolutionary Emigration (1888-1905)," *European Studies Review* 13 (1983), no.1, pp.39-62.

V42.   Schurer, H. "Some Reflections on Rosa Luxemburg and the Bolshevik Revolution," *SEER* 40 (1961-62), pp.356-372.

V43.   Shlapentokh, D. "Drunkenness and Anarchy in Russia: A Case of Political Culture," *RH* 18 (1991), pt.4, pp.457-500.

V44.   Smith, N. "Political Freemasonry in Russia, 1906-1918: A Discussion of the Sources," *RR* 44 (1985), no.2, pp.157-171.

V45.   Smith, N. "The Role of Russian Freemasonry in the February Revolution: Another Scrap of Evidence," *SR* 27 (1968), no.4, pp.604-608.

V46.   Smith, N. & Norton, B.T. "The Constitution of Russian Political Freemasonry (1912)," *JFGO* 34 (1986), pp.498-517.

V47.   Sokolov, O.D. "Mikhail Nikolaevich Pokrovskii," *SSH* 6 (1967-68), no.2, pp.51-56.

V48.   Stone, H. "The Soviet Government and Moonshine, 1917-1929," *Cahiers du Monde Russe et Sovietique* 27 (1986), nos.3-4, pp.359-380.

V49.   Stuart, M. "Creating a National Library for the Workers' State: The Public Library in Petrograd and the Rumiantsev Library under Bolshevik Rule," *SEER* 72 (1994), no.2, pp.233-258.

V50.   Volgyes, I. "Hungarian Prisoners of War in Russia, 1916-1919," *Cahiers du Monde Russe et Sovietique* 14 (1973), nos.1-2, pp.54-85.

V51.   Von Laue, T.H. "Westernization, Revolution and the Search for a Basis of Authority - Russia in 1917," *SS* 19 (1967), no.2, pp.155-180.

V52.   Von Mohrenschildt, D.S. "Lincoln Steffens and the Russian Bolshevik Revolution," *RR* 5 (1945-46), no.1, pp.31-41.

V53.   Wagner, W.G. "Legislative Reform of Inheritance in Russia, 1861-1914," in: W.E.Butler (ed.) *Russian Law: Historical and Political Perspectives* (Leyden: A.W.Sijthoff, 1977), pp.143-178.

V54.   Watson, D.R. "The Krasin-Savinkov Meeting of 10 December 1921," *Cahiers du Monde Russe et Sovietique* 27 (1986), nos.3-4, pp.461-468.

V55.   Williams, R.C. "Russians in Germany: 1900-1914," *JCH* 1 (1966), no.4, pp.121-149.

V56.   Wolfe, B. "War Comes to Russia," *RR* 22 (1963), no.2, pp.123-138.

V57.   Wortman, R. "Property Rights, Populism, and Russian Political Culture," in: O.Crisp and L.Edmondson (eds.) *Civil Rights in Imperial Russia* (Oxford: Clarendon, 1989), pp.13-32.

W

INTERNATIONAL IMPACT OF THE REVOLUTION AND WORLD OPINION

W1.   Alzona, E. "Some French Contemporary Opinions of the Russian Revolution of 1905," PhD diss., Columbia, 1922.

W2.   Anderson, P.H. "The Attitude of the American Leftist Leaders Toward the Russian Revolution (1917-1923)," PhD diss., Notre Dame, 1943.

W3.   Ascher, A. "German Socialists and the Russian Revolution of 1905," in: E.Mendelsohn & M.S.Shatz (eds.) *Imperial Russia, 1700-1917: State, Society, Opposition. Essays in Honor of Marc Raeff* (DeKalb, Illinois: Northern Illinois Press, 1988), pp.260-277.

W4.   Augursky, M. *The Third Rome: National Bolshevism in the USSR* (Boulder & London: Westview Press, 1987).

W5.   Berry, D.G. "The Response of the French Anarchist Movement to the Russian Revolution (1917-24) and to the Spanish Revolution and Civil War (1936-39)," PhD diss., Sussex, 1989.

W6.   Carroll, E.M. *Soviet Communism and Western Opinion, 1919-1921* (Chapel Hill, N.C.: North Carolina U.P., 1965).

W7.   Cowden, M.H. *Russian Bolshevism and British Labor, 1917-1921* (Boulder, Colorado: East European Monographs, 1984).

W8.   Cowden, M.H. "Soviet Comintern Policies Toward the British Labor Movement, 1917-1926," PhD diss., Columbia, 1964.

W9.   Cullen, R.G. "The British Labor Party and Russia, March-November, 1917," PhD diss., Georgetown, 1971.

W10.   Dukes, P. *October and the World: Perspectives on the Russian Revolution* (London: Macmillan, 1979).

W11.   Durham, M. "British Revolutionaries and the Suppression of the Left in Lenin's Russia, 1918-1924," *JCH* 29 (1985), no.2, pp.203-219.

W12.   Eudin, X.J. & Fisher, H.H. *Soviet Russia and the West, 1920-1927. A Documentary Survey* (Stanford: Stanford U.P., 1957).

W13.   Filene, P.G. (ed.) *American Views of Soviet Russia, 1917-1965* (Homewood, Illinois: Dorsey Press, 1968).

W14.   Graubard, S.R. *British Labour and the Russian Revolution, 1917-1924* (Cambridge, Mass.: Harvard U.P., 1956).

W15.   Graubard, S.R. "The Russian Revolution in British Labour History, 1917-1924," PhD diss., Harvard, 1952.

W16.   Hammond, T.T. "The Communist Takeover of Outer Mongolia: Model for Eastern Europe?," *Studies on the Soviet Union* 11 (1971), no.4, pp.107-144 [also in T.T. Hammond (ed.) *The Anatomy of Communist Takeovers* (New Haven and London: Yale U.P., 1975)].

W17.   Hitchins, K. "The Russian Revolution and the Rumanian Socialist Movement, 1917-1918," *SR* 27 (1968), no.2, pp.268-289.

W18.   Holt, C.E., Jr. "English Liberals and Russia, 1895-1907," PhD diss., Kentucky, 1976.

W19.   Hongiwachs, L.H. "The Edwardian Discovery of Russia, 1900-1917," PhD diss., Columbia, 1977.

W20.   Imam, Z. "The Effects of the Russian Revolution on India, 1917-1920," *St. Anthony's Papers* 18 (*South Asian Affairs* no.2) (1966), pp.74-97.

W21.   Isono, F. "Soviet Russia and the Mongolian Revolution of 1921," *Past and Present* no.83 (1979), pp.116-140.

W22.   Kadish, S. *Bolsheviks and British Jews: the Anglo-Jewish Community, Britain and the Russian Revolution* (London: Frank Cass, 1992).

W23.   Kadish, S.I. "Bolsheviks and British Jews: the Anglo-Jewish Community, Britain and the Russian Revolution," PhD diss., Oxford, 1987.

W24.   Lasch, C. "Revolution and Democracy: The Russian Revolution and the Crisis of American Liberalism, 1917-1919," PhD diss., Columbia, 1961.

W25.   Lasch, C. *The American Liberals and the Russian Revolution* (New York & London: Columbia U.P., 1962).

W26.   Lauridsen, K.V. "Revolution in Russia and Response in France: Contemporary Views from the French Far Left, 1905-1907," PhD diss., New York, 1971.

W27.   Lindemann, A.S. "Socialist Impressions of Revolutionary Russia, 1920," *RH* 1 (1974), pt.1, pp.31-45.

W28.   Lindemann, A.S. *The 'Red Years': European Socialism versus Bolshevism, 1919-1921* (Berkeley: University of California Press, 1974).

W29. MacFarlane, L.J. "Hands Off Russia: British labour and the Russo-Polish War, 1920," *Past and Present* no.38 (1967), pp.126-152.

W30. Maehl, W. "The Anti-Russian Tide in German Socialism, 1918-1920," *ASEER* 18 (1959), pp.187-196.

W31. Marchand, R. *Why I Support Bolshevism* (London: British Socialist Party, n.d.).

W32. Meaker, G.H. "Spanish Anarcho-Syndicalism and the Russian Revolution, 1917-1922," PhD diss., Southern California, 1967.

W33. Mitchell, D. *1919: Red Mirage* (New York: Macmillan, 1970).

W34. Naarden, B. *Socialist Europe and Revolutionary Russia: Perception and Prejudice, 1848-1923* (Cambridge & New York: Cambridge U.P., 1992).

W35. Northcutt, W.B. "Contemporary French Evaluations of the Russian Revolution of 1905," PhD diss., California, Irvine, 1974.

W36. Northedge, F.S. "1917-1919: The Implications for Britain," *JCH* 3 (1968), no.4, pp.191-209.

W37. Pastor, P. "The Hungarian Revolution's Road from Wilsonianism to Leninism 1918-19," *East-Central Europe* 3 (1976), no.2, pp.210-219.

W38. Peake, T.R. "The Impact of the Russian Revolution Upon French Attitudes and Policies Toward Russia," PhD diss., North Carolina, 1974.

W39. Renshaw, P. "The I.W.W. and the Red Scare 1917-24," *JCH* 3 (1968), no.4, pp.63-72.

W40. Schinness, R.T. "The Tories and the Soviets: The British Conservative Reaction to Russia, 1917-1927," PhD diss., SUNY, Binghamton, 1972.

W41. Schurer, H. "The Russian Revolution of 1905 and the Origins of German Communism," *SEER* 39 (1960-61), pp.459-471.

W42. Seidman, J. *Communism in the United States - A Bibliography* (Ithaca & London: Cornell U.P., 1969).

W43. Shapira, A. "Labour Zionism and the October Revolution," *JCH* 24 (1989), no.4, pp.623-656.

W44. Snell, J.L. "The Russian Revolution and the German Social Democratic Party in 1917," *ASEER* 15 (1956), pp.339-350.

W45. Spector, I. *The First Russian Revolution: Its Impact on Asia* (Englewood Cliffs, N.J.: Prentice-Hall, 1962).

W46. Strakhovsky, L. *American Opinion about Russia, 1917-1920* (Toronto: University of Toronto Press, 1961).

W47. Thompson, A.W. & Hart, R.A. *The Uncertain Crusade: America and the Russian Revolution of 1905* (Amherst: University of Massachusetts Press, 1970).

W48.   Von Mohrenschildt, D. "The Early American Observers of the Russian Revolution, 1917-1921," *RR* 3 (1943-44), no.1, pp.64-74.

W49.   White, S. "Soviets in Britain: the Leeds Convention of 1917," *IRSH* 19 (1974), pp.165-193.

X

PLACE AND SIGNIFICANCE OF THE REVOLUTION IN RUSSIAN AND WORLD HISTORY

X1.   Carr, E.H. *1917: Before and After* (London: Macmillan, 1969).

X2.   Chamberlin, W.H. "Forty Years of Soviet Communism," *RR* 17 (1958), no.1, pp.3-10.

X3.   Chamberlin, W.H. "Soviet Communism: The Transient and the Permanent," *RR* 10 (1951), no.3, pp.169-175.

X4.   Chamberlin, W.H. "The Jacobin Ancestry of Soviet Communism," *RR* 17 (1958), no.4, pp.251-257.

X5.   Deutscher, I. *The Unfinished Revolution: Russia 1917-1967* (London & New York: Oxford U.P., 1967).

X6.   Dukes, P. "From October 1917 to August 1991 and Beyond: Newer Thinking on the World Revolution," *EHQ* 22 (1992), no.4, pp.569-595.

X7.   Keep, J. "1917: The Tyranny of Paris Over Petrograd," *SS* 20 (1968-69), no.1, pp.22-35.

X8.   Nechkina, M.V. "The Decembrists and the Problem of the Three Revolutions: Toward a Formulation of the Question," *SSH* 17 (1978-79), no.3, pp.52-82.

X9.   Pitt Rivers, G. *The World Significance of the Russian Revolution* (Oxford: Basil Blackwell, 1920).

X10.   Schoenfeld, G. "Uses of the Past: Bolshevism and the French Revolutionary Tradition," PhD diss., Harvard, 1989.

X11.   Shlapentolch, D. "The French Revolution in Russian Intellectual and Political Life, 1789-1922," PhD diss., Chicago, 1988.

X12.   Shlapentolch, D. "The Images of the French Revolution in the February and Bolshevik Revolutions," *RR* 16 (1989), no.1, pp.31-54.

X13.   Ulam, A.B. "Reflections on the Revolution," *Survey* no.64 (July 1967), pp.3-13.

AUTHOR INDEX

SUBJECT INDEX

About the Compiler

MURRAY FRAME is a research student in the Department of Slavonic Studies at the University of Cambridge. He is working on a study of Russian theatre during the Revolution.

ISBN 0-313-29559-X

EAN

HARDCOVER BAR CODE